TOPICS IN MODERN IRISH HISTORY

General Editor: R. V. COMERFORD

Towards a
National University
William Delany SJ (1835·1924)

To the memory of all the nation-builders
great and small

William Delany S.J.

Towards a National University
William Delany SJ (1835·1924)

An Era of Initiative in Irish Education

THOMAS J MORRISSEY SJ

WOLFHOUND PRESS: DUBLIN
HUMANITIES PRESS: NEW JERSEY

First published 1983 by
Wolfhound Press
68 Mountjoy Square
Dublin 1

Published in the United States by Humanities Press
Inc. Atlantic Highlands, New Jersey 07716.

British Library Cataloguing in Publication Data

Morrissey, Thomas
    Towards a national university. — (Topics in
    Modern Irish history, ISSN 0790-0783; v.2)
    1. National University of Ireland — History
    I. Title   II. Series
    378.417   LF872

    ISBN 0-86327-012-3 Wolfhound Press
    ISBN 0-391-02975-4 Humanities Press

Cover design by Jarlath Hayes
Typesetting by Print Prep Ltd., Dublin.
Printed in Great Britain.

TABLE OF CONTENTS

Preface   7

PART I

The making of an educationalist: 1835-1883

I   The background years: 1835-1879   13
II   The Intermediate Act and the Royal University   33
III   From Tullabeg to University College: rejection
        and reinstatement, 1880-1883   61

PART II

From president, University College (1883-
1888) to pastor (1888-1897)

IV   Difficult beginnings at St Stephen's Green   75
V   The fellowship controversy goes public   89
VI   Occasions of conflict: Dr Walsh as archbishop   98
VII   A university settlement undermined   117
VIII   Experiencing vigilant hostility: 1886-1888   124
IX   First term as president reviewed   136
X   The years between (April 1888 to April 1897):
        church work and contacts   143

PART III

Return to Stephen's Green: 'The real work for
Ireland', 1897-1909

XI   'A new internal vigour'   157
XII   The struggle for educational equality: negoti-
        ations towards a settlement, 1897-1905   168

XIII The worst solution possible; divided opinions: 1905-1907   222
XIV Student unrest: a reputation tarnished   244
XV The issue of women's rights   279
XVI Mr Birrell and the final solution   288
XVII The afterglow of the act: explanations, congratulations, and a silver jubilee   314
XVIIIThe compulsory Irish campaign   321
XIX Defending the old, equipping the new   345

PART IV

From provincial to obscurity; 'the propaganda of silence'

XX The man, the provincial, the educationalist in decline, 1909-1912   355
XXI The final years: 'out of the swell of the sea'   370
XXII An appraisal: 'In the gallery of nation-builders'   381

Notes to the text   388
Bibliography   405
Index   417

Illustrations   2; 43-46; 113-116; 275-278; 351-352

Acknowledgements

Many people played a part in the development of this book. Those who helped in reading and research are mentioned in the Preface, but to many others I am also indebted: to the president and authorities of University College Dublin and the Jesuit provincial, for their encouragement and practical support; the Jesuit community at Dooradoyle, Limerick, for their interest and patience, and also the communities at Gonzaga College, Clongowes and Leeson Street; Miss Frances Whyte and her most efficient and generous office staff at C.C.C., Limerick; Ms Gráinne O'Flynn for permitting me to view her collection of the Bithrey papers, and the Sisters of High Park Convent, Drumcondra, Dublin, for their courtesy in providing photographs and background information on Sr Agatha Morley.

PREFACE

The passing of the National University Bill in 1908 brought
to an end over fifty years of protest and negotiation on behalf
of the majority population in Ireland. Its enactment coincided
with the silver jubilee of the Jesuits' connection with University
College Dublin. At the jubilee celebrations, Dr John Healy,
archbishop of Tuam, linked together the achievements of the
old Royal University, the advent of the new national institution,
and the work of Dr William Delany. He concluded his rather
grandiloquent address with a characteristic diapason:[1]

> This is a new era; a new dawn is opening before us . . . and
> I pray to God that the dawn will usher in a brighter day to
> all, without distinction of politics or religion. When that
> day comes, I hope that neither the present nor a future
> generation, nor the historians of the new university, will
> ever forget the labours of the man who led that forlorn
> hope, so to speak, through the desert, through so many toils
> and troubles, and brought his people to take possession of
> that happy land for which they had . . . laboured so zealously.

Many years later, in 1956, the then vice-chancellor of the
National University and president of University College Dublin,
Professor Michael Tierney, judged that 'it was probably due to
Fr Delany more than to any other single man that the National
University was given its present form'.[2]

William Delany's life was largely devoted to winning for the
Catholic majority in Ireland equality of educational opportunity
at secondary and university level. The struggle was a protracted
one. In 1904, during his second term as president of University
College, St Stephen's Green, Dublin, he summarised his arguments on the university question in a pamphlet which ran to
four editions. It was entitled significantly, *A plea for fair-play:*

Irish university education, facts and figures. Copies were sent to prominent English politicians, and to influential friends and acquaintances. One of those friends, Lady Betty Balfour, found it 'a most convincing document, admirably free from bitterness or party spirit, and all the more forcible and telling on that account'; and she almost despaired of democratic government 'that a case of such plain and simple justice supported by all the leading interests of the government should nevertheless be ignored or refused.'[3] Delany had described the government's response, 'after fifty years of waiting', as 'tantamount to a declaration that Ireland could not expect justice from Westminster'.

His personal challenge to justice extended over thirty years. By persistent political lobbying, the enrolment of support among persons of influence, a steady stream of letters to newspapers, evidence before royal commissions of enquiry, and his achievements as an educationalist, he kept before successive governments the need for equality of treatment in education between Catholics and Protestants. His achievements as an educationalist buttressed all other endeavours and presented a challenge which could not be ignored. First at a small intermediate school in Tullabeg, County Offaly, and then at University College, he showed, as his colleague Fr Tom Finlay noted in 1924, 'that handicapped for funds, equipment, and even staff', his students 'could meet and overcome the far more numerous and favoured sons' of state-aided institutions. Step by step, 'he made good his proposition, that Irish Catholics were capable of profiting by, and desirous of, the best education possible. It had been considered an absurdity; in forty years Fr Delany made it an axiom.' What he accomplished, Finlay continued, had 'profoundly affected ... all the secondary schools in Ireland. ... He was a notable figure in that movement of reform in education which has resulted in so many changes and the force of which is not yet spent.'[4]

William Delany sought both 'to raise up the intermediate education of the whole people'[5] and to prepare his university students to become leaders in a new Home-Rule Ireland. In 1930 William Magennis, a former student of University College and one of its most influential professors, reviewed in the *National Student* magazine the recently published *A page of Irish history: the story of University College Dublin, 1883-1909.* Remarking on the cloud which had, of late years, overhung Delany's 'renown as an educator', he declared that retrospectively he saw him 'in truer proportions — a grander and a finer figure in the gallery of nation-builders than when he was first leading us'. Delany had no doubt that he and his college were nation-builders; nor had his students. 'The young cocks were crowing', C.P. Curran observed in his *James Joyce remembered* (Oxford, 1968, p. 61) and, as will appear, that very talented generation did produce many who became famous 'in the after glow of history'. Also bathed in the same glow were members of Delany's teaching staff, notably John MacNeill and Patrick H. Pearse. And in a wider and different context, the 'College on the Green' could boast of one lecturer and one student who achieved international reputations, respectively, as poet and novelist namely, Gerard Manley Hopkins and James A. Joyce.

Delany's interest to a biographer, however, is not confined to his struggle for justice in education nor to his impact on the students and staff of an influential institution at an important moment in Irish history. He was a schoolboy at the time of the great famine, and he lived until after the Irish civil war. In between, he was a student at Rome when Garibaldi was campaigning against the Papal States, was co-founder and first secretary of the Catholic Headmasters' Association, an adviser in the drawing up of the 1878 Intermediate Education Act, and much involved in proceedings leading to the foundation of the Royal University. Thereafter, as president of University College, and senator of the Royal University, he was credited with being chiefly responsible for the emergence of the National University in 1908.

His friendships crossed political and religious divisions, ranging from the Duchess of Marlborough, Randolph Churchill, John Morley and Augustine Birrell on the one side, to John MacNeill and P.H. Pearse on the other. Moreover, throughout his long life, he was an indefatigable writer of letters and memoranda, corresponding with most of the leading British politicians of the day, with Archbishops Croke, Walsh and Healy, and with Bishops Butler and O'Dwyer of Limerick, with the Jesuit General, with members of the Irish parliamentary party, and with a host of other prominent personalities; and as a good Victorian, with an eye to posterity, he preserved drafts of much of his correspondence, and left copious notes on different important and controversial issues in his career.

Of controversy and disagreement there was plenty. At one time or another he was at cross-purposes with members of his Order, with members of the Catholic hierarchy, with the Gaelic League — of which he was an honorary member in recognition of his work for Irish language and history — with the feminist movement, with government ministers, with some of the Irish parliamentary party, with unionists and nationalists, with representatives of Trinity College, Dublin, and the students of University College. Whenever he considered an important principle at stake, or 'fair-play' being flouted, he seemed prepared to court unpopularity in its defence. Hence, success and humiliation, public acclaim and obloquy, came his way; and on the last lap the obloquy predominated. The result was that when, in the late nineteen-twenties and early nineteen-thirties, Fr Lambert McKenna proposed to write his biography and collected material from many of his distinguished correspondents and other contemporaries, the projected work did not get beyond manuscript form. The memory of disagreements was still fresh, many participants were still living. Besides, some of the bodies with which the president of University College had clashed in his final years in office held a dominant position in Ireland of the nineteen-thirties; and views which ran counter to the hallowed principles of that decade were not likely to receive a hearing.

And yet, the remarkable thing was that — despite the many controversies and the opprobrious charges levelled against him at times — Delany was not a contentious personality, and never seems to have made a personal enemy. Even those who disagreed most strongly with him, but knew him as a man, rather than a symbol, conceded that his arguments were principled and his manner of conducting them invariably 'gentlemanly'. He did not have 'any wish to fight at all if he could have avoided it', Francis Cruise O'Brien wrote, but when he did 'he always fought with steel like a gentleman'.[6] The word most frequently applied to him, in the idiom of the day, was, indeed, 'gentleman', not in any derisory sense, nor with any connotation of social pretension, but rather in the context of Newman's 'Christian gentleman', an approximation to the lofty ideal suggested by Gerard Manley Hopkins in a letter to Robert Bridges on 3 February 1883.[7]

> The quality of a gentleman is so very fine a thing that . . .
> the more a man feels what it means . . . the more backward
> will he be to think he can have realised in himself anything
> so perfect. . . . If the English race had done nothing else,
> yet if they left the world the notion of a gentleman, they
> would have done a great service to mankind.

Such words, which echo strangely today, suggest the pervasiveness of religious beliefs and sentiments in Britain and Ireland during the nineteenth and into the twentieth century.

Scarcely in any other century, Professor Kitson Clarke wrote in *The Making of Victorian England* (London, 1962, p. 20), 'did the claims of religion occupy so large a part in the nation's life, or did men speaking in the name of religion contrive to exercise so much power'. In Ireland, the effect was even more marked. Religion, in a broad sense, played its part in the moulding of different cultures, in fostering separation and promoting hostility as, on the one hand, what has been termed 'cullenisation' (after Cardinal Cullen) closed and unified Catholic ranks against colonisation by Protestant or free-thinking influences; and, on the other, the unionists of the north aggressively proclaimed that their southern neighbours were lazy and priest-ridden and that concessions to them only strengthened the expanding tyranny of Rome. The century's regard for education made it the central battle ground for these contending forces; and their struggle, with all the strong emotions it aroused, is part, too, of William Delany's story.

Time, however, has removed the carapace around many hitherto emotional and 'forbidden' topics. Hence, it seems appropriate, as the centenary of Delany's appointment to University College draws near, to look squarely at his personality, work and achievement. In this account a very conscious effort has been made to present the story as objectively as possible. To that end, a Jesuit writing about a Jesuit may not appear the ideal arrangement. But, redressing the balance, it has the advantage of the author sharing an inside understanding of the subject's training and ideals. From the side of personal misgivings, my fear is, rather, that in attempting to paint a living portrait, and therefore a flawed one, I may have been less than fair to the subject as a person, a religious, and even as an educationalist.

The primary source materials for this book are the Delany papers in the Irish Jesuit Archives, Leeson Street, Dublin, and from that rich source most quotations are drawn; relevant papers in the Dublin Archdiocesan Archives, Clonliffe College, and in the Limerick Diocesan Archives; the Clongowes Wood College Archives, Co. Kildare — the section relating to St Stanislaus College, Tullabeg; the minutes of the senate of the Royal University at the offices of the National University of Ireland; the minutes of the Irish Jesuit provincial consultors at Eglinton Road, Dublin; and the Monsell MSS, as also newspaper and parliamentary sources, in the National Library of Ireland. I should like to take the opportunity of thanking all those who greatly facilitated my research work over a period of ten years, particularly Dr Fergal McGrath, S.J., Leeson Street, the Rev Dr Kevin Kennedy, Clonliffe College, Most Rev Dr J. Newman, Bishop of Limerick, who has shown great interest in the subject from the beginning, and the late Fr Charles O'Conor Don, S.J. To Professor V.A. McClelland of the University of Hull, an inspirer of publication, and to my most helpful and challenging readers and advisers, Fr Peter Troddyn, S.J., Dr Fergal McGrath, S.J., Professors James Meenan and T.D. Williams of University College Dublin, and Dr R.V. Comerford of St Patrick's College, Maynooth, I owe a deep debt of gratitude. What is deficient in this work is so through no fault of theirs. Thanks are due also to Mr John Kennedy, M.A., for his skill and cooperation in the preparation of photographs. Finally, a word about presentation. As much as possible in the text the use of capital letters has been restricted to proper names and special titles, except in a few instances where it seemed appropriate to use them to avoid confusion: hence the Chief Secretary and Lord Lieutenant, the Jesuit General, and reference to a religious Order, are honoured with capitals; whereas more general titles like prime minister, pope and bishop, are not.

PART 1

The Making of an Educationalist: 1835-1883

'Nothing is more certain than that our manners, our civilization, and all the good things which are connected with manners and with civilization, have, in this European world of ours, depended for ages upon two principles, and were, indeed, the result of both combined: I mean the spirit of a gentleman, and the spirit of religion'.
Reflections on the French Revolution, by Edmund Burke, in B.W. Hill (ed.), *Edmund Burke* (London, 1975), pp 345-6.

Chapter 1

THE BACKGROUND YEARS: 1835-1879

'By birth and education and character and sentiment, I am an Irishman of the Irish': so William Delany in the *Freeman's Journal* towards the close of a long educational career,[1] when over-zealous critics, reliving an ancient tradition, sought to discredit his arguments by researching his ancestry.

He was born at Leighlin Bridge, Co. Carlow. Today but a scattering of houses on either side of the river Barrow, it was, during his boyhood, a busy post and market town of some two thousand inhabitants and three hundred and seventy buildings. Its central location at a river crossing — six miles from Carlow, twelve from Kilkenny, and forty-six from Dublin — rendered it convenient to coach travel. Hence, through the main street, where William lived, there clattered the day coaches to Kilkenny and Waterford; while at night, and in the early hours of the morning, the mail coaches to and from Dublin stopped, changed horses, and hurried on. The town's location, also, and the sur- round of good agricultural and pasture land, fostered its develop- ment as a market centre. Fairs were held four times a year, and markets three times a week. The presence of a well-known spa nearby brought, moreover, a wider cross-section of people

through the town. The river stimulated further activity. Goods
were sent to Carlow, Dublin and intermediate towns; and, following the expansion of the corn and butter trade in the eighteen-
twenties, the milling industry prospered and butter was trans-
ported down stream to the port of Waterford for the London
market.[2]

Despite the semblance of trade and commerce, however, the
relatively slower life of the countryside was but a stone's throw
away; and most of the families came of farming stock. In the
Delanys' case the transition to the town was quite recent; and,
as with so many others, there was a story of eviction in the background. William's father, John Delany, had been one of four
brothers who held a moderate-size farm in the neighbouring
townland of Coolnakieran. It had been in the family since the
middle of the eighteenth century. Their land, as indeed the town
of Leighlin Bridge, was the property of William R. Stewart, Esq.
In 1825, coinciding with the growing trade in corn and butter,
expulsions took place on the Stewart estate. The Delany brothers
were among the dispossessed. Three of them emigrated to the
United States. John moved to Leighlin Bridge and set up a small
bakery business on the main street. When this began to prosper
he bought some land of his own, and married a girl from Old
Leighlin, a smaller town in the same parish. Mary Brennan, his
wife, proved a resourceful, strong-willed woman, who built a
united home and contributed much to the development of the
business. Ten children were born to them, of whom five survived
to maturity. William, the second child, was born on 4 June
1835, just ten years after his father's eviction.

The picture of the household which has survived is one of
close family affection, frugality and hard work. The children
were expected to play their part in the running of the home
and business. To his mother's eyes, William, from an early age,
displayed an exasperatingly impractical bent. His main interest
seemed to be in reading and music. Frequently he slipped away
from the daily chores to 'waste his time' on books and practising the cornet. To her annoyance, the local clergy, who were
regular visitors to the house, encouraged these interests. He
developed into a precocious, somewhat precious youth, carefully observing the accent and pronunciation, the convention-
alities and manners of the 'nicer' people whom he met among
the local gentry, the professional classes, coach travellers, and
visitors to the highly regarded local spa. He attached much
importance to these social manifestations and sought to re-
produce them. To this almost priggish sense of propriety, how-

ever, there was joined a decided independence of mind when something he valued was in question. It was an unusual mixture in an Irish Catholic boy living in a small country town in the first half of the nineteenth century. A relation of his mother, a Mr Lesmond, had reason to remember the mixture. When William was fourteen years, he brought him with him on a business trip to Dublin and Liverpool. Business concluded, he treated him to an evening at a Liverpool theatre. The programme included a stock Irish melodrama. To his chagrin, his refined young cousin, instead of enjoying the performance, stood up and announced that he would listen no longer to such a travesty of his countrymen: 'Irishmen do not speak in that horrid way!'[3]

Already at this stage, then, many of the features later associated with William Delany were in evidence: intelligence, studiousness, impracticality where business was concerned, a care for the correctness in accent, pronunciation and manners characteristic of a 'gentleman', a fluency of speech, an independence of character to the point of wilfulness but tempered in expression by the requirements of socially acceptable behaviour. All were embodied in a small, compact frame, set off by an alert face and a head of fair, curly hair, which gave him a permanently youthful appearance; years later, at the age of forty-two, the Duke of Marlborough was to mistake him for a divinity student.[4]

His formal education was conducted at the local national school and, from the age of ten to sixteen years, at a pay school in Bagenalstown. Mr Lyons, the headmaster of that establishment, was reputed to be a gifted teacher. At the close of his career, he liked to boast that he had had among his pupils Professor Tyndall of Dublin University, Cardinal Moran of Sydney, and Dr William Delany, president of University College Dublin. The region was indeed rich in ecclesiastical connections. Among the Delanys' neighbours were: their cousins, the Foleys of Old Leighlin, from whom came the future bishop of Kildare and Leighlin, at whose consecration William was to preach; the Cullens of nearby Ballyallen, cousins of Cardinal Cullen; and the Morans, also of the main street, Leighlin Bridge, one of whose sons became the cardinal. Neighbourhood affinity was a factor of life often overriding other differences. One of William's closest supporters at a later date would be Mr Arthur Kavanagh, M.P., a Protestant and the leader of the Irish Conservatives, who came from the neighbouring town of Borris.

From 1845 to 1851 he was driven the few miles to Bagenalstown school, making his way home on foot. They were particularly indelible years for an Irish boy. The horror of the great famine impressed itself vividly on the local towns as the starving country people swelled the population. Their plight overcame social barriers and distinctions of wealth. Those who had sufficient frequently responded to those who had little or nothing. The Delanys with their bakery were in a privileged position. Quantities of soup and bread were made available, and the children, at times of special demand, were kept at home from school to assist in distributing bread at the door, and in carrying bread and soup to the houses of the sick.

At the age of sixteen, William informed his parents that he wished to go to Carlow diocesan college to study for the priesthood. They were much opposed. As the eldest son, he was the natural heir to the family business. In face of protestations he remained adamant.

None of the family, in fact, was to carry on the business. The only other boy, Thomas, also went for the priesthood, served as a curate in the diocese, supported the tenants during the land agitation,[5] and died at an early age in October 1880. Of the daughters, the eldest, Maria, married a cousin, James Maher, and their son, Michael, became a Jesuit of the English province, a distinguished lecturer, and the author of a celebrated text-book on rational psychology. The youngest girl, Elizabeth, entered the Irish Sisters of Charity. The second girl inherited the business which passed to the name of her husband, William Bacon of Carlow. Two of their sons, John and Thomas, were to be prominent members of the student body of University College under William Delany, John becoming in addition a member of the teaching staff and, later, after 1909, a member of the governing body of the new University College, and a senator.

During his two years at Carlow College William displayed signs of that readiness of speech and skill in extempore argument which frequently afterwards stood him in good stead. One of his professors, Fr James Kavanagh, held him in high regard and was to remain a trusted friend. Under the stern rule of the dean, Fr J. Hughes, nevertheless, he found life at the college quite difficult. He went on to the chief Irish ecclesiastical seminary, Maynooth College, at the commencement of the academic year 1853-54. Some years later, when he was studying at Rome and had to revise in two years the entire course of theology, he attributed his success to the excellent teaching he had had at St Patrick's College, Maynooth. His time there afforded him contacts with future priests from different parts of the country. Some of the teaching staff, too, provided links to his later career. Dr Charles Macauley was the uncle and guardian to the MacNeill family, one of whom, John, was to be invited on to the University College staff by Delany, and to achieve distinction as a historian and a national figure, while Dr Henry F. Neville was to become rector of the Catholic University and an opponent, for a time, of Delany's plans for a Jesuit university college in Dublin.

The Delany parents were heartened by the accounts they received of their son's academic progress and general conduct. His extravagance in dress, however, was another matter. They received frequent requests for new clothes, about the cut and texture of which they thought him unnecessarily particular. He did not agree. If God's service called for splendour and beauty in buildings, it was appropriate, too, that his ministers should dress carefully and well! The lavish use of materials in pursuance of what he considered to be desirable and lofty ends was to prove a further characteristic feature. It added considerably both to his influence and to his troubles.

One of the 'nicer' people at Maynooth was Matthew Russell, a young man of literary interests, charm, and impeccable connections. He was a nephew of Dr Charles Russell, the celebrated president of Maynooth, and his brother, Lord Charles Russell of Killowen, was to become one of the most eminent barristers of his time and the first Catholic Lord Chief Justice of England since James II. Matthew and William became close friends. To Russell, in 1854, William confided his intention of entering the Society of Jesus, learning, to his surprise, that his friend had similar plans. Matthew, as editor of the Jesuit magazine, *The Irish Monthly*, was to provide openings for many of the young writers who inaugurated the Anglo-Irish literary revival. It was, as W.B. Yeats saw it, 'a kind of college of the bards'.[6]

William's motives for joining the Jesuits are not clear. He appears to have had no immediate contact with members of the Order. His younger sister, to whom he was close, implied that he was drawn by the desire to be a foreign missioner. Fr Joseph Darlington, his assistant for many years at University College, declared at the close of a long life, in a rather rambling memoir, that already at Maynooth William was very conscious of the need to raise the standard of education among Irish Catholics and saw in the Society of Jesus an effective means to that end.[7] There was also the example of Fr Edmund O'Reilly, a leading theologian at Maynooth, who had become a Jesuit in 1851 and now, three years later, had been appointed to the chair of theology in Dr Newman's Catholic University of Ireland.

Whatever the motivation, William's entry to the Order was deferred for two years. The Jesuit vice-provincial instructed him to continue his studies at Maynooth. He was accepted as a novice in January 1856 and, there being no Irish novitiate at the time, was sent to St Acheul, in the vicinity of Chalons, in France. After nineteen months he moved, for reasons of health, to Beaumont Lodge, near Windsor, in England, to complete his two year noviceship. His first vows in the Society of Jesus were taken in January 1858 at Clongowes Wood College, Co Kildare. Two subsequent years were spent at the college in the role of prefect and teacher of younger pupils. It proved a trying time. He was at first a failure as a teacher. He had no control over his pupils, and did not seem able to communicate knowledge to them. A systematic examination of the causes of his failure was required before he found a remedy for it.[8] By August 1860, however, when he was transferred to St Stanislaus College, Tullabeg, near Tullamore, Co Offaly, the problem had been solved. Apart from three years at Rome, he was to be stationed at Tullabeg for the next twenty years. In this unlikely location in the Irish mid-lands, he achieved the reputation as an educationalist which paved the way to his appointment to the presidency of University College Dublin.

St Stanislaus College, when he went there, had for long been a mere preparatory institution to Clongowes and was just beginning to develop as an independent secondary school. A key figure in that development was its rector-*cum*-prefect-of-studies from 1861 to 1865, Joseph Dalton, who subsequently took a prominent part in the expansion of Catholic education in Australia and was a man of great energy and vision, who communicated a driving ambition for the success of any venture to which he committed himself. William Delany was to reflect many of his rector's characteristics and to surpass him in his ambitions for the school. In 1860 he was put in charge of a third year class. He taught them in a number of subjects and, as was the custom, moved up with them each year. In 1863-64 he took them to rhetoric or sixth year class — the first such at Tullabeg. The following year he was appointed assistant-prefect of studies. At the close of that year he was sent to Rome to study theology. He remained there from 1865 to 1868.

It was an eventful time to be in Rome. The future of the Papal States was in the balance. He wrote regularly to his brother, Tom, then a curate at Monasterevan, Co Kildare. The letters covered a wide field: ordinary family matters, his work, the traditions of the university, its professors, the fluctuating political situation, the expulsion of the Jesuits from parts of Italy, his function as a *cicerone* to the numerous groups of Irish and English visitors to the Holy City. It is evident from the letters that he studied with great intensity. His working day ran from 4.0 a.m. to 10.0 p.m.; and here, one suspects, commenced the problem of insomnia which was to plague him for much of his life. He had a very clear and elevated view of his destined role as a Jesuit priest. He was impressed, too, by the Society's links with Rome and its traditions at the Roman College, and by the high intellectual standards of the latter; and he was not above trying to dazzle his less intellectual brother with it all. On the other hand, his letters played down the considerable academic success he himself achieved. In September 1866 he was ordained at the basilica of St John Lateran; and during his subsequent years of studies he was appointed chaplain to the Irish brigade which had been formed to assist in the defence of the Papal States.

Study in that year was disturbed not only by his duties as a chaplain but 'by the incessant stream of visitors to the Roman College and their requests to go and say Mass for them at altars of saints to whom there is a more particular devotion'. In a letter of 24 April 1867, he named some of the more prominent members of an English party for whom he had recently celebrated mass: 'Lady A. Kerr and Captain Kerr, the Hon. Mrs Douglas, and Mr & Mrs Chadwick'. Nevertheless, a month later, 23 May, he was able to report of his final examination that 'the event came off on the whole satisfactorily, far and away more than I had any hopes of'. The rector informed him that the General of the Order 'was much pleased at the examiners' reports'.[9]

In August he entered on his tertianship, a kind of second noviceship devoted largely to prayer and seclusion in preparation for final vows in the Society. From the end of May to early in November there are no extant letters. Their absence leaves unrecorded his reactions to the continual revolutionary agitation leading up to the critical events of October 1867. On 8 November he wrote to his brother of the failure of the *coup* within Rome; how the Garibaldians had infiltrated the city, 'for the most part with English passports', and how the signal for insurrection which was to have been given at ten o'clock was given by mistake at seven, with the result that 'the assassins' were made prisoners almost without firing a shot. He told of the defeat of Garibaldi's army of eight thousand men at Mentana by a combined force of three thousand papal and two thousand French troops. Hundreds of prisoners were brought back to Rome, and 'French troops, guns, munitions of war, horses, provisions etc' were being poured into the city every day. He himself attended the wounded soldiers in the hospitals. Some months later, 5 July 1868, he related in a sermon at Monasterevan how he had ministered to three young Irishmen who had taken part in the battle and who died cheerfully because they had fought in defence of 'their holy faith'.

He was recalled to Ireland shortly after this and his health once more gave cause for concern. He made his final vows at the Jesuit residence in Gardiner Street, Dublin, on 2 February 1868. The time in Italy was probably most relevant to his future career in bringing him to the notice of the General, in adding to his social assurance and intellectual self-confidence, and in providing an awareness of how the government of the Order and of the Catholic church worked. It also deepened his sense of history and politics, fostered an abhorrence of violent nationalism, and afforded him contacts with Irish and English visitors, some of them titled. Within a few years reference would be made to his influence with his 'Tory friends'.

Soon after his return home he was appointed to Tullabeg. His state of health seems the most likely explanation. In the eyes of the provincial and his advisers, St Stanislaus College was of secondary importance. An easy class and some occasional work was assigned to him. Within a year, however, he was appointed prefect of studies and minister (the provider of the day to day needs of the establishment), and straightaway he became involved in planning and building. A new boys' chapel was built and opened in 1870. On 8 December of that year he was made rector of the college, while retaining the position of prefect of studies.

On a number of occasions in his long career a congenial challenge provided an antidote to poor health. The challenge presented at Tullabeg was formidable. The greater part of the buildings required overhauling; arrangements for cooking, heating, laundry and toilet facilities, were of a primitive nature; the one hundred and twenty or so pupils were more than the school had been built to accommodate; the number and quality of the Jesuit teaching staff assigned to it by the provincial were not commensurate with its pretensions as a secondary school; and, finally, there were the school's remote location and the threatening state of its finances. To the new rector the problems seemed to serve as a stimulus. He had an exalted vision of what

could be achieved, and step by step he improved facilities and
built up a teaching staff to match his ambition. All over Britain,
as the empire entered on its final stages of expansion and openings in the public service increased — at home, in India, and in
the army — more and more schools modelled themselves on
Eton, Harrow and Winchester, the alleged moulders of the elite
who managed the empire. Delany, too, looked to the more celebrated of the English public schools for points of comparison,
and planned to make his neglected institution amidst the midland bogs into the leading college in the country.   Ebb\O .

He set about remodelling the buildings. Hot water was laid
on throughout the school. A new toilet area was constructed.
A section of the nearby river Silver was deepened and enclosed
to provide bathing facilities in the summer. The financial outlay
was met by an increase in pupils' fees. This occasioned support
rather than protest from the parents. He then embarked on
further improvements. Moreover, as part of a continuing effort
to widen the cultural horizons of youngsters, many of whom
came 'from utterly artless homes', he promoted better refectorial
arrangements and manners, introduced drill classes and teachers
of elocution and dancing, and encouraged wide reading, dramatic productions, and an interest in art and music. The library
was considerably enlarged, the school walls were hung with
Roman prints of works of art, the old study hall was converted
into a theatre where monthly productions were staged by the
pupils, and the development of a school orchestra and brass
band was actively fostered.[10]

Not surprisingly, members of his community took fright at
the expenditure and denounced his 'extravagance' to the provincial. But as with Fr Reffé, his distinguished counterpart at
Blackrock College,[11] such denunciation seemed to have little
effect. He considered that he had an obligation to spend money
to provide facilities for the pupils and to expand the reputation
of the college; and he showed no inclination to desist from expenditure unless formally forbidden to improve the school. He
took care, however, to keep the General of the Order, Fr Peter
Beckx, a Belgian, informed of his activities and long-term aims.
During his time in Rome, Fr Beckx had formed a highly favourable opinion of him. He hoped through him to revivify Jesuit
education in Ireland and had personally nominated him as
rector.[12]

Apart from the endeavour to broaden cultural horizons, a
fresh approach to school discipline came into operation. The
new rector placed much emphasis on promptness and punc-

tuality and communicated his concern for an all-round improvement in standards. But — according to a former student, and friend Judge Matthias McDonnell Bodkin — 'he ruled not by fear but affection. Physical punishment was almost unknown. He trusted to the honour of his boys'.[13] A close personal interest in them, their work and activities, was fostered by means of form or class-masters. Serious offences, however, were dealt with severely. The penalty was instant expulsion; and pleadings, or considerations of talent, wealth or social position, were of little avail. The point was made that the school's main concern was not to keep up its numbers, but to achieve and maintain a high standard of study and behaviour.

Organised games were seen as contributing to the school's well-being. The Jesuit prefects were encouraged and financially assisted to work up enthusiasm for games and to keep them going in a lively fashion. A type of football was played in winter. During the long summer months facilities were provided not only for swimming, but also for boating and cricket. He negotiated permission from the canal company to use a long stretch of water between the local locks for boating. A boat house was built and five or six boats installed. Boys using them were required to be able to swim 'in accordance with the rule of Eton College'.[14] Regattas were held on special occasions and every effort was made to make them colourful events, with special prizes, printed programmes, and music provided by the school band. In search of further status, a professional coach was employed to teach cricket. After some initial resistance from the pupils, the school developed a competent side, and a variety of fixtures with outside clubs added to the attraction of the game. Military and Gentlemen's elevens were invited to play the school. They stayed over-night and were lavishly entertained. A steady stream of notable guests and open-handed hospitality became marks of William Delany's term of office.

It was all congenial to his temperament, but it was also part of a deliberate policy to improve the status of St Stanislaus College and, in the process, to enlarge the interests, contacts and ambitions of the pupils and increase their pride in themselves and in their school. The new pride proved expansive. It spread to the teaching staff and the parents, and the latter, in particular, were not slow to publicise the changes brought about by 'the wonderful young rector'. A feature especially appreciated by them was his personal interest in and care of pupils who fell ill. In the case of serious illness accommodation was made available at the college for parents who wished to be near their sons. Not surprisingly, applications for entry showed an increase. In his third year, 1871-72, they reached 142; and rose to 152 the following year. By 1878 there were two hundred on the rolls.

But the growth in numbers was not characterised by uninterrupted progression. On the contrary, between 1873 and 1876, it seemed to many that the school could not survive. There was a serious drop in applications in 1873-74, which he attributed to the depressed financial state of the country. By the close of the following year a virulent scarlatina epidemic had reduced the number of pupils to seventy-five. His response was to inform a widening circle of influential acquaintances of his plans for the future and to incur further expenditure. He had the infirmary enlarged against further outbreaks, and an additional farm was bought to secure a more plentiful supply of milk, butter and meat. His faith in his own judgement and in the future of the college was vindicated by events, but not before critics within the Order, including, it would seem, the provincial and his consultors, linked the school's depressed condition to the rector's deviation from traditional ways — in extravagant expenditure, frequent absence from the college, and the cultivation of influential outsiders. They communicated their anxiety and criticism to the General, Fr Peter Beckx. He relayed the complaints to Delany, reinforced by his own admonitions. The complaints intensified, and the admonitions waxed more severe, as the situation deteriorated.

On 16 July 1873, Fr Beckx wrote that he had received the province's report on Tullabeg, and that from this there appeared to be a good spirit of unity amongst the Jesuits at the college and, generally speaking, they were well disposed towards their rector. It was also clear that he was well thought of by outsiders. On the other hand, it was remarked that he could show 'a greater care for the spiritual well-being of the servants', and that he displayed an 'unduly mundane and secular' attachment to the goodwill of important outsiders. He was said to be 'too frequently, for too long, and without need or permission, away from the college frequenting the houses of externs'. This was 'not edifying' to his fellow Jesuits; and, if the rumours were true, 'such familiarity with externs' was viewed unfavourably by some of the secular clergy. The conclusions drawn by some of those who had written to Rome was that he had little care of the students; and to this they attributed a falling off in studies at the college and the students' failure to come up to expectations. Nevertheless, all were of the opinion that he was 'an excellent man, with all the requirements for a rector laid down by the constitutions' of the Order, and that the reason he had not lived up to expectations was that he did not 'give himself fully to his office'. Delany replied on 5 August, and on 10 October the General thanked him for his letter and 'for the humble spirit in which he accepted the corrections and the prompt manner in which he had set about correcting the defects'.

Two years later, however, on 27 September 1875, the sense of crisis experienced at Tullabeg generated a deeper discontent and a correspondingly more severe letter from Fr Beckx. He opened by expressing his regard for Ireland because of its Catholic faith and religious practice, and his disappointment that Irish Jesuits, despite such a background, were not noted for that sanctity which their institute required, and did not, as a result, achieve the good they should achieve. Then, turning to Tullabeg, he expressed his dissatisfaction with Delany's performance. 'When I knew you at Rome, I saw you to be well disposed and full of love of religious discipline. For the good of the province, I hoped for much from you, but sadly events did not correspond with the expectations. I named you rector, and I don't know what special fruit to yourself and the college that office brought. Many quarrels are referred to me . . . and I ask you . . . to examine yourself before the crucifix if you proceed according to the spirit of St Ignatius, if you always keep before your eyes the rules of your office'. He wrote thus not to upbraid him, but rather to animate him to respond to God's goodness and glory. 'Believe me, dearest Father', he concluded, 'you can do much good if you seriously wish to do so. Study how to please men . . . and how you do not study to please God in all things or to keep the rules perfectly'.

The following year as applications increased the complaints declined. The General wrote briefly to express himself pleased with how things were going. He hoped that the financial debt would be overcome by prudent administration. On 15 February 1878, he was still concerned about the college's debt, but the main burden of his letter centred around the favourable reports he had received of the good spirit prevailing amongst the members of the community and the students, of the increase in pupil applications, of ardour in studies and success in examinations. A dramatic surge forward in academic achievement from 1876 onwards had brought widespread public recognition and disarmed criticism within the Order

Tullabeg, in its early years as a secondary school, had followed the lead of many of the Catholic colleges in presenting its pupils for matriculation in the Catholic University of Ireland, which had been founded by the Irish bishops in 1854. The Catholic University's degrees were not recognised by the government, and its standard of entrance offered little challenge. Delany, concerned at the lack of drive and purpose among his students, sought to substitute the London University matriculation for that of the Catholic University. Receiving no support for his proposal from the provincial and his consultors, he wrote directly to the General. Fr Beckx refused permission. To enter for the London examination might be interpreted as a declaration of no confidence in the bishops' institution. Throughout the years of criticism and bleak prospects, Delany continued to press his case. There was the precedent set by Carlow College. English Jesuit colleges, such as Stonyhurst, had found that London's standards gave a stimulus to study, removed a sense of isolation, and provided a recognised test to fathom the proficiency of the boys. Ahead of his time in Ireland, he underlined the importance of mathematics and science and the emphasis which London University placed on these subjects. Eventually, in 1875, the General acceded to his request.

With an assurance and single-mindedness which belied his relative inexperience, he organised the preparation of the senior classes for the London examinations. The result justified his confidence. A new spirit of work manifested itself throughout the school. The most advanced pupils were entered for the matriculation. Each of the six candidates presented was successful and two 'obtained good honours places'. This hundred per cent success, as he was careful to note, compared more than favourably with the thirty-three per cent success achieved by other Irish colleges taking the examination. The public acclaim which followed took him by surprise. A feeling of inferiority about academic standards in Catholic schools was widespread. Tullabeg's achievement, in the beleagured climate of the time, was seen as a justification of Catholic claims for equal educational opportunity with the endowed Protestant schools. The college's year book for 1875-76 noted that:

> Many of the leading Catholics wrote to Fr Rector to convey their delight at the college's success, and a certain noble lady (Lady Londonderry) donated an annual prize for literature to be competed for by our pupils. Not long afterwards a certain official, as yet an Anglican, offered a similar prize for mathematics.

The advent of the London University examinations ensured that recognised qualifications were available to the students and an increased status for the college. Moreover, 'the manifest benefits of competition and emulation' made a lasting impression on Delany. During his remaining four years at Tullabeg the school was geared increasingly towards university standards. Provision was made for classes up to Bachelor of Arts level. Special quarters and incentives were provided for those matriculating and then staying on to take their arts degree. He went out of his way to obtain specialist lay teachers, particularly in mathematics and science, both to prepare his students and to coach his young Jesuit teachers; and in order to obtain the best available he was prepared to pay salaries well above the going rate. In this, in the number of lay teachers employed, and in his attitude towards them, his college was quite exceptional among Catholic schools. The religious communities or diocesan clergy who ran such schools relied on pupils' fees, and on such other sources of income — if any — as attended the community house or diocesan institution, to keep their schools going. There was no government subsidy. If they raised their fees beyond a certain level, they were likely to lose pupils. Hence, for most of them, shortage of money was a perennial problem. They were able to employ very few lay teachers, and then only at a miserable salary. The lay teacher's position, as a result, was an unenviable one. He was a layman in a clericalist world. He had no security of tenure. And his status was further undermined by the fact that he usually did not have a degree. The absence of a recognised university acceptable to the Catholic bishops meant that very few Catholics had the opportunity of obtaining a university qualification. Those who did obtain such were in a more favoured situation, but the salaries they commanded put them beyond the reach of most schools.[15]

At Tullabeg, from 1876 to 1882, there were between seven and eleven lay teachers on the staff, and the number of graduates amongst them ranged from two to four. In 1880, Delany impressed on his sceptical and unsympathetic provincial, Fr James Tuite, the important rôle played by these men in the college's achievements. Much of its success was due to them, and since this success generated, in turn, an increase in applications from brighter pupils and, thereby, an increase in prospective scholarships, it was not uneconomical to employ so many of them. He went on to argue the need for a mathematics teacher with an honours degree to teach the B.A. students, since only such a man was capable of assisting them obtain high honours at university level. He was prepared to pay the teacher he had in mind £200 a year in the characteristic conviction 'that the best is cheapest'.[16] When it is considered that twenty-five years later the government inspectors, F.H. Dale and T.A. Stephens, reported that the average annual income of a male teacher was only £82.6.7d,[17] the reluctance of the provincial is not surprising. With a similarly persistent advocacy, Delany had his way in obtaining a succession of talented Jesuit scholastics to strengthen the teaching power and fulfil the prefectorial functions at the college.

The school went from strength to strength in its performance in the London examinations and, after 1879, in the matriculation to the new Royal University. It achieved his aim of being considered one of the leading colleges in the country. His own reputation as an educationalist (or educationist – as he preferred) rose with that of his school. His wide-ranging social contacts ensured that his school's success was remarked on in the right quarters. He became more and more involved with educational developments at national level, and was absent from the college for longer periods. Such absences, as evidenced by the General's letters, were not welcomed at Tullabeg and throughout the province and helped create a particular image of him which still lingers in the corporate memory. He is recalled, both as rector at Tullabeg and president of University College, as a gracious but remote and rather magnificent personage, who was frequently away from the establishment and only made his presence felt on occasions of special importance. He was described 'as ruling from beyond the clouds'. The evidence, however, indicates that while there might be some grounds for the implied criticism during his final years at both institutions, these did not apply to the critical early years when it was necessary to motivate staff and students and to establish a well-defined organisational structure. These aims having been achieved, he appears to have felt free to devote increasing time and energy to influencing the wider course of Irish education at both secondary and tertiary level.

In those early years, however, great attention was given to setting the tone and atmosphere of the college. Thus at Tullabeg he kept in close touch with pupils and masters and regularly visited the classrooms. The visits were devoted not so much to superintendence of teaching, or to a search for improved methods, but to the infusion of a spirit of hard work, ambition, and lively rivalry. Given ability and motivation, the teachers would, he believed, find their way to the methods best suited to each of them. To fire the zeal of pupils and teachers regular oral examinations were held for an entire class. He personally attended, accompanied by a number of masters, and the occasion was invested with solemnity and pageantry — features he considered particularly important in the formation of youth. These *concertationes*, as they were called, were introduced by musical items, and diversified by declamations and the reading of essays, in keeping with his desire to stimulate interest in music, elocution, and 'good writing'. He also attended, and occasionally participated in, the meetings of the college debating society, where proceedings were modelled on those of the House of Commons and the House's freedom of expression was encouraged. Thus, an emphasis on hard work was joined to a variety of activities aimed at all round personal development. The atmosphere of the school reflected the blend. 'The golden mean between "cram" and dilettantism was not lost sight of', wrote Joseph McGrath, later registrar of the National University of Ireland, and a former pupil of Tullabeg, 'and there was an easy relationship between boys, teachers, and school authorities'.[18]

A less well-disposed account of the school was furnished by Dr J.P. Mahaffy of Trinity College. As a member of the 1878 Endowed Schools' Commission, he applied for leave to visit Tullabeg. Although his functions extended only to schools enjoying public endowments, and he was known to be strongly opposed to the Intermediate examination system and critical of Delany, one of its staunchest defenders, he was assured of a welcome. He arrived just after the main vacation in 1880 when, as he said, the boys 'were some what rusty in their back work'. His report found room for praise and criticism. He concluded with the observation that 'the various school boards and headmasters throughout Ireland' might find, as he did, 'a certain restraint among the boys' but 'they would all profit greatly by visiting the college and learning from its many good points of management, of neatness and of order, which made it quite exceptional in the country'.[19]

Mahaffy's visit was at a period when Delany was frequently absent. His testimony indicated that the school was not adversely affected. Part of the secret appears to have been clearly delineated functions within the college, and an expectation of co-operation from students and of high professional standards from all members of staff. 'You have shown what spirit a rector can give to his staff, and what energy and spirit in a staff can do', Fr Weld, the General's assistant, wrote to him in September 1878. His own professional outlook was also 'quite exceptional in the country', and in the Irish Jesuit province. Sir Patrick Keenan, assistant commissioner for education, commented in 1875 on the very low standards in Irish secondary schools, but exempted from his strictures the establishments run by the French Fathers at Blackrock and by the Jesuits.[20] The latter, nevertheless, left much to be desired by Delany's criteria. He considered that they were not living up to the high traditions of their Order in their teaching and in their general contribution to education in the country. He sought to remedy these deficiencies at Tullabeg. It was to be outstanding, but not in isolation. Its success was to be linked to the betterment generally of Irish secondary education. In the process the prestige and influence of the Order would be advanced. His wide reading, much of his voluminous correspondence, his style of administration, and his cultivation of many of the important personages of the day, were tributary to these aims; and they extended the range and depth of his personal influence once Tullabeg had captured the limelight and his reputation as an educationalist had become established.

That personal influence grew steadily from 1877 onwards. Politicians sought his advice on educational matters, and his presence was requested in the drawing-rooms of the titled and of the influential Dublin middle class, as well as on public platforms. His genuine interest in others, his capacity to marshall arguments on a wide variety of subjects, and what Judge Bodkin called 'his brilliancy of conversation, his indescribable fascination of manner, ranging from grave to gay, from serious to serene',[21] made him a desirable guest in a city which prided itself on its 'rich talk'. By dint of avid reading, he could speak with some authority on matters of history, literature, economics, philosophy, science, and events of current interest, but he mainly confined himself to those areas where he could speak as a professional, the areas of education and religion. And here, according to the uncompleted biography by his near contemporary, Fr Lambert McKenna, the earnestness of his speech, the orderliness of his thought, the wealth of his facts, the appositeness of his illustrations, joined to a constant courteousness of manner, gave to his spoken and written word a special authority.[22]

A few extracts from a diary kept by him in 1873 give an idea of the extent and character of his reading at that stage, and indicate the background to his reputation as a conversationalist and speaker:

'Nov. 7   Read *All's Well that Ends Well. Much Ado about*

Nothing. Four chaps. *Book of Proverbs*; two chaps.
Life of St. Teresa.

Nov. 10   Trollope's *Vicar of Bullhampton. Novels and Novelists of 18th Century.*

Nov. 11   *The Head of the Family* (John Halifax).

Nov. 12   Mill's *Autobiography. Dublin Review* on *Vindiciae Alphonsianae,* also Frazer's *St. Symeon Sales.*

Nov. 14   Parson's *Hecuba,* 200 lines. Darwin's *Descent of Man.* Vol. 1. Three chapters of *Proverbs.*

Nov. 15   *Henry IV.* Freeman's *Essays. Proverbs* (3 chaps). *Life of St. Teresa* (2 chaps).

Nov. 16   Some *Essays of Elia.* Some *Hecuba, Henry V, Quarterly Review.*

Nov. 23   *Book of Wisdom,* I-VIII. Mill's *Autobiography* (2nd time). Bollandists' *Life of St. Symeon Sales.*

Nov. 24   Rest of *Bk. of Wisdom. Life of St. Teresa* (1 chap.). Faber's *Bethlehem* (25 pp.). *Iliad,* 1. (315 lines). Freeman's *Essays* on Athens and Mediaeval Italy. Essay in *Quarterly.*

Nov. 26   Cicero's *Pro Lege Manilia, Pro Murena, Pro Rabirio. Book of Ecclesiasticus* (8 chaps). *Bethlehem* (31 pp.)'.

These indications occurred during normal working weeks. Much of his reading was probably done at night. It is known that he stayed up till very late. It is not clear whether this practice was a cause, or an effect, of the sleeplessness which was certainly a recurring feature from 1881 on.

Though his reading could scarcely have been very deep, it was not superficial or listless. Notes and short summaries were frequently appended to the names of books read. He was noted for his power of instantly seizing the main points of a narrative or the main lines of an argument; and he had an excellent memory. And these qualities were joined to that capacity, already mentioned, of rapidly marshalling reasons to defend almost any position, clearly stating them, and illustrating them vividly.

The seal on public recognition of Tullabeg's achievements was provided in 1879 with the formal visit to the school of the Viceroy, the Duke of Marlborough, and his wife. The visit had been arranged through the duchess who was already a friend of his. He had frequented Blenheim, the Marlborough ducal home, according to R.F. Foster in *Lord Randolph Churchill* (Oxford, 1981), and had, perhaps, been introduced to the duchess through her Catholic relations, her sister-in-law, Lady Londonderry, or her sister, Lady Portarlington, with whom he was particularly friendly. Delany was a regular visitor at Emo Park, the estate of Lord Portarlington, as were a number of the Catholic hierarchy. Portarlington, though a Protestant, took a strongly Catholic line on educational questions and frequently called on Delany at Tullabeg.[23]

At the time of the duke's visit, the Intermediate Education Act had been passed, and there was hope that the principle it enshrined of indirect endowment for Catholic schools might be also applied to provide university education for Catholics. It was typical of Delany's approach to his titled guests that he availed himself of the occasion both to congratulate the Viceroy on the passing of the Intermediate Act and to point his attention towards an Irish university bill. Students greeted him with elaborate addresses and adulatory verse in Greek, Latin, French and English; and he was reminded in mediocre rhyme that his contribution to intermediate education was but a beginning:

The Irish University is still
Contained within the compass of the Bill.
Safe launched at anchor rides the sparless hull
For Irish schools of hope and promise full.

At this juncture Delany had already had private meetings with the duke and his son, Randolph Churchill, on the question of intermediate and university education, and had been involved in preparations for the Intermediate Bill. Already, indeed, he had acquired in educational circles the reputation of notable influence over his 'Tory friends'. Prominent among these friends were Gerald Fitzgibbon, the solicitor-general, and Edward Gibson, attorney-general. They were key figures in a small, influential group of mainly professional men, who met convivially and favoured wide-ranging, interesting and witty conversation. They befriended Churchill on his arrival in Dublin and made him a grateful member of their company. The circle included David Plunkett, later Lord Rathmore, Dr J.P. Mahaffy, future provost of Trinity College, Michael Morris, who became the first Catholic lord chief justice of common pleas in Ireland (and later Lord Killanin), Lord Chief Justice Ball, and the famous parish priest of Little Bray, Fr James Healy. The key personality in many ways was Fitzgibbon, a committed Protestant and influential Freemason, who had many Catholic friends and worked closely with Catholic clergy. Able and astute, and cleverly critical of government policy towards Ireland, he was particularly friendly with Churchill and favoured him with frequent political advice on Irish questions. For some years after leaving the country, Churchill used to return to Fitzgibbon's annual Christmas house party at Howth, outside Dublin, 'the *haute école* of intelligent Toryism', as his host described it. Part of the function of 'intelligent Toryism', in Fitzgibbon's view, was to promote the natural alliance between Catholics and conservatives; and full denominational education for the Catholic middle classes was a means to that end, and to keeping fenianism in check. It was an outlook that was shared by the Chief Secretary, Sir Michael Hicks-Beach, Lord Randolph Churchill, the Duke and Duchess of Marlborough and, according to Isaac Butt, by many 'Roman Catholics in various positions'.[24]

With 'Tory friends' expressing such attitudes towards education, it is not surprising that Delany's non-conservative friends should attribute much influence to him. What is more revealing, perhaps, is Dr Mahaffy's remark in the official report on his visitation of the school the following year:[25]

> The relation of the college to the university question has constantly occupied the rector, and he has busied himself much in the various attempts to obtain a system of examination for his boys after the London fashion. *The new Irish University will probably be arranged (like the Intermediate) in such a manner as to suit his views exactly.*

This remarkable comment testified to a fairly widespread belief that Delany had a considerable hand in the shaping of the two government bills which changed the face of Irish education.

Chapter II

THE INTERMEDIATE ACT AND THE ROYAL UNIVERSITY

The inequality in treatment as between Protestant and Catholic secondary, or intermediate, schools was a constant source of grievance to Catholic educationalists. Although endowments were available to the Protestant schools, governments, in the climate of the time, did not dare offer direct endowment to schools for Catholics. Religion, in Victorian Britain, was a vigorous, if contumacious, component of society. The Catholic church was viewed with hostility and was still, for many, associated with superstitious practices and foreign dominance. The powerful nonconformist voice, in particular, was critical of public expenditure in support of any form of denominational education, let alone denominational education for papists.[26] As an expedient at third level, the government, in 1845, had sought to meet the needs of nonconformists and of the Irish Catholic majority by the establishment of the undenominational Queen's Colleges of Belfast, Cork, and Galway. But these instruments of 'mixed education' were denounced by the Catholic hierarchy as 'godless colleges' and, as a result, largely failed in their purpose. The bishops had set up their own Catholic University and made it clear that they were opposed to the very principle of undenominational education. Hence, successive governments found themselves, at second as well as at third level, at an *impasse*.

The dead-lock continued until 1878. The arrival of Randolph Churchill, as secretary to the new Viceroy, two years previous to that date, marked the turning-point. He interested himself almost immediately in education at intermediate level. It was an area receiving much public notice. The Irish parliamentarians, following the disappointing defeat of Gladstone's university bill of 1873, had turned their endeavours to seeking relief for Catholic secondary schools. Various educationalists were writing and speaking on the schools' overall needs. It was not just a matter of securing endowmental equality with Protestants, there were also the problems, experienced in many of them, of little motivation, low academic standards, the absence of an educational tradition, and the lack of an ordered, professional approach to teaching. To Sir Patrick Keenan, in particular, but also to others like Fr Delany and Fr Leman of Blackrock,[27] the answer appeared to be to provide a system of competitive public examinations, which would carry money prizes on the basis of results. This, it was claimed, would make available a form of indirect subsidy and would also encourage the schools to lift their standards.

The proposal was attractive to the Chief Secretary, Hicks-Beach, who, as noticed earlier, wished to further Catholic denominational education and had in mind to that end a plan to allocate surplus church funds. Churchill, committed to denominational education for the Catholic middle classes and prepared to seek the limelight by denouncing the government's neglect of Ireland, declared that much though Parliament might like to find a solution on the grounds of undenominational education, such an approach was not practicable. The Roman Catholics had 'never accepted the principle of mixed education'.[28] The schools would have to remain denominational. He proposed that an indirect subsidy, based on examination results, be found for them from the endowments of the Protestant schools and from the surplus funds of the disestablished Irish state church. The latter suggestion proved attractive to the government as involving no extra expense on English and Scottish tax-payers. The resulting education bill was drafted by Gibson, the attorney-general, and Fitzgibbon, the solicitor-general.

Judge Matthias Bodkin was to claim, some thirty years later, that he and the rector of Tullabeg had drafted the proposed measure clause by clause. 'At the time, Fr Delany was hand in glove with the Duke of Marlborough, Lord Lieutenant, and his son, Lord Randolph Churchill, the rising hope of the Tory party. Lord Randolph determined on an Intermediate Education Act for Ireland. Fr Delany was naturally called into council. It chanced that a little while afterwards I visited him at the college, and at his suggestion made a rough draft of the proposed measure. When we next met the measure, almost unchanged, was half-way through the House of Commons.

"Well, Fr Delany", I said, "Our bill is going through".
"Yes, Matt", he replied triumphantly, "and it is our bill".'[29]

It is scarcely to be expected that, after such a lengthy span, Judge Bodkin's recollections were entirely accurate. Delany himself gave much of the credit for the shape of the new legislation to Sir Patrick Keenan: 'It is mainly owing to you that the measure is so thoroughly satisfactory'.[30] Nevertheless, there is some evidence in support of the judge's recollections. Delany *had* discussed the proposed measure in considerable detail with Randolph Churchill and the Lord Lieutenant. He *had* corresponded with friends in the Irish party, such as Judge Little, who had sons at Tullabeg, and the O'Conor Don, in connection with it; and another friend, Lord O'Hagan, had passed on his written views to Lord Cairns who introduced the bill. Moreover, the solicitor-general, Fitzgibbon, had sought his opinion, and on 22 June 1878, remarked that his hints had been 'well ventilated' and had contributed to keeping the draft, as settled by Gibson and himself, 'in its present shape'.[31]

However significant Delany's contribution to the parliamentary measure may, or may not, have been, he did have a key rôle to play in subsequent events. In the aftermath of the act, a board of commissioners was appointed to draw up a common curriculum and to administer the decree. They sought the advice of the headmasters. The Protestant schools were represented by a headmasters' association. The Catholics as yet had no point of unity. The Protestant headmasters invited Delany to join their association. He declined and wrote to his friend, Dr Walsh, vice-president of Maynooth, of the need for an association of Catholic headmasters if the new scheme was not 'to be shaped from the very start so as to suit the Protestant schools'. On 8 October 1878, forty-four Catholic headmasters, representing nearly all the chief Catholic boys' schools, met at Maynooth. The Catholic Headmasters' Association thus came into being. Dr Walsh was appointed its first president and Fr Delany, its secretary. At that first meeting a list of school books was drawn up, and the draft of a programme for submission to the board of commissioners was approved. It had been put together by Delany on the basis of the Oxford local programme.[32] The two headmasters' associations reached substantial agreement on it. The commissioners, in consequence, sanctioned its publication over Christmas to enable pupils to commence their preparation for the examinations, scheduled for the following June.

The outcome of the examinations was awaited with anxiety. It was widely held that the Catholic candidates would be shown up badly by their Protestant counterparts. The anxiety was reflected in the dissatisfaction expressed with a number of the examination papers. Their unsuitability was attributed 'to the predominance of Protestants, mostly Trinity professors or past Trinity men, on the examining board'. In his position as secretary, Delany wrote on the matter to the Catholic commissioners, the O'Conor Don, Chief Baron Palles, and Lord O'Hagan, and produced in support a printed memorandum signed by Dr Walsh and himself. He sent a copy to Randolph Churchill, who added to his disquiet by warning that he would need 'to be constantly on his guard' against attempts by the Protestant headmasters 'to take unfair advantage wherever they can'.[33] What was suspected was that the examinations were being set to cater for a select group of pupils rather than for the majority of the candidates. Delany maintained that he had no fears of such a bias where his own pupils were concerned, his concern was that it ran counter to what the country needed. 'The question in Ireland', he reminded the general conference of Catholic headmasters in August 1883, 'was not how to develop the education of solitary individuals or of a small class, but to raise up the intermediate education of the whole people'. It was not a matter of a system 'fashioned to the special requirements of individuals, or limited to the production of Arnolds, or Mahaffys, or rhetoricians however brilliant' but one which would, 'whilst unduly fostering none, offer scope and stimulus for the development of the tastes, aptitudes, and capacities of all classes', while yet holding out to teachers inducements, 'to exercise their best energies in the producing of this result'.[34]

In the event, there was little cause for anxiety about examination results. The pattern of the immediate future was indicated in the first year. Blackrock came first, Tullabeg second, in the total of exhibitions and prizes won; and a little known Jesuit school, the Crescent, Limerick, produced the student who headed the list of successful candidates.

As principals of the first two Catholic colleges, Fr Reffé of Blackrock and Fr Delany became the natural leaders of their headmasters' association. Delany remained secretary of its standing committee until the end of 1881, when he was succeeded by Fr Reffé. The work of the association was laborious. Correspondence had to be maintained with Catholic headmasters throughout the country, who did not meet as a body between 1878 and 1883. Besides, much of the onus for communication and negotiation between the Catholic and Protestant associations, and with the board of commissioners — regarding the rules governing the Intermediate, the standard of the examination papers and so on — fell to the secretary; and there also devolved on

Delany during his term of office the responsibility of organising two joint deputations from the headmasters' associations to meet the Chief Secretary, and of preparing and circularising memorials to the Lord Lieutenant and members of parliament against a government proposal of financial retrenchment. The work-load, on top of his duties as headmaster, and his increasing participation in correspondence and negotiations regarding a new university, led to a breakdown in health in 1881 and to his resignation as secretary.

Towards the close of 1878 and early the following year, his ascending reputation as an educationalist almost secured him an appointment which would have severely limited his involvement in university developments. Dr T.W. Croke, Archbishop of Cashel, wrote to the three Catholic commissioners urging them to press on the government the appointment of Fr Delany to the full-time post of assistant-commissioner for intermediate education, which had just been vacated by Dr Gerald Molloy, the versatile Dublin priest who was destined to become rector of the Catholic University and a fellow in physics of the Royal University of Ireland. Chief Baron Palles, in turn, requested the lord high chancellor, Dr J.T. Ball, to urge the matter with the Duke of Marlborough. Randolph Churchill wrote to Delany encouraging him to press his candidature. The Lord Lieutenant sent for him. He, however, having grounds for believing that Dr McCabe, the recently appointed Archbishop of Dublin, did not wish a priest to be appointed to the office, informed the duke that he thought it more advisable, both in the interests of the government and of the smooth working of the Intermediate Education Act, that the wishes of Dr McCabe should be consulted. He recommended Major Myles W. O'Reilly, whose name had also been mentioned in connection with the post, as a man of whom the archbishop would approve and whose appointment would be regarded as satisfactory to those engaged in Catholic education. Major O'Reilly was appointed on 24 March, 1879. He was an interesting choice: a dapper, slightly-built Irish country gentleman who bred race horses and prize cattle but held an arts degree from London University and an LL.D. from Rome. He had been leader of the motley Irish brigade which in 1860 went to the aid of the Papal States against Garibaldi's forces, and had distinguished himself at the defence of Spoleto. On his return he became a popular member of parliament for Co Longford, and resumed his interest in educational pursuits. He was the author of a number of articles and pamphlets on Irish education.[35]

Delany had kept Rome informed of developments. Fr Weld,

the assistant to the Jesuit General, wrote on 4 April 1879 approving his actions, but wondering whether Major O'Reilly would be able to inspect schools and examine pupils. He feared that much of his work would fall on Delany without 'pay or honour'. 'However', he continued, 'if we can do some good it is the principal thing'; and he concluded with the significant reminder 'to take care not to let these things take your attention from the college'. It was only half heard. Delany was preoccupied with the prospects of a university bill.

He had devoted much thought over many years to the university question: how to secure for Irish Catholics equality of treatment in higher education with their Protestant fellow-countrymen? The latter had available to them the University of Dublin, which had been the sole university institution up to the late eighteen-forties and was, in practice, a Protestant university for the Protestant people of Ireland. The question was to claim his active attention for a further thirty years; the duration of the struggle testified to the conflicting aims and attitudes of the main protagonists: the government, the Catholic bishops, the nonconformists of Britain and Ireland, and the authorities of the University of Dublin.

To appreciate the difficulties posed by the question, and to better understand Delany's efforts towards a solution, it is appropriate at this point to turn briefly from the chronological sequence of events in order to consider the views of the protagonists, something of the history of the problem, and, finally, the chief proposals put forward for its settlement.

'Her Majesty's ministers have made up their minds as to the nature of the education suitable for Ireland', the Liberal prime minister, Lord Palmerston, informed an Irish Catholic deputation at the beginning of the eighteen-sixties. 'They are firmly convinced that the best system of education for that country is a mixed education.'[36] Successive governments had promoted a system of mixed or undenominational university education since the eighteen-forties; and they had persevered with it in spite of opposition from the Irish Catholic episcopate and laity. They appealed to the principles of freedom of the individual conscience and equality between denominations in support of their policy. English governments, wrote W.K. Sullivan, professor of chemistry at the Catholic University and later president of Queen's College, Cork, to William Monsell (subsequently Baron Emly) in 1866, tended to apply 'general principles' to the solution of Irish problems 'while common sense and experience alone are the guides for English legislation'.[37] The effects of government policy had been, as noted: the founding of the undenominational Queen's Colleges in 1845, with colleges in Cork and Galway to serve the Catholic population and a college in Belfast for the nonconformist minority, and the condemnation of the new institutions by the Catholic bishops and the Holy See, and their establishment in 1854 of a counter-institution, the Catholic University of Ireland. The bishops appealed to similar 'general principles', asserting, under the heading of emancipation and equality of treatment, the right of Catholics to parity with the Protestants of Britain and Ireland in having a system of denominational education appropriate to their beliefs.

Episcopal condemnation effectively nullified the new colleges as a means of solving the university question. The Queen's Colleges of Cork and Galway failed in their purpose, the Chief Secretary, Augustine Birrell, was to tell the House of Commons in 1908, 'for the simple reason that no pains whatever seem to have been taken to find out what Irishmen want. You may in Ireland sometimes succeed in sending a man to prison against his will, but never to college'.[38]

One of the abiding grounds of grievance where Catholics were concerned was the manner in which successive governments subordinated Catholic claims to the demands of the nonconformist minority. The political influence of nonconformism was, in fact, sufficiently powerful to act as a brake on initiatives from the two great English political parties. The Liberals' dependence on the nonconformist vote and their own predeliction for mixed education greatly limited their prospects of putting forward an acceptable solution. The Conservatives, in spite of a more open attitude to the denominational claims of Catholics in keeping with their party's traditional support for denominational education for Protestants, were also restricted in what they could offer by the anti-papist stance of their particular nonconformist supporters — the radicals in England, the orange adherents in Ireland.

The Catholic bishops, who displayed their own brand of intransigence from time to time, were, as a rule, more flexible than their nonconformist opponents in their capacity to adapt to political reality. Their main weakness as a body lay in their absence of unity with regard to precise objectives, a condition which provided unsympathetic governments with an excuse for not taking action, and added to the considerable difficulties facing well-disposed administrations.

The remaining interested party, the authorities of the Uni-

versity of Dublin, gradually moved from a position of antagonism
to any special denominational concessions to Irish Catholics to
one of opposition to any solution of the university question
which would interfere with the constitution and privileges of
their ancient university.

In the course of the long-drawn-out struggle, the protagonists
were subjected to a variety of pressures. The interplay of
political, economic and religious considerations combined to
defy attempts at a settlement, as did such psychological factors
as mutual fear, mistrust, and an anxiety to preserve control over
developments.

The history of the question indicates that the Irish bishops,
in the person of their chief spokesman, Archbishop Paul Cullen
of Dublin, had seen in the policy of the Liberal government of
Lord John Russell, which came to power in 1846, a deliberate
application to Ireland of that aspect of continental liberalism
which sought to take education out of the hands of the clergy
and to divorce it from religion. A conspiracy had been formed,
Cullen believed, 'to rob the Irish people of their faith' by imposing on them a system of secular or mixed education 'calculated
to sow the seeds of indifferentism'.[39] The Catholic University,
as a result, was envisaged as a means of uniting Catholics throughout the empire, of creating 'a large body of learned men' and
preparing 'the rising generation for the combat before them'.[40]
The choice of John Henry Newman as its first rector gave hope
of great achievement. The hope was short-lived. The university
had no source of financial support apart from church collections; and the absence of government recognition of its degrees
undermined its academic standing. The struggle to keep it
going, nevertheless, sharpened in the Catholic laity an awareness
of the value of higher education and increased their sense of
grievance against a government which obliged them to pay taxes
in support of mixed educational establishments, which as
Catholics they were forbidden to attend, while they at the same
time had to tax themselves to maintain the Catholic University.
Representation to the government, as indicated by Lord Palmerston's reply, met with little sympathy. At length, however, the
pressure of Catholic requests evoked a reponse from a Tory
administration and, subsequently, from its Liberal successor.

In 1868 the Chief Secretary, Lord Mayo, put forward a
scheme for a predominantly Catholic university which would
be chartered and endowed but which would give access to students of other denominations. The proposal met with strong
opposition from within the cabinet, and was eventually with-

drawn on the plea that the bishops' demands for control of the governing body was excessive. Two years later a large number of prominent Catholics presented a declaration to the new Liberal government of Mr Gladstone demanding on constitutional grounds equality of educational opportunity between Irish Catholics and the rest of their fellow countrymen. In 1871 William Monsell, an influential Irish Catholic landlord and a disciple of John Henry Newman, proposed a plan for admitting the Catholic University into the University of Dublin on terms of equality with that university's sole college, Trinity College. That year also the bishops issued a pastoral letter in which they pointed out that the Catholic demand for educational equality could be secured in either of two ways: the establishment of a national university having one or more colleges conducted on purely Catholic lines, or the establishment of such a college within the University of Dublin.[41] The latter proposal marked a new departure on the part of the Irish episcopate. The University of Dublin, founded in the reign of Queen Elizabeth as a Protestant institution, but open to Catholics since 1793, was regarded as a bastion of the state religion and, as such, Catholics were discouraged from attending it.

Gladstone responded to these representations with the university bill of 1873. There was to be one university in Ireland, the University of Dublin. This was to have as affiliated colleges Trinity College, the theological department of Trinity College as a separate institution, the Queen's Colleges of Cork and Belfast, Magee Presbyterian College of Theology in Derry, the Catholic University, and any other colleges fulfilling the necessary conditions. The bill met with general opposition. The University of Dublin strongly objected to the proposed interference with its autonomy and traditions. The authorities of the Queen's University and its colleges viewed with alarm the destruction of a large part of their system. The bishops opposed it on the grounds that it granted no endowment to any Catholic institution and thereby rendered competition within the university unfair to Catholic students. They also objected to the secularist character of the new establishment. The most determined opponents, however, were the nonconformists of the Liberal party. Every real concession to the Irish Catholics, Edmund Dease, M.P., wrote angrily to Delany after the division in the House of Commons, had been withdrawn from the bill 'for the sake of nonconformist bigotry'.[42] The Irish members, as a result, joined with the Tories and the unplacated, dissentient Liberals, in voting against the measure. In spite of this opposition, the bill was defeated by only three votes.

Gladstone's bill was to be the last attempt for nearly forty years to legislate for a permanent solution to the Irish university question. It proved a watershed in the history of the problem. Subsequent governments were loath to introduce proposals likely to interfere with Trinity College's autonomy or to rouse nonconformist hostility. They were left, as a result, with the almost insuperable task of providing an alternative institution to that of the University of Dublin which would meet the denominational requirements of the Catholic population and the undenominational demands of the nonconformists. On the Catholic side, on the other hand, there were those, such as Dr William Walsh, the future Archbishop of Dublin, who looked back to the near success of Gladstone's measure and hoped that, with the passage of time, a solution on its lines might be found.

A temporary alleviation of the situation was provided by Disraeli's Conservative government in 1879. The Royal University Act of that year established a purely examining body, the Royal University of Ireland, which made it possible for the students of Catholic colleges to compete for degrees, as Delany's students had done by means of the London University examinations. The Queen's University was abolished (from 1882) but the Queen's Colleges continued in existence with their system of endowments. No direct financial aid was granted to Catholic institutions, though a form of indirect subsidy was engineered for them. The overall result was a makeshift institution which satisfied nobody but was accepted as an expedient until a permanent solution was accomplished. As the years passed, such a settlement took on the character of a will-o'-the-wisp. A generation of intermittent agitation and hopeful schemes was to bring no further tangible improvement to the Catholic position.

During that long intermission three main proposals for a solution were put forward: the establishment of a great national teaching university, independent of the University of Dublin, which would be generously endowed and so structured as to meet the needs of the Catholic majority without danger to their religious beliefs; the establishment of a suitably endowed Catholic college, of equal standing with Trinity College, within the University of Dublin; and, when neither of these goals seemed likely of realisation, the enlargement of the scope of the Royal University to include a central Catholic teaching college suitably equipped and financed.

Catholics were divided in their preferences. The episcopate as

'The Wooden Corridoor', Tullabeg. Classroom doors on right.

St Stanislaus College, Tullabeg

 J. M. J. C.

SAINT STANISLAUS' COLLEGE,

TULLABEG,

TULLAMORE.

DISTRIBUTION OF PRIZES,

1877.

A. M. D. G.

COLLEGE OF ST. STANISLAUS.

PROSPECTUS:

I.—LOWER SCHOOL.

I. THE course of Instruction embraces the Classical and Modern Languages, History, Mathematics, and the Natural Sciences.

Boys are prepared for Matriculation. and for the B.A. degree of the London University, for the Civil Service, for the Army, for the Indian and other public Competitive Examinations. Special attention is paid in all the classes to English Composition, Arithmetic, Writing, and Elocution, and they are regarded throughout as forming the most essential part of the boys' education.

II. Unceasing care is taken to convey to the minds of the Pupils solid instruction in the principles of Religion, and to engage their hearts to the observance of its precepts.

III. The greatest attention is paid to the health and comfort of the Scholars, and they are supplied with abundant means of in-door and out-door exercise and amusement. In Summer they have the advantage of daily bathing within the College Grounds.

IV. Terms: Forty Guineas per annum. to be paid half-yearly, in advance. Entrance Fee, Two Guineas. Music, Dancing and Drawing are extra charges; as is also Medical Assistance, when necessary.

All necessary Books are provided at a uniform charge of One Guinea yearly during the course.

Two Guineas half-yearly will be charged to each for washing, repairs of clothes, linen, shoes, etc.; and One Guinea yearly to those more advanced pupils who attend Lectures on Natural Philosophy and Chemistry.

The necessary outfit for each Pupil comprises, at least, two suits of clothes, six shirts, eight pairs of stockings, eight handkerchiefs, six towels, three night shirts, three pairs of sheets, four pillow-cases, three pairs of shoes, and a dressing case.

V. The Midsummer Vacation begins towards the end of July, and ends on the First Tuesday after the Eighth of September. During this interval no Pupil can remain in College. There are also Three weeks' Holidays at Christmas; a charge of Two Guineas will be made for each boy who remains in College during that time.

Boys not returning punctually on the days appointed after Vacation or Holidays, lose their places for the ensuing half-year; and should satisfactory explanation of their absence be wanting, the Rector shall be entitled to decline re-admitting them to the College.

Previous to the removal of any Pupil, Parents are required to give three months' notice.

The College Station is Tullamore, on the Great Southern and Western Railway, which is five miles distant. Clara, on the Athlone and Streamstown Junctions, and Moate, on the Midland Great Western Railway, are respectively within three and eight miles of the College. The Telegraph Station is Tullamore.

II.—HIGHER SCHOOL.

IN view of the recent decision of the English Catholic Hierarchy regarding the London University, and to meet the wishes of many Catholic parents who desire that their sons should be able to obtain, at moderate expense, the advantages of a recognised University Degree, or to have them prepared for the Public Competitive Examinations, without being subjected to the influence of heterodox or infidel teachers, or exposed to the dangers and distractions almost unavoidable in a large city, the Jesuit Fathers have opened at St. Stanislaus' College an additional School of higher studies, where young gentlemen may be prepared for Degrees in the London University, as also for the Army, the Indian Civil Service, and other Public Competitive Examinations.

The Yearly Pension is 70 Guineas, to be paid half-yearly in advance.

There are no *extra* charges, except that for Medical Attendance when necessary.

The Pupils of the Higher School have a separate table, a private reading-room and reference library, and a separate dormitory, with well-appointed cubicles.

In other respects they are subject to the ordinary discipline of the College, and are liable to immediate removal for any grave violation of the rules, especially for any act of wilful insubordination, or any impropriety of conduct.

It should be clearly understood, also, that the Higher School is established solely for young men who will work, and that a persistence in idle habits shall therefore be regarded by the heads of the College as sufficient grounds for requiring the removal of a Pupil.

No Pupil can be received without a certificate of good conduct from the head of the School or College at which he has previously studied.

Regarding the London University Examinations, it may not be amiss to remark :—

I. That the Matriculation Examination is accepted (1) by the Council of Military Education, in lieu of the Entrance Examination otherwise imposed on Candidates for admission to the Royal Military College at Sandhurst; and (2) by the College of Surgeons, in lieu of the Preliminary Examination otherwise imposed on Candidates for its Fellowship. It is also among those Examinations, of which some one must be passed (1) by every Medical Student on commencing his professional studies; and (2) by every person on entering upon Articles of Clerkship to an Attorney—any such person Matriculating in the First Division being entitled to exemption from one year's service.

II. The B.A. or B.Sc. Degree may be obtained within two years after Matriculation, and at the age of eighteen; and, therefore, whilst boys are still young enough to begin at any calling in life, and within the limits of age prescribed for any of the Military or Higher Civil Service Competitions—for which the University Examinations are an excellent preparation, and in many of which the holders of University Degrees have special privileges granted to them.

At the London University Matriculation Examination, held simultaneously at London, Liverpool, Manchester, Birmingham, Ushaw, Stonyhurst, and (for the first time) St. Stanislaus' College, Tullabeg, Tullamore, in June, 1876, 704 Candidates presented themselves, of whom 311 passed : 83 being placed in the Honour List, 214 in the First Division, and 14 in the Second Division.

At St. Stanislaus' College 14 Candidates from various Irish Colleges offered themselves, with the following results :—

	No. of Candidates.	Honours	First Division	Second Division	Total Passed.
St. Stanislaus' College	6	2	3	1	6
From other Colleges	8	1	1	1	3

In the Intercollegiate Competition between the Irish Jesuit Colleges of Clongowes, Limerick, and St. Stanislaus, the Provincial's Prize of Twenty-five Pounds for the highest place on the University Honour List was won by Joseph M'Grath, of St. Stanislaus', and the second place was gained by Joseph Crowley, also of St. Stanislaus'.

In 1877, at the Matriculation Examination, three pupils passed from St. Stanislaus',—Michael Maher and Patrick Skerrett in the First Division, and John Rochford in the Second Division.

At the First B.A. Examination 263 Candidates presented themselves, from nearly 100 different Colleges in the United Kingdom. Of these, 118 passed. The *only* Candidates who passed directly from any Catholic College or School were Messrs. CROWLEY, M'GRATH, and Ross from ST. STANISLAUS'. At the subsequent Honour Examinations, Mr. CROWLEY was bracketed equal for Second Place in First Honours in Classics, and Mr. M'GRATH obtained a place in Third Honours in Mathematics, being, with the exception of the Rev. Mr. COLLEY, S.J., the only pupil of a Catholic School who ever obtained Mathematical Honours at the London University First B.A. Examination.

The page opposite shows the subjects of the examination.

Prospectus of Tullabeg, including results for 1877

Lord Randolph Churchill

The Duchess of Marlborough

William Delany as rector of Tullabeg

a body, with Bishop Edward Thomas O'Dwyer of Limerick as its most forceful spokesman, favoured the first of these proposals, envisaging the national university as being, in practice, a Catholic institution. With reference to the other alternatives, a majority of the bishops appeared to prefer an enlargement of the Royal University to the prospect of a Catholic college in the University of Dublin. The minority, however, was represented by the most influential figure in the hierarchy, Dr Walsh of Dublin, who, though he expressed his support for the idea of a great national teaching university, seemed mainly concerned with establishing a Catholic college within the University of Dublin in order that, in the short term, Catholics might benefit from the prestige attaching to its degrees and, in the long term, by force of numbers, assume control of the establishment. William Delany was to find himself in the unenviable position of opposing his archbishop. The realisation of a great national teaching university had become his life's ambition. He viewed the scheme for a college within the University of Dublin as both impracticable and undesirable, and strongly supported an enlargement of the Royal in preference to it.

In 1878, however, when Delany first became preoccupied with the prospects of a university bill, he had no idea of the shoals ahead nor that a solution was so far distant. He had hopes, in fact, that the grounds of a settlement could be secured within a relatively short period, though not in the context of government support for the Catholic University.

The Catholic University under Newman's rectorship, 1854-1858, had been associated with high educational aims, and had an air of enthusiasm and intellectual freedom. Any university experience worthy of the name, he had maintained, must involve to some extent a risk of unsettlement. His lofty ideals remained as a stimulus. Following his departure, however, and for the other reasons already noted, the institution suffered a loss of regard. This was contributed to, in the view of W.K. Sullivan, by the bishops' defensive stance against the dangers of 'liberal Catholicism' and their consequent tendency to run the university as 'a seminary under their absolute control'.[43]

By 1872 Delany had no doubt that the Catholic University was virtually defunct and its matriculation certificate 'of no value whatever'.[44] Its handful of students described it humorously as 'an institution of hope, founded in faith, on the basis of charity'.[45] Its position was not far from that described by Sullivan in a letter to William Monsell in May, 1873:[46]

Without suitable buildings, museums etc.; without endowment to pay the professors, without prestige, without the
faculty of giving degrees; . . . with the apathy of a large
number of clergy and bishops; with the unconcealed hostility
of a considerable number of priests; it is not possible to maintain a central Catholic university in Dublin.

Delany could not see any prospect of the government granting recognition to an establishment owned and managed by
Catholic bishops, and providing a low standard of academic
achievement for a small number of students. What was needed
initially, he believed, was something more modest and realistic,
namely, an efficient university college distinguished by the
academic excellence of its students and providing the superior
qualifications of London University. If a considerable number
of young men from such a college, in competition with students of better equipped English establishments, were to distinguish themselves in the London examinations, the point
would have been made in the most effective manner possible,
and in a manner the government could not ignore, that the
Irish Catholics valued higher education, were capable of benefiting from it, and were determined to acquire it. Even if their
case were overlooked for some years, the time would not have
been wasted. The opportunity would have been taken of raising
up a generation of scholars well-trained in every branch of learning, and especially a number of sound university teachers ready
for the day when a proper university would be granted by the
government. Besides, such a policy was one of hope and dignified
self-help as compared to the prevailing practice of idle cries for
assistance.

But where was such an efficient Irish university college to
be found? For a while he had hopes that St Stanislaus College
might be the answer. The relation of Tullabeg to the university
question had constantly preoccupied him, as Mahaffy had remarked. Gradually, however, he came to hold that for maximum
effect the college should be situated in Dublin. By the time
new prospects emerged following the Intermediate Education
Act of 1878, he had arrived at clear opinions on most aspects of
the university issue.

The Act had solved the problem of how to give state aid to
different denominations without violating the undenominational
principle. It was widely believed, he wrote, that the Act 'was to
be followed up by a university bill drawn largely on the same
lines, and giving Catholic colleges a considerable indirect endow-

ment by means of liberal results fees and grants for educational appliances'. The Duke of Marlborough, indeed, publicly announced the existence of such a scheme for an examining-type university.[47] His announcement met with a mixed reception from Irish Catholics. There was still a considerable body of opinion married exclusively to the objective of a directly endowed Catholic University, residential rather than examining in character. Delany sought Randolph Churchill's views. They were quite opposed to those of his father. He saw little prospect of the government doing anything about the university question prior to an election. Besides, if the Conservatives were to risk dealing with it they would need to have 'a clear understanding' that, if Catholic views were met, 'the bishops and the Vatican' would 'support the government at the polling booth consistently and continuously'. He went on to advise confidentially that Irish Catholics bide their time and hold out for 'a national university of a denominational character . . . which should guide and direct Catholic thought and intellect, and which should be able to rank before long with the great Catholic universities of the continent'. A mere examining university would be 'a body without a soul' and 'would never excite national enthusiasm or stimulate intellectual effort'.[48]

Delany found these views impractical. His reply indicated his order of priorities. He favoured, as the ultimate ideal, a fully endowed residential university for Catholics, but saw no prospect of obtaining such in the foreseeable future. An examining-type, national university, meanwhile, would be beneficial and a stepping-stone towards a more satisfactory solution. The immediate need, however, was 'the devising of some practical plan for endowing a central Catholic college, at least, in such a form as would be approved by parliament'. With reference to the suggested alliance between Conservatives and Catholics, he remarked that he had 'always regretted that Ireland was the only country in Europe where Catholics were forced, as it were, to be Liberals', and he feared that this situation would continue 'until Conservatism ceased to mean Orangeism, with which it has hitherto most unfortunately been identified in Ireland'.

His support for an examining-type university became widely known and occasioned misunderstanding and criticism. He held his ground both because he saw such an institution as the only kind likely to be supported by the government, and because it had, in his view, a positive value for an emerging country like Ireland. 'People not engaged professionally with educational work', he told Arthur Kavanagh, leader of the Irish Conservatives in the House of Commons, 'will gauge of university teaching by the best university men', though, in fact, such men rarely owed anything to their teachers in any university or secondary school. Those, however, who were in earnest about raising the education of a people 'look for a system producing the best average results in the mass — whilst leaving to the privileged few full scope for their games.' This was best achieved by means of competition between a large number of rival colleges. Hence, the value of an examining university like London and the quality of its degrees. Their standard was 'not only maintained' but was 'raised by the widening competition'. How different this was from the residential universities! The royal reports on Oxford and Cambridge had shown that pecuniary considerations 'tended necessarily to the keeping of very low standards of education, or rather to the absence of a standard'; while the standards of Trinity College and the Queen's Colleges were such that boys might 'leave school in a low class and enter these universities without difficulty', and were, thereby, encouraged to think that there was 'no need for knowledge to win even distinctions at the university'.[49]

Early in 1879 the widespread expectation of a government bill seemed doomed to disappointment. Edmund Dease, M.P., informed Delany on 28 February that he feared that a settlement was further off than ever. The government could carry a bill by virtue of the support of all the leading Liberals, but it feared to do so because of the extreme 'anti-Irish-Catholic' attitude of its Lancashire members. The government, therefore, was in the impossible position of contemplating a bill which they could only have passed 'by the aid of their opponents but not of their friends'.

Delany saw interesting possibilities in the support of so many Liberals at a time when an election was not far distant. He wrote to the O'Conor Don proposing that as the lines of the intended measure were well known, had the approval of many of the Irish Conservatives, and would be helped through parliament by the success of the analagous Intermediate Act, he ought 'to undertake the bringing forward of a bill drawn on the same lines so as to force the government by pressure from their own Irish Tory followers to deal with the question'. In part it was an effort to play off the Irish Tory vote against the Lancashire vote. At the same time he wrote to Kavanagh, as leader of the Irish Tories, asking him if he would support such a measure and put his name with that of the O'Conor Don on the back of the bill. Both men accepted his suggestions.

A further letter to the O'Conor Don emphasised the need of a clear undertaking between the bishops and the Irish parliamentary party, and the general Catholic body, as to the definite *quid minimum* they would privately accept, as well as agreement on 'the fuller proposals which it is judged prudent and practical to bring forward'. Such a procedure was necessary to scotch 'the never ending charges that the Catholics ask for impossibilities', or the objections of well-disposed members of government who complained that they did not know what Catholics really wanted: 'what one bishop says today another contradicts tomorrow, and the *Freeman*, "the Catholic organ", has its own unpractical proposals which no one disavows'.[50] The O'Conor Don secured the approval of some of the bishops, and of Drs Woodlock and Molloy, the rector and vice-rector of the Catholic University.

The bishops, as a body, were placed in an awkward predicament by the proposed measure. They were divided on its merits, yet they were not disposed to oppose any reasonable proposal which would take off their shoulders the albatross of the Catholic University collections. But they could not openly support it lest they seemed to be plumping once and for all for a lesser settlement and also because their public support might inflame non-conformist opposition and jeopardise the proposal's chances.

The bill was drafted in a few days. Modelled on the Intermediate Act, it envisaged a new university called St Patrick's (Delany suggested 'Royal University' as an alternative title), with a governing body and senate and with affiliated colleges eligible for results fees, exhibitions and scholarships; its professors could be engaged to teach in the affiliated colleges, and additional payments would be available to the colleges for equipment, library facilities and laboratories. The university would be financed by a sum of one and a half million pounds from the church surplus fund. The endorsers of the bill were Arthur Kavanagh, William Shaw, then leader of the Irish party, C.S. Parnell, Mitchell Henry, and, later, Lord Charles Beresford.

Throughout March, April and May, Delany corresponded with the O'Conor Don, Judge Little and Arthur Kavanagh on the progress of the bill and procedures to be pursued. He also sent out a flood of letters, many of them very long, canvassing support for the measure. Copies are extant of letters to such members of parliament as P.J. Smyth, T.D. Sullivan, George Errington, David Sherlock, Edmund Dease, Philip Callan, and Mitchell Henry. Through Judge Little his views reached Shaw and Parnell, and through Kavanagh the attorney-general, Gibson.

Other letters went to Randolph Churchill, the Duchess of Marlborough, Dr Walsh of Maynooth, and various bishops, especially Dr Croke of Cashel whose support he considered particularly important. Friends like Lord Portarlington rallied round with letters to the newspapers. Towards the end of May, Delany was invited to the House of Commons by the Irish members to advise them during the debate.[51]

The bill needed very careful handling if it was not to stir up violent reaction in parliament. David Sherlock, M.P., sketched the contradictions and difficulties surrounding the measure in a letter to Delany on 22 May. He saw no hope of it being passed that session.

> The government are against us; the Lancashire Protestant party have succeeded in their opposition, and the Chancellor of the Exchequer . . . sufficiently showed his determination not to adopt it. The Scotch are against us almost to a man; Chamberlain, . . . though personally favourable, found it necessary to stay away; and if there had been a division yesterday, the division list would have exhibited a remarkable combination of men differing in other positions, but united in their hostility to our church. The complaint that our bishops have not accepted the bill is mere pretence.

By way of illustration, he noted 'how Sir George Campbell, who led the opposition, objected to the absence of any positive statement that the bishops were willing to accept the bill', and then continued 'that if he were assured that they would accept it, that would be in itself a reason for his opposing it'.

Delany, despite his efforts to rally support, had himself little hope of the bill being passed in that session. In an undated letter to the Duchess of Marlborough he wrote:

> When some weeks back I sketched out for the O'Conor Don the project which has now taken this shape, we had neither of us hope that it might be passed this session, but we trusted that the political exigencies of the moment would compel the opposition leaders to receive the proposal sufficiently well to make it easy for the government to deal with the subject next session on somewhat similar lines.

Up to a point, matters fell out even better than he hoped. Robert Lowe, M.P., indicated the opposition's support for the O'Conor Don's bill. This, as Judge Little remarked on 23 May, proved the wisdom of proposing the measure. The government would kill it by evasions if they could; and that was Parnell's objection to participating in the enterprise. 'But I showed', said Little, 'that it was necessary both the government and the opposition should be brought to the test before the elections, as they were both looking for Catholic support'. At the end of June, the Home Secretary, R.A. Cross,[52] mentioned, almost in passing, that the government was bringing in its own bill. The O'Conor Don immediately withdrew his measure. His hopes of forcing the government to declare its policy had been fulfilled. 'The government', Little declared, 'were driven to the alternative that I anticipated and hoped for . . . of being obliged to disclose their policy and their principles, if they have any, ... There is a race between them and the Whigs. Now, if they are not fools, they will make a high bid and bring in a bold measure'.[53]

The government disclosed the bill in the House of Lords on 30 June. It was far from being 'a bold measure'. A new examining board was to be set up, nothing more; no prizes, no teacher payment, nothing but degrees. Lords Emly and O'Hagan, speaking as Irish Catholics, described it as useless. Even so it was received with hostility by the ultra-Protestant party. The Catholic bishops, however, had an inkling that there was more to the bill than appeared on the surface. They deputed Dr Woodlock and Dean Neville 'to go to London to confer with the Irish members of parliament as soon as any substantial concessions' were 'likely to be made by the government'. Judge Little urged Delany to go over himself on the grounds that he 'could do more than either of the clergymen', especially 'with Kavanagh and your other Tory friends'.[54] About the same time, Delany received confirmation from Philip Callan, M.P., that the government might be considering making results-fees available to Catholic colleges to enable them to compete more equitably with the endowed Queen's Colleges and to render the bill more acceptable to Catholics. He replied to Callan on 20 July that if prizes and results-fees were included in its provisions, the bishops would wish the Irish members not to oppose the bill, while yet denouncing it as quite inadequate towards meeting their claims.

He was loath to reject any measure which offered amelioration. In a letter to Edward Dwyer Grey, M.P., towards the end of July, he explained his philosophy. He was personally inclined not to reject any measure that would do even partial good, provided it infringed no religious principle nor compromised any larger rights. Hence, he added: 'I should regret to see refused even a small part of what we are entitled to, in the uncertainty, greater every day, as to when we may have even a part offered us again'. But *'not rejecting'* was one thing, and *'formally accepting as a settlement or expressing great gratitude for a crumb'* was another. He did not hold with people like T.D. Sullivan, M.P., who rejected proposals because they were not perfect. Catholic Emancipation and Gladstone's Land Act were not perfect, yet they were accepted. With characteristic assurance, he concluded:

> I don't know a more untenable, in fact a more absurd proposition in politics than that it is a surrender of one's convictions, or one's principles, to do things bit by bit according as they become possible. I would, therefore, fight strongly to amend the government bill; when amended, I would declare it fell entirely short of just Catholic claims. This would leave entire liberty of action and would still permit the alleviation of some of the grosser existing evils; whilst making more possible the future measure needed to establish equality. . . . By holding out for what the Tories are afraid to propose, we shall fall between the two stools and perpetuate our present miserable state.

He added that he would try to cross over 'for the fight in committee'.

The Irish members were still in a condition of indecision on 1 August when the Chief Secretary, Lowther, provided another dramatic turn in the bill's progress. With an appearance of throw-away indifference, he mentioned that he would introduce a clause empowering the senate of the new university to draw up a scheme of exhibitions, prizes and scholarships. The opponents of concession were taken aback, but had not sufficient material in the vague statement to raise a 'no popery' cry. Why was the clause not mentioned in the Lords? Did not this addition make the bill a substantially different one from what had been introduced? The Chief Secretary remained stolid, apparently unaware of the point of such questions. Would the scheme of exhibitions be laid before the House? Mr Lowther could not conceive of such a possibility. Parliament never undertook such tasks. It would be the senate's business to go into details.

The confusion of his more intolerant followers seems to have been part of Disraeli's intention. 'A just and proper settlement', he explained in confidence to the English Catholic M.P., Charles Langdale, was not possible, given 'the present temper of parliament and of the country'. All that could be achieved was 'an extension of the principle on which the University of London rests'. 'An indirect endowment through the means of fellowships for a Roman Catholic College' would be granted but 'in such a way that it will not be understood'. He hoped that 'when in time the people of Great Britain find that they are virtually accepting the principle of an endowment which is quite inadequate, their sense of justice will cause them to admit that the Irish Roman Catholics are entitled to a properly endowed university college as regards income, buildings, and appliances. In fact', he concluded, 'what we are doing is to place the ball at the feet of the Irish Roman Catholics, and if they do not kick it, the fault will be theirs not ours'.[55]

Although Disraeli's involuted intention remained unpublished for a further seventeen years, Lowther's clause offered hope to the Irish members. Kavanagh saw it 'as a very valuable concession and . . . valuable from its vagueness'. He looked on it 'as carrying results-fees, even to be paid to the heads of colleges indirectly, if the senate embodies that in the scheme'. Mitchell Henry charted the way of reason as the debate drew to a close on 5 August. The bill was not satisfactory but to oppose it would be bad policy. Everything depended 'upon the recommendations made by the senate which is to be appointed under the bill', and if its recommendations were not satisfactory it would be time enough then to take strong action when they were placed before parliament.[56] The Irish party agreed to accept the bill and it was passed on 5 August. The bill is now safe, wrote George Errington, M.P., to Delany on the following day, 'and I fully agree with you as to its vast importance, not so much for itself but as the thin end of the wedge leading to concurrent endowment'.

In the Irish Jesuit archives there is a seventeen page summary by Delany entitled: 'Some Notes on the Irish university question and the position of the Jesuit fathers in relation to it'. With regard to the Royal University Bill of 1879, he remarked that it abolished the Queen's University, yet preserved the Queen's Colleges with all their collegiate endowments and provided no endowments for Catholic colleges. It did envisage, however, that the senate of the new university would submit 'a scheme for the carrying out of the purposes of the Act and for the government and working of the university', and that an endowment would be provided according to the nature of the scheme. Referring to the considerable opposition on the Catholic side to the acceptance of the bill, he recorded that when asked his opinion 'by some of the leading Irish members of parliament, and also by some of the bishops', he replied by letter advocating that the bill be permitted to pass subject to protest on its shortcomings as a just settlement of Catholic claims. He outlined four reasons which he had given in support of his stance. They were more precise than those given to Dwyer Gray, and the first two of them were to greatly influence his policy as president of University College. The reasons were:

1. That under the bill the Queen's Colleges would be compelled to enter into competition with the unendowed Catholic colleges, and their certain failure would make it impossible for the government to defend them. Hence, £25,000 a year, at least, would be withdrawn from the Queen's Colleges of Cork and Galway, which would either be closed or given over to the Catholics.

2. That in this open competition the Catholics, despite every disadvantage, 'would give public proof that they had both students and teachers entitled to a due share in public educational endowments, and their success would afford an irresistible argument in support of Catholic claims to a proper redistribution of those endowments'.

3. That the Liberals had made it clear, in discussing the O'Conor Don measure, that they adhered to the principle that educational endowments should be non-sectarian. Consequently, the return of Mr Gladstone offered little likelihood of a further attempt 'to deal with the Irish University question in accord with Catholic ideas'.

4. That the leading Irish Conservatives had stated that they regarded the bill 'merely as a temporary stop-gap', which was made to appear colourless in view of the approaching general election, but that, if returned to power, 'they would make further provision for Catholic claims by *direct* endowment of at least one Catholic college'.

On the effect of his arguments, Delany noted that Archbishop Croke of Cashel, 'who was at first strongly opposed to the acceptance of the bill', wrote to him on receipt of his letter 'that, on the whole, perhaps it might be as well to let the measure pass'. Moreover, at the conference of the Irish party on the day fixed for the second reading of the bill, 'many members were strongly in favour of obstructing it, but on reading his letter a majority voted in favour of the course he recommended and it was determined to act accordingly and the bill was therefore admitted to pass'. He was careful to note that throughout all his correspondence he had been 'in constant communication with Fr General, through Fr Weld, both of whom took a very deep interest in the question'. It was his insurance against possible charges, from within or outside the Order, that he was acting *ultra vires.*[57]

His confident prognostications on the effects of the bill were to be only partly fulfilled. The government was to resist all pressure to withdraw endowments from Cork and Galway; the Irish Catholic colleges did prove superior and their success — especially that of University College under Delany — did force in the long term a complete change in the university situation; but the hopes of direct endowment from the Conservatives, which were to materialise as a distinct possibility in 1886, were undermined by divisions within the Catholic ranks.

Meanwhile, the senate was the key factor in determining the scope of the new university. Its membership and its course of action were of particular concern to the Catholic bishops. As they saw it, the future of their institution in Stephen's Green was at issue.

Their lordships had ample grounds for concern. The Catholic University, as has been seen, had a name for failure and inanition. Most of its score or less students were supported by episcopal bursaries, which were to be discontinued in 1880. The only efficient professors, Dr Casey, the mathematician, and Dr Molloy, professor of natural science, devoted their time, respectively, to grinding pupils for London University and other external examinations, and to adult education lectures. Most of the remainder of the staff did not attend or else appeared daily, rang a bell, read their newspapers, and then went home having fulfilled all justice. Not surprisingly, in Delany's words: 'the bishops, clergy and people were all sick of the Catholic University collections and protested against the waste of money on an institution that was perfectly useless and did no educational work whatever'.[58] At the same time — though they determined to have no further collection after 1881 — the bishops could not close down the institution.

Quite apart from the admission of failure involved in closure, there was the special position of the professors who claimed to have been appointed for life by Dr Newman and to have had the arrangement ratified by the hierarchy. How were these gentlemen to be provided for? The main hope lay in a sympathetic senate. To show cause for sympathetic consideration, their lordships decided to try to revive the virtual corpse. In succession to Dr Woodlock, made Bishop of Ardagh on 1 June 1879, they appointed, in October, Monsignor Neville as president. He was a man of much ability and of forceful and combative character; but being a parish priest in the diocese of Cork his appointment involved regular commutations between there and Dublin, a circumstance which earned him among his handful of students the musical nick-name 'Monsignor Often-Back'.[59] His hopes were pinned on the securing of an indirect endowment for the Catholic University in the form of fellowships.

The charter of the senate and the names of its members appeared on 27 April 1880. There were thirty-six senators, eighteen Catholics and eighteen non-Catholics. It was almost the last act of the government. No money had yet been voted. Gladstone returned to office, and concern was felt regarding the Liberals' attitude to their opponents' bill. The senate met on 24 June 1880 and appointed a committee to draw up their scheme. It consisted of Lord Emly, Dr W.K. Sullivan, Sir Robert Kane, Monsignor Neville, Dr Molloy, and Mr Redington, representing Catholic interests; together with the Earl of Ross, Rev Robinson Scott, Dr Moffett, Dr Porter, Dr Macalister, and Dr Ball, the lord chancellor.

The committee addressed itself to the delicate area of fellowships. It decided to establish forty-eight of them, each to be worth £400. The senate adopted this proposal on 18 February 1881. How the fellowships were to be allocated, however, was not announced. It was a key question. Delany was drawn into the debate early in January when Dr Walsh, greatly annoyed, informed him that he had heard that the Queen's Colleges were to receive thirty-six of the fellows, leaving only a quarter of the total to the Catholic side. Delany checked out the rumour, found it well based, and reported his findings to Archbishop McCabe of Dublin. A special meeting was called at which he emphasised the basic inequality of the proposed arrangement. McCabe, after consultation, announced that he would not consent to any scheme 'which did not secure for Catholics at least one half of all appointments'.[60]

Dr Walsh and Delany kept each other supplied with such items of information as came their way regarding the senate's deliberations and government plans. Walsh feared that the senate might be used to further the interests of the Queen's Colleges at the expense of the Catholic colleges, and was suspicious of the 'liberal Catholics' appointed to that body by the government. Delany, too, was concerned about the Queen's Colleges, particularly at the support they seemed to be receiving from Gladstone's government, but not to the same extent as Dr Walsh, who appeared to seek all the fellowships for the Catholic institutions and to hold the view that any recognition of the Queen's Colleges was 'a concession to institutions formally condemned by the Holy See'.[61] Delany was worried by his friend's obduracy. Hence, from Bournemouth — whither he had been sent by his doctors in March, to get 'away from worry and work' — he wrote to Fr Reffé expressing his disquiet. By their opposition to any concession Walsh and some of the bishops, were leaving themselves wide-open to counter-attack. The fellowships had been devised as a compromise and there was 'no prospect of the bishops obtaining all the fellowships and excluding the Queen's Colleges from them'. If the argument against giving these colleges fellowships was that they were endowed already, the same applied to the proposal to give fellowships to Maynooth; and if the Queen's institutions were shut out and the Catholic University became the main recipient of the fellowships, might not the question be raised in parliament:

What is the teaching work, who are the students for whose education so much public funds are granted? Catholics, they will say, object to having public money given to the Queen's Colleges, because they allege, they are not doing good educational work. What amount of educational work is being done in the institution for which they claim these public funds?

He saw no answer, and no result save 'a disgraceful exposure'. He would much prefer to base the argument on grounds of equality, and to let time and examination results provide the logic of events to force the government's hands. It was 'plainly indefensible' to have the endowed Queen's Colleges competing on 'equal terms' with the unendowed Catholic colleges. It could not last. 'It must end either in their being disbanded' which he now thought out of the question in the case of Cork as well as Belfast — 'or in the endowment of a Catholic college in Dublin'. Dr Ball, the lord chancellor, saw this plainly 'as the necessary outcome of the next few years'.

At the end of July there was still no decision on the distribution of the fellowships. Delany's insomnia and general health showed little improvement. On his doctor's recommendation he was given leave for a sea voyage to Canada. The same month, W.E. Forster, M.P.,[62] announced that the government had decided to allocate only £20,000 a year to the Royal University. Given the reduced allocation, the Senate committee felt obliged to reduce the fellowships to thirty-two, and later again to twenty-six. Their modified scheme was approved by the senate body on 1 October, but once again no decision was made on the distribution of the fellowships.[63] It was finally taken later in the month; and Delany, according to 'A memorandum on the fellowships controversy' among his papers, had a hand in the decision. On his way back from America, he stopped over in London, called on 'many leading lay senators' and urged on them the views he had previously put to Dr McCabe. His representations 'were finally adopted and it was agreed that Catholics should have half the fellowships and examinationships and other appointments'.

Thus, the bishops, despite their worries about the 'liberal Catholics' on the senate, had reason to be satisfied with the senate's arrangements. Not only were there thirteen Catholic fellowships, each carrying £400, whose holders were to be official examiners to the Royal university, but the senate had also decreed, the previous February, that 'every fellow should hold his fellowship on the condition that, if required by the senate, he should teach students of the university in some educational institution approved by the senate'. This came to mean – thanks to 'a private understanding' between the senate and Monsignor Neville, according to Delany – 'that the Catholic fellows should be required to teach at the Catholic University'.[64] Hence, the bishops' university was now in the happy position of having available to it an indirect endowment of fellows, paid by the senate, who would teach its students and serve at the same time as their examiners. Its prospects had changed dramatically. The fastening of the fellowships to the college in Stephen's Green was to be the decisive factor in the Jesuits agreeing to run it two years later; but it was also to beget an estrangement between Delany and his friend, Dr Walsh, the future Archbishop of Dublin.

Chapter III

FROM TULLABEG TO UNIVERSITY COLLEGE: REJECTION AND REINSTATEMENT, 1880-1883

While the senate had been deliberating about fellowships, Delany had suffered a number of personal setbacks which seemed likely to terminate his career as an educationalist. His troubles came to a head in 1880. Many of them were of his own making. From 1878 to 1880, as has been seen, he had been involved in a welter of overlapping activities. His primary obligations, as rector and prefect of studies, were to the pupils, community and staff of Tullabeg; yet he had been deeply engaged in the negotiations and correspondence prior to the Intermediate Act and, subsequent to it, had carried the workload of secretary to the Catholic Headmasters' Association; he then had immersed himself in a flurry of letters and many-sided involvements relating to the O'Conor Don's measure and the later negotiations leading to the acceptance of the Royal University proposal and its implementation. Increasingly, his time and attention had been diverted away from Tullabeg. In his role as a much-consulted personage he sometimes stayed over in a Dublin hotel and even had an office in the city. Not surprisingly, members of his community resented his multifarious commitments and complained again to Rome of his absences and expenditure. The combined pressures took toll of his health. Insomnia became an increasing problem. And then in close succession came the death of his father in June 1879, and, in October 1880, quite suddenly, that of his brother, Thomas, to whom he was deeply attached. The final pressure which heightened tensions to a pitch which made sound sleep a rarity and brought him to the point of physical and mental exhaustion, was the unfriendly attitude towards him and Tullabeg experienced from the new provincial, Fr James Tuite. Shortly after his appointment on 31 July 1880, Fr Tuite received an instruction from Rome to take efficacious means to bring to an end 'the unapproved prodigality which was driving the college to ruin'.[65] Under this head, William

Delany was the architect of his own downfall.

His Order's financial resources were, and are, to a considerable extent in its colleges and residences, each of which is by long tradition responsible for its own solvency. Except in very special circumstances, each institution is expected to pay its way. A rector who runs his college into debt, and continues to do so without much hope of recovering his expenditure, is almost certain to be removed from office. In letter after letter from 1878 to 1880 the General's assistant, Fr Weld, had urged Delany to take steps to reduce the school's financial debts. As late as February 1880 — after congratulating him on his successes in the matriculation examinations — he had pointed out that pupil numbers were down and that he had insisted on Delany diminishing his debt while his numbers were up. It seemed to have little effect. Nemesis came in the form of Fr Tuite, whose vision did not extend further south than Clongowes Wood College, Co Kildare, and who had a dread of 'unnecessary' expenditure. He moved into action on receipt of the General's letter. Delany was informed that money was being thrown away on extern teachers, that they should be visiting rather than resident masters, and that it seemed wise to send away the B.A. students from the college. The provincial demanded a detailed statement in response.

To Delany two things seemed clear: that there had been some mis-representation of the situation at Tullabeg; and that the future of the college was at stake. With his facility for marshalling arguments, he wrote a lengthy reply on 30 August explaining the apparent extravagant expenditure in connection with the college, and making a strong case in favour of the extern teachers. He trusted that his letter might 'be found to remove some erroneous impressions'. With regard to the B.A. students, their introduction had been sanctioned by the General and he presumed that any change in their regard would have to come expressly from him. But, he concluded, 'having expressed our views fully and frankly, we shall be prepared to do promptly whatever your reverence, having weighed all, shall determine'.

The well-reasoned but respectful letter did not disarm Fr Tuite, but it prevented sweeping changes. Deciding it would seem, that suggestions were lost on Delany, he responded the following day in a peremptory manner. After derogatory remarks about keeping lay teachers in their place, he issued a restriction on the number to be appointed, and laid down a list of other regulations to be attended to. These were as much a commentary on the provincial as on the rector. Thus, the scholars' diet was to be strictly planned, 'substantial enough but no waste'; the community were not to have whiskey at supper, and 'punch days' were to be cut to a minimum; food and drink were not to be given 'to workmen or hangers-on about the place without express permission from the minister — who will seldom grant it'; travelling expenses were to be cut down to what was strictly necessary, 'and no one should stay in a hotel anywhere without the provincial's permission, nor take his meals there'. He positively forbade 'having an office . . . in any city for the transaction of any business of any kind', without his express consent. 'In a word, I wish that no extra expense should be undertaken without my knowing it beforehand and consenting to it'. The implementation of the regulations, many of which were aimed at himself, was committed to Delany, as rector.

The same day Fr Weld wrote to say that the General had written to the provincial 'to explain his order in such a way that I trust your interests will be cared for'. But he reminded Delany that he would have to retrench expenses that he could not afford, however 'nice and taking' they might be. On 27 September, Fr Sturzo, the former provincial, sent his congratulations on the Intermediate results, which, in proportion to the size of the school and the numbers entered for the examination, were the most successful of all the colleges. Delany wrote to the General enclosing the examination results, listing other favourable developments, expressing his concern about the school debt and his fears that Fr Tuite was intent on down-grading the college. Fr Beckx's reply on 19 October was strangely out of tune with the tone set by the provincial. He was pleased at the examination results, at Delany's care of the students and his provision of expert teachers, all of which had 'brought renown to the college and the Society'. He was pleased likewise at the spiritual well-being of the students and at the large number of them at one time entering the Order. He was not overawed by the school's very heavy debt; but he was saddened to learn of Delany's fears of damage to the college from the new provincial, and that such damage had already occurred through the allocation to it of less suitable Jesuit teachers. The college was dear to him and he would write to the provincial to send more outstanding teachers as soon as possible.

The provincial meanwhile, on 5 October, and presumably on authorisation from Rome, informed Delany that he was being replaced as rector by Fr Sturzo, but that he was to continue as prefect of studies and to give every support to the new superior. To Sturzo's embarrassment, Delany was not appointed as one of the house consultors. A little over two weeks later, 23 October, came the news of the sudden death of Fr Tom Delany. William, who by this had been struggling with insomnia for over six months, maintained his correspondence on the university question and in connection with intermediate education, and continued as prefect of studies, until the following spring. At that stage his condition was such that his doctor insisted on a complete break. He was sent to Bournemouth in England, where the Society had a parish, to recuperate. The General wrote to him on 17 April 1881 to say that he had heard from the provincial of his illness — 'due, perhaps, to excessive work and insomnia' — and that he had been ordered by his doctor to recuperate 'under a foreign sky'. He prayed that God would restore him to full health, for his own sake but also for that of the college which owed so much to him and still expected much from him.

During July he was offered the opportunity — already referred to — of a sea-voyage to Quebec. As his doctor considered it likely to be of benefit, he wrote for permission to the General. The provincial informed him on 21 July that the General had given his approval. He hoped that he would return 'quite restored in health'. He was to apply to Fr Sturzo for what he needed and to remember 'to observe holy poverty' as strictly as he could in the circumstances in which he found himself. Delany moved about between Canada and the eastern part of the United States until October. His pursuit of sleep was not aided by anxious letters from Sturzo. No one seemed to know what to do at St Stanislaus College — an indication that despite his past absences he had kept a firm grip on administration and policy. The provincial's annual allocation of men had seen Clongowes secure a much stronger teaching staff than Tullabeg. And, agitated by the college's debt and Fr Tuite's stern eye on expenditure, he drew Delany's attention to the very heavy bills which he had incurred in England and urged him to be more economical. Hopes for any change in life-style, however, were scarcely encouraged by a reply from Montreal mentioning that 'Lady Dudley invited me to dine'.

In August, not feeling much improved, Delany wrote to the provincial for guidance. On 2 September, the latter requested him 'to return home to Ireland by the most direct route'. 'I feel confident', he added, 'that native air will do much for you now that you have had this foreign outing'. He told him that the General had placed him 'at the disposal of the provincial'. Delany's reply was sent from New York on 17 October. 'I shall

January 1882, and mentioned that it was being opened 'with the approval of His Grace the archbishop', there was an immediate reaction from Dr McCabe. He wrote to the provincial that he had given his approval to a hostel for country pupils from Jesuit schools and did not understand the proposal to extend to a university college.[66] Fr J. Walsh, who accompanied Tuite on his visit to the archbishop, had a distinct remembrance of informing His Grace that the new foundation was not intended to be a mere hostel but also a place where young men would be prepared for degrees. He believed McCabe had been 'got at'. Delany inclined to the same view. He feared, he told the provincial, that 'there must be some very strong influences at work against us'.[67] The General's new assistant, Fr G. Porter, in his confidential letters to Delany spoke of 'enemies' to the Society's plans among the bishops and clergy, and saw signs of a continuation of 'the less friendly feelings of Cardinal Cullen's later years'.[68] Delany suspected that the archbishop was influenced by Monsignor Henry Neville, who had so far failed to revive the Catholic University and was upset at the prospect of a rival university college which would render his task of attracting students even more difficult.

On 17 January Delany wrote to McCabe regretting that the original proposal had not been submitted to him in writing and appealing to him to heal whatever was 'defective or misconceived'. 'We ask,' he said, 'and this alone: that the Jesuits, who have had the largest share in the intermediate schoolwork of the country for the last sixty years, should not be shut out from higher education in Catholic Ireland'. He readvertised in the *Freeman* in such a way as he thought would meet His Grace's wishes. The following day the provincial received a letter from the archbishop expressing his regret that 'your good Society has deemed it right to treat me with such discourtesy'. He was not conscious 'of having done anything to deserve it'.[69] Deeply upset, Delany wrote a most submissive letter. Nothing would induce him knowingly 'to be wanting in respect to any bishop — most of all to a prelate in Your Grace's exalted position'. He was innocent of any fault in this regard and placed himself in the archbishop's hands with 'most unquestioning obedience and with the deepest personal respect'. It seemed the Jesuits' fate, he added, 'to have even the most upright-minded and most holy misconceive their actions'.

The *impasse* lasted for almost nine months, despite efforts to have sympathetic bishops and lay friends influence His Grace to a change of attitude. In the meantime, a number of impor-

be glad to be back at work. I am tired of idleness'. As has t
seen, he stopped over at London on his way home. By the t
of November he was back at Tullabeg 'at the disposal of t
provincial'; and, in a further strange twist to the story, was me
by the news that the Order was planning a university college in
Dublin and that he was to be appointed to it. The General, conscious of the opportunities opened to Catholics by means of
the new Royal University, was eager that the Order should play
a leading rôle in forming the new generation of graduates. Consequently — and influenced, perhaps, by Blackrock College
opening a university department in September — he instructed
the provincial to embark on a university college in Dublin, and
recommended Fr Delany's appointment to it in glowing terms.

Delany was not happy about his appointment. He had grown
tired of educational challenges. 'My personal liking', he told the
provincial, 'would be for missionary work, but I must prefer to
have obedience rather than personal liking mark out my work
for me'. His unease was increased when Fr Tuite outlined his
rôle to him on 7 December. He was to be prefect of studies at
a new university establishment in Temple Street, but he was to
be subject to the vice-rector of the college who 'would have
charge of the expenditure, the accounts, the housekeeping, and
the discipline', and to Fr T. Kelly, rector of Belvedere College,
who was also to be joint rector of the new institution. In the
circumstances, he told the provincial, it was of 'comparatively
small importance' who was prefect of studies. He wrote to the
General outlining the problems of the new college, including its
location on the unfashionable north side of the river Liffey. On
22 December, word came that he was to be both vice-rector and
prefect of studies of the college, which was to be entitled 'St
Ignatius'. He moved to Dublin the following day. Five days later
he had his prospectus ready, and was immersed in plans for the
staffing and equipment of the institution. Suddenly, however,
all plans had to be suspended. The first of the misunderstandings
which were to obstruct the Order's plans for university education in Dublin had arisen.

What had been envisaged at Temple Street was an establishment which would be both a college and a hostel catering for
the social and moral well-being of students from country areas.
Fr Tuite had visited the Archbishop of Dublin to obtain his
approval for the enterprise. Unfortunately, he did not submit
his proposals in writing. Convinced that His Grace approved, he
forthwith leased three houses in Temple Street. When, however,
Delany advertised his college in the *Freeman's Journal* on 12

tant developments intervened. The episcopal committee to administer the Catholic University approached Fr Tuite on 7 February 1882 to offer him the opportunity of establishing 'a college of the Catholic University in the Catholic University buildings'. The university would remain under episcopal control 'with the rector, vice-rector, and professional staff appointed by and dependent on the episcopal body'. Any Jesuit granted a fellowship was 'to lecture in the halls of the Catholic University, and a portion of the said fellowship' was to 'be applied to meet the general expenses of the Catholic University'. Fr Tuite was told by Dr P.F. Moran, Bishop of Ossory (and future Archbishop of Sydney), the spokesman for the committee, that the Jesuits would be entirely free in the administration of the college and the direction of its studies, but that if they declined the offer the bishops would 'have to look out for others'. The bishops, he added, perhaps significantly, were of the unanimous opinion 'that in the city of Dublin there should not be more than *one* such Catholic University College'. Negotiations continued during February and March. Delany conducted a survey of the buildings at nos. 82-87, St Stephen's Green, and at the request of the episcopal committee outlined the programme he would envisage running in the institution.[70] The bishops appear to have been impressed. Fr Tuite, however, was not enamoured of their lordships' terms and dismissed the Catholic University as 'a dingy old barrack that would require a vast outlay, the floors all rotten, dosed; the woodwork, window-sashes, crumbling with powder'.[71] Delany, though not impressed by the buildings, recommended to Rome that the bishops' offer be accepted. On 1 March word came from Fr Porter that the General had instructed the provincial to accept the offer, but that he was to try to obtain better conditions, insist on 'perfect independence', and 'have the terms of the agreement carefully drawn out'.

It was a time of intense competition between Catholic colleges, with the successful ones publishing their results to assert their competence and to attract the brighter students. The schools run by the French Fathers, or Holy Ghost Congregation, especially Blackrock College, were natural rivals to those of the Jesuits. On 12 March, Fr Tuite indicated his belief that Monsignor Neville had turned the archbishop around 'in favour of the Blackrock people for the University College'. Delany replied that Dr Neville was certainly working against the bishops' proposals. He might be working in coalition with Blackrock to that end, but he was not in favour of the French College as

such. He had said frankly that he disliked any of the religious
orders 'getting education into their hands'. The bishops met on
21 March. All seemed ready for agreement when word came
that the archbishop, about to depart for Rome to receive the
cardinalate, wished to defer agreement until his return. At
Delany's suggestion, the General invited the new cardinal to
accept his hospitality at Fiesole. His Eminence did not accept,
and was alleged to have remarked to Mr Langdale, M.P., during
a stay over at Florence, that he had no intention of giving the
university to the Jesuits.[72]

Early in August, Fr Tuite called on the cardinal to impress on
him the urgency of a decision. Temple Street, with scarcely any
income, was in serious financial straits. He was asked to have
patience until the bishops met in October, and told that, meanwhile, 'Dr Neville would carry on the St Stephen's Green institution as well as he could'. What all this signified became clear
at the beginning of October when 'Dr Woodlock's plan', drawn
up by the bishop of Ardagh, was circulated. The Catholic University, henceforth, was to be but a moral body with some
six constituent colleges of which one, University College, St
Stephen's Green, was to occupy the buildings of the Catholic
University. On Dr Woodlock's recommendation, however, the
bishops agreed 'that all the fellowships allotted to Catholics
at present should be centralised in the Catholic University
College, Stephen's Green'. Monsignor Neville, fortified by the
episcopal centralisation of his 'private undertaking' with the
Senate, felt certain that the presence at University College of
fellows-cum-examiners was sure to attract students. Hence he
advised the bishops on 3 October that the establishment of a
Jesuit College, near Stephen's Green, would be an advantage:
'the students . . . would frequent the lectures of our fellows'.[73]

On 6 October, on the advice of Dr Butler, Bishop of Limerick,
Frs Tuite and Delany paid a visit to the archbishop. They were
very amiably received. Not only was permission granted to open
straightaway at Temple Street, it was also envisaged that the
college could be transferred within a year to a southside location
near Stephen's Green. His Eminence explained that University
College was to be under his control and that the Catholic fellows
of the Royal University would teach there. The students of St
Ignatius were welcome to attend the lectures of the fellows, but
not obliged to do so. Rather remarkably, according to Fr Tuite's
memo of the meeting, he went on to state 'that he wished us all
along to have the college, but that he did not wish to interfere
with the interests of the bishops, hence his delay. He had the

power at the same time of sanctioning it all through'.

Delany immediately set about building up faculties and staff, but once more ran into difficulties with his provincial. Fr Tuite refused to forward sufficient money and refused to pay a number of outstanding bills. Delany offered his resignation, and wrote to Fr Porter outlining the situation. Porter replied that Irish Jesuits submitted too easily to inaction on the part of their superiors. It was the General, not the provincial, who had appointed him; and it was to the General, if anyone, he should have made his offer of resignation. If there were complaints about money, these were to be made to the General. He was to continue on at Temple Street, keeping in mind that the Catholic University in its present form was not likely to last long. He had done good work at Tullabeg. Let him gather his energies now 'to do a far greater work, one which will have consequences in the province for many days to come'.[74] Delany had no further major difference with Fr Tuite. He turned to the task of acquiring well-qualified teaching staff, especially in the areas of mathematics and classics. The provincial promised him Rev Michael Browne, who was 'a good head at classics and mathematics' but who had still to complete his philosophical studies. He made enquiries of Jesuit provincials in England, France, Germany and Italy with little success. Fr Porter had suggested that Fr Gerard Manley Hopkins of the English province might be available. He had done very well at classics in Oxford. 'He is clever', Porter wrote, 'well trained, teaches well but has never succeeded well: his mind runs in eccentric ways'.[75] The English provincial, Fr Purbrick, pointed out to Delany on 10 November that six of the seven men he had asked for were 'the cream of the province' whom he could not spare. Hopkins, however, was a possibility. But he warned: 'Fr Hopkins is very clever and a good scholar — but I should be doing you no kindness in sending you a man so eccentric. I am trying him this year in coaching B.A.s at Stonyhurst, but with fear and trembling'. Delany continued his search.

In the second half of November he informed the provincial that he had secured Dr Casey of the Catholic University for mathematics, but had held back 'on religious grounds' from employing Trinity College scholars who had privately offered their services 'at moderate salaries'. The appointment of Dr Casey brought him into renewed cross-purposes with the archbishop.

He was not unaware that he was on difficult terrain. His able young colleague, Fr Tom Finlay, had been made a fellow of the

Royal University in classics, the previous April; and even though he lived at Temple Street where a classics teacher was eagerly sought there was never any question of he teaching there. Delany, in fact, had carefully questioned Dr Casey as to his availability in his capacity as a fellow but had been informed that there was no difficulty to he taking part-time hours at St Ignatius, and that he still retained his engagement at the Teacher Training College. He told this to Dr Egan of University College, when the latter informed him that he felt obliged to report Casey's position to the archbishop. He had accepted Dr Casey's statement, he said, and appointed him as a part-time teacher, mainly for the benefit of the six Jesuit scholastics. He failed to see how this could be considered inimical to the interests of University College, still less to those of Catholic education; and it did provide a substantial addition to Dr Casey's limited income, and obviated 'the need otherwise practically unavoidable of employing a Trinity College man whilst so good a Catholic is available'.[76]

Monsignor Neville was not disposed to accept such explanations. Apart from suspicions of Jesuit trickery, he found it difficult to be objective where Dr Casey was concerned. They had had a head-on clash the previous August. He had insisted that Casey teach matriculation students on 14 August. Dr Casey had claimed that this was work during vacation time and brought the matter before the senate. The senate ruled that it could not oblige a fellow to teach during the ordinary summer vacation.[77] Hence, hearing of Casey's work at the Jesuit college, Monsignor Neville, on 30 November wrote a rather peremptory letter from Cork to Cardinal McCabe.[78]

> Dr Egan will call on you tomorrow to let you know some of the tactics of the 'Fathers'. They have Casey teaching at Temple Street. As a *fellow* he can teach no where except in Stephen's Green. If the Jesuits want his services as such they should send their young men there for his lectures. As a private tutor he is under engagement to the Royal University not to teach students preparing for any Royal University examinations. You must deal strongly with this breach of faith on the part of all concerned — otherwise all your efforts for the University College will be thwarted.

The cardinal sought the advice of the secretary to the senate, and was informed that the position was not clear. On 2 December he wrote to Fr Delany. The employment of Dr Casey, he said, was not in accordance with the extraordinary circumstances in which he had consented to the opening of St Ignatius College. By employing him, Delany was 'making the staff of the University College fight against the college'. The cardinal was 'personally satisfied' that Casey was not free 'to accept such engagements' and felt obliged to 'bring the matter officially under the notice of the senate'. With regard to Delany's reference, in his letter to Dr Egan, to 'bringing in a Protestant professor from Trinity College', he considered this as 'really too bad' and couldn't see how he 'could set such a bad example to other schools'.[79] Delany replied two days later. He had learned of His Eminence's disapproval with regret and surprise. Dr Casey taught seven students at St Ignatius College; one, a lay student, a former Tullabeg boy, was doing a course for Woolwich and, therefore, quite different from the courses of the Royal University; the other six were Jesuit scholastics who were training to be teachers, were not free to attend the university lectures in the forenoon and, besides, required more advanced teaching. 'The crying want in Catholic colleges at present', he continued, 'is that of trained and competent mathematical masters. The intermediate and university results show this, for whilst Catholics have won first places in everything else, they are beaten always in mathematics': hence his anxiety to have the young scholastics trained 'by the one competent Catholic in Ireland', so that the Jesuit colleges might have masters capable of sending up pupils 'able to hold their own against the Protestants in the intermediate and university competitions'. The only alternative to Dr Casey was Protestant teachers from Trinity College. He did not like the alternative anymore than His Eminence but, he concluded, 'we cannot condemn our pupils to the stigma of perpetual inferiority in mathematical studies. In these days they would not submit to it, but would themselves go to the (Protestant) grinders and crammers who would make them succeed'.

McCabe wrote to the provincial to say that Casey's engagement should cease. On being told, Delany informed Casey that, 'no matter what his legal right in the question might be', he wished to give effect at once to His Eminence's wishes. Casey replied that he held himself perfectly entitled, legally and morally, to continue at Temple Street, but that in deference to Delany's 'strong desire and determination' to comply with the cardinal's wishes he would waive his legal claim to three months notice. In considerable trepidation, Delany decided to call on Dr McCabe in the hope of overcoming any ill feeling which might persist. They had on the whole 'a very friendly and satisfactory conversation'. He had come round, he told Dr

Walsh, towards accepting that the archbishop might be 'quite entitled to forbid Casey teaching outside University College', and was relieved to find that Casey was to be permitted to stay on at St Ignatius provided he did not train people who would compete against students of University College. It was clear to him that there were 'influences strongly hostile' working on 'the cardinal's peculiarly impressible character'. But he added: 'Casey holds on at least *for the present*. How long the cardinal may be let alone of course I cannot guess — but I don't expect the opposition will give up at once'. He was happy 'to have this little breeze calmed down'.[80] The 'little breeze', nevertheless, was sufficient, on top of recurring worry about Temple Street's finances and the various pressures of the previous months, to bring on a recurrence of insomnia and a general decline in health. Once again, he was sent away to recuperate.

Following his return in January there came the good news that the episcopal board of the Catholic University had enrolled St Ignatius College as a college of the Catholic University. The other colleges were: St Patrick's, Maynooth; the University College, St Stephen's Green; the School of Medicine, Cecilia Street; the French College, Blackrock; Holy Cross College, Clonliffe; St Patrick's College, Carlow; St Kieran's College, Kilkenny; and the College of Mount Carmel, Terenure. Further favourable news was the success of a student from St Ignatius College, and a former pupil of Tullabeg, Michael J. O'Dwyer,[81] in the examinations of the Royal University. After 'only two months of preparation', he had taken first place in modern literature and second place in classics. Delany, with considerable delight, wrote to Cardinal McCabe to inform him of the college's success. Other comforting features of the new year were the replacement of Monsignor Neville as rector of the Catholic University by an old friend, Dr Molloy; and, in May, the appointment of Fr Thomas Browne as provincial.

On the reverse side, there was an accumulation of worries and anxieties. On the one hand Delany was obliged to appeal to Fr Tuite, with little prospect of success, for a loan to meet financial commitments at Temple Street; on the other, he was being regularly reminded from Rome of the need to 'make St Ignatius a success' and that he 'must leave no stone unturned to get the clear lead in the educational movement'.[82] Fr Porter, indeed, had urged him, despite the province's dearth of money, to acquire a site for the college on the fashionable south side of the river Liffey. Delany visited a number of possible places to the palpable unease of Fr Tuite.

Hard financial reality disposed of Fr Porter's proposals. By August it looked as if the college's sole chance of survival was to move to the south side, not as an independent institution but as an adjunct to the Jesuit house of studies at Miltown Park. Delany saw only a bleak future ahead for the Jesuit colleges. His normal confidence deserted him, and with it much of his competitive spirit. During the summer he informed the acting-provincial (the new provincial being away in Rome) that Temple Street seemed 'likely to die out speedily'. He did not see how he could advertise for new students; yet the staff had to be kept up. Where the money was to come from was 'a question more easily asked than answered'. Tullabeg was falling off and, given its present staff, faced 'a downright collapse next summer'. Clongowes, with its comparatively small numbers, was unlikely to make much of a show. Hence, 'the French College would be not merely first, but we should not be second, perhaps not even third nor fourth, without prestige or position. At present, no doubt, the Irish province is in a sea of difficulties and the way out is visible only to providence'.[83] Fortunately, providence had a life-line ready!

During 1883 the cardinal became disillusioned at the lack of progress at University College and at the financial costs involved. Early in September he discussed the situation with Dr John Egan, the president of the college, who urged him to hand over the institution to the Jesuits. Egan had the impression, he told Delany, that the archbishop accepted his views.[84] The matter would certainly be raised at the bishops' meeting in October.

Delany wrote to the provincial, still in Italy, on 3 October, for permission to negotiate with the bishops. With the assistance of Dr Walsh, he lobbied episcopal support. The bishops met on 10 October. Their proposals, so far as he could find out, were the same as those 'ratified by the General last year'. Dr Corr, the new Bishop of Galway, proposed that the college be entrusted to the French Fathers. 'Dr Croke proposed that it should be given rather to the Jesuits to whom it had been offered already by the unanimous vote of the bishops. On a division there were twenty for the Jesuits, four for the French College'.[85] The matter was referred to a committee composed of Cardinal McCabe, and Drs Moran, Butler, Gillooly and Woodlock, which was instructed to offer the place first to the Jesuits, and failing them to the French College. If the Jesuits got it, Delany wrote to the acting-provincial, it would be 'a very big undertaking, indeed, in every sense, and needs a good deal of thinking about'. On the other hand, if it fell into the hands of Blackrock, the

Jesuits might as well 'retire from Irish education'. The following day he relayed information from his friend, Dr Kavanagh,
formerly of Carlow College, that 'the greatest efforts' were
being made to keep the Jesuits out of St Stephen's Green and
to put in Blackrock. He grew increasingly restless at the absence
of the provincial at a time when 'the most important and vital
interest of the Irish province for the present and future' was at
stake. He feared, besides, that Fr Browne's 'timidity and slow-
ness' would 'throw away our chances'. His insomnia returned
and he suffered from a tendency to dizziness. Towards the end
of the month, however, the rector of Miltown Park, as the
acting-provincial, accepted the bishops' offer and conditions.
On 26 October, 1883, Fr Delany, on behalf of the Society of
Jesus, signed an agreement with the episcopal trustees of the
Catholic University.[86]

Two days later his energies had flooded back to meet the new
challenge. He wrote to Fr Browne that the issue had been in
doubt to the end, due to 'the efforts made by the cardinal's
advisers'; and that Dr Kavanagh (now parish priest of Kildare)
rendered 'most valuable service at a critical moment'. It was
imperative to take possession on the 1 November. 'The professional lectures of the fellows' were advertised to take place
early in November. It was essential, therefore, to appoint an
acting-president to take over the next Thursday and ensure that
the winter lectures commenced by 15 November. He would
need an active and useful assistant. Help was required straightaway in the heavy work of reorganising the premises and clean-
ing them up. He, Delany, was prepared to move into Stephen's
Green immediately, as acting-president, if such was the Provincial's wish. Not surprisingly, Fr Browne agreed.

Part II

FROM PRESIDENT, UNIVERSITY COLLEGE (1883-1888) TO PASTOR (1888-1897)

'On its trial and suspected'
Delany to Lord Emly

'Our empire is less and less christian as it grows. . . . Of course those who live in our civilization and belong to it praise it . . . but . . . it is good to be in Ireland to hear how enemies, and those rhetoricians, can treat the things that are unquestioned at home'.

Gerard Manley Hopkins, S.J., to Coventry Patmore, 1886, in W.H. Gardiner (ed.), *Poems and prose of Gerard Manley Hopkins* (London, 1953), p. 204.

Chapter IV

DIFFICULT BEGINNINGS AT ST STEPHEN'S GREEN

The agreement signed by Delany laid down the conditions under which the Jesuits took over the management and most of the buildings which had constituted University College. They were to pay an annual rent of £200, plus rates and taxes, for no. 84 St Stephen's Green, no. 85 (excluding the *Aula Maxima* or great hall), and the two upper storeys of no. 86. The tenancy was to be terminable at two years' notice on either side. They were to have perfect freedom in all matters administrative and scholastic. No fees were to be required from matriculated students of any of the Catholic University colleges. The existing staff of fellows and other professors was to be retained.[1] As regards the Catholic fellows yet to be appointed, it was understood (though unfortunately — in the light of subsequent events — not expressly formulated) that they were to be assigned exclusively to the college in a teaching capacity.[2]

Just prior to the Jesuit community moving into the buildings, a strange occurrence of doubtful legality caused much upset. The entire library of the Catholic University, apart from the medical volumes, was removed to the archdiocesan college of Clonliffe, presumably with the cardinal's approval.[3] It was a token of a curious change of heart on the part of a number of the bishops. Now that the buildings of the Catholic University were handed over, they seemed to regard University College, not as a promoter of university education for Catholics, but as somehow a foreign institution to be overseen with a critical eye.[4] Despite the representations of Dr Butler, Dr Croke, and other episcopal friends of the college, the library was never restored.

On 1 November, the day before the college opened, Delany invited Dr Walsh to dine and stay at Stephen's Green when he was in town. 'The work here is so big', he wrote, 'and so much is to be done at once, that I am tested to the utmost, and many things are sure to escape my attention which your quickness would advert to at once. I am in a rush to make some sort of beginning tomorrow — and what with transferring from Temple Street and the doing up of this neglected old barracks, I am obliged to let many things wait that I should like to deal with'. Nevertheless, with his accustomed capacity for rapid work, he had engaged all his immediate staff within a week of the transfer, had made all arrangements for lectures, and published his prospectus. It appeared in the press on 8 November, and was hailed with enthusiasm by his friends. Dr Walsh described it as 'splendid'; Dr Woodlock wished him a *'prospere procede'* and to his work an *'esta perpetua'*;[5] and Dr Phelan of St John's College, Waterford, in a letter matching congratulations with guarded confidence, wrote: 'To my mind Irish Catholic higher education had never got such a chance before. I say 'chance' advisedly; I have some idea of the still precarious condition on which the issue may depend'. The cardinal remained aloof. To Delany's invitation to Clonliffe students he made it clear that they would not be attending lectures at University College.[6]

The obstacles to success were formidable. The accommodation was more limited than Delany had expected. The tenant in no. 84 refused to leave, hence it was unavailable. No. 85 had a few rooms which could serve as lecture halls, but no. 86 had only small rooms, mainly bed-rooms. Yet this limited space had to be encroached on for sleeping space for the community and some resident students, for a chapel and two dining-rooms. To these drawbacks were added buildings full of dry rot, no laboratories, no library, no museum, no university church, no endowment; and a university staff of whom many were no longer capable of effective teaching, so that, in effect, the college had to supplement them with a large number of tutors. Combined with shortage of accommodation was shortage of money. The furniture taken over at a valuation, had to be paid for; a chapel had to be fitted out; the eight members of the community had to be fed and clothed; the bills of the tutors had to be met; and dilapidated buildings repaired. In fact, because of financial difficulties, insufficient repairs were effected. To meet these costs, plus the annual rent of £200 and £30 in rates and taxes, Delany had Fr Finlay's salary as a fellow (£400), Fr O'Carroll's as examiner (£75), and such students' fees as were not included in the agreement between the bishops and the provincial. Of the fees paid, however, one-third (or £5 in each £15) went to the fellows and not to the college. Little wonder that Fr Denis Murphy, a practical man of affairs as well as a historian of some note, looked upon his president's enterprise as quixotic. 'I am his librarian and his bursar', he said dejectedly to one of the professors, 'yet I have not a penny in my burse nor a book in my library'.

Despite this background, Delany viewed the college as the heir to Newman's lofty ideals and consciously preserved the link with the past. Indeed, within a few months of arriving at Stephen's Green, and in conjunction with the staff of the college, he wrote to Newman on his favourite church feast of the Purification and in anticipation of his birthday on 21 February, 1884. He envisaged his institution becoming the leading university establishment in the country, an institution which by its success would highlight the ability of Catholic youth and, in doing so, virtually force the government's hand into providing a fully-fledged, generously endowed, central university for Catholics. It is doubtful if anyone else shared his dream in 1883. Yet his confidence and work-rate were infectious. Lectures began immediately, and within two months he had on the rolls 109 students, of whom nine were resident — the most that could be accommodated. The examination results at the end of the year justified his confidence.

For the meeting of the episcopal committee on 29 January, 1884, he presented a printed memorandum on the college.[7] It commented on the shortage of accommodation, the condition of the buildings, the cost of maintenance, and stressed that for its efficient operation the college required:

1. A sufficient staff of thoroughly able teachers to meet all the requirements of the university course.
2. Suitable accommodation and fitting educational appliances for effective university teaching.

Having indicated what constituted 'a sufficient staff', he pointed out that his deficit, counting staff, maintenance and repairs, came to £1,500. Some means had to be devised to meet this serious situation. An increase in residential students was not the answer because of lack of accommodation. The only other means immediately available was that Jesuits be elected to the vacant fellowships, provided they were 'in every way qualified for the vacant appointments'. The salaries of such fellows would go directly to the support of the college and provide 'the supplemental funds necessary to maintain the large staff of supplemental professors who will be always a necessity'. Besides, unlike other fellows who gave a maximum of eight hours a week to University College, these men would give 'all their time and energies, as well as their salaries'; and having on the staff an influential body of fellows whose sole object was the good of the college could not but assist the overall 'unity of purpose and harmony of action'. Hence, he respectfully commended to their lordships the candidature currently before the senate of Robert Curtis, S.J., in mathematics, and Fr G.M. Hopkins in classics, each of whom he believed 'to be the most qualified of the candidates, independently of the considerations above given'.

On the matter of 'educational appliances', he raised 'the grave inconveniences and expense entailed' by the removal of the library. The fellows complained that they had no books of reference, the students that they had no collection of books within their reach, and many of the students were too poor to make frequent purchases. He understood that the former library 'consisted in large part of donations made to the Catholic University . . . when it was identical with the central Catholic University teaching college in Dublin', and as University College was now doing the same work in the same position, he considered that 'it would seem to have some claim to at least the use of the educational appliances given expressly for teaching purposes to the institution with which it is substantially identical'.

The memorandum went on to outline what was being done for the religious training of the students, who 'needed help more than any other class in the community'. He sought faculties for weekly sodality meetings, benediction, and a students' mass on Sundays. Finally, he drew attention to an innovation which was meeting a real need and of which he was particularly proud. A complete course of evening classes had been introduced 'at the charge of six guineas for the whole course, or two guineas a term'. These catered for students of limited means and for people working during the day; and, from the earnestness of those who formed the classes, they gave 'promise of good educational results'.

It is clear from the foregoing how much Delany pinned his hopes on the appointment to fellowships of suitably qualified Jesuits. He took for granted that the senate would allocate the fourteen Catholic fellowships to the college. His experience with Monsignor Neville, the cardinal, and the senate, with regard to Dr Casey and Fr Finlay, confirmed this assumption. Five fellowships remained to be filled. He had proposed to the senate that two of them be immediately allocated in the areas of classics and mathematics, for which he had ready the two Jesuit candidates recommended to the episcopal committee. Robert Curtis had been one of the leading mathematical scholars of his day at Dublin University. He was highly regarded by Dr Casey and considered generally as one of the outstanding Irishmen in his field. Gerard Manley Hopkins, whatever his eccentricities, was an exhibitioner and first class honours graduate of Balliol College, Oxford, and had been described by Professor Nettleship as 'one of the cleverest and most original men in Oxford'.[8] Of the qualifications of the two candidates, therefore, there could be no question. Delany knew that the lay members of the senate, moreover, sympathised with his problem and aims. All seemed plain sailing. Unexpected by him, however, a storm was brewing.

He had been aware that St Malachy's College, Belfast, had put in for a fellowship two years previously, and he was not averse to making a concession to it because of its special circumstances amidst a large non-Catholic population in the north of Ireland; but he had not paid much attention to more recent reports that other colleges, like Blackrock, Clonliffe, Fermoy and Dundalk, sought a similar concession for themselves. The first indication that there was afoot a serious challenge to his hold on the fellowships came when he learned that his friend and confidant, Dr Walsh of Maynooth, was an advocate of their dispersal among the different Catholic colleges. It was the prelude to a bitter and far-reaching controversy.

On 22 January 1884 Blackrock College submitted a request to the senate for approval 'as a college in which fellows of the Royal University may be authorised to lecture'.[9] The following day, Dr Walsh sent Delany an invitation to a meeting at Maynooth to discuss university affairs. He mentioned that Fr Reffé of Blackrock would be present, as well as Fr Burke of Carlow, and Dr Egan late of University College. His letter crossed one from Delany in which he told of a visit to the cardinal to seek his support for Hopkins's candidature. He thought that His Eminence was impressed by the fact that Hopkins had a talent for classical verse writing, an important factor 'on account of the competition with Trinity College which prides itself on its verse writers', and he mentioned that Bishop Butler would urge Hopkins's case at the meeting of the episcopal committee on the 29 January. The next day he wrote to accept the invitation and, still unsuspecting, related that there was good support for his two candidates but that the cardinal's support was a vital point since he, Delany, 'should not like a struggle — even if we were sure to win'. On 25 January Dr Walsh obviously decided to remove any misconceptions about the purpose of the meeting. It was his view, he wrote, 'that the French College people ought to be *recognised* to the extent of getting one fellowship . . . let it be classics or modern languages'. He would prefer the latter. Fr Reffé could be put forward as a good candidate for that. 'We must see', he concluded, 'that your people and theirs do not fall out over it, and that the interests of neither suffer'. The cardinal agreed 'that they ought to get one'.

Delany was placed in an embarrassing predicament. When at Temple Street he had been in favour of a fellowship being given both to Blackrock and his own college. Dr Walsh was aware of this, and seemed to presume, despite recent indications to the contrary, that he still felt the same way. There was the presumption, too, that the senate would grant a fellowship to Fr Reffé, even though it had rejected a previous application from him on the ground of insufficient qualifications. Delany considered that he was being put in an unreasonable and unfair position in being asked, just a few days before the senate met, to face a concerted lobby pressing for the withdrawal of Fr Hopkins in favour of Fr Reffé, and in the latter's presence. He decided to write at length to Dr Walsh to make his views quite clear.

He had been in favour over a year previously of a fellowship being given to the French College and St Ignatius College, since both held similar relations to the central college in Stephen's Green. Now, however, the situation had changed. Help given to the Jesuits went 'directly to the maintenance of the central college itself', and that institution if it were to be made 'a working place worth preserving' needed all such help that could be given it. Hence, he would not *advocate* the appointment of Fr Reffé, since the presence of one who was 'the very guiding spirit of an avowedly rival institution' invited 'a considerable risk of divided counsels' in the working of University College; but he would not object to the appointment, if His Eminence and Dr Walsh deemed it advisable, provided it was 'under the same conditions as Fr Finlay and the other fellows' namely, that he be freed 'from all and every duty of every kind' in connection with Blackrock. He then went on to make a distinction central to the whole question. 'Giving a fellowship is one thing, approval of the French College is a totally different thing'. Where the latter was concerned, he felt it a duty to University College and to the bishops, for whom he was to some extent in a fiduciary position, to offer every opposition in his power. There were a number of reasons for this.

Approval of the French College would involve, as you know, the liberty of choice to Catholic fellows to lecture here or there. It would be at once open to the French College to induce fellows to exercise their choice in favour of Blackrock by the offer of salaries. Hence competition on our part to retain them, and consequent expenditure — and the practical abolition of the whole fellowship scheme.

Approval, moreover, would put an end to the chances of securing state recognition which, he believed, could be obtained by a few years successful work at University College. Should such recognition come, the Jesuits would 'not allow their presence to be made an obstacle in the way of realisation'. Again, if Blackrock were approved, what of the claims of St Malachy's, of Carlow, of Mungret, and of the other colleges which had or might have from time to time, 'a goodly show in the lists of the Royal University'? Finally, were the French College open to fellows the whole status of University College would be altered, 'and it would be necessary to revise the conditions of tenure, as the bishops' property would have seriously deteriorated in value actually and prospectively'. He concluded with the hope 'to go down by train' the following day.[10]

No account remains of what must have been a rather tense meeting. The day after, however, Dr Walsh attended the preliminary session of the standing committee of the senate and found himself in a minority of one in his support of the Blackrock submission. Lord Emly made 'an admirable little speech' in explanation of its almost unanimous rejection. Dr Kavanagh, Delany's informant, counselled him 'to look well to the proposer and seconder of Curtis and Hopkins' and to rally his forces. He had heard that His Eminence 'intended to propose Reffé' at the next meeting of the standing committee in two days time, 30 January 1884.

The episcopal committee met, meanwhile, on 29 January.

One of the items on the agenda was the filling of the fellowships. Delany, as has been seen, had requested the committee's support for his two candidates. It was a crucial meeting. Dr Walsh had received permission to attend. Bishop Butler, however, Delany's chief supporter, was unable to be present. Dr Walsh's advocacy succeeded in gaining majority support for Fr Reffé. The cardinal, although opposed to the decision, let it go forward as unanimous. The meeting came to an end around five o'clock, and Dr Woodlock was instructed to contact the Jesuit provincial to have Hopkins's name withdrawn. The committee, according to Bishop Gillooly, was confident that the cardinal's support of Fr Reffé would prove decisive as the senate had postponed the appointment the previous October due to His Eminence's inability to attend.[11] At six o'clock Delany encountered Lord Emly, who told him that he had had a conversation that day with McCabe who declared his intention of proposing Curtis and Hopkins, and that as he (Emly) would second them there was nothing to fear. On hearing this, Delany telegraphed the news to Hopkins, then at Stonyhurst, and to some of the senators, and stayed out for the evening. Dr Walsh was out also. He spent the evening at Blackrock preparing the case in support of Fr Reffé.[12] Late that night Delany learned that the cardinal had expressed the wish that Hopkins's name be withdrawn. He deemed the hour too late to communicate with Stonyhurst, and as the senate could not recognise any withdrawal except from Hopkins himself, he decided to let matters take their course.

His opponents found it difficult to accept his story.[13] To them it seemed like a jesuitical subterfuge to hold on to the fellowship. On the other hand, Delany at this stage was not sure how the voting would go the following day, and besides, given the absence of Bishop Butler, and the yielding dispositions of Drs McCabe and Woodlock, he had reason to believe that the committee's decision had been stage-managed by Dr Walsh and was not expressive of the overall view of the hierarchy.

Prior to the meeting on 30 January, the lay Catholic senators urged the cardinal not to propose a candidate who was sure to be rejected. He replied that as the representative of the committee of Catholic bishops he had to persevere with the proposal, but that his personal preference was otherwise. Before the division, several senators, both Protestants as chancellor Ball, and Catholics as Dr Kavanagh, Dr Cruise and Lord Emly, explained the reasons for their votes, namely the importance of building up a great central Catholic institution, and, secondly, the complete absence of any evidence that the cardinal's candidate had the necessary qualifications in the classical languages.

In the subsequent election, Dr McCabe first proposed Mr Curtis, who was elected by eighteen votes to eight, and then, seconded by Dr Walsh, Fr Reffé, who was rejected in favour of Hopkins by twenty-three votes to three. To Mr Redington, who immediately afterwards expressed his regret at having himself bound to vote against His Eminence's candidate, the cardinal said 'I am just as glad things turned out as they did'.[14] Before the session ended, Dr Woodlock gave notice that he would move at the next meeting for the recognition of the French College as a college where the fellows of the university might teach. The next day McCabe resigned from the senate. On a number of occasions he had expressed his sense of inadequacy as a bishops' representative on the senate, but had permitted fellow prelates to persuade him against resigning.[15] Some days later, following a special request from Lord Spencer, the Lord Lieutenant, he withdrew his resignation. Dr Walsh, who had favoured His Eminence's action in resigning, showed no inclination himself at this stage to imitate him.

The succeeding weeks placed great strain on Delany. The provincial, Fr Browne, received a letter from Dr Gillooly on 4 February which deplored his 'opposition to the *coetus episcoporum*, represented by the episcopal committee', in not withdrawing his candidate's name and, thereby, bringing about the resignation of the cardinal. The bishop requested him, for the sake of his 'great undertaking at Stephen's Green as much as for wider and weightier reasons', to remedy his mistake at this stage by withdrawing Hopkins. He had used his best efforts to secure for the Society an eminent position in the university system, but if the result were to be from the outset a conflict on the Society's part with the *coetus episcoporum* and a ruinous division among the Catholic senators of the university, then he would heartily repent of what he had done and persuaded others to do. Fr Browne's reply explaining what happened and the difficulty at this stage of withdrawing Hopkins, left the bishop unmoved.

Faced with such a strong reaction, and sensitive both to the interpretations being put on his own part in the proceedings and to the challenge presented by Dr Woodlock's proposal for the next senate meeting, Delany sent letters to some members of the episcopacy and of the senate. To the bishop of Limerick he wrote a detailed report of all that had happened. Dr Butler replied on 14 February that his letter would enable him do some good at future meetings of the episcopal committee and with individual bishops. He considered it 'very fortunate that Fr Hopkins *could not* be advised to withdraw beforehand'; while to withdraw him after the election 'would have been an aimless and stupid proceeding, seeing that it would not tend in any degree to carry out the cardinal's view of helping Black-rock, for the senate would not have Reffé.' He hoped that with his three fellows Delany would achieve, in the near future, such a success as to silence his enemies and satisfy his friends. Dr Croke, in reply to him on 19 February, was of the opinion that the episcopal education committee's powers were limited 'to matters of comparatively inconsiderable interest'; and he was clear that it was not competent 'for Dr Woodlock to speak before the senate at the next meeting, *in the name of the bishops of Ireland*', seeking approval for the French College. Besides, he characteristically stripped away non-essentials — pointing out that two exceptionally favoured university colleges could not effectively co-exist in Dublin. 'Let the French College *or* the Stephen's Green College be *the* University College, sustained and fostered *as such*: but let us not have two competing establishments in or near Dublin at least, both certain to lack vigour, because both lacking funds.'

The next meeting of the standing committee of the senate was scheduled for 29 May. In the months between, amicable relations continued between Delany and Dr Walsh. The latter was engaged, by means of letters in the *Freeman's Journal* and questions in parliament, in attacks on the Queen's Colleges. He and Delany exchanged letters. On 15 March he announced that he was pressing for a royal commission to enquire into the colleges, and on 7 April from London, after the commission had been announced, that he had hopes of the Queen's Colleges being handed over to the Catholics. Delany, with a clearer grasp of the situation, was taken aback. There were not enough trained Catholic teachers for existing colleges, let alone finding additional staff for the Queen's Colleges.

Shortly after this, his easy relationship with his Maynooth friend received an unexpected jolt. He was preparing material for the senate meeting, and as had been his custom, sent a draft-copy to Dr Walsh for his perusal. The latter took strong exception to the wording of one sentence. Delany had written: 'As it is contemplated, I believe, to assign to this college three of the fellows who are to be appointed'. Dr Walsh replied bluntly that such a statement should not be made without the cardinal's approval. To do so was to 'simply invite the Protestants and the lay members of the senate, not merely to differ from the cardinal, but to ignore him'. Surprised at the interpretation, and even more at the excessive reaction, Delany altered his words to read: 'In the event of it being determined to assign. . . .' Dr Walsh declared himself happy with this version as it did not prejudge the case. On reflection, Delany saw his friend's previous reply as 'the *first* letter that showed any trace of wounded feeling'.[16]

As the 29 May drew near there was intensive lobbying of senators by both sides. At the meeting of the standing committee a surprise was sprung by the joining of Dr Woodlock's proposal seeking approval for the French College to a proposal in favour of Fr Reffé for a fellowship, this time in modern languages. Delany was later to regard this dual proposal as a tactic inspired by Dr Walsh to obtain full recognition for Blackrock. Dr Kavanagh responded with notice of a counter-motion. Should Bishop Woodlock's proposal in favour of Blackrock be adopted, he intended to propose that Carlow College be approved by the senate 'as a college wherein the fellows of the Royal University may lecture'.[17] In face of this complication, there was no seconder for the dual proposal. That evening Dr Walsh sent in his resignation from the senate. At the senate meeting on the following day, Dr Woodlock, who presided, announced that he was withdrawing for the present his motion on the recognition of the French College. Lord Emly then proposed, and Mgr Neville seconded, the appointment to modern languages of the Abbé Polin, the only candidate remaining and an examiner at the college. He was elected.

The cardinal resented the fact that Dr Walsh had resigned without first consulting him on the matter. He wrote to Dr Healy, a professor at Maynooth, asking him to allow himself be proposed for the vacant place. When Dr Healy queried the propriety of this, he being a member of Dr Walsh's staff, McCabe informed him that he was to be appointed Bishop of Clonfert. Dr Healy, having conferred with Dr Walsh, concurred.[18] He was to prove one of Delany's staunchest supporters on the senate.

Following this challenge, all subsequent fellowships went to University College as a matter of course. Mgr Patrick J. Walsh, in his *William J. Walsh, Archbishop of Dublin* (1928), was later to represent the fellowship dispute as one between Dr Walsh, as champion of Catholic nationalism, and the Whigs, ecclesiastical and lay, on the senate. In fact, there was no justification for applying the term 'Whig' to the policy of concentrating the fellowships at Stephen's Green. It was the policy which the bishops as a body had initiated, and had insisted on while University College was in their hands. It had never been challenged until Dr Walsh did so on 25 January, 1884. His alternative policy of scattering the fellowships was never subsequently sponsored by any of the bishops. It was one of the two important matters of university policy – the other being the nature of the final solution to the university question – on which he held a view differing from the majority of the episcopate. On this occasion he had carried the episcopal committee with him; but Dr Croke, scarcely a 'Whig', had considered that they had exceeded their powers; and neither he, nor Dr Butler, nor the cardinal, agreed with his stand.

Delany was relieved at the success in the senate, but he deeply regretted being forced into opposition to Dr Walsh. When the announcement of the latter's resignation appeared in the *Freeman's Journal*, he wrote back to ask if it were correct and to express his concern. Dr Walsh replied on 31 May that he had himself written the account in the newspaper 'so as to shut out the possibility of any effort being made by Lord Spencer' to induce him to do 'what the cardinal was unfortunately induced to do after his resignation'. It had been a source of great pain to him as a senate member to take a course at variance with what Delany regarded as the interests of University College. Hence, he found it a relief to be rid of the responsibility imposed on him by the senate. He had not acted precipitately. Though he had not posted his letter of resignation till after the senate meeting, he had, in fact, written it the night previous, having a distrust of his own judgement 'on any matter, when formed under anything like excitement, or without the fullest consideration'.

Thus, the dispute over the fellowships appeared to have ended. But Dr Walsh's 'relief' at being off the senate was to prove short lived. Ironically, but humanly, he resented not being officially requested to reconsider his resignation; and the memory of his senate defeat rankled to the point of virtually blinding him to any side of the question but his own. The senate became a *bête noire*. Before the close of the year he was to carry the confined senatorial disagreement into the public arena.

In the meantime, he was engaged in harassing an older adversary. For some months, as has been noted, Dr Walsh had been waging a vigorous campaign, by letters in the press and questions in parliament, to expose the waste of money involved in the running of the Queen's Colleges. This resulted in the appointment of a royal commission of enquiry (1884-5). During the month of June 1884 Delany and he were busy preparing their evidence for the commission. 'I read your evidence today before the commission with great pleasure', Dr Kavanagh wrote to Delany on 27 June. 'It was terse, cogent, and beautifully expressed. Dr Walsh's evidence also was very good'. Still, he did not think much would come from the commission. He feared, correctly, that it would rehabilitate the Queen's Colleges. 'Have you yet solved the riddle of Dr Walsh's resignation? It is the wonder of all whom I hear speaking of it'. In July came the formal announcement of the appointment to the senate of Very Rev John Healy, D.D., 'in the room of Very Rev William J. Walsh, D.D., resigned'.[19]

Delany was ill over the summer. He went to a house of the Order in Bournemouth, a favourite place, to recuperate. His recovery, in time for the new academic year, was encouraged by the college's remarkable examination results. Their comparative significance he underlined some time later for the benefit of the government's Under Secretary, Sir Robert Hamilton.

> University College in its first year, and labouring under great disadvantages, won more distinctions in classics and modern languages than the three Queen's Colleges taken together. In science it excelled Cork and Galway, and nearly equalled the two together — falling behind Belfast alone in subjects where educational appliances, laboratories, museums, and library are absolutely essential.

It was an auspicious start for the new college, and people were not slow to draw comparisons between it and its predecessor; a procedure which Delany, conscious of episcopal sensitivities, was careful to avoid. The current assistant to the General, Fr Keller, wrote to him in triumphalist terms on 4 November. 'Your triumphant success has consoled us very much. Considering the time you had and the means at your disposal, you have shown what Jesuit education can produce, in a manner perhaps never surpassed in the whole of our history. God be praised!' He had seen all the praise Delany had received in the *Freeman's Journal*, and he trusted 'that the bishops will be moved to show you favour . . . and help the cause, e.g. giving you the church and restoring the library'.

There was another type of reaction, however, in the same month. It took the form of a harsh public attack by Dr Walsh. The latter had clearly been brooding over his experience in the senate and over the treatment of Blackrock, a college which had supported the Catholic University to the end, its pupils doing the university's matriculation when others, like Tullabeg, had turned elsewhere. Delany received his first indication of his friend's state of mind when Dr Higgins of Navan sent him a copy of a letter he had received from Walsh. It declared that 'the disorganised condition of affairs' had forced upon him 'the very painful necessity of withdrawing from the senate of the Royal University', and that he had determined 'to have nothing more to do with any organisation for Catholic educational interests' until he saw 'some prospect of justice being done in the matter of university education to those who successfully fought our battles in the critical time, and who had now been left out in the cold by the unnatural alliance of certain Catholic members of the senate of the Royal University with those who, to say the least, are not friends of Irish Catholic interests'.[20]

Chapter V

THE FELLOWSHIP CONTROVERSY GOES PUBLIC

The fellowship dispute was expanded into a public controversy in the last weeks of November and the first week of
December 1884. The rather unseemly struggle was waged
mainly in the pages of the *Tablet*, the Belfast *Morning News*,
and the *Freeman's Journal*.

The president of Maynooth fired the first shots with a letter
to the *Tablet*. The *Morning News* drew attention to his remarks; and soon there was a series of letters and articles attacking or defending the special position of University College.
Dr Walsh, himself, argued with eloquence and vigour, but, as
the controversy developed, it was not easy to see where exactly
he stood. His power of emphasis was not matched by clarity of
expression. Briefly, he did not approve of the Royal University
and was opposed to the fellowship scheme, as such, because it
created the illusion that Catholics enjoyed an endowment.
University College, he maintained, could manage without fellowships. Blackrock had shown that a college could do brilliantly
without such aids. But given that there were fellowships, it was
unfair for University College to have a monopoly of them; and
it was doubly unfair — a strong point — to have the fellows who
taught at Stephen's Green also acting as setters and examiners
of the Royal University examinations. Rather than all the
fellowships being concentrated in University College, some
should be granted to Blackrock in recompense for its splendid
contribution to Irish education. To grant it a fellowship would
lessen to some degree, at least, the unfairness of the examination system.

His denunciation of monopoly struck a chord in other
Catholic colleges which felt unfairly treated at having no form
of indirect subsidy. The *Morning News* eagerly stirred the discontent. On 22 November it made reference to Dr Walsh's
letter in the *Tablet*, went on to state that many Catholic edu-

cationalists were concerned at the scandalous waste of teaching power at Stephen's Green, and commented on the unfair proportion of teachers to students there compared to Belfast and other colleges.

Dr Butler sent a copy of the article to Delany that day and asked him how he would answer the charges. Delany in reply noted the reference to the *Tablet* and said that he had contemplated a public answer but hated the prospect of a newspaper squabble between priests. He feared 'that Dr Walsh's propensity to newspaper writing' might lead him to begin a controversy no matter how mildly the opposition case was put. With regard to the actual charges, he pointed out that his student numbers were not a mere seventy, as given in the paper, but 168 in all; that at this early stage University College's classes were naturally small compared to Belfast, but that a small class took as much time and labour for lectures as a large one; and that, moreover, University College, with its pass and honours divisions, had actually more classes than Belfast, hence its greater percentage of honours successes than Belfast in classics, English and mathematics. As to having an excess of teaching fellows, this was so far from being the case that he was obliged to appoint a number of tutors. The full reality of the situation, in this respect, he could not make public 'because of the pain it would cause unoffending persons'. Thus, three of the fellows were seventy years of age or over and could do little work; another, Dr Molloy, was absent nearly all last year and he had had to employ a substitute for him; and two others, ascribed to Stephen's Green by the *Morning News*, actually taught at the Medical School in Cecilia Street. Besides, the full value of all the fellows at the college was less than £1,000 a year in terms of their teaching hours. Their combined teaching hours each week did not exceed eighty-four hours. If he had not the allocated fellows and was in a position to pay masters of his own choice, he could obtain from six men, teaching eighteen hours a week and paid £150 a year, the equivalent of 108 hours weekly for £900 a year. 'Our assailants', he said, 'know all this well, and it is not the fellows they want but the fellowships'. And, with rising indignation, were University College not harassed by 'this insane jealousy' it would have more arts students in two years than Belfast. It was a tragedy that at a time when the Queen's Colleges of Cork and Galway were collapsing the Catholics were not joining together for Catholic interests.[21]

On 24 November the *Morning News* proceeded to question the monopoly of fellowships at University College. 'It was the scandalous one-sidedness of this arrangement which caused the resignation by the distinguished president of Maynooth College of his position on the senate of the Royal University'. Asked to comment, two senators of the university expressed the view that University College had special benefits because it was 'the college of the bishops of Ireland'. The bishop of Down and Conor, on the other hand, was recorded as declaring that the bishops' connection with Stephen's Green had ceased 'for some time past'. 'The institution is now the private concern of the Jesuits, who have taken a lease of the place, and conduct it at their own risk and peril'.

On the 24th also, Dr Butler expressed his satisfaction with Delany's response. But, he added, 'the attack on the Royal University senate for giving you all the Catholic fellows should be answered by some Catholic members of the senate — such as Dean Neville, Dr Cruise or Lord Emly, and whoever answers should show that the Jesuits undertook to work the Stephen's Green school under an express arrangement with the bishops that all the Catholic fellows should teach at Stephen's Green'. It was strange 'that Dr Walsh should close his eyes to the fact that this inviolable principle, for whose sake he has resigned his place on the senate, has been wholly overlooked by the cardinal, the bishops of Ardagh and Clonfert, and by Dr Neville'.

For the president of Maynooth, however, emotion and 'inviolable principle' seemed to have become intertwined, and he returned to the charge on 29 November with contributions to the *Tablet* and the *Freeman's Journal*. He continued to hammer at the injustice perpetrated by the senate in allocating all the Catholic fellows to University College, and queried the college's right to have them. Delany sat down and wrote a long reply to which he attached 'not for publication'. He discussed what he had written, however, with his two senatorial friends, Dr Kavanagh and Dr Cruise, both of whom now took up the cudgels. Cruise's response to Dr Walsh showed many similarities to Delany's private reply.

Kavanagh took Walsh to task on the issue of University College's monopoly. The president of Maynooth replied at considerable length on 1 December. By this, his persistence was occasioning some episcopal unease. On the same date, Dr Butler commenced a letter to the Jesuit provincial with the words: 'the attacks of Dr Walsh on the university school, Stephen's Green, are becoming simply intolerable'. He distinctly remembered that when Fr Tuite, the provincial, and another Jesuit, discussed with the committee of bishops the arrangements regarding Stephen's Green, 'it was clearly set forth, as an important factor in the contract', that the college 'was to have, so far as the bishops could control it, the advantage of the teaching of all the Catholic fellows of the Royal University'. Hence, he had 'pointed out to Dr Walsh some months ago that if there was anything wrong in giving the Catholic fellows to Stephen's Green, it *was the fault of the bishops*, and that to attack the arrangement was to attack the bishops', but Dr Walsh had 'either forgotten or disregarded' his reminder.

Up to this point, the weight of public criticism had been directed at the senate and at the Jesuits in University College. That both had merely continued what had been demanded by the bishops, and that to attack them was to attack the bishops, was something that nobody had yet ventured to say in public. The nail had been hammered to one side by Dr Walsh. To make it straight, it needed to be hammered in the opposite direction. The required polemic was provided by Dr F. Cruise in the *Freeman's Journal* of 2 December. His letter was protracted and inflated, but it made a number of telling points and so upset the president of Maynooth as to virtually terminate the public controversy. Ranging over the history of the fellowships and the background to Dr Walsh's opposition, and indicating the strength of feeling generated by his newspaper campaign, it is worth presenting at some length.

The Royal University, Cruise wrote, was accepted by the bishops and established in 1880 mainly to meet the needs of Catholic aspirants for university degrees. The most pressing want, in the opinion of the Catholic senators, and of the educated Catholic laity, was a central college for Catholic candidates combining 'the highest training with suitable religious supervision, such a centre as we see for non-Catholics in Trinity College, Dublin, and in the various colleges of Oxford and Cambridge'. In furtherance of this 'very intelligible view', the Catholic senators obtained for University College — 'formerly the Catholic University College, and still in the hands of the bishops of Ireland' — some thirteen fellowships.

'After a brief trial the bishops deemed it wise to hand over to the Jesuit Order the task of organising and working this college, subject to certain conditions, of which the most important was that the college should retain the staff of fellows allotted to it by the senate'. This condition had held from the start and was so zealously guarded that, as many would remember, when one of the fellows, Dr Casey, wished to give instructions in his leisure hours to students outside the college, he was not permitted to do so. 'The Jesuits accepted Stephen's Green college, with its staff of fellows, under these conditions from the bishops'. They took possession in November 1883; and a glance at the table of results given in Dr Walsh's letter of 1 December 1884 showed 'what fruit had come of their efforts within an extraordinary short period, justifying the hope that the disastrous failure of the old Catholic University of Ireland' was 'not likely to be repeated, and that after thirty years of darkness and confusion' there was 'good prospect of brighter days and of a better order of things'.

Having thus set the scene to his own satisfaction, he turned a sarcastic eye on Dr Walsh's behaviour. In April 1883, he said, just before the transfer of the college to the Jesuits, Dr Walsh was appointed senator and 'forthwith set himself to work with all his well-known vigour and ability, to accomplish, if he possibly could, the subdivision of the fellowships allotted to the Stephen's Green college'. He did not pretend to judge his motives, but he could not suppose 'that he was ignorant that this subdivision of teaching and financial power, if obtained, would speedily paralyse and ultimately destroy the youthful college, handed over by the bishops of Ireland to the Jesuits, and now being nobly worked by them at great pecuniary sacrifice'. He noted that Dr Walsh had held back 'the undisguised fact that his real contention was for the formal recognition of Blackrock College, which would have enabled all the fellows to fulfill their statutory obligation of teaching there in place of the Stephen's Green college'. The senate at its meeting in May last differed from Dr Walsh 'and were not prepared to take a step which would endanger the breaking-up of the bishops' National College'. Whereupon, Dr Walsh, 'foiled in his attempt, threw up his senatorship on the spot'. To all who knew these facts, Cruise continued, 'it will not be a matter of surprise that the Rev ex-senator should now endeavour to organise an attack from without to accomplish what he so signally failed in doing while on the senate'.

He regretted the loss of a man of such ability from the senate. He also regretted his charging the senate with a policy 'essentially based on unfairness and injustice'. 'Surely,' he said, 'in these days of enlightenment, men may differ without taxing each other with base motives, and the fact that the senate was not prepared to accept his *ipse dixit* cannot justify even so accomplished and distinguished a churchman as the president of Maynooth College in this accusation against a body of gentlemen

whose time and energy, as well as his, may be worth something
— and who may be presumed to have, as well as himself, some
conscience, some education, some interest in the great question
of Catholic higher education, and some little knowledge of university affairs'.

He pressed on:

> To a layman, like myself, it must remain a puzzle that Rev
> Dr Walsh should find himself constrained to withdraw from
> the university senate, while we find His Eminence Cardinal
> McCabe, Most Rev Dr Woodlock, Right Rev Dean Neville,
> and Very Rev Dr Kavanagh still holding their seats; and more
> remarkably still, while the Most Rev Dr Healy, co-adjutor
> Bishop of Clonfert, a most distinguished professor of May-
> nooth College, does not hesitate to step, without condition
> or stipulation, into the vacancy created by Rev Dr Walsh's
> retirement, showing that the Very Rev President's withdrawal
> cannot have been based on any point of principle.

> Rev Dr Walsh dwells strongly upon the supposed iniquity of
> 'monopoly'. Dr Kavanagh has let in so much light upon this
> fallacy that I need not touch it. I will ask only one question.
> Is not Maynooth College a monopoly, and a very big one?
> What reply, then, would its Very Rev President make if I
> or anyone else declared that the monopoly of Maynooth
> should be broken up in order that justice may be done, and
> its professors and funds divided amongst the provincial
> colleges throughout Ireland, engaged in training young men
> for the priesthood?

But, Cruise asked, 'what is the iniquitous policy of the
senate?' In summary, 'it is to support the bishops' college —
University College, Stephen's Green — in order that it may be
what Catholics want, an efficient training college for undergraduates, under perfect religious discipline'. What Dr Walsh
wanted, on the other hand, was to divide the fellowships throughout Ireland. But

> if this monopoly to which he so inconsistently objects, being
> a huge monopolist himself, is to be abolished, then all will have
> equal claims, and it needs little foresight to see that such a
> course would destroy the bishops' college, without materially
> serving any other, or making it what Catholics want.

He (Cruise) yielded to no one in his admiration for the work of Blackrock and its splendid staff, but 'as the bishops of Ireland did not select it to represent them at their college, Stephen's Green, but, on the other hand, confided that institution to the Jesuits', he, as a Catholic senator, felt that he had no option but to give his best support to the University College, Stephen's Green.

Faced with this strong mixture of hard facts, special pleading, and sustained reproof, Dr Walsh was deeply stung but did not immediately grasp its implications. He made a detailed rejoinder the following day to demonstrate that Dr Cruise had given an inaccurate presentation of the facts and an inaccurate exposition of his motives. Two days later, however, it seems to have come home to him that what Cruise was actually saying was that he was acting out of pique in publicly supporting Blackrock and that in reality he was opposed to the Jesuits and to the policy of the Irish bishops. He wrote a private and rather disjointed letter to Delany. He was in a state of some distress and the humiliation he experienced in writing was not conducive to easy relations between them in the future.

'I really fear', he wrote, 'that if I do not write to you to ask you not to be led away by all the terribly false things that Dr Cruise has written about me in reference to your college, even you may be carried away by the current into the belief that I am in reality one of the deadliest opponents of your great work'. He then went on, to Delany's astonishment: 'I can quite *understand* the view taken by some and, I dare say, not unnaturally by yourself and many of your Fathers, that the appointment of anyone but a Jesuit, as fellow of the university, even with the obligation of teaching as fellow in Stephen's Green, involves as a necessary consequence the paralysis and destruction of the college. Preposterous as the notion seems to me, I can make allowances for the influences, as I believe of prejudice, etc, which led to its being adopted by those who hold it'. What he most objected to, however, was that 'a man like Dr Cruise' had publicly charged him with opposition to the bishops. He hoped Delany, at least, would believe that if he (Walsh) had 'even a *slight* fear that the success of Stephen's Green college would be in the least degree endangered' he would not be a party 'to the line of action that would involve such a consequence'. Delany knew how much he had done to remove obstacles to the transfer of the college to the Jesuits, but not even he knew that were it not for one particular step which he went out of his way to take 'at the very last and most critical moment' the Fathers would not now be in the college. He had written a further reply to 'Dr Cruise's shocking misrepresentation' showing that he had been from the beginning an advocate of the transfer of the Stephen's Green college. He felt it a great humiliation to have to write this in public about what he hoped would have been taken for granted, 'but the bold assertion of a respectable Catholic like Dr Cruise' made it impossible for him 'to remain silent under his misrepresentation'. 'I really would prefer', he concluded, 'that when next writing to me you would make no reference to all that I have written now. I only want you to know my real position. And may I ask you to show this letter to the provincial? I would not venture to write so freely to him'.[22]

As he closed the letter, Delany was not at all clear as to the 'real position' as Dr Walsh saw it. He seemed to want two conflicting things, the continuing success of University College, and the dispersal of the fellows on which it depended for continuance. The one thing that did seem clear to Delany, from Dr Walsh's actions as well as his words, was that he sought above all recognition for Blackrock, that everything else was tributary to that, and that that, and not the election of an individual fellow — which Delany was prepared to accept — was the real issue; it was only when such recognition was categorically rejected that he had resigned from the senate.[23]

In his public letter of 5 December 1884, the president of Maynooth declared that he was writing again because some friends urged him to defend himself against Dr Cruise's indictment of his action as a senator and of his apparent opposition to the policy of the Irish bishops. It was quite false to suggest that he had been in anyway opposed to the transfer of the Stephen's Green college. On the contrary, he had been one of the strongest advocates in its favour, and he saw it as 'the most practically useful step' taken by the bishops in the cause of Catholic university education. Far from being opposed to the bishops in his action in the senate, the two episcopal members, Cardinal McCabe and Dr Woodlock, voted with him. The vote was 21 to 3. He also wished to point out that the candidate in question was voted for on the understanding that if elected he would fulfil the statutory obligations of teaching at Stephen's Green. As to his alleged aim to obtain recognition of Blackrock, the proposal was Dr Woodlock's and it was withdrawn. He had used the cardinal's and Dr Woodlock's names without their permission, but he was sure they would support his doing so in the cause of the president of Maynooth College. He concluded his rather evasive letter with the hope that Dr Cruise would now 'have the propriety to let the matter drop'.

Dr Cruise closed the public disputation two days later. He was brief but scarcely merciful. He noted that Dr Walsh had not consulted the two prelates before writing. This was to be regretted, as was his omission to consult them before resigning, as any layman would have done. Since Dr Walsh had appealed to him to let the matter drop, he, as a Catholic layman, would gladly do so. Dr Walsh had written many letters to English as well as Irish newspapers. He had written only one, and that in self-defence of the senate of which Dr Walsh had been a member and 'many of the highest dignatories in the country are members'. He observed that Dr Walsh wanted him to desist even though he had not withdrawn his charges. He (Dr Cruise) was doing so in respect, while, at the same time, restating his belief in the accuracy of the picture he had drawn of Dr Walsh's policy and its effect on the bishop's college. 'I deeply regret', he concluded, 'the grave imprudence which originated such a controversy and conducted it so strangely'.

A curious foot-note to all the publicity and emotional ferment was provided a few days later when Delany paid a visit to the cardinal. The latter informed him that he had told Dr Walsh that his letter of resignation 'was most uncalled for and inopportune', and he expressed the view that it had been a mistake to put forward Fr Reffé's name.[24]

Dr Walsh was large-minded and not prone to nurse grievances, but his public humiliation in the fellowship controversy rankled deeply and, thereafter, his attitude to the Royal University and its senate was dismissive or openly hostile. University College, as an institution favoured by the senate, experienced, inevitably, some of this disapproval. He had 'closed his eyes' as Dr Butler remarked, to the consequences of his actions in the fellowship affair. Something similar had happened with regard to the Queen's Colleges. It was to recur on at least two other occasions: an *ideé fixe* would be asserted in defiance of all arguments to the contrary and the prestige of his office as archbishop of Dublin to which he was appointed in 1885, would add special weight to his advocacy.

The criticism and strong feeling generated by the fellowship question did not end in a period of quiet for Delany at University College. The next two years were marked by a succession of issues in which he and his college came under fire. The first of these was on a matter of philosophy.

Chapter VI

OCCASIONS OF CONFLICT: DR WALSH AS ARCHBISHOP

The bishops at their meeting in Clonliffe College on 1 October 1884 complained of the questions set in the metaphysics examinations of the Royal University as 'questions practically necessitating the reading of anti-Catholic works, most dangerous to Catholic faith', and they called on the episcopal education committee to seek a remedy to the situation without delay.[25]

The questions had been set by Fr T.A. Finlay of University College, in collaboration with Professor Park of Queen's College, Belfast. They sought to cater for all candidates, those who studied under professors acquainted only with modern systems of philosophy and modern terminologies, and those who attended Catholic institutions and studied both scholastic philosophy and modern systems. But they made what Fr Finlay admitted to be 'a deplorable blunder'. They did not take account of the fact that in the Catholic seminary colleges the main emphasis was on scholastic philosophy and little was done on the modern systems; and that, besides, there were as yet no text-books in English dealing with the modern philosophies from a Catholic point of view and none on scholastic philosophy. Hence, the Catholic students were placed at a disadvantage; and it was feared that were the form of examination to continue, particularly at honours level, they would be tempted to ignore the study of scholastic philosophy and devote their attention to modern text-books by non-Catholic writers. In such circumstances, it was not unlikely that the bishops would withdraw their students from the Royal University's philosophy courses. As soon as the episcopal remonstrance was issued, therefore, all members of the senate showed the utmost willingness to remedy all grounds for complaint. On 24 October they appointed a sub-committee to devise a programme which would give equal advantage to all candidates. Dr Woodlock was the bishops' representative. Before a revised scheme was ready, however, the issue became one of public controversy.

Dr Thomas McGrath, who professed philosophy at Clonliffe seminary college, impugned the fairness of the papers in the November issue of the *Irish Ecclesiastical Record*. This was followed by attacks in the *Tablet* which Delany believed were 'inspired by Maynooth', as Dr Walsh was known to be very hostile on the matter and was prepared to appeal to Rome 'to assail us on our programme'.[26] Dr Kavanagh, formerly a professor of philosophy at Carlow College, explained and defended the philosophy programme in a pamphlet in January 1885, but his argument was not considered fully convincing and he was answered in the *Irish Ecclesiastical Record* of February and March by Dr Walsh and Dr Walter McDonald.

Eventually, a satisfactory and effective compromise was worked out. It was largely the work of Fr Finlay. Some changes were made in the courses and a choice of alternative questions was offered. These proposals, drawn up by the sub-committee, were approved by the senate on 6 February, 1885.

Delany felt very keenly the importance of the question. To Lord Emly, who had argued in favour of the papers and seemed prepared to challenge the bishops' stance, he wrote that he regarded it 'as *absolutely essential* to satisfy the bishops, even at the risk of narrowing temporarily our course of mental philosophy'. He used the word 'temporarily' because he hoped that within a few years there would be suitable handbooks available, and that by then the university, '*now on its trial and suspected*', would have grown and established itself, and that Catholics would have won such a position at University College that it would be plain that the system involved no unfairness and no religious danger. All that the bishops asked ought to be done readily so that they might be '*thoroughly satisfied*'. The Royal University, and still more University College, would be in 'an insecure position' so long as an active minority of them were dissatisfied; and 'the paramount consideration' of embracing 'in its system not merely our young lay Catholics, but also our ecclesiastical seminaries and our future priesthood', would not be secured. So far as he was concerned, it was his 'primary object' to make University College 'deserve the confidence of the Catholic ecclesiastical authorities', and he would subordinate his own views to those of the bishops wherever he might happen to disagree with them. On the matter of mental philosophy, however, there was no disagreement. He followed the lines laid down by the pope and was fully committed to making the college's philosophical teaching 'distinctly and thoroughly scholastic and thomistic' whilst doing his best to make his young students 'able to defend their faith against the errors of the day'.[27]

His 'paramount consideration' echoed, in restricted circumstances, Newman's view of the Catholic University as 'a middle station where clergy and laity can meet and from which as from a common ground they may act in union upon an age which is running headlong into infidelity'.[28]

Despite his 'primary object', instances of disharmony between himself and an 'active minority' of the episcopate continued. The college remained 'on its trial and suspected'. Dublin gossip fanned the embers. The appointment of Dr Walsh as vicar-capitular for the diocese, and the likelihood of he being appointed archbishop, in the place of Cardinal McCabe who had died on 11 February 1885, offered immediate scope for conjecture and rumour. Delany, meanwhile, responded favourably to the offer of a seat on the senate, and on 20 June, 1885, he was formally appointed by royal warrant 'in the room of His Eminence Cardinal McCabe deceased'.[29] As in the case of Dr Healy, Coadjutor Bishop of Clonfert, the government had not consulted the body of bishops about the appointment; and neither had Delany.[30]

Dr Walsh was the choice of the Dublin clergy for archbishop and he enjoyed wide support throughout the country. His appointment was challenged by the British government, and by those unkindly labelled by the *Nation* newspaper as 'orange papists', because of his strong Home Rule views and his reputation for outspokenness.[31] Delany, despite their differences, argued in favour of the appointment with many of his political friends and with the General's assistant in Rome. Dr Walsh might not always be easy to understand, his line of action not always easy to foresee, he might at times attach undue importance to details of phraseology, prove stubborn and heavy handed, and curiously insensitive to the hurtful impact of his utterances; nevertheless, he was clearly the ablest ecclesiastic of the day, and his support for popular and national rights had given him a general standing which was likely to be of great advantage to the church. Hence, Delany was deeply upset when Dr Kavanagh informed him in May that there was a widespread belief that Jesuit influence was being exerted against the elevation of the president of Maynooth owing to his supposedly unfriendly attitude to University College. Vehemently denying any such opposition, he wrote straightway to Dr Croke, then in Rome, and to Mgr Kirby of the Irish College, to scotch the rumour. 'The absurd rumours,' he told Mgr Kirby, 'that the

Jesuits are opposing the nomination of Dr Walsh, fearing he might not be friendly to them, are utterly without foundation. Make whatever use you wish of this letter'.[32] The Jesuit assistant later told him that the contents of his letter became widely known amongst all the Irish at Rome and did 'a great deal of good'.[33]

Dr Walsh was appointed archbishop of Dublin on 23 June 1885, and consecrated in Rome on 2 August. He returned home to enthusiastic acclamation. A public meeting at Kingstown (now Dun Laoghaire) greeted the elevation of a prelate 'whose aspirations are in unison with those of the Irish people.'[34] He never forfeited that image. For the next thirty-five years he was to wield immense influence and to hold an unparalleled position among Irish bishops. William Delany could no longer hope to compete on equal terms in any future contest on university affairs. Determined, however, to secure His Grace's good will towards University College, he invited him to pay a formal visit on 22 September. The occasion passed with every external mark of harmony.

Delany began the address of welcome by expressing the college's joy at the elevation of one who had been a student within its walls. Education, he continued, had been the staple work of His Grace's life. He felt confident it would hold a foremost place in the future. Ireland, 'on the threshold of a new era,' needed to secure 'a reversal of the past education policy' which had been 'as blind as it was unjust'. The helps which the state had given with lavish hands to the few, must be shared by the many without sacrifice of their principles as Catholics and as Irishmen. After contrasting 'the conditions of this state-neglected institution, outcome of a national aspiration and of a nation's sacrifice, with those of Trinity College, with its royal revenues, its buildings, and its wealth of educational appliances, or with those of the Queen's Colleges, against which it has so successfully maintained an unequal contest', he ventured to express the confident hope that under His Grace's 'powerful influence and fostering care', there might be created 'from this college, which boasts of you as her child, a great national home of learning and religion, renewing in no distant future the glories of Ireland's better days, a centre of civilization — Catholic and Irish — to which Irishmen in all lands will look with pride as worthy representatives of the faith and the patriotism and genius of their race'.[35]

The balanced eloquence of the address was calculated to stir the archbishop's sympathies for the college by evoking his own student ties with it; and it was carefully phrased to divert his attention from questions of inequality between Catholic colleges to the wider inequality between them and the state-endowed institutions. The idea of University College as 'a centre of civilization', a 'great national home of learning and religion', was not just idle rhetoric on Delany's part. Complain as he did about the total inadequacy of finances and facilities, he was sustained by a vision which looked beyond disabilities to the potentialities of his students and staff. He consciously, as has been seen, sought roots in Newman's ideals and hopes; and preserving the past for pride, present achievement for encouragement, the future for inspiration, confidently predicted on every suitable occasion that from the beginnings at Stephen's Green would flower a national university and a new era of Irish learning.

It soon became evident, however, that Delany's appeal, and in particular that aspect of it which virtually identified the Catholic University with the college, was not welcome to His Grace.

Can you tell me 'what line Dr Walsh will take? Not long ago he, in the presence of a friend of mine, did not show himself very friendly to us'. So, Lord Emly to Delany on 29 June, after the appointment of the new archbishop was announced. Emly had been elected vice-chancellor of the Royal University; and Delany, having received an honorary degree of L.L.D. in April, had in June, as previously mentioned, been elevated to the senate. The answer to the question came very clearly only two days after the reception at University College. His Grace, in a speech at Blackrock, vigorously assailed the senate once again for its fostering of inequality among Catholic colleges. He was clearly availing of his position to make himself the authoritative spokesman on all aspects of education. Already he had made pronouncements on primary education and on the endowed schools. His comments on the latter were too harsh, Captain Ross of Bladensburg (later Lord Ross) informed Delany. In the light of the current expectation of Home Rule, the Protestant population was likely to interpret them as meaning: 'if we Catholics ever get our way in Ireland, we will drive you Protestants out of the country'. That, he added, was 'the thought in the minds of many Ulster Protestants'.[36] Within a short while, Delany experienced difficulties himself with the forceful archbishop. It arose out of his quest for a grant-in-aid from the government.

At the end of his first year at Stephen's Green, University

College was in serious financial straits. There was a debt of £1,500. The Society of Jesus, which had already suffered a loss of nearly £4,000, could not be expected to go on financing the institution indefinitely. The bishops had shown little interest. Recent events indicated that it was unwise, at least for some time, to seek further Jesuit fellowships. What was to be done? A meeting in a friend's house at Killiney, Co. Dublin, in November 1884, gave promise of a temporary solution. Sir Robert Hamilton, the Under Secretary at Dublin Castle, was present. Much taken by Delany, his exposition on the university question and on his college's achievements and needs, he asked him 'to put the facts of the case in a memorandum' which might prove useful if shown 'in certain quarters'.

Delany prepared the document with great care, and had it printed and ready for forwarding by 11 December. It analysed the results' lists of the undergraduate examinations in arts in the five colleges approved by the senate of the Royal University – the Queen's Colleges, Magee College, Derry, and University College. The successes of the last named, in spite of so many disadvantages, were compared with those of the Queen's Colleges with all their facilities, educational appliances and scholarship funds, and the comparative failure of Cork and Galway was particularly emphasised. It was pointed out that there were many young Catholics, well qualified and eager for university education, who, for reasons of conscience, could not attend the Queen's Colleges, but who could obtain a higher education at University College, 'an institution established by the Catholic bishops', if it were suitably developed and aided. A detailed list of the college's requirements was given: all of which could be covered by a government grant of £6,000, or little more than half the endowment of one Queen's College. Such a provision would have the effect of 'producing very great educational results'.

Buoyed up by hopes of financial independence, Delany, deliberately or inadvertently, did not inform the episcopal education committee of his discussion with the Under Secretary. When he confided in Dr James Kavanagh, however, he was counselled to be 'most cautious' in his dealings with Dublin Castle, and to 'inform the cardinal of the fact that the castle asked for reports' and that he had sent them on. 'Everything you do', Kavanagh warned, 'will necessarily come out, and it would be a perfect defence to say that you acted under the instructions of His Eminence'.[37] Delany acted on the advice. He called on the cardinal on 12 December, the day after he had sent the memorandum to Sir Robert Hamilton. He was well received: Dr McCabe expressing the view that the Jesuits at Stephen's Green 'were doing a national work', and that 'the burden' ought not to fall upon them.[38]

On his return home, he summarised the memorandum and sent it with an explanatory letter to His Eminence. He wished to make it clear that he would not have sought temporary aid if there was any indication that the government proposed, at present or proximately, 'to deal largely with the whole university question', or if on the Catholic side 'we were prepared to press forward a large scheme'. In the absence of such, he thought it 'most desirable for Catholic interests to secure now such temporary aid, without in any way prejudging our claims — because we should thus enable the college to win and hold such a position in the next two or three years that it would *force* the solution of the question upon the government'.[39]

In the spring of 1885, Justin McCarthy, M.P., approached him for material which might be useful in the debate on the Queen's Colleges' estimates. As the bishops had made the Irish party their voice in parliament on educational matters, he entrusted the memorandum to him, stipulating, however, that any pressure for such a temporary measure was in no way to weigh against the permanent settlement of the university question. On 11 April McCarthy informed him that his paper would be of considerable assistance when they raised the question on the Queen's Colleges' estimates. He agreed that it was better for the party not to put forward any scheme of its own for the present, but rather to prepare for the final settlement 'by exposing the utter unfairness of the present system'. Parnell was anxious to meet with Delany. The latter, meanwhile, had sent copies of the memorandum to the bishops and to Dr Walsh, still president of Maynooth. Soon afterwards, he sent copies to other Irish members of parliament,[40] the chief representatives of the two great English parties, and to the Lord Lieutenant. During May, Henry Campbell Bannerman, M.P., and Charles Dilke, M.P., replied in a sympathetic vein. In July, Delany crossed over to Westminster to discuss his memorandum in greater detail with members of the Irish party.[41] Parnell seemed well disposed to it.[42]

On his return, he visited Sir Robert Hamilton who suggested that the government might be more disposed to make the grant if supervision of its administration was in the hands of a governing body. Delany then discussed his quest for aid with Dr Walsh, now appointed archbishop, and outlined his experiences with the Irish party. Dr Walsh, apparently, saw no objection to the temporary provision and especially agreed with a remark of Parnell — whom he greatly admired — that a grant of this kind could not be withdrawn afterwards and would, as a result, be so much additional money to divide *pro rata* when the final settlement came. Together they drew up a tentative governing body, or board of visitors, to administer the grant; Dr Walsh authorising him to inform Hamilton and the Irish members that he had no objection to the temporary provision.

As the date of the debate on the estimates drew near, Delany called on the new Lord Lieutenant, Lord Carnarvon,[43] sent copies of his paper to McCarthy for distribution in the House, and personal copies, with covering letters, to John Morley, Mr Gladstone, Randolph Churchill, and Lord Salisbury, prime minister. To the latter his letter was quite trenchant. Successive Lord Lieutenants, and the great mass of the Irish people, had agreed as to the 'undeniable justice' of the Catholic claims for equality in university education. Would the English government 'take action on the merits of the case?', or had Irishmen 'to wait for the setting right of inequalities until violent pressure is brought to bear on the government inside or outside parliament?' Identifying his college with Catholic educational needs in the manner criticised by Dr Walsh, he pointed out that 'under the new state of things coming into existence with the new electorate' the contrast between Trinity College's enormous revenues and the unaided state of University College must necessarily give rise to political antagonism. There had to be, he said, 'either a levelling up or levelling down', and it seemed to him that the wisest friends of Trinity College must see the point of decreasing the existing glaring inequality 'in the direction indicated in the memorandum'. He had good reason for confidence that there would be no serious opposition from the Liberal side.[44]

The debate took place on 28 July, 1885. Justin McCarthy, in Parnell's absence, urged the provision of the temporary grant-in-aid. The chancellor of the exchequer, Sir Michael Hicks-Beach, answered on behalf of the government that a most convincing case had been made; that, however, a temporary grant would be an unsatisfactory way of dealing with the grievance complained of; and that the government, if in office next session, would undertake 'a full examination of the whole question'. Delany was told by Lord Carnarvon that the cabinet had actually agreed to the provision, but changed their minds on the eve of the debate.[45]

Despite Hicks-Beach's promise, Delany was very disappointed with the outcome. Still, he felt that the Catholic cause had benefited from the debate. It came as a rude shock therefore, to learn from Dr Butler on 25 September that his motives and actions were being misconstrued in some Catholic quarters, and that the bishops had on the agenda for their October meeting a notice querying the action of the Jesuit Fathers in seeking a public endowment for University College, which had been entrusted to their care by the Irish bishops, without consulting the body of bishops or the episcopal education committee. It was also implied that he was seeking special financial aid for his Order.

He immediately drew up a statement of the facts relating to his grant-in-aid proposal, had it printed, and on 4 October sent copies to Bishop Butler and to Archbishop Croke, accompanied by a letter giving measured vent to his feelings.

University College, he wrote, had so far had a remarkable success, 'a success that was admitted by the government in parliament to have made the speedy settlement of the question quite inevitable'. But it had been at a price which the Jesuit Fathers, with their very limited means, could no longer afford to carry. Most of the bishops did not seem to realise how onerous were the conditions of tenure imposed on them.

> Their predecessors in Stephen's Green had rent free at their disposal all the Catholic University buildings, a library and a church, and a subvention from the bishops and people averaging £7,000 a year. The results produced were not deemed satisfactory. Yet now when the results are eminently satisfactory, the Jesuit Fathers, who have undertaken as serious a responsibility, far from receiving any such yearly help, have been given but a small portion of the necessary buildings, hold even that small portion under rent, are left without a church or a library, to build up, as best they can, a great Catholic university college, and, strangest of all, by way of encouragement to them to lay out the money necessary for such an attempt, a clause is held over their heads making them liable to eviction at two years notice, without compensation for the losses that they may have incurred in making the college a success.

Had the body of bishops or the episcopal committee 'given any intimation that they held themselves in any way responsible for the welfare of the college, and would take measures to promote its interests', he would only have been too happy to leave matters to their lordships' initiative. But so far the only in-timation ever made to him by the episcopal committee was a prohibition of his describing the college as the 'Catholic' University College — 'a prohibition, by the way, which has since had the effect of depriving us of a legacy' — and a prohibition on his using the great hall for religious purposes.

Consequently, he felt that the responsibility had been thrown on him of doing what seemed best for the college, 'so far as anything could be done without prejudice to Catholic interests, and in perfect accordance with the educational policy marked by the bishops, and by the Irish party under their lordships' instructions'. He had placed the whole matter in the hands of Mr Parnell and his party — at the same time making clear re-peatedly 'that no temporary measure should be allowed to weigh against the permanent settlement of the university question'. In every step he was guided by their advice and acted, he believed, for the interests of Catholic education. 'I leave the matter with perfect confidence', he concluded, 'in their lordships' hands, and I shall carry out in all cases any instruction they may be pleased to give me with entire fidelity'.[46]

Dr Butler replied the next day that he had 'never read a stronger case, or one better put'. It was 'simply impregnable'. He himself would not be able to attend the bishops' meeting on 6 October because of an attack of sciatica, but he would have no apprehensions about the meeting. 'Your case is too honest and too clear'. He misjudged the situation.

Delany had sent his report on his actions and aims to Justin McCarthy, asking him to inspect the account and forward it to Archbishop Walsh with a covering letter as to its accuracy. McCarthy did so, affirming its 'absolute accuracy'. The report mentioned Delany's consultations with Dr Walsh and the latter's approval of his action. On 4 October Delany left a copy of his report at the archbishop's house, together with a note explaining how he had asked McCarthy to write to him, and requesting a brief interview before the bishops' meeting. The only response from His Grace was an unexpectedly curt letter on the morning of the meeting. He had received Fr Delany's 'extraordinary document', and in view of the statements in it regarding himself he must 'in self-defence' say 'that for the present it is better that any communication between us on this question should be in writing'. He felt it necessary, 'on a question of such import-ance as this,' that he should be in a position to produce, should the occasion arise, 'unquestionable evidence' of the precise nature of any views expressed by him.[47]

Mystified and much upset, Delany contacted Dr Croke, in Dublin for the meeting, and the archbishop promised 'to do all that lay in his power to have fair play done'. Delany then wrote to Dr Walsh. He was 'deeply pained' by His Grace's letter. He believed 'most thoroughly in the absolute accuracy' of the statement he had made to the bishops and to him, and in earnest of that he had asked Mr McCarthy to inspect it and write directly to His Grace in 'the simple belief' that with his letter, 'and Your Grace's own knowledge of the facts', the matter would have been settled to the satisfaction of the bishops. He then took Dr Walsh step by step through all the circumstances of his consultations with him down to the day when he had set out for Rome and Dr Molloy, following a request from Sir Robert Hamilton, gave it as his opinion in writing 'that he had reason to believe that the grant would be acceptable to His Grace, and that the other bishops had not discussed the question but he had no reason to think it would be unwelcome to them'. His Grace's judgement on the matter was final, Delany concluded, and if he was mistaken he could only express his 'very deep regret at the unconscious blunder' and humbly request that His Grace would forgive it.[48]

The episcopal meeting took place at Clonliffe College on 6 October. Delany spent the day at the college 'to be at hand for any explanation that might be demanded'. He was present again the following morning as the meeting continued. After a short time he received word 'that the whole matter was ended'. He subsequently learned that a resolution — 'that the committee on education be instructed to inquire into the action of the Jesuit Fathers in seeking an endowment and to report on it to the bishops' — had been vigorously opposed by Dr Croke, who, in Delany's words, 'declined to be a party to any action of the kind, deprecated strongly the bishops placing themselves in seeming antagonism to the Jesuits, and stopped the whole transaction'.[49]

The final comments on the unhappy story came a few days later. On 9 October, 1885, Dr Walsh, without reference to his previous letter, wrote that the difficulty had been disposed of. In partial explanation, he declared that the greatest source of difficulty was 'the publication of the board of visitors'. He had never supposed that any such project would have been put before the Irish party 'without some authorization for the use of those names being given by the bishops and others concerned'. In a post-script he added that Dr Molloy could tell him that, after the July meeting of the bishops, when Lord Carnarvon asked him (Dr Walsh) what he thought of the project, he had stated that he could express no favourable opinion of it as it had not come before the episcopal body.[50]

Delany, determined to justify fully his motives and actions, replied at length. Had he had the opportunity of meeting with His Grace, as he had requested, he could have cleared up the points he had made. He would point out that the names of the board of visitors was not 'published'; the list was made out at Hamilton's request to show the 'kind' of governing body that might be submitted to the cabinet 'rather than the selection of particular names'. It was only a 'proposed' board, and the 'proposed' names were made available only to the members of the Irish party and to the government. It had never entered his head to have such a board established permanently. He was happy that in the entire negotiations from first to last 'there was not a word or a proposal for any personal or selfish ends, not a word or a proposal that touched in the smallest degree on the rights of the bishops, or their interests here or elsewhere, or that tended to interfere with absolute freedom in further dealings with the question'. Hence, he failed 'to see anything in the whole transaction to modify in the least . . . . there was no attempt at secrecy or private negotiations'. The members of the Irish party would endorse his statements, and he ventured to hope that so too would His Grace and the bishops 'when all the facts of the case' were 'fully and fairly weighed.'[51]

The tone of his letter indicated the change that had taken place in his attitude to the archbishop. Some time later when a new assistant general, Fr Whitty, was visiting Ireland and due to call on Dr Walsh, Delany wrote to him to acquaint him with 'something of His Grace's line of action and mode of thinking'. He was also, perhaps, providing himself with insurance against possible complaints from the archbishop. He enclosed the two peremptory letters of Dr Walsh previously noted. The first, from April 1884, presented, he said, 'a curious mental study'. The vehemence of the reply 'quite startled' him. 'It was the *first* letter that showed any trace of wounded feeling'. After he had made 'a most trivial change in the form of one sentence', Dr Walsh 'then approved it without any difficulty'. The tone of the second, on 5 October 1885, insisting that all future communication between them be in writing, was now as much as then 'absolutely unintelligible'. He went on to say that when he had replied at great length, repeating more strongly what he had written in the memorandum, His Grace made no attempt to meet his statements but tried 'to get off on a side-wind about what he said to Dr Molloy'. He explained why he considered the archbishop's foot-note 'a side-wind' or evasion. He was aware that His Grace had spoken as he said to Lord Carnarvon, but His Grace had not mentioned his subsequent remark to Dr Molloy on leaving the Viceregal Lodge, namely, that 'it would be a good thing to have the grant-in-aid'. Dr Molloy was so sure that this was His Grace's mind that he had sent the written assurance to Hamilton. Subsequently, as he had told Delany, he had read to the assembled bishops, in the presence of Dr Walsh, the text of his letter to the Under Secretary and had explained how it came to be written. Dr Molloy, moreover, confident of the archbishop's approval, had advised the Irish party in the House of Commons regarding the grant-in-aid, while Dr Croke had telegraphed Parnell asking him to support the proposal. 'Anyone knowing the Irish episcopacy', Delany concluded, 'might prudently believe that a project supported by Dr Croke, Dr Walsh, and the rector of the Catholic University, had ecclesiastical sanction sufficient to ensure its being accepted by the Irish bishops'.[52]

Delany, with all his adroitness, tended, in the view of his colleagues, to be overtrusting. Where His Grace was concerned, he was henceforth on his guard and became increasingly critical of his judgement on university matters. The source of much of their disagreement, as became evident before long, was a conflicting view as to what constituted an acceptable final solution to the university question.

In the meantime, he found himself under fire on yet another issue. In August 1885 when the Education Endowments Bill was being prepared, Lord Justice Fitzgibbon proposed that Fr Tom Finlay, S.J., be appointed as assistant commissioner. The *Freeman's Journal* indicated that the government had accepted the proposal. Early in October, when he was already anxiously preoccupied about the outcome of the bishops' meeting, it came to Delany's notice that rumours were circulating 'in certain Catholic quarters in Dublin', and believed by many, that he had put himself foward to the government and to the Irish party as a mouthpiece for Catholic education, and that he had made it a condition of supporting the bill that Fr Finlay be appointed assistant commissioner. In fact, far from supporting the appointment, he had, after reading the *Freeman*, telegraphed two of the Irish members in London, Thomas Sexton and T.M. Healy, advising opposition to the measure, and had written to Captain Ross at the Viceregal Lodge and others in the same vein. In the light of the rumours, however, and the insecure position of Uni-

versity College, he felt himself obliged to request those he had
contacted to express in writing their view of the charges. He
considered it imperative, he told Capt. Ross, 'to meet these false
statements by a crushing refutation'.[53] His correspondents
readily exonerated him. As it turned out, there was no need to
appeal to their letters. The rumours never developed beyond
Dublin gossip and dissolved when Dr Molloy, rather than Fr
Finlay, was appointed commissioner.

The feeling of being under siege continued. In the *Tablet* on
3 November, Dr Walsh took exception to the paper praising
University College while not mentioning the successes of the
other Catholic colleges, especially Blackrock. He noted a similar
distortion of the truth by Sir Michael Hicks-Beach during the
grant-in-aid debate in singling out the performance of the same
'favoured college' as compared to Cork and Galway, and making
no reference to Blackrock's impressive achievement. Three days
later at the University School of Medicine, Cecilia Street, the
archbishop delivered a speech which was taken as highly
critical of University College and of the Royal University. At
the same time, he appeared to advocate the extension of Dublin
University as the only satisfactory solution to the university
question. 'You claim for yourselves', he declared, 'no exceptional
privileges. You do not claim to have degrees conferred on you
by a university which could be jeered at as an upstart institution, the growth of a few months or years. The object of your
ambition is not to be the graduate of an institution which would
never, in my time or yours, win the prestige so honourably
won by the still Protestant University of Dublin'. He found it
impossible 'to discover in any other principle the foundation
of that absolute equality' which he regarded 'as the essential
element in any satisfactory settlement of our admitted claims'.[54]

During November the debate on endowments proceeded in
parliament. The prospect of a grant to University College was
being mooted anew. Its chances seemed likely to be upset,
however, by the insistence of the archbishop of Dublin that
any endowment obtained be divided between the different
Catholic colleges. Lord Emly spoke out in a way that made
Delany concerned for him. His lordship's blunt views on His
Grace and the educational situation were expressed in his reply
to Delany on 15 November:

Don't trouble your head about me. If Dr Walsh does you no
harm I shall be quite satisfied. Now at all events, you know
what he is about, on the best authority. I told you he was

implacable and irreconcilable. If you want to win you must fight.

He advocated a visit to Bishop Butler of Limerick. What Delany required was a resolution from the bishops in favour of a grant of endowment for University College. What he had to fear was it being shared out. It would be an excuse for the government to refuse and be able to say 'Dr Walsh is hostile, the other bishops are silent'.

The question of endowment faded as it became likely that a new university scheme was being contemplated by the government. Already on 12 October, in a private letter, Randolph Churchill had made it clear that the government were prepared 'to deal very liberally and very fully' with higher education in Ireland if they received 'fair and reasonable co-operation from the Catholic hierarchy'. He warned, however, that they would not be able to go forward in the matter if 'an unfriendly and suspicious attitude' was persisted in by Catholic prelates. To Delany it seemed clear that he had Dr Walsh in mind. The government, in the absence of an alternative episcopal voice, attached special significance to his pronouncements.

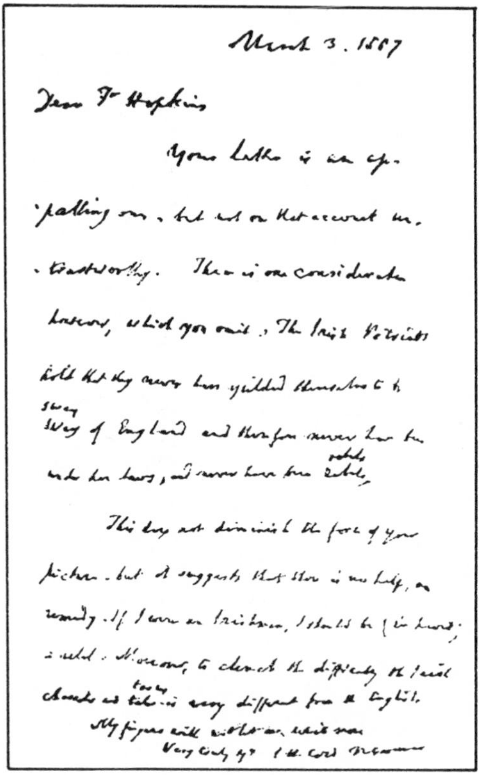
March 3. 1887

Dear Fr Hopkins

Your letter is an appalling one, but not on that account untrustworthy. There is one consideration however, which you omit. The Irish Patriots hold that they never have yielded themselves to the sway of England and therefore never have been under her laws, and never have been rebels.

This does not diminish the force of your picture – but it suggests that there is no help, or remedy. If I were an Irishman, I should be (in heart) a rebel. Moreover, to clench the difficulty the Irish character and tastes is very different from the English.

My fingers will not let me write more

Very truly yrs J H. Card Newman

Letter from Newman to Hopkins in which he states: 'If I were an Irishman, I should be . . . a rebel'.

John Henry Newman

The Royal University, Dublin

Clongowes Wood College staff with guests. On the immediate left of the rector is Gerard Manley Hopkins; next to him is William Delany. On the rector's immediate right is the provincial, Fr Browne, and on the extreme right is Fr Finlay, rector of Belvedere College.

William J. Walsh,
Archbishop of Dublin

John Morley

Sr Agatha, stepdaughter of John Morley

Chapter VII

A UNIVERSITY SETTLEMENT UNDERMINED

Delany and the archbishop represented two very different points of view with regard to a suitable settlement. Ideally both would have welcomed a fully-endowed Catholic university for a Catholic people, even as Dublin University was endowed to serve a Protestant population. In practice, it was evident, despite Churchill's advice to hold out for a great Catholic institution, that neither the Tories nor the Liberals dared risk such a proposal. Anti-Catholic prejudice in Britain was too strong. The most that could be achieved, and that with great difficulty, would be a university which was outwardly undenominational but in essence Catholic, just as Dublin University was outwardly undenominational but essentially Protestant. But how was this to be accomplished? Through a revival of Gladstone's plan or in some other way? Delany was opposed to reviving Gladstone's scheme of one university for all Ireland, Dublin University being so remodelled as to contain within itself not merely Trinity College but a number of other colleges in different parts of the country. He opposed it on educational, religious and national grounds, and because it would never be accepted by the Protestants nor seriously proposed by the government. It was much more realistic to think of a separate *de facto* Catholic University, with a great central college in Dublin and other colleges elsewhere, and to allow the Protestants of Belfast also to have a university of their own. This involved a levelling up of the Catholic position to equality with that of the Protestants, without interfering with Dublin University; and it was in line with proposals made by the Tory party in 1867. He had been given to believe by Lord Carnarvon, late in 1885 or in January 1886, that such an approval would be acceptable to the government.[55]

Dr Walsh's point of view was more complex. Once again he appeared to favour two opposing positions. In public speeches and letters he insisted that it was not the business of Irish Catholics to propose a solution to the university question: it was the part of the government to put forward a plan, that of the Catholics to decide on its acceptability. At the same time he declared publicly that the only acceptable solution was the equivalent of Gladstone's plan; and, in spite of Protestant opposition and the government's unwillingness to introduce such a scheme, described any alternative government pro- posal as but a bribe to preserve the ascendancy bastion at College Green and to defer the only just and lasting settlement. He was careful to point out that he was expressing only a personal view, but his prestige was such that he was generally assumed to be speaking for the hierarchy: 'Dr Walsh is hostile, the other bishops are silent'.

Early in 1886 Delany put together an extensive document designed to win episcopal support for his proposals. The cir- cumstances of its compilation were unusual. In the early morning of 14 January he was called on by Dr Kavanagh who, with Dr Walsh, was going on a visit that day to Archbishop Croke at Thurles, where they planned to arrive at a unified policy on the projected bill. The chief question was whether they should press for the Gladstonian scheme of one university (with appro- priate collegiate provision for Catholics), which both Kavanagh and Walsh would prefer, or seek a separate university for Catho- lics, as Delany had advocated. He urged Delany to go at once to his desk and to put on paper a statement of his views and of the arguments in favour of them, and to send it down to Thurles that evening. He would read it to the archbishops next morning. They would give it their fullest consideration; and then, what- ever decision might be come to, he hoped Delany would accept, so as to avoid divided counsels. Delany promised to abide by the decision. He then went to his desk and 'wrote the livelong day', sending on his statement that evening by the mail train.[56]

His long letter was a remarkable example of his capacity to work under pressure. Its lucid presentation of his views on the university question remained a testament which he could still maintain more than twenty years later and point to as an adumbration of the eventual solution.

The plan of the document was comprehensive: a preliminary section on the Jesuits' involvement in university education, which was, in effect, a defence of himself and his colleagues against misrepresentation; his reasons in favour of Catholics having a university separate from Dublin University, presented under four headings — 'Religious, Educational, National,

Political'; an outline of the difficulties inherent in a joint university, and some arguments in favour of a joint institution proposed and answered; and finally, a summary of the reasons for a separate university and against a common one. The complete text, when printed, ran to almost thirty quarto pages. It was to prove an important contribution to the continuing debate. A brief résumé will serve to illustrate the range of his views and his manner of presenting them.

By way of preliminary he requested that if any of his views called for an explanation, he should have the opportunity of giving it. He did not wish to be credited with opinions he never held, as had happened in the past. More than once in the past, the wholly 'groundless statement' had been made that he, on behalf of the Jesuits, claimed exclusive privileges at University College, and in the great central Catholic college which was expected to supercede it. He wished to make it clear once again, that where University College was concerned he had always expressed the view that the senate should appoint as fellows only those with the best qualifications, and he would 'deem it a calamity for the college, if a Jesuit, merely because he was a Jesuit, were named fellow in preference to a man showing higher qualifications'. In the future central Catholic college, he asked for the Jesuits 'only the same fair play, which should be given to everyone else, namely, that they should be judged on their merits and treated accordingly, without any special favour or disfavour'.

Having cleared any suspicion that his support for a separate Catholic university was linked to an expectation of special treatment for members of his Order, he turned to what he termed 'the great fundamental position': whether Catholics should opt for a new, state-recognised, fully endowed university under Catholic management, with a great central college in Dublin and other colleges elsewhere, or agree to be incorporated with Trinity College in one joint university. He adduced a host of reasons in support of the first alternative.

The 'religious' reasons were four-fold. In a separate university 'the entire scheme of education could be drawn on purely Catholic lines' and include degrees in Catholic philosophy and theology. This would not be possible in a mixed university which would necessarily be a purely secular institution. If Trinity College were joined with Catholic colleges in one common university, the confidence of Catholic students must necessarily be undermined. The tone of Trinity would be dominant: 'They count, and must for some time count a dozen eminent scholars to our one'. Again, if they had an independent, fully-recognised university of their own Catholics would attend it in preference to the common, 'godless university'; but if all were part of the 'godless university', many Catholic students, to the detriment of their faith, would find excuses for attending Trinity 'as the oldest and most successful of the university colleges'. Finally, in support of the principle of distinctively Catholic education for Catholic youth, he appealed to the practice of Catholics in Belgium and France, to a pastoral letter of Cardinal Manning, Archbishop of Westminster, and to the declaration of the American bishops at the plenary council of Baltimore.

The 'educational reasons' in support of his viewpoint threw some further light on his idea of a university. The experience of mankind, he declared, showed it to be of greatest importance 'to avoid as far as possible the despotism of undue centralization and the moulding of all the minds of a nation in one groove, and according to one system'. The 'disastrous influence' of such despotism in France had often been referred to, as compared to the benefits enjoyed by England and Germany through having several universities of distinct types. In the last named countries there was a rivalry between several institutions which became 'a comparison of excellence and thoroughness in varied branches of learning', as distinct from what happened in a common university, as the experience of the Royal University showed, where colleges had to conform to a common programme and where, in consequence, there developed between them 'a merely examinational competion' that tended 'to develop cramming to the injury of real learning'. What happened under the Royal would necessarily occur in a new mixed university, but on a larger scale and with greater injury to the nation. A mixed university, besides, would tend to produce neutral and colourless programmes and hold neutral and colourless examinations at the expense of any educational policy, or of any special phase of intellectual or moral culture. Finally, a new mixed university would either have to form its educational system from *tabula-rasa* or else shape it largely according to the well-marked lines and established traditions of Trinity College. The former 'would be an act of tyranny totally indefensible' where Trinity was concerned, while the latter approach was not desirable in the interests of Catholic education.

In that heyday of imperial expansion and confidence, Delany shared the prevailing regard for hard work, fair play, social proprieties, and Her Majesty, the Queen; but, as with many of his contemporaries, these sentiments subsisted with a deep sense of 'Irishness' and of concern for things Irish. In keeping, however, with a dominant trend then and later, he tended to identify the Irish nation with its Catholic population. This was evident in his 'national reasons' against incorporation with Trinity College.

Self-government was likely 'at no distant date'. It was vitally important, therefore, to create as rapidly as possible a generation of highly educated young men who would be thoroughly Catholic and thorough Irishmen. In any education seeking to produce such an outcome, religion and nationality would have to be the foremost and predominant influences. These could not be the predominant influences in a neutral university. Trinity College 'would lead the way intellectually for several years', and was, and would probably 'remain for years non-national as well as non-Catholic'. Again, in a new university, of the kind Catholics wanted, 'the Irish language, and Irish history and archeology, as Catholic Irishmen understand them, would evidently hold an honoured place in the curriculum, and be duly rewarded on the honours list'. In a mixed university it would not be possible to find a programme in those subjects which would be satisfactory both to the Catholics and to the non-Catholics of Trinity College and of Belfast's Queen's College. Finally, a national university which was thoroughly Catholic and Irish, could become one of the foremost Catholic intellectual centres in the world, drawing to it Catholics, Irish and others, from many lands. This would not be the case if the university were 'godless', with its degrees borne by men known throughout Europe as champions of Protestantism or infidelity.

Under the heading of 'political reasons', he argued that since one of the chief grounds of opposition to any measure of self-government was the fear that the rights of Protestants would be violated, interference with Trinity College would be taken as a proof of such a disposition. Any effort to bring Trinity into the university scheme would meet with stern opposition, even from people otherwise prepared to support any measure making equal educational provision for Catholics. The practicable solution was 'a scheme for a separate university, making provision for Catholics equal to that enjoyed by Protestants at Trinity College', which 'would involve comparatively little matter for discussion.'

Having outlined his reasons, Delany drew attention to a crucial problem in any joint university, namely its manner of government, the proportion of Catholics to non-Catholics on its senate, and the difficulty of achieving a generally acceptable balance. Then, after proposing and answering some of the chief arguments used in support of a common university, he summarised briefly the reasons favouring the alternative preferred by him.

If Trinity College, he wrote, was left altogether untouched and Catholics merely insisted on being equally well provided for, they would gain in many ways: resistance would be minimised, as no vested interest would be injuriously affected; the new measure would be much simpler and much easier to carry through parliament; no colour would be given to the cry that self-government in Ireland involved injustice to Protestants; the endowment and equipment of Trinity College would become 'the measure of what must be done for Catholics in order to give them fair play', and thus a liberal provision would be secured for Catholics — the advocates of Trinity College helping them in order to safeguard their own college.

But over and above the intrinsic merits of the two schemes, there were other cogent considerations. The proposal for a separate university might be carried this session if the bishops and the Irish party, in their name, accepted it. It was very unlikely that the government would propose, or could carry through, any joint university scheme. Delay might lead to the question being put off indefinitely, 'with corresponding loss to Catholic students and Catholic institutions, condemned to wait still further for the justice so long denied them, and to carry on under crushing difficulties the all-important work of training the Catholic leaders and teachers of the future'. Trinity College, meanwhile, would enjoy 'its enormous revenues', and the Queen's Colleges of Cork and Galway, 'now proven and admitted to be failures', would continue to have public funds squandered on them with a lavish hand.

He concluded with the reminder that it was unwise to reject a proposal that established substantial equality for Catholics, 'whilst granting them that perfect independence and exclusive control of their higher education' which they had always claimed; it was unwise above all because there was a real risk that rejection might result in the question being shelved for years to come, 'and perhaps less satisfactorily settled in the end'.

The mammoth letter achieved little in effect beyond clarifying its writer's views. Dr Kavanagh, on his return to Dublin, told Delany that he had read it to the two archbishops and that he and Croke, but not Walsh, had come around to his views.

Dr Croke, indeed, had expressed a strong desire that Delany would have the letter printed for private use,[57] and would send him a copy. The real damage, however, had been done the preceding day (14 January) on their arrival at Thurles. They had visited the diocesan college and, in reply to an address, the archbishop of Dublin had declared that no scheme of educational settlement could be accepted which would leave Trinity College — 'that standing monument of conquest' — in its privileged position.[58] 'The government scheme', Delany recorded, 'did not propose to touch Trinity College or the Dublin University, and therefore when this declaration of the leading Catholic ecclesiastic in Ireland appeared in the Irish newspapers the following day, the government abandoned their intention of dealing with the Irish university question'. The Conservatives went out of office a fortnight afterwards.

Chapter VIII

EXPERIENCING VIGILANT HOSTILITY: 1886-1888

The year 1886, which commenced so inauspiciously, brought many other set backs and ended with a positive rebuke from the episcopal education committee.

In preparation for the December meeting of the committee, Delany produced a lengthy document entitled 'A memorandum regarding University College, and the work done there since it was entrusted to the Jesuit Fathers, its present position, and its relations to the Catholic University'. He outlined the history of the arrangement with the Society of Jesus and pointed out that the college's position was a false one. It was the bishops' college, not the private property of the Jesuits. Yet — and despite its success compared to its predecessor — it no longer enjoyed the *insignia* which in days gone by had stamped it as the national Catholic institution, such as a university church, library and great hall. He emphasised its perilous financial condition, showing that the Society of Jesus was carrying a loss of £120 a year on their lordships' college, and suggested that some alleviation might be given in the rent, some extra rooms and a part of the library be made available, and permission be granted for the use of the large hall and the Catholic University's teaching appliances. The education committee, whose guiding figure was now Dr Walsh, was neither impressed nor pleased. Their reply on 9 December was sent not to Delany but to his provincial. It stated that with reference to the memorandum signed by Dr Delany 'and purporting to represent the views of the Jesuit Fathers', it was inconvenient to receive such communications from persons who could not speak with authority, or treat finally with the bishops. With regard to the specific proposal submitted, they saw no reason to depart 'from the arrangements that were made on 26 October 1883'. Besides, they regretted to find in the memorandum statements derogatory to the Catholic University of Ireland, and they could not acquiesce in the assumption that it had become merged in one of its colleges. They were the trustees of the entire university and could not entertain the proposal to allocate the funds and teaching appliances pertaining to the whole university to the use of one college. Finally, they wished to point out that they were 'fully alive to their responsibilities in the matter of higher Catholic education, and would deprecate, as calculated to lead to inconvenience, unauthorised interference with the conduct of negotiations connected with it'.

The calculated deflation of himself and of the achievements of University College, and the unsubstantiated implication of 'unauthorised interference with the conduct of negotiations' on his part, combined to undermine Delany and make him feel isolated. His hopes of forcing a speedy solution to the university question by means of success at Stephen's Green now seemed a chimera. The sense of isolation and ill-regard were heightened by the unexpected deaths during the year, first of Dr Butler[59] — his mainstay on the education committee —, and then of his close friend and confidant, Dr Kavanagh. The latter had the most unexpected of all demises, being killed by a fallen angel! He was fatally injured while saying mass when a statue above him fell off its pedestal.

There were, nevertheless, some redeeming features. Dr Croke managed to obtain from the general body of bishops, subsequent to the meeting of the education committee, the use of the great hall for religious purposes, and the promise (never fulfilled) of the restoration of a portion of the Catholic University library.[60] Also on the positive side where Delany was concerned, was the sympathetic, if circumspect, support he received from Dr Healy, both as a senator and a bishop; and the fact that Dr Butler's successor was displaying a lively interest in the university question.

Edward Thomas O'Dwyer, the new Bishop of Limerick, was to prove an independent voice on many matters. In the sphere of higher education he was to challenge the ascendancy enjoyed by the archbishop of Dublin. Small in stature, fiery of temperament, sensitive of his authority, and frequently autocratic in manner, he had great intellectual ability and was eloquent in speech and with pen. Above all, he displayed an assertive independence which was to make him the *enfant terrible* of the hierarchy. This trait became particularly marked whenever he suspected that an effort was being made to browbeat him. It was exercised in his first year in office with reference to higher education.

The Liberal government had given way to a Tory administration after its failure in June 1886 to carry Home Rule. The
new government was prepared to grant widespread concessions
to Ireland, but not self-government. Parnell was opposed to the
seeking of any settlements which might lessen support for Home
Rule.[61] The archbishop of Dublin, in consequence, publicly
deprecated any attempt at a political bargain with the Conservatives on the university question. Dr O'Dwyer did not
agree. 'It would be highly deplorable', he wrote to Dr Walsh on
18 October 1886, to postpone the question of a university
settlement much longer. If Parnell and His Grace agreed on a
university bill it would be passed 'and Home Rule need not be
touched one way or another'. He wished to draw Walsh's attention to the presence of 'a very strong body of Queen's College's
men' in the professions in Ireland, and to the fact that His
Grace might find in his Irish parliament when it came less
'consideration for ecclesiastical authority' than he expected.[62]
He followed up his letter with a public pronouncement in favour
of negotiations on the university issue. Dr Healy wrote to congratulate him and express his agreement; observing that there
was a vacancy in the senate 'for a cleric', which might be offered
to him if he were interested.[63]

The bishop of Limerick returned to the charge in further
letters to the archbishop.[64] The matter was one affecting millions
of Catholics. He was prepared to consult 'with representatives
of any shade of politics, nationalist, Whig or Tory' with a view
to organising public meetings 'to agitate the question'. 'The
Protestant press' had taunted His Grace 'with being the only
man in Ireland who cared about the question'. Mr Parnell was
clearly of the same opinion. It was time for the bishops as a
whole to make their views felt. And, returning to a preoccupation
which he knew was unwelcome to Dr Walsh, he asserted 'that a
more disastrous policy to religion was never manifested than to
postpone this question to an Irish parliament'. The archbishop
eventually gave way and entered into negotiations with the Chief
Secretary, Sir Michael Hicks Beach, in December 1886. The discussions produced no result. They appeared to break down on
two grounds: the inadequacy of the government's offer, and the
ambiguity surrounding what Walsh wanted or was prepared to
support as a solution.

Meanwhile, on 24 November, O'Dwyer informed Walsh that
he had accepted from the Lord Lieutenant, Lord Londonderry,
an offer of nomination to the senate of the Royal University.[65]
He saw the appointment as putting him in a position which

might make him 'more useful in working for a settlement'. He had made it clear to Lord Londonderry, however, that he did not see the Royal University, or any conceivable development of it, as a settlement of the just claims of the Catholics of Ireland which it would be his duty as a bishop to urge. To Walsh, whose policy it had been to studiously ignore the senate except when it was appropriate to attack it, O'Dwyer's acceptance was unwelcome. He informed him that since the Lord Lieutenant had not paid the bishops the courtesy of asking them to nominate one of their number, his nomination had not 'a representative character'. On 8 December the royal warrant announcing the appointment was issued.[66] Pressure was brought to bear on Dr O'Dwyer to resign. Following the bishops' meeting in December, he was on the point of doing so.[67] Both Lord Emly and Dr Healy, however, counselled him to leave his name stand, even if it meant, as Healy said, that like many other senators he did not attend any meetings.[68] A letter from Dr Kirby of the Irish College, Rome, urged him to fulfil his promise at the bishops' meeting of resigning and thereby preserve the 'compact unity of mind and heart amongst the supreme guardians of the faith in Ireland'.[69] Other pressing letters followed from Archbishop Walsh;[70] but O'Dwyer still delayed his announcement. Then, on 3 January 1887, the *Freeman's Journal* did it for him. At the same time, Dr Walsh informed him that there was a question of advocating a total break with the Royal University because of the 'breach of faith on the part of the government' in not first approaching the bishops for their nomination; and shortly afterwards he wrote that 'arrangements were being considered for filling up the vacancy'.[71] Irate at the pressure and feeling that he was being pushed aside, O'Dwyer put an end to the whole matter briefly and bluntly. 'To prevent any further misunderstanding', he told the archbishop on 8 January, 'I wish to say explicitly that, notwithstanding the announcement in the *Freeman*, I have not resigned, and as things have gone, it is less likely than ever that I shall'.[72] The following day he assured the editor of the *Freeman's Journal* that his paper's announcement was 'utterly untrue'.[73]

Thus, the bishop of Limerick became a member of the senate; and though he took Dr Healy's suggestion about not attending meetings almost literally, he was to avail of his position in the long term to contribute powerfully to the final solution of the university question.

During 1886, Delany was put in touch with him through a Mr W.H. Keating, an ultra-Catholic layman, who had written ably, if at times injudiciously, on issues of higher education. On 25 October, Keating wrote to Dr O'Dwyer to congratulate him on his speech which, he noted, showed how much his views differed from those of His Grace of Dublin. The latter had recently declared that, on the one hand, 'union with Trinity College' was the only way to solve the university question, and on the other, that educational equality could not be attained in Ireland until Trinity was 'removed'. 'The positions', said Keating, 'are destructive of each other: and neither brings us one step nearer to the satisfaction of our needs'. He enclosed a 'confidential' letter which he had received from Delany. He also mentioned the latter's long letter to Dr Kavanagh, and the different reactions to it of Archbishop Croke and Dr Walsh. 'In His Grace's well-known views', he wrote, 'will be found the chief difficulty to be surmounted 'ere solid ground be touched or any real progress made'.[74] A few days later he sent, with Delany's permission, the letter to Dr Kavanagh and some other communications, and declared that Delany had once favoured union with Trinity College but that a closer and deeper examination of the situation had 'converted him to the views he now puts so forcibly'. At the same time, Keating was forwarding to Delany letters he had received from Limerick.

Some time later, Delany wrote personally to the bishop. His Lordship's views, as passed on to him, commended his notice and most cordial assent. He wished to make clear, however, that while in substance he agreed with Keating on general principles, he could not accept him in any way as an exponent of his views. He filled in the background to his document to Dr Kavanagh, and enunciated the step by step principle which he applied to political negotiations and which found an echo in the bishop. Although he believed, he said, that for religious and patriotic, as well as educational reasons, 'we ought to *aim* at establishing a great National University, distinctly Catholic and under Catholic management', he was nevertheless clearly of the opinion 'that we ought to secure *now* anything that we can obtain consistently with our principles, and without prejudice to the realisation of that ultimate aim'.[75] The communication marked the beginning of a fruitful relationship, which continued unstrained despite His Lordship's prosecution of a cold war in his own diocese against Delany's *confrères*.

While William Delany, from 1886 to 1888, was preoccupied with university education and its immediate amelioration rather than its final solution, the archbishop of Dublin had other priorities. He saw Dublin University with its large endowments, its lack of sympathy with Irish self-government, and its dominant position in the heart of Dublin, as a constant reminder of inequality. He was determined to remove this particular symbol of inequality, but he considered that this could best be achieved by means of Home Rule — the panacea for all ills. The country generally was in a condition of economic depression. Evictions were being enforced on a wide scale. An agrarian eruption prior to 1886 was only held in check by belief in the imminent prospect of self-government.

> We simply want to manage our own affairs, stock, lock and barrel. We are satisfied to live for ever more under the sceptre of England's king or queen, yielding all due obedience to the same, provided that Irish administration be in the hands of the sons and friends of the Irish people. *Voilà tout.* We have a right to that and . . . any compromise on that right we will not accept. When that right is conceded, all other good things will, in due course, come to us.[76]

These aims and hopes expressed by Dr Croke in 1888 were shared by the archbishop of Dublin and, with less conviction, by Delany. The bishop of Limerick was more ambivalent. He was for Home Rule but had no time for John Dillon, M.P., and many of its other political promoters. He was like, he said, the small boy at the salvationist meeting who did not rise when the preacher asked all who wished to go to heaven to stand up. Asked did he not wish to go to heaven, he answered: 'Yes, but not with that crowd'.[77]

The defeat of the Home Rule bill in June 1886, the subsequent fall of the Liberal government, and the failure of Parnell's Tenants' Relief bill in the autumn, caused a reaction in rural areas proportionate to the previous expectation. The Irish party members, Dillon, Smith-O'Brien, and Harrington published their Plan of Campaign to control and channel the agrarian anger. If a landlord refused to lower his rents voluntarily, his tenants were to combine to offer him reduced rents. If he declined these, the tenants were to refuse to pay any rents. Instead, what they offered was to be paid into an estates' fund for the maintenance and protection of the tenants who were morally certain to be evicted for following the Plan. Anyone who moved into the farms from which tenants were evicted, was to be boycotted. The new programme, which operated most widely in the counties of Tipperary, Limerick and Kerry, gave rise to a bitter and tense struggle.[78] The health of Sir Michael Hicks Beach was not equal to the strain. His successor, Arthur Balfour, introduced a ruthless and relentless system of coercion.

The clergy were divided. Many in the disturbed areas sided with the tenants. Mr Montague-Griffin, writing to Fr Matthew Russell from Kerry, during 1888, related how at a Land League meeting the local curate had exhorted the crowd to 'shoot low' so that the victim would have the benefit of the priest before he died![79] Drs O'Dwyer and Healy publicly attacked the violations of the rights of property, the extensive use of boy- cotting, and the active involvement of clergy on the side of the tenants. Drs Walsh and Croke, on the other hand, conscious of the hardships of the tenants, of the feelings of many of the priests, and of the danger of the official church becoming alienated from the majority of the people, gave qualified support to the Plan of Campaign. The government sought to enlist papal support against the movement, with the active assistance of the Duke of Norfolk and other prominent English Catholics. A papal envoy, Monsignor Ignatius Persico, was sent to Ireland to investigate the situation in July 1887. His report was not wholly unfavourable to the tenants' cause.[80] The pope, Leo XIII, felt obliged, nevertheless, in April 1888, to issue a rescript condemning the Plan of Campaign. Popular feeling against the rescript was intense. The bishops were in a delicate position. They had to uphold the papal condemnation without inviting further tenant reaction. At a special episcopal meeting it was agreed, according to Dr Croke, that no 'written com- munication' would be issued, not even to priests. All directions were to be given orally. It came as a bombshell, therefore, when shortly afterwards, in June 1888, the bishop of Limerick issued what came to be called the 'Limerick manifesto': 'a verbal pronouncement' against the Plan of Campaign, in which he stated that in his action he was at one with the other bishops.[81] The archbishop of Cashel, writing to Dr Walsh, was moved to un- episcopal language. Despite the unanimous agreement to which he was a party, 'see what the little ceer has done! It is un- accountable. The general impression is that he has lost his head, how else account for his eccentricity and audacious egotism. 'Tis hard to hold one's tongue under the circumstances'.[82]

In the emotion-charged atmosphere of the late nineteenth and early twentieth century in Ireland, to have reservations about the benefits of Home Rule was to be considered anti- nationalist and unpatriotic, while to express dissatisfaction with aspects of government policy was to invite charges of disloyalty. In July 1886, Fr Whitty, the assistant general, then in Dublin, informed Delany that he had been told by some people that he was on the anti-nationalist side.[83] A year later he was reported to the General for expressions of disloyalty to the queen. The charge well illustrated, in Delany's words, 'the manner in which very grave misrepresentations are at present made and propagated about Irish affairs by, I presume, well-meaning but misinformed and imprudent persons'. What had happened, he informed Rome, was that Dr Healy had interrupted proceedings at the senate of the Royal University with a proposal that the senate present an address to the queen. The archbishop had the address already written. Dr Porter of Queen's College, Belfast, a Presbyterian minister, seconded the proposal and spoke of 'the debt that was owed for the Royal University, of the unexampled prosperity of the community under Her Majesty's reign, and of the great boon granted to education'. Delany intervened to request that the address be read to the senate before being passed. When this was done, he and others proposed some amendments which were accepted by Dr Healy and the address was passed unanimously. Delany declared, however, that he could not agree with Dr Porter's speech in support of the proposal. He recognised Dr Porter's right to express his views, and felt that he had the same liberty to express his while still remaining a loyal citizen. For him, as a Catholic priest, loyalty was 'a solemn duty of conscience'. As a direct representative, however, of the interests of Catholic education, he felt it right 'to dissent from any statement that implied that the Irish nation was satisfied, or had reasons to be satisfied, with the provision made in the Royal University and elsewhere for Catholic education'. He was sure that even Dr Porter would agree that Catholics were 'miserably and scandalously provided for'. He regretted that he was also 'unable to recognise in this country any signs of the unexampled prosperity that Dr Porter spoke of'. Delany's account of the incident was received by Fr Whitty as 'most satisfactory'.[84]

In August 1887 a somewhat different charge occasioned considerable upset, though it had a lighter side to it. The English provincial, Fr Purbrick, announced that he was recalling Fr Klein, one of Delany's science professors, because of his father's state of health but also because of 'the political action of some of those around him' in not permitting him, though invited by the senate, to perform 'a dutiful act of loyalty'. As it turned out, the provincial had been misled by Fr Klein. The latter was a most unusual character. An eloquent writer and preacher, and an agreeable man to deal with, he had served as a surgeon throughout the Franco-Prussian war, and had excellent qualifications for the position of fellow which he obtained in 1885. He spoke English, French, German, Italian and Spanish, and had a good manner and address. He had been recommended by Lords Emly and O'Hagan. Delany, who had been sceptical at first, was quite won over once he 'had seen and spoken with him'. What he did not realise, however, was that Dr Martial L. Klein had delusions of grandeur and a fertile imagination. It was only some years after he had left Stephen's Green that he learned that Dr Klein, also during 1887, had falsely persuaded Cardinal Manning that his superiors in Ireland wished him to send in 'false returns to the Royal University', and had informed a friend of Manning, Dr Butler, 'that he was a grandson of Napoleon's Marshal Klein' (*sic*)![85]

The English provincial's avowed reason for withdrawing Fr Klein — that he was refused permission to act on behalf of the senate in presenting an address of welcome to the royal princes of Saxe Weimar — led Delany to fear injury to relations between the Jesuits and the senate to the detriment of University College. He wrote to the General for 'a judicial investigation' of the reasons for the recall. He wrote also to Fr Purbrick to explain his action and to furnish an exact account of what had taken place.

The princes of Saxe Weimar had given a garden party in June 1887. Dr Klein, along with some two thousand others, had certainly been invited to it. He liked to speak of 'his connections with the Saxe Weimars', much 'to the amusement of Dublin's drawing rooms'. The invitation was sent to him from London through the good offices of his friends Lord Emly and Lord O'Hagan. There was no question, however, of the senate making a presentation, and if there was they were not likely to appoint as their representative one who was 'merely a paid official . . . and not even an English subject'. Fr Klein approached the Irish provincial for leave to attend. The permission was refused. The provincial had grounds for believing that the garden party had political overtones, that the occasion was linked with a memorandum being put together by the leader of the English Catholic Tories, the Duke of Norfolk, to protest against the Irish bishops' attitude to the Plan of Campaign; and he considered that the attendance of a Jesuit at such a function was at variance with the General's recent instruction to avoid identification with any of the political parties[86] and might easily be misconstrued by nationalist supporters. Delany, when approached by Klein, was even more explicit as to the source of a likely attack. He told him that if left to him he would have held himself passive and allowed Fr Klein to act on his own responsibility — 'neither forbidding him to go, on account of his regard for Lord Emly, nor on the other hand giving him leave and thereby implicitly approving of a Jesuit professor of the college taking a position at variance with that adopted by the whole hierarchy and clergy of Ireland at a moment critical for this college, and *with so keen and hostile a critic as Archbishop Walsh watching over every movement*'. To this Fr Klein replied 'that if the responsibility had thus been placed upon him, *he would not have gone to the party*'.[87]

During October Fr Purbrick wrote to say that he had been misinformed on the whole matter. At the end of the month Fr Whitty, replying for the General, announced that the English provincial had been justified in recalling Fr Klein 'in the circumstances', but that he had written to the General 'acknowledging and withdrawing the mistakes' of which Delany had complained.[88] The last reference to Dr Klein came many years later, when he had left the priesthood and had a wife and family. Alice Stopford Green wrote from London to Delany in 1904, that she had met him a few times 'before and after his change and never disliked anyone more. He is now a Positivist, having taken that unfortunate family that road too, and is trying to get the head of Congreve's branch of the Positivists'.[89]

Evidence of the archbishop's vigilant hostility, to which Delany had referred, was again forthcoming during that October. As secretary of the episcopal education committee, he wrote to the provincial regarding articles on 'The Royal University of Ireland' appearing in the college magazine, the *Lyceum*. The second article had promised to deal in the November issue with proposals regarding a system of endowments for Catholic education in connection with the Royal University. The archbishop took exception to this. The question of endowments pertained strictly to the hierarchy. Were Fr Finlay, as editor, to print the projected proposals it might appear that his views had the approval of his Order and of the Irish bishops. Hence on behalf of the *coetus episcoporum*, he told Fr Browne, 'I must request that you kindly exercise such supervision over the public acts and utterances of your Fathers, especially those connected with the university, as will enable the committee and the bishops to maintain with them, publicly and privately, those cordial and confidential relations which have hitherto prevailed'. The provincial forwarded to him the proofs of the third article, which did not, in fact, treat of endowments for Catholic education.[90] Dr Walsh returned them unread. The article was not published.

As the year drew to a close, His Grace's cold-shoulder treatment was crystallised in print. In spite of his numerous commitments, he published on 3 December, *A memorandum on the Irish education question.* It ran to seventy-nine pages. Twenty-four were devoted to university education; and of these more than twelve were devoted to an historical summary, seven were concerned with reiterating his views on the senate and the fellowship issue, and four were given over to possible lines of solution of the university question. On the senate and the fellowship issue he made much of the actual inequality between Catholic colleges arising from the fact that one college alone, University College, enjoyed the benefit of having on its staff people who were at the same time both teachers and examiners. Apart from this objective point, he was quite selective in his presentation of the occurrences surrounding the fellowships. The bishops' desire to have the fellows concentrated at University College, before even the college was entrusted to the Jesuits, was passed over; the absence of Dr Butler from the education committee's meeting and the unhappiness of the cardinal with its decision were ignored; the sudden change on Dr McCabe's part from Hopkins to Reffé, and the latter's lack of acceptable qualifications, were not mentioned. Moreover, the Jesuit provincial was represented as turning down 'the request of the bishops' as a body for the withdrawal of Fr Hopkins's name, and no reference was made to the lateness of the hour or to any other qualifying factor. As to University College itself, its growth in numbers was attributed solely to the presence on its staff of fellows who were both teachers and examiners; and no reference was made to the fact that this advantage had existed before Delany became president, or to the quality of the fellows he had inherited. The senate was represented as generally disregarding the influence of the episcopate, and it was indicated that it followed a 'policy of ignoring the wishes of the bishops in matters of exclusively Catholic interest'. In evidence of this, he pointed to the appointments of Bishops Healy and O'Dwyer and of Dr Delany 'without the episcopal body being in any way consulted or referred to'.[91] The Catholic senate members, indeed, could be considered as somewhat lacking in due respect for their religious leaders, since all of them had opposed the wishes of the cardinal and some, in addition, were proponents of the principle of 'mixed' education.

Three months later William Delany's first period as president of University College came to an end. At a meeting of the province consultors on 27 March 1888 – the visitor from the

General, Fr Fulton, being present — Fr Robert Carbery was chosen as superior of the Jesuit community at Stephen's Green and president of the college.[92] A pleasant man, in poor health, he had been a chaplain in the old Catholic University and enjoyed amicable relations with the clergy of the archdiocese.

The normal term of office for a Jesuit superior is six years. Delany had fulfilled that length of time if his period at Temple Street was added to that at Stephen's Green. Were it considered necessary to the well-being of University College it is likely that his term as superior would have been extended or, alternatively that he would have been allowed continue as president while Fr Carbery acted as superior of the Jesuit community. There is no evidence, however, that such alternatives were contemplated. The college was on a firm footing. The archbishop and the episcopal committee had been unfriendly to the institution under his presidency, relations might be easier after his departure; as, indeed, would be the financial drain on the Order. He himself, besides, welcomed the prospect of more directly priestly work. He was appointed to Gardiner Street church as a preacher and confessor, while retaining his function as senator of the Royal University. So far as he was concerned, his work as an educational administrator was over. Ironically, in his new role he was to find himself invited to dine from time to time at archbishop's house, and something of their old relationship was restored between Dr Walsh and himself.

Chapter IX

FIRST TERM AS PRESIDENT REVIEWED

By 1888 it was evident that Delany's aim of forcing a speedy solution to the university question had failed. University College would have to make its impact over a longer period. That it managed to do so to great effect was due to the foundations laid in its first years. It is instructive, therefore, at this point, when Delany believed that his work in education was at an end, to take stock of his time at Stephen's Green: not only in terms of the conflicts and achievements already noticed, but also with reference to the staff, students, and temper of the college.

From the start, as has been seen, he attributed an importance to his ramshackle college which seemed to many, not least the episcopal education committee, quite inappropriate. He chose to see it as a national institution, heir to Newman's university, and the chief means whereby the government would be brought to recognise the justice of Catholic claims for higher education. The teaching staff and students came to share his vision, and to respect what Thomas Arnold, one of the fellows, termed his 'vigorous and watchful administration'.[93] The new spirit of work in the college was reflected in its examination results: the supreme yardstick of the day in measuring success, and the means by which the government could compare the Stephen's Green institution with its own Queen's Colleges. The achievements of the first year were the start of a trend. In subsequent years University College demonstrated in the quality and number of its successes that it was the leading Catholic educational establishment and a long way ahead of the Queen's Colleges of Cork and Galway. By 1894 it was to outdistance all rivals, including Queen's College, Belfast.

But the college's attentions were not confined to academic achievement. Those other aspects of university life were actively fostered which were considered part of a liberal education, and which were part of the heritage from Newman's day. Thus literary

136

and debating societies were encouraged. One extant record shows Delany speaking at the inaugural meeting of the Literary and Historical Society for 1884 on the theme 'The Influence of Irish genius on English literature'. Moreover, the president's expansive views on the role and obligations of his college as an important university centre ran to the provision of scholarships and prizes, paid out of Jesuit salaries, and to the introduction of evening classes providing degree courses.

These manifestations of vigorous life underlined Delany's main achievement as president of the .young institution: solid foundations had been laid, in face of financial worries and almost constant criticism, which enabled the college to progress even in the absence of basic facilities. These remained largely unprovided. The library was not restored. The students and staff of Stephen's Green managed by courtesy of a generous arrangement with the National Library and, to a much lesser extent, by means of books obtained by the president. The president's books, indeed, were no more than a token, if the deprecatory humour of his assistant, Fr Joseph Darlington, is to be relied on. He recalled that when Delany took over No. 86 Stephen's Green there was not a book on the shelves. So, 'he went down to the quays and bought several lots at auctions; the good books were picked out and went to his own room, the rest filled the library!'[94] Facilities for science remained equally primitive. Up to the establishment of the National University, 1908, there were no laboratories and scarcely any appliances for teaching chemistry and physics. The remarkable fact was that the college's students, nevertheless, secured notable successes. The handicaps under which the college laboured in this field were encapsulated for some Cambridge students when they came to call on Professor McClelland in 1903. They had worked with him previously at the Cavendish laboratory. Not finding him at the college – it was vacation time – they expressed a desire to see his laboratory. One of the Jesuit fathers brought them to the physics theatre. 'But the laboratory?' 'There it is,' said their guide, pointing to a small book-case in which there were a few instruments. 'And', he added, 'there is the Irish university question in a nut-shell'.[95]

The clash, however, between the absence of basic facilities and Delany's high ambitions for the college, led him once again to incur debts which he felt would be repaid once success was assured. It was the policy which had given rise to anxiety about his financial administration during his years at Tullabeg. It had a similar effect at Stephen's Green and was a factor in the provincial's decision to change him from there in 1888.[96] Where Delany and the college were concerned, nevertheless, the chief source of anxiety and frustration in the early years was the opposition of influential prelates and clergy, and of Dr Walsh in particular. Delany, along with his staff and many members of the senate, felt that at such a critical time for his institution and the cause of Catholic higher education he had a right to expect the whole-hearted support of the bishops for what was really their own college. The encouragement he received from Bishops Butler and Healy, and Archbishop Croke, confirmed him in this view. Instead, he found that much of his time and energy was taken up defending the college, or himself, against criticism from the episcopal education committee. It is important to keep in mind that it was the committee, not the bishops as a body, which was at loggerheads with the college. Dr Walsh, its guiding force, often gave the impression, by referring to 'the bishops' or the *coetus episcoporum* in support of his arguments, that he was speaking for the entire hierarchy. In practice, it was largely a case, as Lord Emly observed, of 'Dr Walsh is hostile, the other bishops are silent'.

The frustration generated in the college by the constant opposition was reflected in a letter from Thomas Arnold to Delany on 27 January 1887. The great success of Louvain University, he declared, had been due to two factors: the ability of its rector, 'and the unanimous, steady support of the bishops from the very beginning'. The latter factor was missing at University College. He hoped that the Society of Jesus would 'confront the situation boldly' and let the bishops know that if their lordships did not see their way 'to according to the college the same kind of hearty and unflagging support which their episcopal brethren in Belgium had extended these fifty years to Louvain, they, the Society,' would 'as soon as the terms of agreement permit, retire from the undertaking'. The occasion of Arnold's letter was the negative episcopal response to Delany's memorandum on the college, and a reply which he himself had received from Dr Walsh in response to his request for the return of the Catholic University library to Stephen's Green. The archbishop informed him that the practical difficulty about restoring the library was that University College had, from the beginning, exhibited a tendency to identify itself with the Catholic University and to virtually ignore its other colleges.

Dr Walsh's reply indicated part of the grounds of opposition from the side of the episcopal committee and of some individual bishops. Further factors were Delany's assurance in taking on a college which for years under the episcopate had been a failure, and the success he made of it; the suspicion of religious orders generally in the field of education, and particularly of the Jesuits with their complex image of independent privileges, influence at Rome, corporate pride, and imputed duplicity — the latter feature being visible, to those wishing to find it, in the misunderstanding about the opening of the Temple Street College, in the appointment of Dr Casey, and later in the fellowship issue; and finally the alleged defiance to and humiliation of the cardinal at the senate, as regularly reissued by Dr Walsh, was neither forgotten nor forgiven. As might be expected a certain amount of dualism operated on both sides. Delany proclaimed that he was running the 'Bishops' National Catholic College', and he was conscious of holding it in fiduciary trust from them. At the same time he acted with an assured independence, negotiating personally with many of the political leaders of the day, opposing the education committee, as not being representative of the episcopacy, on the issue of Fr Hopkins's election as fellow and of the recognition of Blackrock, and not referring to it when accepting nomination to the senate. The committee, for its part, veered between considering University College as 'the private concern of the Jesuits who . . . conduct it at their own risk and peril',[97] and stepping in to curb the ambitions of the college's president and to reprimand him for seeking aid for it. And like any other committee given a specific function by a powerful, traditional body, it tended to expand its area of interest and to arrogate to itself the over-all authority of the larger body and, in consequence, to resent any suggestion of challenge from a subordinate institution. It was sensitive to signs of dualism in others, while prepared to justify such, if recognised at all, within itself. The over-all result was that the Stephen's Green College during Delany's presidency, like the Royal University and its senate, was 'on trial and suspected'; and the trial was being conducted by Dr Walsh, no longer as president of Maynooth and challengeable but as the virtual leader of the Irish hierarchy.

The difference in personal style and temperament between him and Delany facilitated their estrangement. Where Walsh — in the recollection of C.P. Curran, who was a student at University College at the turn of the century — was direct and resolute, using an almost sledgehammer approach to problems, Delany, though equally tenacious, was 'more accommodating', more indirect and suave in style, able to press his case with charm and 'complete, persuasive lucidity'.[98] The contrast was tailor-made for misunderstanding once cross-purposes appeared. In Dr Walsh's eyes, it would seem that Delany had come to appear not quite trustworthy, too smooth perhaps, too much a man for all seasons — content to adapt himself to a variety of persons and situations in order to achieve his ambitions; and hence the provincial's decision to transfer Delany from University College was probably the best decision for the college at that point of its development.

Much of the success of University College was due to the varied and talented staff which Delany had brought together. The group of nine fellows which he had inherited were, as has been seen, a mixed blessing; but they did include men of eminence like Dr Casey, the mathematician, and Thomas Arnold. The latter, who professed English, had had like Fr Klein, an unusual career. A younger brother of the poet, Matthew Arnold, he had taken his degree at Oxford and then spent some years as an inspector of schools in Tasmania. In 1856 he was received into the Catholic church, and came to Dublin to lecture at Newman's invitation. Six years later he followed Newman to Birmingham, teaching classics at the new Oratorian school there. He left the church subsequent to Pius IX's pronouncements on Liberalism, but returned to it later and was to die a Catholic. In 1882 he became a fellow of the Royal University and professor of English language and literature at University College.

Among the Jesuit staff, too, Fr Klein apart, there was an unusual mixture of background. Père Mallac, who lectured in philosophy, had practised at the French bar and had been at one time a confirmed free-thinker. Fr Kieffer, from the German province, was a specialist in electrical science. The Irish members included the extremely able and widely talented Tom Finlay, who had taught classics, moved to philosophy, and later professed economics, and was conspicuously successful in each; Denis Murphy, the author of a number of historical works; Edmund Hogan, whose pioneering work in the field of Irish language and history has frequently been acknowledged; and John J. O'Carroll, who claimed competence in eighteen European languages. From the English province came Joseph Darlington and Gerard Manley Hopkins. Darlington, a convert instructed by Newman, became almost a legend for his interest in the students and closeness to them, his sense of tact carried to the point of agreeing with everyone, power of organisation, almost alarming energy, and droll humour. Open to every new idea, he was in later years a strong, if unlikely, supporter of Sinn Fein, and characteristically suggested that the history of the Jesuits at

Stephen's Green should be entitled 'Whigs on the Green'! He was assistant to Delany and was in many ways the pivot of the college. Gerard Hopkins's contribution to University College was mainly posthumous: providing it with one of its three claims to literary renown – the others being John Henry Newman and James A. Joyce.

The brilliant but eccentric Hopkins displayed from the first a different approach to teaching. Apparently scrupulous about the much publicised advantage University College was said to enjoy by having fellows both as teachers and examiners, he undertook at the beginning of each year not to teach anything which would be asked in examinations! Not surprisingly his lectures were attended only by those who loved learning for its own sake, and those who occasionally dropped in to find out what they might safely omit; and as discipline was a problem for him, he sometimes found his students rude and disinterested. Darlington retailed how, hearing uproar from his classroom, he found that Hopkins, 'anxious to explain the death of Hector, lay on his back on the floor and got a student to drag him around the table!'[99]

'I am in Ireland now; now I am at a third remove'.[100]

Gerard Hopkins considered himself an exile in Dublin. His darkest poetry was written there. He was drawn towards 'the carrion comfort' of despair; and he felt intensely his own inadequacies as a teacher, and the apparent waste and pointlessness of being where he was. His sensitive, highly-wrought temperament recoiled from the pragmatic pressures of preparation and correction, of lectures and competitive examinations, and from the crude and inadequate furnishing and facilities of a university institution which was, in Dr O'Dwyer's blunt words, but 'a burlesque. A house on the side of a street'.[101] Distressing, too, were the current anti-English sentiments of Irish Catholics which he allowed affect him personally. Irish writers, he wrote to Dr M.F. Cox on 26 March 1887, tended to dwell on what was most honourable to Ireland and most dishonourable to England, following the dictates of passion rather than of truth. To Newman he complained of the country's 'appalling' state of rebellion, and how the tactics of the Land League were reducing good landlords almost to poverty. The cardinal's reminders that 'the Irish character and taste is very different from the English', that 'Irish patriots hold that they never yielded themselves to the sway of England and therefore never have been under her laws, and never have been rebels', and his addendum that 'if I were an Irishman I should feel (in my heart) a rebel' did little to dispel his sense of alienation and depression. There were times when the clouds lifted and he experienced himself as 'immortal diamond', but mostly each new day heralded further misery: 'I wake and feel the fell of dark, not day'.[102] The house on the side of the street, indeed, precipitated the final darkness. He died on 8 June 1889 of typhoid, said to have been contracted from inadequate plumbing in the Jesuit quarters at Stephen's Green.[103]

William Delany, by contrast, was blessed with a resilient, sanguine temperament. At the age of fifty-three he turned to church work with enthusiasm and assurance. Directly apostolic activity, as noted earlier, had always been his first preference. In the midst of his educational preoccupations he had used every opportunity of giving spiritual direction and preparing sermons and retreats. For many years already he had been in demand as a preacher and retreat giver. It is a measure of his priorities that among the voluminous papers found in his room after his death by far the greatest proportion of them consisted of his sermons, spiritual notes, instructions and lectures. The influential Gardiner Street church, therefore, gave him the opportunity he had long wished for. No appointment ever pleased him so much as his transfer thither in 1888; and none was to cause him sharper pangs than his recall from there to Stephen's Green in 1897.

Chapter X

THE YEARS BETWEEN (APRIL 1888 TO APRIL 1897): CHURCH WORK AND CONTACTS

Like all men Delany played many parts; and none of them was more or less real than another. The years at Gardiner Street illumine aspects of his personality and outlook not easily observable in his public career. The evidence for those years is to be found in his sermons and letters and, especially, in Fr Lambert McKenna's manuscript biography, already referred to, 'Fr William Delany and his work for Irish education'.[104] McKenna had the advantage both of examining Delany's papers and of interviewing many who had worked with him or had sought spiritual advice from him.

It seems clear that despite the hurly-burly of university negotiations, disputes and meetings, of day-to-day administration, the pressure for examination results, and the cultivation of public relations, he preserved an inner calm; and with those with whom he came in close contact he enjoyed a reputation for deep spirituality. 'Those with whom he spoke more intimately on the things of God', McKenna remarked, 'bore away, and still retain, a deep impression of his extraordinary piety and whole-hearted devotion to God's interests'. These basic qualities, allied to a certain largeness of mind — bringing all subjects of doubt and trouble under the light of the great principles of religion — kindness, a joyous buoyancy of spirit, and the powers of rapid, clear-cut, decisive judgement, won him the confidence and affection of numerous people. The scope of his effectiveness, however, was limited by other aspects of his personality. Although he was, in McKenna's judgement, 'sympathetic to the point of tears, and generous to the point of extravagance towards those on whom the ordinary afflictions of life had fallen', he was rather slow to appreciate the pain which small trials can inflict on chafed or highly sensitive temperaments. Moreover, his own instinctive respect for high principle and apparently easy loyalty to it 'made it difficult for him to place himself at

143

a lower angle of vision'; and 'just as he had little power of interesting people by small talk and could not speak to children in their own language, so he could not easily understand the mentality of the wavering, the petulant, the disingenuous, the lower types of spirit.' Not that he did not strive to do so. He professed never to be surprised at any human divagation. But it seems likely, as McKenna concludes, that many of the weaker clients 'preferred someone who with heart as well as head could understand them'.

As a preacher and public speaker his reputation stood high. 'He was recognised for more than thirty-one years as one of the best pulpit orators in the country, and one of the most success-ful conductors of retreats — especially of retreats to the clergy and to ecclesiastical students.'[105] He was in great demand, also, for charity sermons. There were few charitable institutions in Dublin for which he was not asked at some stage to appeal to the generosity of the public. On the more important church feasts, and on other special occasions, his name was sure to attract large congregations. The press reproduced many of these sermons and lectures. Among the sermons reproduced were: charity sermons for High Park convent, 24 January 1892 and 8 January 1899; a charity sermon for the Assumptionist Sisters, Camden Street, 21 April 1892; a sermon on the consecration of Dr Foley as Bishop of Kildare and Leighlin, 31 May 1896; on the beatification of Blessed Peter Chanel, 26 October 1890; a funeral sermon on Baroness Von Hugel, 1 April 1901; a charity sermon for St Michael's hospital, Kingstown, 26 May 1901; a charity sermon for Harold's Cross hospice, 8 May 1897; the funeral sermon on Dr Egan, Bishop of Waterford and Lismore, 28 July 1901; and the nuptial sermon of Lord Ninian Crichton-Stuart, 23 June 1906.[106] Three or four other sermons, as well as lectures on 'Christian reunion' — delivered in October 1895 and Lent 1896 — were printed in pamphlet form. The talks on 'Christian reunion' aroused much interest at the time. Delany traced the history of the movement for reunion across the Christian churches, but saw little likelihood for a long time of anything in the nature of corporate reunion. He believed, as he told the students at Maynooth in 1896, that individual conver-sions to Roman Catholicism would go on increasing steadily.[107] The fact and prospect of conversions coloured his views on the whole matter. On 10 May 1896 he wrote to Fr Meyer, Assistant-General, to express disagreement with the appointment of a committee to report of proposals for the reunion of the Anglican and Roman churches. He could see little merit in the venture.

It would act as a brake on conversions and was, besides, quite unrealistic since many of the supporters of reunion were uncompromising opponents of papal supremacy and infallibility. [108] In the spirit of the age, his was a rather militant Catholicism, interested in defence and expansion rather than in negotiation and adaptation. 'The battle of the faith in these days', he reminded the students of Maynooth at the close of a lecture on 'Christian reunion', 'is to be fought not merely in the pulpits, as in former times, but in the newspapers, the magazines, the pamphlet, the book: in all the places where falsehood so easily makes its way must it be met and conquered with its own weapons'.[109]

As may be seen from the list of sermons above, his presence as a preacher, and indeed as a retreat-giver, was sought by a number of bishops; and some welcomed him also as a guest and friend. Thus, Dr Foley of Kildare and Leighlin invited him in November 1897 'to come down on Sunday' to Carlow to meet Dr Barry, the Burke centenary lecturer, adding the interesting tit-bit — 'Dr Barry like your own Fr T. Finlay sadly lacks dramatic power. I fear the people won't hear a word from him on Sunday.'[110] Delany's own attraction as a preacher or lecturer, lay not in magnetic force or passionate intensity but in a quiet form of 'dramatic power' joined to lucidity and a persuasive fluency which, delivered in a resonant, soft musical voice, had the capacity to carry conviction.[111] Despite his remarkable readiness of utterance, his ease in *extempore* speech with the exact word always to hand, it was characteristic of him to take great care with all his sermons. Something of a perfectionist by temperament, he could not be negligent about the exercise of preaching which he viewed as being, in a special way, the work of God. Consequently, each one of his many sermons was written out fully and scored all over with the marks of preparation.

Throughout his life he devoted a great deal of time to correspondence. During the years in Gardiner Street he received numerous letters on spiritual matters. Such communications as have survived indicate that his replies were full and rounded, imparting general exhortations or exposing a central principle with a sweep of vision which linked together different facets of knowledge. His advice was not of the pious-manual variety. It frequently carried the ring of personal experience and wide reading, and was adapted to each individual's needs. No marks of a harsh, negative theology were in evidence. His message was one of confidence in God's love, and of peace and joy in his service.

As well as such letters, however, he maintained contacts and correspondence appropriate to his position of senator and his standing as an educationalist. Some of his communications with persons of influence arose out of approaches to him of people in need or people seeking to avail themselves of his advocacy in obtaining improved positions of employment. Thus, during March and April 1899 he corresponded with A.J. Balfour, the highly unpopular Chief Secretary, on behalf of an applicant for the position of local postmaster. This type of communication apart, he continued from Gardiner Street his long-time practice of keeping in personal touch with government representatives at the Viceregal Lodge; and they in turn, by virtue of his name being known to them from previous occupants, and out of regard for his educational reputation and his attraction as a conversationalist, were not slow to invite him to meet with them. In this way he came to know many of the leading English politicians at close quarters. His interest in their work, his readiness to praise what he considered beneficial to the country and to criticise what he deemed harmful, his genuine desire to appreciate their points of view on a variety of topics, and his expressed interest in their families, resulted in close personal relationships which frequently persisted over many years. The popularity or otherwise of a Chief Secretary seemed to make no difference. So, on 27 January 1890, Arthur Balfour, known in Ireland as 'Bloody Balfour' for his repressive measures, invited him to a stag-dinner at the Lodge; and on 3 May wrote to thank him for a letter which expressed a 'good opinion' of a recent speech of his. It was specially gratifying 'as coming from one who on certain very important questions connected with Ireland does not share the views which I hold'; and it was a sincere pleasure 'that at all events with regard to the social problems which the country presents' they seemed to be in close agreement. He added that he entirely agreed with the general views he had put forward on the university question.[112] The issue of university education was brought up again and again by Delany in informal meetings with successive Chief Secretaries and Lord Lieutenants: an exercise which helped to school a whole generation of public figures to the country's educational needs.

His own self-assurance and self-acceptance helped him to see beyond the dignity of office to the human needs of the office-holders and their families. His interest in a man's wife and family, given the circumscribed life of the English in Ireland, and his desire to make them feel at home, was particularly appreciated. Thus, in the case of the family of Mr West Ridgeway, the Under Secretary, he loaned books to Mrs Lina Ridgeway and, at her request, took her over the Mater Misericordiae Hospital, and brought gifts to their children.[113] Not surprisingly, West Ridgeway, a moderate Unionist, maintained his interest in Irish educational affairs long after he left Dublin, invited Delany to his daughter's wedding, and corresponded with him up to 1908 — sounding him for his views and feeding back to him views and developments in the House of Commons. It was a further appreciated characteristic of Delany to take the trouble to write to any of these friends or acquaintances, even after the lapse of years, who suffered a family bereavement.

His closest relationship, despite his 'Tory friends', was with the Liberal M.P., John Morley, a professed agnostic, and his family. Their friendship went back at least to 1885.[114] During Delany's time at Gardiner Street, Morley was appointed Chief Secretary. On 23 September 1893, he wrote to remind Delany that he was expecting him to dinner at eight o'clock, and that a bed would be at his service if this was convenient to him. Less than a month later he wrote that Mr Asquith was due to arrive and he was sure that Delany would wish to talk with him. Arising out of their talk that night, he wrote to express his thanks 'for the book on psychology' which Delany had sent him. In March 1894 he was grateful for a letter which gave him comfort in his distress at Gladstone's departure — 'a noble voice for noble ideas, hopes, feelings'. On 30 December he wrote from Cannes conveying his thanks for the 'little book' sent him as a Christmas gift. After leaving Ireland, the correspondence continued, Delany writing to Mrs Morley also. On 23 April 1905 — at a time when the Liberal party was bitterly divided and could not much longer stay in power — Morley commented to him that his wife had read him some of Delany's letters, and then recollected their breakfast together in 1885 and how little either of them had foreseen what was to happen. 'But at any rate you and I are still friends, and that is something, and even much'. He concluded on a note which characterised their relationship: 'If you come to London, be sure to let us know. The Fr General, with special politeness, placed the whole of the Society at my disposal last year. . . . So I have authority over you'. On 25 November he announced that he was likely to be in Rome in a fortnight's time, and asked if Delany could furnish him with an introduction to anyone there. The day before setting out, he gratefully acknowledged the letter of introduction and wished that he would find Delany in Italy.

The final extant letter to an English politician during these years was on 29 October 1896. It was to 'Mr Gerald Balfour and Lady Betty Balfour' accepting an invitation to dine with them on 7 November. He took the opportunity to congratulate Balfour, as Chief Secretary, on his 'very remarkable success' last session in carrying through the Irish Land Act, and sincerely hoped that this 'signal success' might be the augury of a brilliant career in which some of Ireland's remaining grievances would be coped with 'no less successfully'.

The centres of British power in Ireland were Dublin Castle, in the heart of the city, and the Viceregal Lodge in the Phoenix Park. The latter was the residence of the Lord Lieutenant, usually an English nobleman, about whom swirled a make-believe court. He was the head of a social pyramid which reeked of snobbery. The place of gentry and middle class in society tended to be measured by their standing at the Castle or the Viceregal Lodge. To Home Rulers and separatists, on the other hand, such social attitudes were anathema; and to be friendly with British politicians and government officials and to seek their company, at the close of the nineteenth and the early part of the twentieth century, was to incur the slur of 'Castle Catholic' – one who aped English ways, sought social kudos, and generally displayed what Arthur Griffith termed 'the slave mind'. Delany clearly enjoyed such company, and went out of his way to cultivate it; but, despite the taunt of 'Castle Catholic' later thrown at him, he could not be described as subservient or termed a social climber in either his correspondence or his behaviour. It was part of his philosophy not to dismiss a politician or official because he disagreed with his views, but rather to relate to him on a personal level and thereby foster goodwill and a better understanding of the needs of Irish Catholic education and of the country generally. This certainly led to easy relations with Dublin Castle, and these relations adhered, in his absence, to the Jesuit administration at University College. Hence, prior to Balfour's reopening of the university question early in 1897, Fr Carbery appears to have been consulted. On 31 December 1896, Dr Walsh wrote to the Bishop of Limerick: 'It is strongly rumoured the government is going to give us a Catholic University. What do you think of Fr Carbery, S.J., having been sent for the other day to the Castle? This is an undoubted fact'.[115]

The archbishop's comment mirrored an anxiety lest control over educational affairs slip away from him. He had clashed with the Christian Brothers over their independent action in the field of primary education. A government initiative on university education without consulting him was a blow to his prestige. 'If the bishops don't take some definite action', he had written to Dr O'Dwyer in June, 'we shall simply be effaced as a power even in such questions as that of education'.[116] At its October meeting, 1896, the hierarchy came out with a strongly worded statement. They pointed to the increasing number of Catholics availing themselves of intermediate education, the lack of government support for university education, and the exclusion of Catholics from certain government appointments because of lack of university training, and concluded that, in effect, the people were being 'crushed by law into a position of inferiority'. They asked for nothing excessive: only equality of treatment, that the same amount at least be done for the three and a half million Catholics as was done for the half million Protestants of the disestablished Church of Ireland. The government's indecision had given rise to seething discontent. It was twenty-three years since the issue of university education was made a cabinet matter and since then very little had been achieved. Such a miscarriage of legislation was unthinkable in England. There parliament responded to public opinion. It was not so in Ireland.

> Our wishes and demands count for very little. We get whatever the cabinet, which has been formed by English public opinion, thinks good for us; and we are made to feel bitterly the uselessness of constitutional agitation on our part.

It was not surprising, therefore, that the minds of the people were alienated from the government 'and that everyday they lose confidence in constitutional methods'. Their lordships hoped that reflection on the history of this one question might 'make clear to Englishmen why Irishmen desire the management of their own affairs, and stand aloof from the actual government of the country in a spirit of distrust and alienation'. As to how the government should achieve equality for the Catholic majority, it was not for the bishops to decide. They were not, however, 'irrevocably committed to any one principle of settlement', and were prepared 'to consider any proposal with an open mind, and with a sincere desire to remove rather than to aggravate difficulties'.[117]

Despite the vigour of their pronouncement, the bishops' appearance of unity was illusory. They were not 'irrevocably committed to any one principle of settlement' because there was no semblance of unanimity as to how best to solve the issue. 'What is the use of talking', Tim Healy, M.P., wrote to

Dr O'Dwyer on 18 March 1897, 'when some prelates want colleges in their own cities and others wish a central one only? Surely the bishops might at least pronounce unitedly as to this idea!'.[118] Dr Walsh, too, deplored the absence of unanimity but was himself a key instrument of disunion. On 17 December 1896, at Blackrock, he led out once more the old hobby-horse, the issue of the Catholic fellows, which had been ridden into the ground years before and now, after the run of successes by University College, claimed few supporters. Bishop Foley, writing to Delany the following day, deplored His Grace's insensitivity to 'the pressing principle of not dissipating the teaching power of the Catholic fellows'.[119]

Delany remained largely apart from the educational debate during his time at Gardiner Street. His involvement in university affairs, with the exception of informal discussions, was confined to regular attendance at senate meetings of the Royal University. There he played an active part. 'He brought to the board' — in the not unbiased judgement of Professor Henry Browne, S.J., of University College — 'a broad knowledge of university organisation which was shared by few Irishmen outside of Trinity College. His personal gifts were of a kind specially suited for the senate; he was ready of speech, clear in exposition, and had a capacity for carrying conviction, and if need be conciliation. His very manner gave the impression of dignity, devotedness and broadmindedness.'[120] He was a member of the finance committee; and made his presence felt in motions, amendments and observations. On 29 May 1889 he achieved something which he had had at heart for some years. A fellowship in Irish language and literature was established, and he successfully moved the name of Fr Edmund Hogan for the position.[121] It was an appointment of consequence for Irish language and Irish historical studies. In 1896, his nephew, John Bacon, obtained a temporary appointment in English and French at University College. It was a measure of his improved relations with the archbishop that he requested his support for the appointment.[122]

Delany's standing with his fellow-Jesuits remained high. At the provincial congregation in June, 1892, his contribution and reputation were such that he was chosen as one of the province's two delegates to Rome for the election of a new General. His estimation of himself, however, was not so exalted. A diary entry for 23 September 1891 reads:

Completed today twenty-five years since my ordination. Looking back, how rapidly it has passed by. And how little it shows done for God. Had it been well spent, how different I should be now! How much more fitted for God's work! What need for making up in future for wasted time and opportunities!

There followed a set of resolutions to counteract his failings. 'I must try especially:
1. To have a fixed order of time — ensuring: a. Spiritual duties properly performed; b. Regular systematic study and preparation of sermons; c. Care of souls of which I have the guidance — confessional, visiting the sick; d. Acts of kindness and charity.
2. To keep things in a more orderly way: books, papers, letters.
3. To observe poverty more strictly.
4. To ask leaves more regularly'.

An entry of 24 September cast further incidental light on his outlook and values. By way of comment on a sentence in St John's Gospel — 'I have finished the work which thou gavest me to do' (17.4) — he noted: 'a. Christ the perfect pattern. b. Life is for work. c. For some specific work. d. Which ought to be completed'.

The diary of 1891 soon lapsed. The next extant daily journal was dated six years later. It made reference to what, unknown to him, was his 'specific work. . . to be completed'.

At University College the superior and president, Fr Carbery, had exceeded a superior's normal term of office, and was in poor health. In June 1896 the provincial and his consultors, as was customary, forwarded a *terna* to Rome.[123] The first of the three names proposed as a replacement was that of Fr Thomas Finlay, described by an Irish historian as 'pre-eminently the Renaissance Man of the Irish Renaissance'.[124] On grounds of sheer ability, energy and reputation, he was the obvious choice. His influence with the students was exceptional. "We strove to talk like him', wrote William Dawson, a lively contributor to the college magazine *St Stephen's* and in later years a barrister, 'perhaps even to think like him'.[125] The General and his consultors, however, had reservations. 'One must pay no attention to criticism', Fr Finlay had told the novelist, George Moore, 'but go on doing what one has to do'. His independent outspokenness when he felt a principle was at stake make him enemies in different quarters. There were members of the Irish party who did not forgive or forget his vigorous criticism of Parnell at the time of the Parnell split (1890-91) and his support of Tim Healy, M.P, in calling for the chief's deposition in the interests of moral standards in public life. Parnell, it would appear, had previously been suspicious of Finlay; and John Dillon was to describe him as 'one of the damndest intriguers in Ireland', an emphatic expression of a point of view not confined to Dillon.[126] Again, the self-improvement policy of the Irish agricultural co-operative movement was seen by members of the Irish party as diverting people from Home Rule as the primary objective; and Fr Finlay, as a co-founder of the movement with Sir Horace Plunkett, subsequently vice-president of the Irish Agricultural Organisation Society and founder-editor of its publication the *Irish Homestead*, and known throughout the country as an apostle of self-help and co-operative effort, was seen as opposing the party's priorities; and he necessarily shared to some degree, besides, the hostility generated by the 'sublime tactlessness' of Sir Horace. Moreover, as founder and editor of the influential college magazine, the *Lyceum*, he seemed to dangerously challenge the *status quo*. It was noted for its variety of progressive ideas, helped by the anonymity of its contributors, and received regular notices from W.H. Stead in his *Review of Reviews*. Finlay's own contributions covered a wild field. On education his articles had frequently a searching quality which make them still relevant a century later.[127] On social and religious matters he exhibited an independence of thought and expression not likely to endear him to established opinion. Thus, in a laudatory article on Cardinal Manning, he pointed out that ecclesiastical training tended to live a good deal in the past, and that the clergy ran 'the risk of growing up more intimately conversant with ways of thought and conditions of existence' which had passed away than 'with the realities around them'. This was particularly true in the social order where there was a process of ceaseless change, and 'the most commonly accepted social truths today were innovations yesterday' and objects of suspicion to good men. And he concluded:[128]

> Rapidity of communication, the diffusion of books, the daily press, above all the spread of education and combination for common ends, have lifted the masses from the position of hopeless inferiority in which they lay. They are the true masters of the modern world, though they scarcely realise their power, and have not yet learned to use it. And religion, if it is to carry on its mission must join forces with them.

As editor of the *Lyceum* he had twice been brought directly to the General's attention. First, when he earned the archbishop's displeasure for the contributions on the Royal University; and secondly when an article of his critical of *Our Christian Heritage*, by Cardinal Gibbons of Baltimore, had been taken up by a Chicago newspaper, and gave rise to such complaints from some American Jesuits that the General felt obliged to send a personal apology to the cardinal, much to His Eminence's surprise.[129]

The provincial consultors drew up a fresh *terna* on 4 March 1897. This time they opted for the known and tried. William Delany was first choice. They were worried, however, by what they termed 'his ignorance of or unsuitability for the administration of financial matters'. The General accepted their recommendation suggesting that Fr Delany be required 'to do nothing of any moment in such matters' without first having the approval of his house consultors. He was also to have an admonitor who would keep the provincial informed as to his financial administration.[130]

The onerous and unwelcome responsibility was imposed on Delany at an age when most men contemplate retirement. He chronicled the effect on him of the General's decision in his diary entry of 25 March:

> Fr Provincial came to my room and told me that Fr General had named me rector of University College. I asked if there was any chance of the nomination being withdrawn at my solicitation. He said, no: that the consultors had been unanimous and Fr General had at once made the appointment. I received the news with very great surprise and regret, much preferring the work at Gardiner Street with its limited responsibilities. Received 'congratulations' from many inside and outside on my supposed 'promotion'. Condolences from some who judged more wisely.

On 27 March he dined at University College at Fr Carbery's invitation. The latter left the college on 31 March. On that and following days Delany transferred his belongings to Stephen's Green, but kept his confessional at Gardiner Street at the request of the superior, Fr Ronan. On Sunday 4 April he wrote: 'Came finally to take my residence at Stephen's Green. Found Fr Wheeler — minister. Fathers T. Finlay, E. Hogan, H. Browne, J. Darlington, M. Russell, and Brother Mulrany making up the community'. There were 'nine resident students of whom five had been at Clongowes'.

During the intervening years the assurance and stability of the Victorian world had been shaken. The year of his return to

University College saw the publication of Kipling's *Recessional*. The old queen still ruled. The empire's far-flung 'dominion over palm and pine' seemed unchallengeable; the departure of 'the captains and the kings' but a homiletic reminder of the inevitable decline of all human greatness. Nevertheless, there had been many significant changes since the eighteen-eighties. A growing unrest was being felt in English cities. A weakening in morals and religion was noted. There was a general decline in evangelism and an increase in nationalism, Anglo-Catholicism, and hedonism. The weakening in religion, as indicated by a falling off in church-going and vocations to the ministry, was paralleled by a spreading tolerance, or indifference, towards the different religious creeds. The *Daily Mail* had just made its appearance; responding to the large semi-literate population which had benefited from Foster's Primary Education Act, and now enjoyed the extended franchise. The older, more dignified presentation of the news was yielding to a re-writing of it in a briefer, more palatable and doctored form. At the same time the demand for higher education was growing steadily. A number of new universities had been established. Going with this advance in education was the sig-nificant social change effected in the status and rôle of women. Increased educational opportunity, and a sudden variation from large to smaller families had given rise to an expanding, relatively leisured class, among young married women; and, on the same social levels, to a considerable body of leisured unmarried women.[131] The fuel was being stacked for the combustible feminist politics of the early twentieth century.

Much of this necessarily influenced British attitudes towards Ireland, and the attitudes of Irish people towards themselves and towards the empire. Within the country the bitterness caused by the land war still smouldered, and the divisions opened by the Parnell split were only beginning to be healed. The increased emphasis on tolerance and liberal indifferentism found supporters and opponents. To the latter it offered a further argument in favour of Home Rule. The traditional values and beliefs of the people were being endangered by a too close association with Britain. Moreover, the self-conscious glorification of empire seemed to act as a counter-stimulus. The Celtic note in literature, the remarkable growth of the Gaelic Athletic Association, and the Gaelic League, proclaimed the coming together of various strands in a revived national pride and consciousness as the new century approached. And central to this new Ireland was a more discerning, more self-confident generation of young people, who had had the experience of universal elementary education and of a more widespread, competitive secondary system.

The university question, too, reflected changes in attitude. The issue of an outwardly undenominational but *de facto* Catholic University had given rise to political opposition to those factors which were deemed synonymous with an essentially Catholic institution, namely strong episcopal influence on its governing body. The degree of episcopal influence thus became a crucial point for governments seeking a university settlement. To the bishops and many Irish Catholics, looking at the overwhelming Protestant control of the 'undenominational' Dublin University, the opposition to episcopal influence appeared as a further instance of sheer bias and discrimination against the Catholic majority, and led to a hardening of attitudes on their part. In 1889, indeed, the Irish hierarchy rejected all compromise and publicly demanded a separate Catholic university under exclusive Catholic control.[132] When, however, Balfour had announced in January 1897 that he proposed to 'put all sectarian pressure aside and attempt to meet the wishes of Ireland,' and the question of episcopal control was raised, the hierarchy came forward with an accommodating response.[133]

The government sought clarification on four particulars, namely: What proportion of ecclesiastics their lordships required on the governing body? Did they require theological teaching to be endowed? Were they prepared to accept the religious Test Acts? And, what security would professors have against dismissal, especially non-Catholic professors? At their June meeting, the bishops showed themselves not intransigent on any of the four issues. They were prepared to accept a lay majority on the governing body. They did not require an endowment for theological teaching and were prepared to assent to any guarantee which would ensure that the money voted by parliament was applied exclusively to the teaching of secular knowledge. They had no objection to the test acts. And as regards the dismissal of professors, they suggested that any difficulties in this regard might be settled by the establishment of a well-chosen board of visitors in whose independence all parties would have confidence.[134] In short, as Dr Healy was to emphasise before the Fry Commission in 1906, the bishops made it clear that they had abandoned their demands of 1889. They required merely that the new institution be as Catholic as Trinity College was Protestant.

Much had changed, but much remained the same. Mr Balfour acknowledged in July 1897 in the debate on the Queen's Colleges' Estimates, that their lordships' pronouncement had done a great service to the cause of a Catholic university. Four months later, however, Dr Walsh felt obliged to summon a conference, to which he invited Delany, to discuss means of stirring the government to action.[135] The conference decided to call a public meeting at the Mansion House, for January 1898, 'to protest against the continual inaction of the government'.[136]

Thus, within a short time of his return to University College, William Delany found himself engaged once more in the struggle for an acceptable solution to the university question. His return also coincided with the presence at the college of a new generation of brilliant but critical students who were to signalise 'the golden age at 86' (St Stephen's Green).

Part III

RETURN TO ST STEPHEN'S GREEN:
'THE REAL WORK FOR IRELAND', 1897-1909

To the sculptor, August Suter, who asked him what he retained from his education, Joyce replied, 'I have learnt to arrange things in such a way that they become easy to survey and to judge'.

For the skill of his Jesuit masters, whose teaching he rejected, he always held the greatest esteem. 'I don't think you will easily find anyone to equal them', he said long afterwards to the composer, Philipp Jarnach.
                                — Richard Ellmann, *James Joyce* (Oxford, 1959), p. 27

Chapter XI

'A NEW INTERNAL VIGOUR'

He was in his sixty-third year when he resumed the presidency. To his friend since student days, Matthew Russell, now a member of his community, he had become a figure of note and admiration. In the bantering relationship which existed between them, Russell wrote for his benefit '*a musa domestica*', a quatrain on no account to be published.[1]

A man of light and leading, king of men,
Strong in speech, yet potent too with pen;
Skilful alike at Bluebooks and at whist —
A sensational Educationist.

Among the traits which he envied in his friend were his order and self-discipline. Having difficulty himself in getting to bed and in getting up, and frequently finding, as a result, that late at night he had still to read the morning and mid-day sections of the obligatory divine office, he noted with wonderment in his diary: 'Fr Delany succeeded Fr Carbery as our rector in Stephen's Green, a week ago. He says persistently all his office to the end of compline immediately after breakfast'.[2]

157

Bacon observed that 'to choose time is to save time'. Delany's capacity to order his time and use it with singleminded effectiveness was a strength which continued, almost unimpaired, up to the age of seventy, and was highly regarded by his associates. Dr W.J.M. Starkie, professor at Queen's College Galway and a former classical tutor at University College, writing to congratulate him, remarked:

> I am glad to see that you are back again at scholastic work. Your friends will say: 'They shall learn the difference, now that Achilles has come back'.

The difference was soon felt within the college; and outside he soon became prominent again in negotiations and argument on the university question. The crowded canvas of the second presidency can best be viewed from three vantage-points: that of the interior life of the college; that of the public arena where the wider issues of the university problem were joined; and, interspersed with these and resounding to them, that of the college and its conflicts.

Fr Robert Carbery was a man of much talent and culture, but he lacked a capacity for organising and energising. During his presidency the college continued to achieve outstanding examination results, but the intellectual and social life, which Delany had fostered, lost its colour and vigour. 'I spent four years at University College', Sir Charles Griffin, Q.C., recalled, 'and as things were then there, I looked upon it merely as a place where one attended classes. There was no sense of a community about it and there was little of what one associates in one's mind with university life'.[3] The Literary and Historical Society had lapsed so completely that in 1898 a copy of its rules and constitution was found only after a long search. The Sodality of the Blessed Virgin, which had formerly been so well attended, had ceased to function; as had almost all other college societies. Delany set about recreating a spirited intellectual and aesthetic community, and the interior life of the institution immediately commenced to burgeon.

The sodality was reorganised and, under the active guidance of Fr Henry Browne,[4] its meetings were soon well attended by staff and students, past and present. Besides the regular Saturday evening devotions, there were monthly or bimonthly conferences on matters relating to Catholic doctrine and practice. In February 1898 Fr George O'Neill, with the president's encouragement and financial help, founded a choral union, and in 1901 an orchestral society. The same year a philosophical society was established under the title of the Academy of St Thomas Aquinas. A scientific society encouraged interest in scientific research, and a *Légion Francaise* was set up which organised excursions and reunions of various kinds where French was exclusively used. The Irish language was catered for, in addition to the regular subject classes, by special weekly lectures of an advanced kind and by more popular elementary sessions open to all comers. These were conducted by John McErlean, S.J., Padraig H. Pearse, and James Clandillon.[5]

The Literary and Historical Society rose from the tomb with remodelled rules and constitution. Delany sought to emphasise its constructive rôle. Among 'the fruits of a debating society', he had told the inaugural meeting of 1886, were that it helped its members understand that great events and great principles were 'commonly many sided in their bearing on practical life' and had to be examined 'under all their aspects' if they were to be justly appreciated. Hence, it was important 'to give a courteous hearing to those who may honestly differ from us, and from the expression of whose views we may often learn much, even though we may remain, as not seldom happens, more convinced than before of the truth of our own'.[6]

He presided at the first inaugural meeting of the renewed body on 2 November 1897, and continued to occupy this position at almost all subsequent inaugural meetings. Present on that first occasion were three members of staff who had held office in the L. and H. during the eighteen-eighties, Fr Darlington, H.C. McWeeney, and W.P. Coyne. Among the students in attendance were Frank J. Skiffington, James Joyce, Arthur E. Clery, and H.B. Kennedy. The first auditor was Skeffington. He was succeeded the following year by Thomas Kettle, just up from Clongowes, and already, in the memory of a contemporary, 'giving proof of that strange magnetism by which he attracted people to him. The audiences at the debates steadily increased.'[7]

The society met fortnightly during Michaelmas and Hilary terms. Its meetings were open to the public and were frequently presided over by distinguished outside speakers. The subjects of debate were generally the actualities of the day, especially those of Irish interest, and at its discussions many of the public men of the next generation won their spurs. Each year from 1899 its inaugural meeting was one of the important annual events and, as such, was fully reported in the press. The report of the 1899 meeting has a special interest as reflecting some of the diverging views and emotions in a year when one age was dying and another was coming to birth. National feeling had been reinvigorated by the centenary celebration of the 1798 insurrection; and the Gaelic League and the Anglo-Irish literary revival were making their influence felt. It was noticeable during the debate how almost every reference to the League and the restoration of Irish language and literature was loudly applauded.

The theme, once again, was: 'The influence of Irish genius in English literature'. The guest speakers were John Dillon, M.P., M. McDonnell Bodkin, Q.C., County Court Judge Adams, and Rev Dr Hickey of Maynooth, a staunch supporter of the Gaelic League. Among the students noted as present were F.J. Skeffington, James Joyce, and James Clandillon. To a distinguished gathering the auditor, Arthur E. Clery, read his address on Irish writers in English, with particular reference to Goldsmith, Berkeley, Steele, Swift and Burke. Of the guest speakers responding to the paper, the most popular appears to have been Judge Adams, who was celebrated for his wit at Limerick court. He ranged far and wide, and some of his comments, applauded then, seem peculiarly imperceptive in the light of subsequent developments. Having expressed his support for those who encouraged the Irish language and then declaring, to a mixture of applause and dissent, that he saw little chance of its restoration, he proclaimed that there had been a marked decline in English literature as the century advanced and at the moment, in his opinion, no one could doubt that 'the general literary decadence of the age was, to say the least of it, fully shared in Ireland' (hear, hear). We had come, he reminded his audience, 'to an age when little men cast long shadows, because the sun was setting' (loud and prolonged applause).

Delany, summing up, gave high praise to Arthur Clery's paper but doubted if any of the great writers mentioned could be considered adequately representative of Irish genius. 'They were exceptional children of a class' rather than of the race. 'For any adequate exposition of a nation's thoughts, for any true representation of a nation's genius, we must have not merely the children of a class, we must have also men who are in every sense children of the nation, . . . men whose life and words give fullest expression to all the great human passions that shaped the history of a nation's life'. In Irishmen these included love of country and even more 'the passion for the religion of their fathers'. Then, after a reference to the country's dark history, and a critical comment on Trinity College's part in it, he concluded on a characteristically buoyant note: 'Our lot is happily placed at the dawning of better days. In an age, too, when events move so fast that we may venture to hope that even in our times a literature thoroughly Catholic and thoroughly Irish, truly representative of Irish genius, may ripen with envigorated national life into a glorious maturity'.[8]

The sonorous sentiments and optimistic vision were scarcely fresh. He was repeating almost word for word what he had said on the same subject, in the same place, on a similar occasion in 1884! His attenuated view of what constituted being truly Irish was, however, widely shared across the country. The consistent opposition of orange unionism to Home Rule and to university education for Catholics, had helped create two Irelands; and the Gaelic Athletic Association, with its vast influence, and the growing Irish Ireland outlook, mirrored the reaction which was equating Irish with Gaelic and Catholic.

His idea of a university included the widest possible provision of opportunities for adult education. Hence, in addition to the Irish language classes, there were provided, on Thursday afternoons in the spring of each year, public lectures of an occasional kind. Their object was that of Newman in launching similar lectures forty-one years previously, namely, that the professors be not mere teachers of students but heralds of Catholic views on the whole range of human learning. In 1899, moreover, special extension lectures of a continuous and systematic character were introduced. The subjects offered were English, French and German Literature, History, Political Economy, and Mental and Moral Science; and they were so presented as to prepare students for the examinations of the Royal University, while being, at the same time, useful and interesting for the public generally. These lectures were held in the evening, even given a second time in the evening, to facilitate those who wished to take the Royal University examinations but were involved in other occupations by day. They became widely known as the 'night classes'.

The availability of the *aula maxima*, or great hall, made these lectures possible. A further use of the hall during his second term of office was to provide lecture facilities for women students. The Royal University, like London University, had made its degrees available to women, even though Dublin University and the older English universities were not yet prepared to do so. Facilities for lectures, however, were not readily available. In 1885 and 1888 women students had applied to the senate for permission to attend lectures at University

College. The senate had been unable to facilitate them. Delany pointed out that he had not sufficient space in the classrooms at his disposal for his own students; and that even if he had the space he was not in a position to permit women to attend, given the location of the classrooms and the current requirements of canon law. The rooms were placed in various parts of a house which was at the same time a house of residence for members of a male religious community and the boarding students. After 1894 the demand for lecture facilities increased. Catholic pupils of the Loreto convents and of the Dominican convent, Eccles Street, had begun to enter in large numbers for the Royal University examinations. On his return to Stephen's Green, Delany arranged that some of the advanced classes, those in which the numbers were not too great, should be held in the great hall so that women students could attend. The arrangement was widely availed of, but the problem was alleviated not solved. The numerous First Arts students remained unprovided for. At the turn of the century this was to give rise to charges of discrimination against Delany and the college authorities.

The tradition of Newman's *University Gazette* and *Atlantis* had received little attention during Delany's early years as president. Towards the end of his first term, however, it had been revived with the establishment of the *Lyceum*, a monthly educational and literary magazine. This foundation of Fr Tom Finlay lasted for seventy-seven issues from September 1887 to February 1894, when it was succeeded by the *New Ireland Review*, which ran from March 1894 to February 1911.

The title of the new magazine was indicative. Its editors announced that they proposed to cater for 'the new Ireland' which was growing up around them. Political and social changes, educational developments, the stirring of new ideas, and the growth of new wants had made Ireland of the day a very different Ireland from twenty years previously. Moreover, they stood upon the threshold of days that might even quicken the pace of social evolution. Hence, it was important 'that outward expression should be given to the notions that are abroad, and temperate discussion be bestowed upon the questions with which the public will occupy itself.'[9] The influence of Tom Finlay was maintained through his contributions and the contributions of others who had been students of his, or in varying degrees of closeness to him. These included W.P. Coyne, William Magennis, Tom Kettle, Arthur Clery, P.J. Hogan, James Meredith, and Frank Little.

The *Review* set itself a high academic standard, and proved an influential success. In its pages there appeared, over a period of ten years, some outstanding contributions from Irish scholars. Douglas Hyde's *Religious songs of Connacht* made its appearance there; as did much of Professor John McNeill's epoch making *Phases of Irish History*, and *Celtic Ireland*.

Delany was naturally pleased to have his college associated with such a publication. Its emphasis on 'temperate discussion' was particularly welcome after the turn of the century, when dissatisfaction with the delays over Home Rule kindled a *sinn fein* mentality and evoked in the student body a growing spirit of independence and impatience of authority. He found himself divided. On the one hand, he sought as an educationalist to encourage critical thinking and a free spirit of enquiry; on the other, he was preoccupied with the public image of the college as the chief argument for an equitable solution to the university question, and as the training ground of the future leaders of the new Ireland, and he was concerned lest any action or utterance of his staff or students give offence to the bishops or provide occasion to the government to defer further the long-awaited university solution.

Something of this dichotomy, as well as of his appearance and manner, was captured in James Joyce's rather malicious portrayal of him, as the Rev Dr Dillon, in *Stephen Hero*,[10] written about 1904. Depicting an encounter between Stephen and the president of the college, he described the latter as urbane, fluent, a bit old-fashioned; and he saw him, saying his breviary outdoors, as 'a small figure wrapped in a loose Spanish-looking black cloak' presenting 'over the edge of the breviary a neat round head covered with curly grey hair and a very wrinkled face of an indescribable colour: the upper part was the colour of putty and the lower part was shot with slate-colour'.

> Stephen raised his cap. 'Good evening, sir'. The president answered with the smile which a pretty girl gives when she receives some compliment which puzzles her — a 'winning' smile:
>
> 'What can I do for you?' he asked in a (wonderfully) rich, deep calculated voice. . . .

Discussion followed on a paper on Ibsen, which Stephen wished to read at the student society. Ibsen was associated with a social doctrine of free living, and an artistic doctrine of unbridled licence. The president had censored the paper, even though he was known by the students to be 'liberal minded'. The president said:

'I am very interested in the enthusiasm you show for this writer. I have never had an opportunity to read Ibsen myself but I know he enjoys a great reputation. What you say of him, I must confess, alters my views of him considerably. Someday perhaps I shall —

— 'I can lend you some of the plays if you like, sir,' said Stephen with imprudent simplicity . . . .

. . . 'I shall be very interested,' said the president with an amiable intention, 'to read some of his works for myself, I certainly shall. . . .'

The president was beginning to exhibit the liberal side of his character, but with priestly cautiousness.

'Do you intend to publish this essay? —

— 'Publish it!'

— 'I should not care for anyone to identify the ideas in your essay with the teaching in our college. We receive this college in trust.'

'Surely a student of this college can pursue a special line of study if he chooses.'

— 'It is just what we always try to encourage in our students but your study, it seems to me, leads you to adopt very revolutionary . . . very revolutionary theories.'

Joyce and Tom Kettle were, undoubtedly, the two men of genius at the college. Kettle has been described by a contemporary as 'the most brilliant intelligence of his generation',[11] but his was a brilliance enlivened by wit and glowing with warm humanity. Joyce, on the other hand, seemed wholly indifferent to questions which excited the general body of the students. He was aloof, self-preoccupied, and in his conclusions frequently oracular and assertive; and this, to those who did not know him, lent an appearance of arrogance. He was held in some awe by many of his contemporaries, but not taken seriously. One of them recalled how after he had read his paper 'Drama and life' to the Literary and Historical Society, he defended it unrelentingly against criticism from all sides, even from Professor Magennis in the chair; and how at the end James Clandillon, later celebrated in the field of Irish music, summed up the opinion of many when he pounded him on the back and said: 'That was magnificent, Joyce, but you are raving mad'. In the same vein, he was frequently referred to in the student journal as 'the hatter'.[12]

Unlike Kettle, Joyce retained few pleasant memories of his days at St Stephen's Green or of those he knew there. A couple of lines in a letter from Rome to his brother, Stanislaus, in 1906, some two years after *Stephen Hero*, reflected his bitterness. He had just received some Irish newspapers in which figured Fr Delany, Dr St John Gogarty, Frank Sheehy-Skeffington, John Marcus O'Sullivan, M.A., and Tom Kettle, now a member of parliament. 'They are all in the public eye and favour', he wrote, 'and here am I (whom their writings and lives nauseate to the point of vomiting) writing away letter after letter for ten hours a day . . . on the off-chance of pleasing three bad-tempered bankers'.[13]

Despite the tight rope which he walked, Delany overcame 'priestly cautiousness' and the wariness of age in approving the publication of a student journal in 1901. It made its first appearance on 1 June, with the president's assurance of making good any financial losses the first issues might incur. Its launching coincided with the growth of the new spirit of independence within the college, and with a general perception of the Gaelic language as the symbol of national identity. That year the number of students taking Celtic Studies more than doubled. *St Stephen's* survived for five years. It was the occasion of many headaches, but for much of its span was creditable to the college. Lambert McKenna wrote of it:[14]

The format of the paper, which was moderately but often cleverly illustrated, was distinctly attractive. What is more important is that all through its career the ability shown by the student editors and contributors was exceptionally high, with marked variety in the style and spirit of the matter communicated. And as writers of eminence (members of staff and others) also contributed articles, the interest and real value of the journal was considerable.

Delany was among the many members of staff who contributed. Among the students there were outstanding papers from Tom Kettle, James Joyce (on James Clarence Mangan), and Francis Cruise O'Brien;[15] and other contributions from such as Hugh Kennedy (later Chief Justice), Arthur Clery (later Professor of Law, and author), James A. Murnahan (later Justice of Appeal), Felix E. Hackett (later Professor of Physics, and author), John M. O'Sullivan (later Professor of European History, and Minister for Education), and Thomas Bodkin (later Curator of the National Gallery of Ireland).

When it is remembered that the small student body at the early years of the century, no more than 180 students, also contained among its members the names of George Clancy, Francis Sheehy-Skeffington, C.P. Curran, Agnes O'Farrelly, T.F. Rahilly, P.J. Little, Alfred T. O'Rahilly, Maurice Healy, Eamon de Valera, Patrick McCartan, 'Ginger' O'Connell, Rory O'Connor, the Sheehy brothers and sisters, Patrick McGilligan, and John A. Costello, and had among its lecturers John MacNeill, Patrick H. Pearse, and Fr Tom Finlay,[16] it is not difficult to appreciate the perceptiveness of W.P. Coyne in 1900 when he assured a former colleague 'the real work for Ireland is being done over there', pointing to University College.[17]

With Delany's encouragement, therefore, there was an intensely-lived social, cultural and spiritual side to the serious academic life of University College. That academic life continued to flourish. The solid organisation which he had first provided, the motivation and excellence of most of the staff which he had collected, and the quality of the students, had resulted in the college outstripping all its rivals in the Royal University examinations. In 1908 the number of its successes were to exceed those of all the other colleges combined.

Although there were differences with staff members about aspects of policy during his final years at Stephen's Green, there existed overall a strong spirit of unity and an appreciation on their part of what had been achieved, of his confidence in them and his interest in their work. 'With admirable tact and judgement Dr Delany never interfered with my biological teaching during the whole term of my residence as professor in the college', wrote Dr Klein in the *Times* on 30 June 1899. W.P. Coyne assured Delany that he had spent his happiest days as professor of economics at the college. 'Certainly', he continued, 'you have left nothing undone to emphasise the importance to Ireland of a Christian economy and I doubt if any of your manifold contributions to education in this country is calculated to have such far-reaching results'.[18] Tom Kettle in the *Nationist*, 2 November 1905, wrote proudly of the college, as 'incontestably ... *the* university college of Ireland ... a centre of vital thought and culture'. In later years both professors and graduates recalled nostalgically those 'golden years at 86'. William Magennis, reviewing in 1930 *A page of Irish history: the story of University College, Dublin, 1883-1909*, looked back upon a life 'that was so vivid in its emotional intensity, and filled with such fervent moments of joy in enterprise'; and he could not resist adapting Wordsworth's lines on the French Revolution — 'Bliss was it then to be alive: And to be young was very heaven'. Arthur Clery, too, writing in the same magazine, *The National Student*, harked back to 'the great age'. For him it was the age of men whose names had become bywords in the afterglow of history.

In the wider area of plans and negotiations towards a university settlement, Delany began to play a prominent part from 1901 onwards. The developments towards the eventual settlement of 1908 are most conveniently considered in three phases. The first covers the years from 1897 to 1905, and includes the watershed in the whole debate, namely, the Robertson Commission of 1902, and developments up to the fall of the Tory government. The second phase from 1906 to 1907 includes the Fry Commission on Trinity College and the disagreements as to the form the new university should take. The third concerns the achieving of an acceptable solution by Augustine Birrell as Chief Secretary. In between the second and third phase, the impact of developments on the student body at University College will be looked at.

Chapter XII

THE STRUGGLE FOR EDUCATIONAL EQUALITY: NEGOTIATIONS TOWARDS A SETTLEMENT, 1897-1905

As has been noticed, the Conservative government raised hopes of a solution in 1897 and then seemed to lose interest. In January 1898 Dr O'Dwyer contributed an article in *The XIX Century* magazine which dealt in detail with the proposed measure and the bishops' efforts to meet the government's requirements. There was no question, he insisted, of discrimination on religious grounds in a university for Catholics, as witness the presence of twenty to thirty Protestants at University College which, though the property of the Irish bishops and conducted by the Jesuits, was undisguisedly undenominational. The following month he was pleased with the country-wide agitation in support of a Catholic university.[19] Signs of a government response, however, were deferred till October. Then R.B. Haldane, though a Liberal, crossed over to Ireland to examine, with the prime minister's approval, how far a bill embodying Balfour's plans would find acceptance. He received assurances from Dr Walsh and Cardinal Logue, and from the heads of the Presbyterian Assembly. He also met with Delany. On his return to England he drafted, with Balfour's assistance, a university bill, which was to be introduced when a favourable moment presented itself. The prospects looked bright. 'You delighted Haldane, and I really think that something may be done', Morley wrote to Delany on 11 November. Eight days later, however, he was less hopeful. When Delany visited him at his home in England on 20 November, he reported that he had met Balfour at one of the Rothschild residences and the prime minister had stated that he feared great difficulty from the side of the Radicals. Moreover, where the Whigs were concerned the measure had very few friends. At the recent debate the chief whip had told him that seven members at the outside were prepared to vote for it.

The anomalous attitude of the Liberals, on the face of it, was difficult to follow. They were prepared to grant Home Rule, and their bill included a future university, yet they scrupled to vote for the university on its own. On closer examination their hesitation was understandable. They had a tradition of opposition to denominational education, and like many British politicians had been jolted by the reality of 'ecclesiastical government' in Ireland when the bishops exerted their influence against Parnell. Home Rule was one thing, a distant objective blessed by Gladstone; but to endow a university for the Catholic majority, and thereby, perhaps, increase episcopal influence, was a very different matter. The Conservatives, for their part, though their tradition favoured denominational education, were likewise nervous of episcopal influence, and had to reckon, besides, with the almost hysterical fears of the 'loyalist minority' in Ireland and, more importantly, with non-conformist opposition in Britain. 'The Orange drum may be more or less silenced in England', E.H. Knox, M.P., told Dr O'Dwyer, 'but there is a vast amount of ancient prejudice which we have to avoid rather than attempt to fight'.[20] Arthur Balfour's celebrated 'Letter to a Manchester constituent' in January 1899 was an attempt to test the force of this 'ancient prejudice'. He felt obliged to resort to a form of special pleading.

He hoped, he said, to set up two new teaching universities, one for Catholics in Dublin, and one in Belfast for Protestants. Then, after outlining the conditions and restrictions that would have to be complied with in the Catholic institution, he continued: 'There will thus be in Ireland two Protestant universities and one Catholic one, which, as there are nearly three Roman Catholics in that country to one Protestant seems not unfair to the Protestants. We have not here, be it remembered, a proposal for making Roman Catholics but only . . . for educating them'. The scheme did not confer new powers on the Roman Catholic priesthood or augment what they had. 'On the contrary, unless we Protestants are strongly mistaken, whatsoever of evil priestly influence carries in its train must surely be mitigated by broadening knowledge and a more thorough culture'.[21]

Meanwhile, the opposition to the government's proposal from within the ranks of Irish Unionists generated among concerned Irish Catholics a mounting resentment. The unionist minority seemed to stand in the way of justice for the Catholic majority. The resentment was strongly expressed to Fr I.J. Flanagan, the parish priest of Adare, Co Limerick, by the volatile Dr O'Dwyer, whose emotions were stabilised by a notoriously short fuse. Fr Flanagan informed Lord Dunraven on 28 January 1899 that the bishop had told him, in considerable anger, that he would 'make it impossible for a Catholic to vote for a Liberal Unionist (or no doubt Conservative)' if the government they were supporting did not pledge itself at once to deal with the university issue. Hence, 'men like Lord Dunraven and Monteagle' might as well retire; and he instructed Fr Flanagan to tell Lord Dunraven this. He had already instructed the parish priest of Croagh to publicly oppose Dunraven. Fr Flanagan passed on the ultimatum with the comment — 'there is a bit of clerical tyranny!'[22]

Balfour's proposals met, in fact, such an outcry in England against 'endowment of papacy' and 'priest domination' that the cabinet declined to press ahead with them; and Haldane wrote to Dr Walsh on 7 February 1899 that the old spirit of intolerance was abroad, and that Balfour's attempt had failed at least for the time.[23]

While the controversy raged over the proposals, an important development took place within the senate of the Royal University. In October 1898 the Belfast Medical Students' Association had formally complained that some of the fellows of the Catholic Medical School, Dublin, who were also examiners, had given extra lectures so as to favour their students. Although the senate, after an investigation, absolved the incriminated fellows from all intention of acting in an unfair manner, it was clear that there was a widespread feeling that the presence of the fellows from the Queen's Colleges, University College, and the Catholic Medical School, on the examining board of the university, gave an unfair advantage to students attending these establishments. The ensuing discussion resulted in a motion from the O'Conor Don on 2 February 1899, which was passed unanimously, that 'in the opinion of the senate, the present provisions for university education in Ireland are not satisfactory, and we therefore recommend the subject to the early attention of the government'.[24] This condemnation of the Royal University by its own governing body marked the beginning of a tirade of criticism, often unmerited, hurled at the Earlsfort Terrace institution. It inevitably heightened dissatisfaction among the student body, whose members were now encouraged to feel that they were being cheated of a proper university education.

O'Conor Don's motion had been seconded by the president of Queen's College, Belfast, Dr Thomas Hamilton. His wider aims and his ambitions were disclosed a week later when he advocated in the *Belfast Newsletter* a solution to the university problem on the lines of Balfour's 'Letter to a Manchester constituent'. The outcry about giving state money to Catholic education was quite ridiculous. Everyone knew that University College was already receiving public money, though in an underhand way. Why not, then, act in an above-board manner and endow a Catholic University in Dublin, and resuscitate the Queen's University and place its chief college in Belfast? Then everyone would be satisfied. His case was strengthened by the publication of a resolution from the governing body of Queen's College, Belfast, expressing its dissatisfaction with the Royal University, and especially its examination system, and calling for the reestablishment of the Queen's University in the north.

Thus Catholics and northern Presbyterians seemed to share common ground on the reorganisation of the university system. What mainly preoccupied the government, however, was the strength of opposition in England and Scotland; and it was chary of any action, with a general election in prospect, which would jeopardise its position. Besides, Trinity College, which up to this had made no pronouncements, now availed itself of the government's hesitations to lodge further obstacles in the way of Balfour's scheme. A senior fellow, Dr Anthony Traill, in the *Contemporary Review*, opposed a Catholic university in Dublin as likely to take students from Trinity College. Dr George Salmon, the provost, in the same publication, argued that a Catholic University was unnecessary since Dublin University was open to Catholics, and if they did not avail of it it was only because they were too subservient to their bishops. To establish three universities in Ireland would lead, moreover, to a lowering of standards and the undermining of higher education in the country. He had no objection, however, to endowing and equipping University College, if its students attended the lectures and took their degrees in Trinity or in the Royal University.

As the government wavered and deferred commitment to its proposals, the Irish bishops began to shift and waver in their stance on the university. Dr Walsh called up again his dream of an extension of Dublin University and, for the rest, discouraged any definite proposal on episcopal policy. Dr O'Dwyer strongly disapproved. He wanted an independent Catholic university — *de facto* if not *de jure* — and deplored the absence of a clear-cut policy on the part of the bishops. 'The whole university business is heart-breaking', he wrote on 27 March 1899. 'It is well for the political and material interests of the country that they are not in the hands of the bishops'. By 9 May he was even more depressed. 'As to our university question', he informed Dr

Donnelly, auxiliary Bishop of Dublin, 'I have almost come to despair. All we bishops have no definite policy. We do not even agree as to an aim'.[25] Depression, however, could not long survive the fire of Dr O'Dwyer's temperament. The general apathy arising from the government's inaction spurred and exasperated him and finally drove him, unwillingly, towards advocacy of self-government. The annual address to the Catholic Truth Society provided the occasion. His paper was published under the title: *A university for Catholics in relation to the material interests of Ireland*. It was a *tour de force* of reasoned argument and bellicose rhetoric.

Despite all the agitation and all the promises in the past, he said, the entire issue of university education had dropped out of sight in recent months. There was widespread apathy because the public seemed to accept that it was 'a rich man's question', and did not realise the material, social and practical benefits of a university. The deprivation of a Catholic university was not only an insult to Irish Catholics – 'a brand of inferiority as a lower race' – but a great national and material injustice which denied the country the possibility of industrial progress. A university was necessary to raise secondary school standards, and the standards of industry and of public life at local and national level. In education Ireland was 'a century behind civilization'. Unless it had access to knowledge it would be as it had been 'all through the ninety-nine years of this century, the mendicant of the world, and a disgrace to English government in Ireland'. But the days of Protestant ascendancy were over. 'Equality must come'. Self-help, 'steadiness, earnestness, perseverance' would hasten the issue. And, he concluded, if the imperial parliament 'is so dominated by English bigotry that, in the great matter of education, it can take no account of the religious convictions of the great majority of the nation, then no one can deny that it has forfeited all right to legislate for us. . . . Such a government is a cruel tyranny. . . . I cannot see how any Irish Catholic . . . can regard it as anything but an usurpation'. There were many roads to nationalism. Exasperation was one. It was yet to make this most unlikely of candidates into the most influential of all episcopal supporters of *Sinn Féin*.

William Delany's energies, during these years, were mainly directed to making University College the launching-pad for the new national university, which he saw as imminent. Following consultation with the General, he proposed to the provincial and his consultors in October 1899 some changes of government 'to bring the organisation and procedures of the college into line with public colleges like the Queen's so as to pave the way for government recognition of a new public university emerging from University College'. His proposed college council eventually secured approval in 1901. It consisted of six members, elected by the whole body of professors, and was supposed to govern the college conjointly with the president. 'Supposed' because, apart from disbursements and the passing of accounts, it enjoyed little executive power, and proved to be mainly an advisory body to which the president referred such matters as he thought appropriate. It did not really modify the character of Delany's government, which he described before the Robertson Commission as 'autocratic'.[26]

He continued to expand his contacts and his correspondence. His communications with the archbishop indicated distance between them but no strain. University College had become an established part of Irish life and had academically so far outdistanced its rivals that comparison with other Catholic colleges no longer seemed relevant. With the Viceroy Lord Cadogan; with the Chief Secretaries of the time, Gerald Balfour and George Wyndham; with old acquaintances and with occasional visitors such as Haldane, he maintained his practice of welcoming opportunities of discourse and of extending to them his interest and regard. Of such, during 1898 and 1899, John Morley and his wife had occasion to experience in a very personal way his humanity and kindness. Their daughter Florence (really Morley's step-daughter, his wife's child by a previous marriage) had become a Catholic while studying in Paris as an art student. The conversion had been accepted with difficulty by her mother. Now in 1898, at the age of thirty-nine, Florence decided to become a religious sister in Ireland. Her mother was distressed. Morley, who habitually wrote God with a small 'g', told his daughter that he did not think she was suited to such a life, but that the decision was hers and she would always be welcome at home. Delany, as a friend of the family, was consulted. He spoke at length with Florence, who was clearly a most determined woman, thought it likely that she had a religious vocation, discussed the matter with Dr Walsh, and sent back a lengthy report to England. Writing to thank him on 11 November, Morley declared that while he would like his daughter to have a vocation he felt that in her case 'the root and mainspring' was 'a restless egotism of the most insatiable kind'. To have archbishops consulted and so forth was delightful food for such an appetite. He had great trust, however, in Delany's 'good sense'. He and his wife were most grateful to him. Delany introduced

Florence to a variety of Dublin convents. Despite her competence as a musician and an artist, she did not choose a teaching
congregation but one concerned with the care of orphans and
of unmarried mothers and girls at risk. She entered High Park
convent, Dublin, as Sister M. St Agatha. The mistress of novices,
rather overwhelmed at the prospect of trying to form as a
religious a woman of middle years who was also a recent convert
and from a distinguished family, had placed starkly before her
the difficulties of the life and tried to dissuade her from entering; but to no avail. Florence settled in happily at High Park.
Sensing the loneliness of her parents as Christmas approached,
Delany wrote a long letter to her mother. Morley replied on
28 December, his wife being ill, expressing her thanks for his
'most kind and considerate letter'. It was 'a real comfort to her
in the depression of our solitary Christmas'. He had a lively
sense of Delany's kindness. Some people were so thoughtless.
In August 1899, Mrs Morley came to Dublin to visit her daughter.
Afterwards, Morley wrote to thank Delany for his kindness to
his wife while she was in Dublin. She sent glowing accounts of
the convent and of Florence's happiness. He had to admit that
it came as a surprise to him. Sr Agatha kept in close contact
with Fr Delany until his death. To her he was 'my own dear
Padre', a figure of joy and holiness, towards whom she always
felt deep gratitude and affection.[27] She herself died in 1936,
after thirty-eight years in religious life.

The government's inactivity continued into 1900, the election
year. 'The skies are black', Morley wrote in May. In June, as if
to underline the collapse of hope of a settlement, a meeting of
the graduates of Dublin University passed a resolution against
the endowment of any sectarian university. The same month,
however, the skies took on a temporarily brighter hue for
Delany with the visit to Ireland of Queen Victoria. Thirty-nine
years had elapsed since she had previously visited her Irish
subjects. In the interval she had become the symbol of the prosperity and stability of the world's largest empire. Against the
background of feelings roused by the Boer war and disappointed
hopes at home, there was a mixed reception to her visit. The
Dublin Corporation voted to present an address of welcome,
provided it did not mention loyalty to the crown. The elderly
queen, however, heard only the loud cheers from 'this warm-
hearted sympathetic people', and missed the background booing
detected by some of her entourage. She set about pacifying
Ireland in her own way, 'meeting the cardinal, and criticising
Dublin Castle for being so gloomy looking'. In her journal she

expressed her regret 'that the proposal for a Roman Catholic
university had not been agreed to in parliament', adding — 'Lord
Salisbury said that many of their supporters in the House of
Commons were much against it, which I could not understand'.[28]

Delany had been enlisted in the preparations for the visit.
During March, the Lord Mayor invited him to act as vice-
president of the Citizens' Reception Committee which was
engaged in decorating the streets in honour of Her Majesty.[29]
In June he was one of those who accompanied the royal party
on visits to certain Catholic institutions. It was a participation
that was open to criticism and ridicule from nationalist supporters: nationalist sensitivity more than matching that of the
'well-meaning and misinformed' loyalists of whom he had
occasion to write in 1887. There were so many tight ropes to
walk. Episcopal vigilance had its analogue within his own
Order. The years 1897 to 1905, during the generalate of Fr L.
Martin, were featured by a series of cautions which must have
appeared unduly restrictive to one who was president of a
university college and advanced in years. In 1899 and 1900
he was reminded that unnecessary visits to the houses of secular
people, especially without a companion, were to be avoided. In
1900 and 1902, when the college and the community were
barely surviving financially, there was a reminder of the need of
preserving the spirit of poverty in the community;[30] and also
in 1900 — 'for several grave reasons against such journeys out
of the province' — he was refused permission to represent the
senate, at the senate's expense, at the centenary celebrations of
the Catholic University of Cracow, Poland.[31] In December of
that year, nevertheless, his standing in the province was acknowledged by his appointment as one of the four consultors to the
provincial.[32]

The return of the Tory government in the autumn of 1900
with an undiminished majority restored the university question
as a live issue. Within a short time two interesting suggestions
were put forward for its solution. Dr W.J.M. Starkie — formerly
tutor at University College, later president at Queen's College,
Galway, and Commissioner of National Education, proposed
that there should be four universities: Dublin University; the
Royal — with a reduced endowment; a Catholic university; and
one for the Presbyterians. He would also have, however, an
independent Council of University Education to ensure the
establishment of 'genuine university courses' and '*bona fide*
examinations' of the courses. Mr J. Pigott, a Catholic and a
graduate of Trinity College, caused a stir by an article in the

Contemporary Review, January 1901, critical of Trinity and calling for changes within it. It was a harbinger of future pressures on Dublin University. The atmosphere there, Pigott argued, was too saturated with Protestantism to be beneficial to Catholics. Yet it was essential to the country's peace and prosperity that Catholics and Protestants be educated together. Hence, it was the duty of Trinity College to make such internal changes as would make Catholics feel at home there. These, he suggested, should include: the removal of the divinity school outside the walls; the establishment of a Catholic chapel within the grounds or that Protestant services be conducted outside the college; the right of supervision of religious instruction to the authorities of the various churches; and the endowment of separate Catholic chairs of mental and moral philosophy.

The next real step towards the solution of the university problem came, however, from within the senate of the Royal University. It was felt necessary to employ external examiners to allay the dissatisfaction expressed with the system of examining. Hence, a proposal was placed on the agenda for 21 February 1901, requesting the government to allocate additional finance to this end. Dr O'Dwyer thought the moment right for forcing the whole university question to an issue. He exchanged letters with Delany about the wording of an amendment which would 'induce the Royal to make an attempt on its own life',[33] and, after much persuasion, agreed to appear personally for the first time at a senate meeting. It turned out that a reason for his non-attendance was an embarrassing affliction, which he sought hard to conceal. 'I fear', he wrote a few days after the meeting, 'I was a great bother to you on Thursday on account of my deafness, and for myself it was most disagreeable not to be able to follow the discussion'.[34] His important amendment, seconded by Dr Healy, was passed unanimously.

The amendment declared that the members of the senate considered that the ultimate cause of any inequality which might exist regarding the conditions under which students were examined was not to be found in the peculiar constitution of the examining boards but in the anomalous constitution of the university itself. Hence, the senate contended that the university's relations with its own colleges and with other colleges and students were unsatisfactory, and that it was most desirable 'that a royal commission should be issued to inquire into the working of the university as an examining and teaching body in relation to the educational needs of the country at large, and to report as to the means by which university education in

Ireland might receive a greater extension and be more efficiently conducted than at present'.

A committee was appointed to present the amendment to the Lord Lieutenant. The bishop of Limerick feared that the deputation might be 'put off with a Lord Lieutenant's commission', and he urged that three of the members, Delany, Healy, and Hamilton of Belfast, should have an understanding to press for a royal commission. 'Nothing less than the report of a royal commission', he wrote to Delany on 26 February 1901, 'would carry so big a reform as what we seek. And I should say that the more Englishmen and Scotchmen on it the better'. Irishmen, he thought, would be less likely to judge the question purely on its merits, and their report would carry less weight as seeming to reflect a partisan spirit. On 9 March a royal commission was conceded. On 20 March, Dr O'Dwyer was even more concerned about the composition of the body. 'If this commission,' he wrote, 'reports against us we're done for, and unless we get a safe and strong chairman, with a compact body of men to sustain him, we should be terribly at the mercy of the Protestant elements'.

On 28 June the names of the members of the royal commission were published. They were: Lord Robertson, chairman, a Scottish Lord of Appeal; Professor H. Butcher, fellow of Trinity College, Cambridge, and University College, Oxford; Dr. John Healy, bishop of Clonfert (later Archbishop of Tuam) and senator of the Royal University; Professors Ewing and Jebb of Cambridge; Mr Justice Madden; Lord Ridley, late Home Secretary and fellow of All Souls College, Oxford; Prof. Rhys, professor of Celtic in Oxford; Dr W.J.M. Starkie, resident commissioner of national education and late president of Queen's College, Galway; Professor Dickie, Magee College, Derry; Professor Lorrain Smith, Queen's College, Belfast; and Mr Wilfrid Ward, examiner in Mental and Moral Science, Royal University of Ireland.

The commission was destined to commence its hearings in September. Delany, meanwhile, found himself and his college the subject once again of serious criticism. His involvement in the lead up to the commission, some remarks of his as a leader of the deputation which met the Lord Lieutenant, and, in particular, some articles by Michael Drummond, K.C., which markedly supported the establishment of a great central Catholic college in Dublin, gave rise to questioning among members of the episcopacy as to his intentions and those of the Jesuit Fathers.

It had all started rather innocuously the previous January
(1901) when Drummond spoke at the Catholic Club to a paper
by Delany's assistant, Fr Darlington. He proposed a personal
solution to the university question, which involved leaving
Dublin University untouched and having an over-all university
with colleges at Dublin, Cork, Galway and Belfast. The northern
institution would be Presbyterian in character, the staff and
government of Cork and Galway would be changed so as to
make these colleges as Catholic as Belfast was Presbyterian, while
the Dublin Catholic College would take over the Royal University buildings at Earlsfort Terrace and the Royal University
funds. Darlington, who was a byword for always agreeing with
whatever was said to him, registered approval. Drummond
put forward his scheme in the newspapers on four occasions
from January to March. The occasion on which his proposals
were first made, the relative favour shown to a Catholic college
in Dublin, and Fr Darlington's seeming approval, appear to have
provided grounds for those 'well-meaning but misinformed
persons' to whom Delany had previously referred and in which
Dublin seemed to abound, to pass on their conclusions.

The provincial, Fr James F. Murphy, received a hint during
August from Dr Gaffney of Meath, and the archbishop of
Dublin's secretary, Fr Pettit,[35] that a number of the bishops
were under the impression that Drummond's articles were
inspired by the Society of Jesus. He raised the matter with his
consultors and, following further discussion with Delany, it was
agreed that Delany would write a letter to the provincial which
would be sent to Cardinal Logue and Dr Walsh under a covering
letter from the provincial. Delany's lengthy communication,
written on 19 August, clarified his position with regard to
Drummond's proposals and outlined once again his views on an
acceptable solution to the university problem.

The 'erroneous notions' which many of their lordships entertained 'regarding the attitude of the Jesuit Fathers', and especially of himself, were based, he believed, on the assumption
that the scheme put forward by Drummond was put forward
with his knowledge and sanction. At the present time of crisis in
the university question, he was particularly anxious to dispel
such an impression; and hence he had asked the provincial to
convey authoritatively to Cardinal Logue and Dr Walsh his
'most clear and emphatic repudiation of, any connection with,
or sympathy or agreement with, that scheme'. He had more
than once communicated to Mr Drummond his strong dissent
from his proposals and had shown in detail 'how utterly in-

adequate and unsatisfactory they were'; and on hearing that Drummond and Fr Darlington had been in communication on the subject, he had repeated his repudiation to Darlington 'and remonstrated strongly with him for having anything to do with such proposals'.

His own views on the university issue could be reduced to this: 'that whatever scheme the bishops proposed or whatever they are prepared to accept, to that scheme I subordinate most cordially all my own views, and I shall support and advocate it to the best of my ability'. He adhered to the claim, 'put forward so clearly and justly by Archbishop Walsh, demanding equality with the Protestants, that is: 1. A university without tests, but controlled *de facto* by Catholics just as Dublin University has no tests but is *de facto* controlled by the Protestant Episcopalians — as the Presbyterians complain just as we do. 2. A college, teaching and residential, as well provided and equipped as Trinity College, and *de facto* governed by Catholics just as Trinity College is *de facto* governed by Protestant Episcopalians'. As to whether a separate university was more desirable for Catholics than a college in the University of Dublin, he would refer their lordships to his long letter to Dr Kavanagh in 1886. He would correct it in only one particular. He had then referred to 'the so called prestige of Trinity College degrees'. He now believed that such prestige was 'absolutely nil so far as the mere degree goes, far below that of the Royal University', and hence he now held even more strongly than in 1886 'the desirability of holding entirely aloof from the University of Dublin'.

Some concern had been felt about remarks of his relating to the Royal University, the possible outcome of Lord Robertson's commission, and 'a great central teaching college' in Dublin. With regard to his views on the Royal University, he would point out that that institution was looked upon from the start, 'even by its own conservative creators', as 'a mere stop gap . . . partly as a preparation for a larger measure, partly as a political dodge to get admitted without notice the *principle* of endowment of a Catholic college in the hope that the results might show that a larger measure would be not only justifiable, but even imperative on the grounds of fair play and equal justice'. As to 'the Royal University in relation to the royal commission', his views on this were expressed on the occasion of the deputation to the Lord Lieutenant when he had said 'that no mere reconstruction of that institution was contemplated in the resolution submitted by the senate . . . that its constitutions would have to be radically changed, and that it would need far wider powers and much more abundant provisions'. With reference to 'the great central teaching college', which was 'the most important item in any scheme of settlement', he wished once again to remove misunderstanding and to repeat emphatically what he had said in 1886, namely, that there was no intention on his part 'to claim for the Jesuits any control of that institution, or any share in its working beyond that which may be assigned to them on their individual merits'. Finally, in relation to the evidence he would be called on to lay before the royal commission in his position as president of University College, he should be most grateful for any instructions that might be given him on the part of the bishops, and he would 'most cordially cooperate with their lordships in furthering their wishes'.

The provincial's covering letter was even more conciliatory. He had been given to understand that at a recent episcopal meeting the impression was conveyed 'that the Society in its views on the matter of university education was at variance with those of the bishops of Ireland'. This was 'absolutely false'. He would be the first 'to condemn, and so far as possible to prevent any action taken or any view expressed by any of our fathers, which would seem to conflict with what the bishops of Ireland shall think best for the interests of Catholic education'. He had written 'a very strong letter of disapproval to Fr Darlington' for even speaking in private with Mr Drummond 'in a way that seemed to support . . . his proposals'. He had spoken with Fr Delany but found he was of the same mind as himself, as the enclosed would show. The Order's desire was to work cordially with the bishops. 'We have no aims or views of our own but that any resolutions adopted or clauses proposed by the bishops of Ireland shall have the loyal support of any little influence our fathers have in this matter'.[36] The bishop of Meath told the provincial that his letter 'did much good and was badly wanted', since some did think the Society was behind Fr Darlington.[37]

The great difficulty still was, however, how to establish where precisely the bishops of Ireland stood on the university question. The majority seemed to have no particular position. Dr Walsh and his immediate followers were evasive, and remained hostile to the senate and any suggestion of a solution coming through its efforts. Drs O'Dwyer and Healy were in agreement with Delany. O'Dwyer, writing to his friend Dr Donnelly, the auxiliary bishop of Dublin, on 18 November 1901, was appalled at their lordships' casual attitude to something so important as the royal commission. Feeling the responsibility of his rôle as the episcopal witness before it, 'and the strangeness of the bishops making no preparation for the commission', he had written a strong letter to the cardinal. A special meeting of the education committee was called. It passed a series of resolutions 'covering pretty well the whole case I had to make'. He was thus able 'to give authoritative information to Dr Delany, Nixon and Ross, and so we were all on the same line'. One of those who approved the line he was to follow was Dr Walsh. Yet Bishop O'Dwyer concluded his letter with the hope that His Grace would not 'upset the case'.[38] His premonition was well-founded.

The aim of the commission was set out as follows:[39]

> To enquire into the present condition of the higher, general and technical education available in Ireland outside Trinity College, Dublin, and to report as to what reforms, if any, are desirable in order to render that education adequate to the needs of the Irish people.

The commission spent from September 1901 to June 1902 in hearing witnesses (147 of them) whose evidence was published in three instalments.

Assessing his fellow commissioners' mode of acting during the depositions, Wilfrid Ward found ample grounds for criticism. The chairman, Lord Robertson, was vehemently anti-Catholic, and was convinced that the bishops were seeking control of education and were 'using their position and influence not in the interests of religion but as party politicians'. He was also bad-tempered, according to Ward, and frequently tried to browbeat Catholic witnesses. The bishop of Clonfert, Dr John Healy, though genial and popular, tended, on the other hand, to be unpleasant towards Presbyterian and Episcopalian witnesses. Dr Starkie was embarrassing in his anti-clericalism, lectured the witnesses instead of taking evidence, and was generally 'very tactless'. Professor Henry Butcher, Sir Richard Jebb, Mr Justice Madden, and presumably Ward himself, seem to have been the members who were most earnest and detached in their desire to discover 'the existing state of things, with a view to furnishing the best form of university education to the people of Ireland'.[40]

One of the most outstanding witnesses was the bishop of Limerick. He astonished the commissioners, George Wyndham informed Balfour, 'by a consummate statement of the Catholic case, unshaken during three days' cross-examination'.[41] That reforms were 'desirable' in higher education was put beyond doubt on the very first day by his eloquent and powerful presentation of the evidence.

O'Dwyer quickly exposed the shortcomings of the chief university colleges serving the Catholic population. The Queen's Colleges at Cork and Galway stood for 'a downright waste and squandering of public money', and taking Cork, in particular, he outlined its attendance figures in different faculties and remarked that 'for anything in the nature of university education, in the ordinary sense of the word, Cork College might as well not exist'.[42] With reference to University College he conceded that it had 'for its size and circumstances, considerable success' but it was 'infinitesimal in its effects on the general educational conditions of the country'. As an university institution, materially speaking, it was 'simply a burlesque'.[43] It and the discredited Queen's Colleges were the only opportunity for higher education in the whole country for three million three hundred thousand Roman Catholics. University education was, in fact, so thin over the country as to make scarcely any impression. 'Gentry, merchants, professional classes (except, to an extent, the barristers), clergy, have no education corresponding to their position' and the teachers of Catholic secondary schools had no opportunity of university training.[44] Pointing to the successes of the Catholic schools in the Intermediate examinations, he called attention to the fact that 'the political centre of gravity in Ireland' had 'shifted towards the Catholics'. 'In three provinces, practically all political and municipal power, with the control of technical education in the latter, have passed into their hands. It is a dangerous thing to have them uneducated'. To lead and guide them there was required a large number of men with the wisdom and trained reasoning power acquired in a proper university.

Delany and Dr O'Dwyer maintained a detailed interchange of views during the commission. In one such interchange, Delany warned that he had reason to know 'that though Trinity College, Dublin, is shut out from the purview of the commission, there are powerful persons anxious to bring it in and to resuscitate Gladstone's scheme, or rather to substitute the much more objectionable one of having a Catholic college in the University of Dublin'. He added that 'after a life of educational work and more than twenty years anxious thought over this university question', he was 'absolutely convinced that the *very worst* solution of the question for Irish Catholics, and for *education generally*, would be the establishment of a college for Catholics in the Dublin University'.[45]

Dr O'Dwyer, in line with the approval received from the

bishops and his consultations with Delany, argued eloquently for a university which was not Catholic in the strict sense, but which in its arrangement and personnel would be as acceptable to Catholics as was Trinity College to the Protestants: for one, in fact, such as Balfour had suggested. He accepted the conditions laid down by the prime minister, and offered a number of suggestions as to how they might be carried out to the satisfaction of all parties. Such a solution of the problem, he assured the commission, would be regarded by the whole Catholic body as final. Questioned as to his views on an endowed Catholic college within the Royal University, he did not completely rule out such a contingency, but in an effort to describe its unsatisfactory character used an image which caught the public imagination. It would lack, he said, the element of finality: and Catholics would not be satisfied 'to be put off with a mere college in a second-class university, in which we and the Dissenters like second-class passengers travelled together, while the privileged body of Episcopalians had a first-class institution to themselves'.[46]

Of Delany's evidence the author of the biography of Archbishop Healy wrote: 'The splendid abilities of this man shine out in every line of those twenty-five pages of his which greatly enrich the minutes of that commission'.[47]

In a way, his whole life had been a preparation for his appearance before the commissioners. He ranged over the whole history of the university question from the period of his connection with the Duke of Marlborough at the time of the Intermediate Act right up to the sitting of the commission. He showed that the Royal University was never meant to be more than a temporary substitute for a proper university. In the course of answering a variety of questions, he touched on a multitude of topics. He outlined the history of University College; its absence of equipment when he took over — 'I received empty walls and no furniture of any kind';[48] its examination successes; its form of government — 'up to the present it has been practically autocratic, that is governed by the rector';[49] the constitution of the staff — of the twenty-two members, 'eight are Jesuits, five professors and fellows and three in administration, the remaining fourteen are laymen, of whom ten are permanent professors and fellows and the other four are tutors'.[50] In a supporting letter he pointed out that there had always been, since 1883, some non-Catholics on the staff, and that 8 to 12 per cent of the students had always been non-Catholics—Protestants, Presbyterians, Methodists, Jews — 'among them being not infrequently Protestant clergymen'.[51] During his years in the college there had been no instance of a student leaving his own faith to become a Catholic. To the probing question whether the teaching was affected by the attendance of non-Catholics at lectures, his incisive answer gave some indication of his relationship with his professors. He replied:

> I do not think there is any difficulty which I could appreciate.
> . . . Our students come to us with the knowledge that our teaching is of a certain stamp in certain subjects like history; and our philosophy is the scholastic philosophy of the Catholic Church. They come with the knowledge that the books we prefer in history are those which we deem free from the errors of other histories. With regard to other teaching, I know no other subject which we teach where there is any difference. During the ten years which I have been president, and actually responsible, there has been nothing of this kind and never once from the beginning have I ever interfered with the teaching of any professor, and never once have I had to interfere with his liberty of teaching.[52]

Other points on which he had to try to satisfy the commissioners included the age-old question of the Jesuits' allegiance to the British government,[53] and whether he envisaged the college under a new arrangement continuing under 'the management of the Jesuit Fathers'.[54] Dr Starkie commented that a teaching career was practically closed to Catholic laymen because 'Catholic clergy can do educational work much more cheaply' and because Catholic educational institutions, having no direct endowments, employed clergy in preference; and he asked if Fr Delany agreed that there was a great need in the country for a sufficiently remunerative educational career for Catholic laymen. The reply covered an aspect of the question dear to Delany: 'I have already stated that in my evidence; and I have pointed out that the reason we have not Catholic professors of eminence in certain branches of education, especially in mathematics and the natural and physical sciences, is that we, Catholics, have not what exists in Trinity College, an inducement to take up the study of those branches of knowledge, with the prospect of obtaining a dignified position, or even a competency in life. Catholics have nothing of that kind. I am strongly in favour of having that inequality removed'.[55] As regards the arrangements for fellows, these were quite inadequate. Fellowships had to be renewed every five years and, so, gave no security. Besides, he went on, 'I regard £400 a year as, after all, only a beggarly income for a man of distinguished ability to look forward to as a provision for life'. In his supplementary evidence he pointed out that he himself as president had no salary and received nothing from the fees, and that neither did the vice-president, nor the lecturer in religion. The fees for the evening classes were paid directly to the tutors, who were all laymen.[56]

Asked for his views on the deficiencies of the Royal University, he made three points which underlined some of his own priorities in university education. 1. It offered no opportunity of a degree in religion. 'I should like that educated laymen should be given an opportunity of getting a scientific knowledge of their religion'. The first faculty in the new London University, established for non-conformists of various sects, was the faculty of divinity. Yet by act of parliament examinations in religion were forbidden at the Royal University. 'If a college was being established in South Africa or India cognizance would be taken of the religion of the inhabitants; but no cognizance was taken of the religion of the people of Ireland'.

2. 'My second point is,' he continued, 'that the Royal University provides no opportunity of collegiate life, and the educational culture such life carries with it. . . . I thoroughly agree with Cardinal Newman that for many men the social life of the college is of more importance for their education than the lectures of the classroom'.

3. Its degrees should bear testimony 'as to whether a man has had the advantage of a collegiate training' or had merely passed its examinations by private study. 'I have had a long experience in educational work', said Delany, 'and I attach very little importance to a great deal of the higher examination results. . . . I should value a man much more who has had a collegiate training than the man who has simply passed the examination'.[57]

Finally, on the injustice done to Catholics in the distribution of educational endowments, he resurrected his finely honed arguments against the Queen's Colleges and pointed to the inequitable manner in which the secularists' anti-religious test was applied. 'It is made to tell entirely against Catholics. University College is ignored as being denominational merely because it is under Catholic government, and teaches the Catholic religion to Catholics: whilst Trinity College is supported as being undenominational, although it is thoroughly Protestant in government, and teaches Protestantism to Protestants'.[58]

'What, then, do the Catholics claim?' he was asked. He replied:

The answer is short and simple: justice and fair play. Nothing more. The state funds belong to all its citizens equally; Catholics claim their due proportion of them; they will rest satisfied with nothing less. They ask for nothing for themselves which they are not perfectly willing to see enjoyed by others; but they cannot acquiesce in any educational arrangements which leave others privileges and advantages denied to Catholics.

The state claimed the right to see that the public funds set aside for educational purposes were duly administered; the Catholics, said Delany, admitted the right, indeed held it a duty 'which the state has hitherto almost entirely neglected in Ireland'. They further held that the state violated impartiality and the right of conscience when it excluded all religion from education, just as effectually as when it confined its gifts to those who held a particular creed. Provision would have to be made to meet the requirements of Catholics in the provinces, especially in the large centres of Cork and Belfast, but it was fundamental that in Dublin, as the chief Catholic centre and the capital of the country, 'a suitably equipped and endowed college should be established, under such conditions that Catholics might have confidence in its administration, and conscientiously benefit by its teaching', and where they might also enjoy, so far as it depended on the state, 'educational advantages and university status equal to those provided by the state for any other Irishmen'.[59]

'Fr Delany', Wilfrid Ward wrote on 22 November 1901, 'though not equal to O'Dwyer – or nearly equal to him – in eloquence, was extremely able and interesting. Butcher says that in the course of seven years commission work he had never heard anything to equal the evidence of those two'.[60]

The scheme for a separate Catholic University, as outlined by Dr O'Dwyer, proved acceptable to a fairly large body of Protestants and to virtually every Catholic witness. In many instances, however, it was not their preferred solution. Some Protestants favoured, as less radical, an endowed Catholic college under a reorganised Royal University. An influential group of lay Catholics, which included Chief Baron Palles, the O'Conor Don, and N.J. Synnott, were permitted by Lord Robertson – as Delany had feared – to argue for a Catholic college in a reorganised Dublin University. To add to the confusion, the Dublin University witnesses opposed any concession to the Catholics, while the Presbyterian witnesses exhibited an unexpected reluctance to support any change in the *status quo*. Thus, the commission found itself faced with a situation in which: a majority of Catholics favoured a separate Catholic university; a smaller, but influential group, preferred a Catholic college in a reorganised University of Dublin; a majority of Protestant witnesses were prepared to support a Catholic endowment within the Royal University; and the body of Presbyterian evidence opposed any concession to Catholics.

This division of opinion was further extended by the fact that among the commissioners themselves, apart from those who were clearly anti-clerical, there were some who had genuine reservations about a separate Catholic university because they feared 'that the bishops would be so eager to control the education given in a Catholic university in the interests of the students' faith that the university would become second-rate educationally'.[61] Hence, the prospects of a satisfactory settlement became more and more remote as the commission's enquiries went on.

Delany and Dr O'Dwyer were incensed at Lord Robertson permitting discussion of a Catholic college in Dublin University, since this was expressly excluded by the terms of the enquiry and he had precluded earlier witnesses, such as Dr O'Dwyer, from a detailed discussion of any proposals relating to Dublin University. The only effect of urging such an issue would be to divide Catholic opinion and offer the commission 'an easy outlet from giving any solution'.[62] Dr Walsh, however, was determined that the Dublin University scheme be urged. In the *Freeman's Journal*, 17 November 1900, he had acknowledged that the Irish bishops had always preferred 'the establishment of a separate university for Catholics', but he had frequently made it clear that his personal preference was for a national university including Trinity College or, alternatively, for a Catholic college within Dublin University. He did not appear before the commission to be questioned on his views, but he sent a letter which added to that body's confusion. He associated himself with the bishop of Limerick's evidence 'in so far as he (Dr O'Dwyer) had an opportunity of expressing himself', and then added that 'on one important aspect of the case', namely the matter of the Dublin University scheme, Chief Baron Palles had said everything he would wish to say. The disarray in Catholic preferences became public knowledge in November and December 1901, with the publication of a series in the *Freeman's Journal* entitled 'Points from the evidence'. It provoked Delany to an annoyed and eloquent response.

'Points from the evidence', which appeared from 16 to 23

November, represented the Dublin University scheme as 'that which many, probably a majority of Irish Catholics prefer'. Subsequent articles, on 6 and 13 December, over the pseudonym of 'Reviewer', developed the educational, social and political advantages of the scheme and claimed as supporters the names of Isaac Butt and Gladstone, the archbishop of Dublin and the bishops of Ireland. Delany replied in four strongly polemical letters on 17, 18, 20, 21 December.

First he took issue on purely educational grounds with the policy of centralisation advocated by 'Reviewer', and with the argument that if all denominations were competing together in a common university they would soon grow to love each other. He pointed to the failure of centralisation in France and Scotland and its abandonment in England, and argued that twenty years of competition between different denominations in the Royal University had not shown 'any perceptible growth of friendly feeling'. The 'Reviewer', he went on, appeared to recognise the inferiority of the educational system he was advocating and hence, 'in order to recommend his *omnium gatherum* to popular favour . . . would write in large letters over its doors the magic scroll: Truly national'. 'Not so', Delany responded, 'do the struggling nationalities of Europe, that have been conquered by more powerful neighbours, understand the word "national". They have learned by experience that the university that moulds the intellect of the nation must inevitably affect the character of the race. They have seen in the mixed university controlled by their conquerors . . . their sons become denationalised and not infrequently dechristianised'; and hence they were demanding and obtaining, as in Bohemia, Galicia, Wales and elsewhere, 'separate universities in which their language and their history and their national traditions shall hold an honoured place'. Had Irish Catholics abandoned that ideal? He for one did not think they had.

'Reviewer' had appealed to 'Butt's ideal'. He obviously had not read Butt's speech in the House of Commons. It was a brilliant speech, but it was evident that it was 'a Trinity College man who speaks'. His concept of equality for Catholics was a small corner of the grounds, and a small endowment of £30,000 for buildings and grounds within Dublin University, while the greater part of the grounds, buildings and equipment of Trinity College remained in the hands of the Protestant minority. So much for Butt's 'great National University of Ireland', and for equality! He resented, moreover, 'Reviewer' persistently invoking the authority of the bishops of Ireland in defence of 'Butt's

ideal', as if it was he, Delany, and not 'Reviewer', who was
proposing a different goal to that of the bishops. 'The ideal of
the Irish bishops is now, and has always been, a university for
Irish Catholics, governed by Irish Catholics, where their children
may have secured to them the best secular education in surroundings that would tend to keep them good Catholics and true
Irishmen'.

With regard to the arguments that in a common university
there would be 'greater political advantages', 'kindly feelings'
would be fostered, and Catholics would benefit from 'the
prestige of Dublin University'; he would reply that for many
years to come Protestant graduates would greatly outnumber
Catholics, and it would scarcely be to the latter's political
advantage to 'be represented in parliament, whether in England
or at home, by men of whom the present representatives,
Mr Lecky and Sir Edward Carson' were 'fairly good types';
the 'prestige' value of Dublin University degrees he, as an
educationalist, was 'utterly unable to recognise'; while as regards
the growth of friendly feelings, which he greatly desired, he saw
no reason for thinking 'that men are made friendly merely by
competing at examinations in a common university', rather
would he agree with Bishop O'Dwyer that if a university were
given to the Catholics, removing their present grievance, friendly
relations would soon be established between the two universities.

He wished to emphasise, moreover, that whatever his views
about the origin and history of the University of Dublin, or 'the
action taken by its more prominent spokesmen today in regard
to Catholic claims, or to Irish national sentiment', he had 'no
hostility whatsoever towards that institution as a Protestant
university for Protestants'. If equal justice were done for
Catholics, he would 'not lift a finger to curtail any of its privileges
or to withdraw a penny of its endowments'. He felt, indeed, a
certain sympathy with the Protestants who were proud of it.
It had been 'the living embodiment and the faithful custodian
of their Protestantism, the unfailing champion of their political
views and the bulwark of their political ascendancy'. Why
should they not be proud of it and struggle to maintain it?
Were he a Protestant, he should probably do so with all his
might. But, he added in peroration:

I am a Catholic priest, of the Irish people, sharing their
beliefs and proud of their sad history, and I ask in all earnestness, what is there in the origin or in the past history of the
University of Dublin, or in the tone of its champions today,

that we, Irish Catholics, should be invited to admire its prestige? Or to seek 'political advantages' by linking our fate with it? Or that it should be even remotely suggested that 'a majority of Irishmen and Catholics' would prefer to a university Catholic and Irish, governed by themselves, 'Butt's ideal': that is to say — a centralised university condemned by all educational experience; a mixed university, neither Catholic nor National; a university in its first beginnings and throughout all its history down to the present day, entirely out of harmony with the religious convictions and with the national sentiments of Irish Catholics?

'You are bold enough', he addressed 'Reviewer', 'to claim that the Irish bishops are with you in that contention. I have too much respect for their lordships even to discuss the assertion; but I venture to express a doubt whether you can find a single Catholic priest in Ireland who will endorse your position'.

Faced with this blend of educational argument, patriotic fervour, and heady rhetoric, 'Reviewer' wilted to the extent of stating that he had been arguing for Dublin University as a second-best solution, only to be sought if a separate Catholic university could not be had. The controversy, however, publicly aired the Dublin scheme and caused concern among Delany's fellow Jesuits. Quite apart from the fact that some of them disagreed with his views, it was felt that he had placed himself on a collision-course with the archbishop and that in doing so might be seen as the spokesman of the Society. When he continued to use every opportunity, in public and in private, to press for a separate university, one distinguished member of the province reproached him personally but received little satisfaction.

Perturbed at his stance, and echoing the current confusion of opinion, Fr J. Conmee, rector of Gardiner Street Church, wrote to the provincial on 4 February 1902. From what he had learned from a number of sources, Fr Delany had overestimated 'the depth and extent of the feeling for his side of the question'. A prominent man had told him that he had heard that 'the commission would recommend a Trinity scheme' and that it was now 'understood' that the heads of Dublin University had expressed formally to the government 'their willingness to further such a scheme and welcome it'. There were conflicting accounts as to what the bishops might do. Even Fr Delany admitted that he could not be sure they would not plump for Trinity. Public opinion in Dublin was certainly settling in that direction. 'Herein', he concluded, 'lies the peculiar fatuity (as I think) of Delany who does not see the possibility of his being defeated'. Delany had agreed, however, not to do anything further in public.

The provincial wrote to Delany, and sent a copy of his reply to the rector of Gardiner Street. Fr Conmee, on 7 February, declared himself 'very edified' by Delany's letter. He was sure that he meant 'to obey in spirit and in fact', but from a conversation which he had had with Fr Pettit, the archbishop's secretary, he gathered that considerable damage had been done already. 'The archbishop was much pained by everything', and Delany's view was generally accepted as 'the Jesuit view'. Dr Walsh, Fr Pettit said, was aware that he was 'most eager and zealous in private propagandism for his theory', and in 'privately speaking against the archbishop'. His doings and those of Fr Darlington were communicated extensively to His Grace, and, Fr Pettit alleged, 'the want of truth and equivocation of Fr Delany' was known to laymen and much commented on by them. He believed that the university question would not, however, be influenced by him since he had 'very little support', and he anticipated 'the triumph of the Trinity plan and a bad beating for Delany'.

The following day, Fr Conmee wrote again. He had spoken very frankly to Fr Delany, 'making him see that the archbishop was much offended, in danger of being substantially alienated, not improbably victorious in the present struggle, and being supplied with his (Delany's) opinions even by some in whom he confided'. The reproof was well taken, but did not seem to have much effect. 'He took refuge in a torrent of argument and would seem, indeed, to be almost a monomaniac on the view he takes'. Fr Conmee also recalled further details of his meeting with the archbishop's secretary. Fr Pettit had said that there was no good in explaining to the archbishop that the Society as a whole was not involved. 'The harm is now done and he does not want to hear anything'. And, turning sharply to Fr Conmee, Fr Pettit had added: 'The archbishop knows well he hates him'. When Conmee deprecated this, the reply was: 'Well you see you were very wrong in your views of the Drummond and Darlington affairs before. You don't know all'. He believed that Fr Pettit's confidence that Delany would be defeated was an indication that episcopal opinion must be against Delany's view. He concluded with an appeal:

These and similar things make me regard the situation as

grave. And in these days when the Society has so much to suffer and accusations of intrigue and insincerity against it are common, isn't it common sense to cut ourselves off from even the appearance of it now when the issue at stake is really of no importance to us at all. The spectacle of Fr Delany in open conflict with his bishop will not gain us the favour of priests and prelates *anywhere* let him think what he likes.

The main effect of the correspondence seems to have been that Delany merely refrained from attacking the Dublin University scheme in public. He remained a conscientious objector, and in the course of a letter to the provincial on 3 March drew his attention to 'the *Mail* of Tuesday' which indicated that the archbishop was an exception among the bishops in his views on Trinity College.

That His Grace was not without a measure of support from the bishops was brought home sharply to him a few days later. A committee of lay Catholics met at the Shelbourne Hotel to press for a Catholic college within the University of Dublin. Its moving spirit was N.J. Synnott who had given evidence before the commission. Feeling that the commission's decision might be adversely influenced by this development, Delany expressed his fears in a letter to the cardinal. Dr Logue replied that he did not see the danger as real. The commission had given no indication of seriously considering any interference with Trinity College. Besides, he himself would prefer a Catholic college attached to Dublin University and equal in status to Trinity College, to a Catholic college engrafted to the Royal University; and he was not sure that he would not prefer such to the scheme of the bishop of Limerick with its 'very large concessions to meet prejudice'.

On 9 March 1902 Dr O'Dwyer expressed similar concern about the Committee of Lay Catholics, in a letter to Dr Donelly, and wondered to what extent the archbishop was with them. 'We were winning all along the line', he wrote, but now the opportunity was being given to 'Cadogan, or Wyndham, or Balfour to say "you have raised the very issue we sought to avoid and in such a way as to increase the weight of Irish Protestant opposition".' That, he concluded, 'is the position towards which we are being driven: and very probably that is the result which is being desired in more quarters than one'.[63] Later in the month, Dr Walsh published a pamphlet which pressed for equality between Catholics and Protestants either within Dublin University or in a common university including

Trinity College; and Mr Synnott's committee forwarded a petition to the commission signed by a thousand lay Catholics. The bishop of Limerick publicly attacked the petition in the *Freeman's Journal* on 20 March. It was not true, as had been implied, that the authorities of Dublin University supported the scheme advocated by the petition: on the contrary they were solidly opposed to it. What the signatories were asking, in effect, was for the commission to make no recommendation, and thereby they were destroying all chance of a settlement.

Almost a year more was to pass before the commission's report appeared. In the intervening months various rumours circulated as to its likely recommendations. Already before the hearings had concluded, Delany seemed to feel that the most that could be hoped for was an endowed Catholic college within the Royal University. He saw possibilities in this which made it preferable to a college in the University of Dublin. He wrote to the Chief Secretary, George Wyndham, with whom he had become friendly, in support of the Royal scheme. Wyndham replying on 26 June 1902, expressed his determination to do all in his power to provide university education for the Catholics of Ireland. He thought the prospect was 'rosier than at any previous period'. His personal preference, however, was for 'adding a Catholic college, equated with Trinity, to the Dublin University', but he quite saw 'the tactical advantages of looking rather towards the Royal'. Dr O'Dwyer, as the year drew to a close, had heard that the commission was hesitating in its recommendation and, in a sarcastic letter to Wilfrid Ward, concluded that an equitable solution would be shirked in the interest of the 'twenty-six per cent of the population who are Protestants'.[64] Ward forwarded the letter to fellow commissioner, Henry Butcher, whom he thought of as 'the perfect educationalist, as free from religious bias as any Irish Protestant could be'. Butcher replied that the difficulty lay not so much in what Presbyterians or Protestant Episcopalians thought or said in Ireland 'as in the fact that educated thought, no less than popular opinion, in every part of the world' had set itself against a denominational type university strongly influenced by ecclesiastics. The most effective way, he suggested, to combat this 'undenominational view' was for the Church to support the setting up of a great autonomous college which, if it worked genuinely for the advancement of learning, would remove 'theoretic objections to founding a university which *in essence* cannot but be denominational'. But Dr O'Dwyer, he concluded, seemed 'unable to appreciate the difficulties, except from the narrow Hibernian view of contending sects in that island'.[65]

The commission's report appeared on 23 February 1903. It was indecisive. Although all but one of the commissioners signed it,[66] they added reservations which in most cases were equivalent to withdrawals of signatures. A Catholic university was declared inadvisable. It was agreed that it would establish equality, that it would be strongly supported by Catholics, and would raise up 'a strong academic class' likely 'to exercise a liberalising influence and to compete in influence with the clerics', but there was an 'intrinsic objection' to giving the right to confer degrees 'to an institution intended for one religious denomination and largely controlled by ecclesiastics', and there was the 'insoluble' difficulty that its establishment entailed the opening of another university in Belfast, which would be unfavourably received because it would be seen as a consequence of the much disliked Roman Catholic university.

The suggested alternative was a reorganisation of the Royal as a teaching university, having the Queen's Colleges and a new college for Catholics as its constituent institutions. This compromise scheme had a number of features likely to recommend it to Catholics. It granted considerable autonomy to each college, and proposed machinery likely to remove the former grounds for complaint against the system of examinations and to assure the bishops that nothing would be taught or published in the Catholic college contrary to the teachings of the Church. On the other hand, Maynooth and Magee College were to be excluded from affiliation; and Queen's College, Belfast — though not Cork and Galway — was to receive more money, a larger staff, and additional buildings. The result was a hotch-potch. Lord Robertson, in a rider which seemed to have Dr Walsh in mind, conceded that it would not satisfy 'those who determine Roman Catholic opinion', and that most authoritative opinions contrary to it had been expressed.[67]

Thus, Dr O'Dwyer's bold stroke had failed. It had had, in fact, little chance of success. However well founded the indignant allegations of Irish Catholics that their just demands had been sacrificed to Presbyterian 'intolerance' and to the 'ascendancy bigotry' of the senior fellows of Trinity College;[68] and however insensitive many of the commissioners showed themselves to the Catholic nature of the country and unsympathetic to its views,[69] the reality was that the 'consolidated opinion' of the time, in Professor Butcher's phrase, considered such control as the bishops sought — limited though it had become — to be unacceptable, and felt itself committed, where Catholics were concerned, to a system of education which was expressly

undenominational. The privileged form of undenominationalism
in operation in Trinity College was not for them.

The royal commission, nevertheless, had brought the cause of
university education a long step forward. It had conceded that
outside Dublin University there were no higher education
facilities worthy of the name, and that the Catholic majority,
unable to attend Trinity College because of conscientious convictions, suffered, in consequence, severe disabilities which were
a source of evil not only to Ireland, but even to the empire.
Much valuable information, moreover, had been brought
together and rendered accessible. 'I really hope', Ward wrote
to Arthur Balfour, 'that Dr O'Dwyer and others have forged
weapons which you will be able to use with effect in parliament'.[70] Five years later, in fact, on the occasion of the
national university bill, Mr Birrell and other speakers were
to make considerable use of the information supplied to the
Robertson Commission.[71] Finally, the idea of an autonomous,
national university had been well aired by witnesses before the
commission and in written submissions to it.[72] Meanwhile,
however, the commission's recommendations were an embarrassment to the government and were received with disappointment
and disillusionment by the Catholic bishops and interested laity.
Activity on the university question was virtually suspended for
some months.

The preparations for the Robertson Commission and the
subsequent controversy took their toll of Delany's health. Over
the next few years recurring bouts of exhaustion would oblige
him to leave the college for a time. His usual places of recupera-
tion were the Lucan Spa and his niece's house at Raheny, then
quite remote from Dublin. At each he received permission from
the archbishop to celebrate mass privately. His Grace's approval
was also readily obtained, in very different circumstances, when
Delany sought permission to say mass from time to time at the
home of Sir Anthony MacDonnell, the Under Secretary at Dublin
Castle, for the sake of Lady MacDonnell who had a serious
heart condition. Indeed, at Delany's request he overruled the
parish priest and permitted her to receive Communion without
fasting.[73] Thus, despite the jeremiads of Fr Pettit, relations
between him and Dr Walsh were maintained at a cordial level.
As his friendship with Wyndham remained undisturbed by the
Chief Secretary's preference for a Catholic college in Dublin University, similarly, differences on educational policy with the
archbishop were not allowed to sour their personal relationships.

During 1904, in particular, a variety of pressures sapped his strength. His sister, a nun, suffered a nervous break-down and required his help for a considerable time — and here again he experienced much sympathy and support from Dr Walsh;[74] the students at University College, following the severe criticisms of the Royal University during the commission's hearings, were adopting a belligerent pose towards the university and the government and thereby, in Delany's view, playing into the hands of hostile critics; and he was very actively engaged in writing and negotiating on the university question. Hence, when in May 1904 the archbishop invited him to give the annual retreat at Maynooth he had to regretfully decline on his doctor's orders. 'Sir Francis Cruise puts a peremptory prohibition on my attempting it. My heart has been again a source of trouble and my old ailment — want of sleep — comes back pretty often and leaves me quite exhausted, and incapable of any sustained effort'.[75] He was in his seventieth year. His incapacity 'for any sustained effort' did not prevent him, nevertheless, in that year, and for another six marked by even greater pressures, from getting through a herculean amount of work. His resilience was remarkable. The following autumn, subsequent to an instruction from the General to take all possible care of his health, he wrote to the provincial:

> I am not equal as heretofore to any prolonged strain involving spells of insomnia, but on the whole by taking things quietly I get very fair health, thank God, and I really see no necessity for any 'coddling' — all the less, as everyone here, and your Rev. with them, quite overwhelm me with kindness and consideration.

Meanwhile the summer of 1903 brought a pleasant distraction. A visit from King Edward VII and Queen Alexandria was scheduled for July. Delany was called on to assist in the arrangements and seems to have enjoyed himself immensely. On 10 August he sent an account of it all to Rome, together with a report on the college's outstanding examination results for that year. Fr J.P. Chandlery, replying for the Jesuit Assistant-General on 2 September, thanked him for his letter, the contents of which he had communicated to the General, 'and for the illustrated paper *Ireland*, full of exquisite illustrations of the king and queen's visit to Ireland'. He had read to the General, he continued, 'the part of the letter in which you speak of the arrangements for visits to Catholic institutions, and of the part you had in these arrangements; also of the visit to Maynooth and to the Hospital of Mercy, in which latter place the arch-bishop and your Rev. accompanied the queen around the wards. The king's visit has left an excellent impression in Ireland, and I hope it will be repeated next year'. Then turning to the examination results, he extended from the Fr Assistant and himself 'hearty congratulations . . . on the brilliant success' and continued warmly — 'I doubt if there is a Jesuit college in the world (now that the *Rue de Postes* is gone) that gives so much glory to the Society as yours. Fr General will write soon and send *his* congratulations. It is marvellous how, year after year, you are able to achieve such extraordinary results, overtopping the results of the three Queen's Colleges taken together'.

Fr Chandlery's response reflected the euphoria generated by the royal visit. Even 'the chief justice', Wyndham informed his mother, 'makes jokes about the millenium from the bench'. The king and queen, on 22 July, were greeted by 'eleven miles of bunting and cheering crowds' as they travelled in an open carriage from Kingstown to the Phoenix Park. Too seldom, the Chief Secretary exulted, had the Irish 'been given a channel for their loyalty'.[76] Many of the younger generation of Irish subjects, however, if some of their Jesuit contemporaries were any indication, treated the occasion with less enthusiasm and the excitement of their elders with a degree of condescension. One such indication was Michael Egan, a lecturer in mathematics and a member of the Jesuit staff at University College. He became noted in later life for his astringent wit and tall stories, and his gifts as a spiritual counsellor. As the most junior member of a seasoned Jesuit staff, he seemed to have felt aggrieved at being put regularly in his place by older associates and har-boured resentment against the rector. Hence, many years later he still retailed with satisfaction the following anecdote at Delany's expense.[77]

The royal procession was scheduled to pass along Stephen's Green. The entire Jesuit community waited on the steps of no. 86, with the rector on the top step wearing a silk top hat above his Jesuit gown. Michael Egan was in front a few steps lower down. 'Presently the royal carriage passed and William Delany took off his hat and with a superb and sumptuous gesture swept it towards the ground, bending forward courteously at the same time. The king had not seen, but the queen had. She returned the salute and nudged the king, who then took off his hat with a most royal gesture and bowed most regally. The carriage moved on, but the Rev William Delany remained bent in reverence.

'Did you see the queen nudge the king?' asked the Rev O'Neill.

'I did indeed, and what is more I heard what she said to him,' responded Michael Egan.

'What did she say?' asked the Rev William Delany eagerly. 'What did she say?'

'Oh, she said: Do you see that young man in front? That's young Egan, the mathematician!'

'Young Egan', apparently, chuckled with delight. His audience was not amused.

It is not clear to what extent the anecdote was embellished by the teller's puckish sense of humour, but it captures something of the special atmosphere of those weeks. The excited optimism of the time, following on his successful Land Act, seems to have quite intoxicated George Wyndham. 'They do believe in me', he wrote, 'and tremble towards a belief in the empire because of belief in me. By "they" I mean the whole lot — Unionist, Nationalist, Celtic, Norman, Elizabethan, Cromwellian, Williamite, agriculturalist and industrialist, educationist, and folklorist. . . . We must give the Irish something sensible to think about and work for. Otherwise they relapse into the position of being mere pawns in the game between rival politicians'.[78] Seldom had a politician so misread a political situation, or so misjudged his personal influence.

Wyndham's desire, nevertheless, to give the Irish 'something sensible to work for' brought the university question to life once more. Urged on by his Under Secretary, Sir Anthony MacDonnell, he believed the time was right for a solution. The hierarchy was now 'in a mood to take what they can get'.[79] *The Times* reported in October 1903 that the Chief Secretary had plans for a national university consisting of three institutions on an equal footing: Trinity College, Queen's College, Belfast, and a third college so constituted as to be acceptable to Catholics. On 1 January 1904 the same paper carried an appeal from Lord Dunraven to his fellow Irish Protestants to support a scheme on the lines of Wyndham's reported plans. The Earl of Dunraven, who had played a prominent part in the lead up to Wyndham's Land Act, combined a reputation as an international yachtsman with that of an improving landlord. He was particularly sympathetic to Catholic claims, his father having been one of a remarkable triumvirate of converts to Catholicism who owned neighbouring estates in County Limerick — Dunraven, Emly, and de Vere — and who were gifted with high moral and intellectual qualities. His proposals on university education became known as the Dunraven-Wyndham scheme.

Three days later the Bishop and Mayor of Limerick called a public meeting 'in support of the claims of the Irish people for a reform of the existing system of university education'.[80] Other bishops followed Dr O'Dwyer's lead, summoning gatherings addressed by Protestants as well as Catholics. Dr Walsh, too, indicated that the hierarchy was in a mood to take what they could get. He informed J.J. Clancy, M.P., on 3 February 1904, that their lordships were prepared to accept 'either the settlement known as the Dunraven scheme or that proposed by the Robertson Commission';[81] and he presided at a large public meeting at the Mansion House. Mr Wyndham's known commitment and the conjunction of Catholics and liberal Protestants raised high hopes of a solution.

The new proposals were not welcomed, however, by the Dublin University authorities or the governing body of Queen's College, Belfast. Dr J.P. Mahaffy informed the bishop of Limerick in a 'private, confidential' note on 14 February, 1904, that he would find the Trinity College governing body 'the most determined opponents' of what he might consider 'the legitimate Catholic claims'. 'Do not imagine that you will get any help from them. They have spoken out against the Dunraven scheme because it seemed the most reasonable, and therefore to them the most danger'.[82] The governing body of Queen's College, Belfast, meanwhile, had embarrassed the government by sending in a memorial to the Lord Lieutenant on 30 December 1903, requesting increased aid from public funds, in line with the Robertson Report, and urging that the consideration of their claims be given priority and not be postponed until the more complicated question of Irish university education was dealt with in its entirety.

Delany, in a public letter to the Lord Lieutenant on 11 January 1904, protested against Belfast's claims receiving prior consideration to the educational needs of the majority population. He did so, he declared, 'on the plain and simple issue of educational fair play, and of the equitable and economic distribution of public educational funds'; and he assumed — 'as an admitted principle of equitable, economic administration of public educational funds' — that 'the endowments granted to public teaching institutions should bear some reasonable proportion to the quantity and quality of the educational work which they accomplish; that institutions which have proved their success should be fostered and developed; and that where institutions after years of trial have proved a failure, the public funds should no longer be wasted on them'. He then went on to point out that while the total Queen's Colleges' estimates for 1903-4 came to £34,966, University College had to survive on £4,500, gained entirely from the fellows' salaries, and that despite this inequality of treatment it had obtained over the previous nine years more distinctions than any of the Queen's Colleges and had gained more first-class distinctions than the three colleges together. In the light of these facts and figures he failed to see how Belfast's request for priority of treatment could be maintained; and in the face of such evidence, also, he would ask: 'what becomes of the charges so flippantly made of "limitations of thought", of "clerical obscuratism" with regard to scientific teaching, of the "danger of low standards in a Catholic college or university"?' University College had been variously accused of 'sectarian exclusiveness', being a 'clerical seminary', 'a college for private profit', and subject to 'episcopal and clerical domination'. Did these bear scrutiny, and how did the college compare with Belfast in their regard?

The Stephen's Green institution was open to all denominations and had a much larger percentage of non-Catholics than Belfast had of Catholics. Its professional staff was composed of fifteen professors and six tutors. Five of the twenty-one were priests; but on the professional staff there had always been 'one or more Protestant professors'. On the college's governing council of six members, five were laymen and one of them a Protestant. In Belfast, by comparison, there had never been a Roman Catholic professor in the faculty of Arts, and this was by express policy accepted by the government. In Cork and Galway, though set in almost entirely Catholic areas and originally established to serve Roman Catholics, there was not in the Cork college a single Roman Catholic professor in the faculty of Arts, and in Galway, out of twenty professors, there were only two. It was not surprising, then, that the Catholic bishops 'discountenanced the attendance of Roman Catholic students at colleges so constituted'; and the charge of 'illiberality' and 'sectarianism' did not come well from those who practised an open sectarianism accepted by the government. He went on to give clear instances of government appointments to Belfast, and even to Galway, based 'on purely religious and denominational grounds', and wondered if it was too much to ask that the religious convictions of the vast majority of the Irish people 'receive at length some small measure of the consideration' that had been given 'so abundantly and for so long a time to Irish Protestants and Irish Presbyterians?'

The remaining charges were disposed of briskly. A 'clerical seminary'? Over ninety-five per cent of the students were preparing for purely secular pursuits, and they included often from twenty to thirty women students; while in Belfast, by comparison, a large proportion of Arts graduates were preparing to enter the Presbyterian ministry. As to the college making 'private profit', he outlined its resources and showed that far from making profit there was, in fact, a deficit for which he as president, though receiving no salary, made himself responsible. With reference to 'episcopal and clerical domination', he carefully pointed out that the Catholic bishops had never once interfered in the administration of University College even though it was their property.

He dealt with these charges, he said, to correct the erroneous notions which many seemed to entertain of what the spirit and management was likely to be of such a college as the Catholics sought. And, with the Dunraven-Wyndham scheme in mind, he spelled out once more the nature of such an establishment: 'A college as satisfactory to Catholics in every respect – in its faculties, in its equipment, endowment and autonomous government – as Trinity College is to Protestants; a college without tests, and open to all, the best man winning, whether priest or layman, and administered, not as University College has been, by any section of Catholics, but by an academical body truly representing and enjoying the confidence of the whole Catholic community – bishops, clergy, and laity alike'. To prevent any possible misconception, he repeated his evidence before the Robertson Commission that he did not see the new Catholic college as in any way under Jesuit management.

In conclusion, he insisted that it was evident that Belfast's claims for priority could not be maintained; that the heavy expenditure on Cork and Galway, 'in their present condition', was indefensible 'on any principle of just and economic administration of public funds'; that the prevailing distribution of public funds for higher education was both economically and educationally unwise and unjust and that, in consequence, it was a matter of urgency 'that the question of higher education in Ireland be dealt with at once by the government'.[83]

The cabinet found itself in a delicate situation. It could not very well grant Belfast's request, which had been recommended by the Robertson Commission, without implementing the commission's proposal regarding the Catholic college – a proposal which would not be universally accepted in Ireland as a final solution and would prove unpopular with many English and Scotch members of parliament. The upshot was that, despite the government's large majority in both houses, Mr Wyndham was obliged to announce on 3 February 1904 that while it was his opinion that Ireland required 'greater opportunities for higher education' these could not be obtained until there was 'substantial agreement between all parties interested'. 'The government', he added, 'do not mean to bring in any measure dealing with the Irish university question'.

Disappointment at the government's apparent tergiversation was intense. Archbishop Walsh, according to his biographer, was so disgusted that he came to the point of giving his support to Arthur Griffith's abstentionist 'Hungarian policy'.[84] Delany's disappointment was tinged with the hope that Wyndham's declaration might be just a temporary expedient, and he determined to keep the issue alive. Thus, on 6 March he wrote to the Chief Secretary in connection with newspaper reports that Ulster Unionist members of parliament were to see him to press again for an increased endowment for Queen's College, Belfast. His letter ran to twelve pages. He hoped that no such endowment would be given except as part of a general settlement of the university question. He reminded Wyndham of the lines of solution he had proposed to him some weeks previously at Castle Bellingham. He should point out to the Ulster members that 'the attainment of their object rests with themselves'. At present it was Belfast, in practice, that blocked the scheme of the royal commission. They feared 'they would be hopelessly defeated in the competitions of the joint university' if there was 'a fully endowed Catholic college'. The solution was for them to have their own university. Then there would be equality of conditions for Protestants (Trinity College), Presbyterians, and Catholics. Hence he suggested that Wyndham, in his 'masterly way', should urge them to prevail on 'the Belfast Corporation and the local bodies which they themselves represent and local magnates — like Lords Londonderry, Dufferin and Shaftesbury — to join with them in putting before the government the claims of a great, progressive, industrial city like Belfast to have a separate university of its own, such as Manchester, Liverpool and Birmingham have got, and Sheffield has just been promised.' Such a university 'could evolve on its own lines in harmony with its own environment as a great modern university, where practical and industrial science would hold its proper place; whereas, by remaining in the Royal University where other ideas and other influences find a place, such development could not be worked out at all so satisfactorily'. In short, he was urging the Chief Secretary to convince them that they should face at once 'the necessity of a distinct university of their own for Belfast and the North, governed, not by Dublin and "the bishops and the Jesuits", but by Belfast and the North themselves'. Such an arrangement, he added, would also solve the university question for Catholics without raising 'the denominational bogey'.

Dr O'Dwyer, writing to Delany regarding the Ulster M.Ps., two days later, commented in more austere terms:

> The Belfast deputation will be a great chance for Wyndham; but you may make up your mind that, having come down on the wrong side of the fence, he will stay there. The one thing to do is to turn him and his party out.

John Morley was even more pessimistic. 'The government', he wrote on 4 April 1904, 'dare not in their present mess touch a question which would complete their ruin in• Scotland and alienate Orangemen in strongholds in Lancashire'. The Liberals, on the other hand, were 'anti-denominational in principle or profession' and were currently 'vehemently anti-denominational in respect of the battle over the schools'. Hence, in his view, it would be easier at this particular time to propose Home Rule itself 'than Catholic endowment in any shape'. The government would probably hold on until Easter, but whenever the election hour struck, this year or next, they would certainly be replaced. The tragedy was that their successors had 'not a rag of Irish policy'. He would continue his efforts without faltering, he concluded, but 'it is not necessary to tell you the stars are fighting in the courses against you'.

Delany, meanwhile, had determined to keep the issue alive by canvassing as widely as possible for an acceptable settlement. To this end he hurriedly put together a pamphlet making a strong case for the just and equitable treatment of the Catholic majority. It appeared in April 1904 under the title *Irish university education, facts and figures, a plea for fair play*. It was well received and ran to four editions. It had four main sections.

The first was a re-print of his open letter to the Lord Lieutenant. The second concentrated on the Queen's Colleges, and on Cork and Galway in particular, as a means of meeting the needs of the Catholic population. They had not only been educationally unsuccessful, he argued, they were an imposition by the government on the overwhelming majority of the Irish people in support of 'a mere handful of secularists' who, under the guise of removing the old system of religious ascendancy and intolerance exercised by a Protestant minority, had built up 'a new and, to Catholics, a much more objectionable ascendancy of *anti-religious* intolerance'. The third section dealt with the argument that Trinity College, as an 'undenominational' institution, offered a way forward. He pointed out that although Fawcett's Act of 1873 had abolished religious tests, Trinity, on the testimony of its own supporters, was 'distinctly Protestant' in its government and policy. The governing body in that year, 1904, consisted of a provost and seven senior fellows, all of them Protestants and four of them clergymen, and all holding office for life. There was but one Catholic junior fellow who, on the average, would have to wait forty years before becoming a senior fellow and having a place on the governing body. He appealed to all those Anglicans, nonconformists, Protestants and Orangemen who, however hostile to the Church of Rome, 'did not permit their hostility to blind them to reason', whether they would require Catholics, in such circumstances, to attend Trinity College. The incongruity of such a requirement was spotlighted by two apposite analogies.

> If a Roman Catholic priest were appointed president of Queen's College, Belfast, with all the professors also Catholic, would you tell the (Presbyterian) General Assembly that they must accept such a situation, and hold that their students were at no disadvantage? And would they listen to you?

Again, if in an English town, where three-fourths of the population was nonconformist, the only school, and maintained by public funds, was an Anglican school originally founded for the spread of Anglicanism amongst the nonconformists, and since then entirely controlled by Anglicans, with Anglican teachers and Anglican reading books — 'would you, I ask, hold that nonconformist parents and children in that town were at no grievous disadvantage? Would you call them "sectarian" and "illiberal" and "priestridden" if they protested that as taxpaying citizens they should have fair play; and that they, who were the majority, were surely entitled to equal privileges with the minority — to at least an equally well-provided school of their own?'

He moved from there to the reasonable claims of the Irish bishops. 'For educational as well as for religious reasons they would prefer a separate university for Catholics', but they had declared their willingness 'to accept an undenominational joint university, either a modified University of Dublin or a Royal University modified according to the suggestions of the University Commission'. Moreover, far from seeking an episcopal or clerical dominance over the university, they had declared again and again that they would accept 'a governing body predominantly lay'. Hence, the old excuses were obsolete. The Catholic bishops could no longer be dismissed as 'impracticable'. Where, then, did the obstacle lie? Successive Lord Lieutenants and Chief Secretaries for thirty years had acknowledged the justice of the Catholics' claims. The Robertson Commission had recommended a solution which the bishops were prepared to accept. Yet, a sympathetic prime minister, Lord Lieutenant and Chief Secretary had declined to take action upon that recommendation, and the Chief Secretary had informed the House of Commons that the matter 'could not be settled until there was a general agreement about it in Ireland'. This, Delany commented, was equivalent to saying in other words 'that three million Irish Catholics must wait for the removal of their acknowledged educational grievances, until it shall please some thousands of Ulster Orangemen generously to concede it'. 'Was not such a reply,' he asked, 'after fifty years waiting, plainly tantamount to a declaration that in the matter of higher education Irish Catholics cannot expect justice from a parliament at Westminster?' Surely that declaration could not be regarded 'as the final word of English statesmanship in reply to the demands of Irish Catholics for educational fair play?'

A brief concluding section dealt with the objection that there was not a sufficient number of Catholic students qualified for university education. With facts and figures he made the case that the number of Catholics 'thoroughly qualified to receive profitably a university education, if suitably provided for them', was larger than that of all other denominations. By 'suitably provided' he meant that the university facilities should be 'suitable to the social conditions and to the manifold, urgent, industrial needs of the Irish Catholic population'. It was a theme to which he was to return with increasing urgency as a settlement drew near. Neither Trinity College nor the Queen's Colleges provided a type of university education geared to such practical and social requirements.

A plea for fair play was generally acknowledged as a skilful presentation of the Catholic case: 'admirably free' — in the judgement of Betty Balfour, wife of the former Chief Secretary,

Gerald Balfour — 'from bitterness or party spirit'.[85] It earned
for its author congratulations and support from people of
different religious belief, some of them members of the government. He sent copies to each of his many friends and acquaintances in Ireland and Britain with a view to clarifying for them,
if not converting them to, the reality of the Catholic grievance.
He urged them to disseminate the publication. He was left in no
doubt as to the need for such clarification. 'It is impossible to
overestimate the prejudice here,' Mrs Alice Stopford Green
wrote to him from London on 23 April 1904. 'I find that even
a man like Mr Bryce is saturated with it'. A week or so later,
3 May, Delany told the archbishop that Sir Anthony MacDonnell
had informed him that people were dinning into the ears of
the authorities that 'there was really no need of a university
measure, that there was no one qualified to profit by it . . . that
Catholics were all illiterate peasants'.

MacDonnell was still seeking a solution to the university
problem. On 29 April he informed Delany that he had drafted a
scheme on the basis of the royal commission's report, but was
faced with the objection that if Roman Catholics had a university they would be unable to fill it; that, therefore, the provision
of such could not be justified financially, and that Trinity
College was quite sufficient for the relatively few who sought a
teaching university. The objection had already been met in *A
plea for fair play*. Replying to MacDonnell on 1 May, however,
Delany geared his answer to undermine the limited and exclusive
concept of university education which had fathered the objection. It had its origin, he believed, in those better class 'educated
Roman Catholics' of the Trinity College type. Hence, having
reiterated some of the information supplied in his pamphlet, he
emphasised the social and practical rôle of a modern university
and represented this personal vision, not then widely shared, as
that of the Catholic majority. Catholics, he said, did not want a
university of the Trinity College type at all. They sought 'a
university to fit Irish Catholics of every sphere in life to live and
to prosper in Ireland today. . . . They want *to live* and therefore
want a university of today to suit the life of today'. They did
not want a university of the better classes to manufacture a
larger number of barristers or office-seekers, they wanted 'to
give every boy of all classes the best possible education in each
and all the manifold, daily increasing branches of knowledge
that play such a leading part in promoting the industrial welfare
of the country'. As to the financial investment involved, no one
questioned 'that the prosperity of Scotland at home and the

demand for Scotchmen abroad' was largely due to its four teaching universities. He would ask Sir Anthony's objectors what was the annual expense of students at any of those four universities, and whether they would hold that only a few Irish Catholics could afford it? He would also ask at what figure they estimated the average cost of a Trinity College degree? The great majority of Trinity students were not resident. They lived in lodgings in town; the average cost of these during term need not exceed £60 to £70, and many students, as he knew, managed on £30 to £40; and this in a situation where there were no scholarships or student exhibitions to help them. Hence, he did not see that the financial argument presented a major difficulty.

As the months passed, however, it became apparent that no amount of persuasive reasoning would move the government. MacDonnell's and Wyndham's hopes of salvaging something had to give way to the cabinet's fear of extreme unionist opinion in Ireland, Scotland and Lancashire. Hence, on 3 August 1904, in the course of the debate on the grant-in-aid to the Queen's Colleges, the unhappy Chief Secretary reiterated that the government would do nothing on the university question, and declared that it had never pledged itself to do anything. He was championing his colleagues at his own expense. It was a turning point in his career. Some six months later — following a storm of opposition from Irish Unionists to his plan to grant a measure of local authority within the existing constitution — he felt obliged to resign. The resignation came more than six months too late. 'The whole lot' no longer believed in him. Ironically and sadly, they were convinced they were being used 'as pawns in the game between rival politicians'. Orangemen viewed him as part of a conspiracy to force Protestantism out of Ireland. Catholics were indignant at being sacrificed to Orange prejudice. There was hardly a statesman of first rank, Dr O'Dwyer thundered in a pamphlet on *The present condition of university education in Ireland*, who did not admit the justice of the Catholic claims. But that was not enough for Mr Wyndham.

We, Irish Catholics, must submit our claims to the judgement of the Orange opposition. They are a handful; we are the nation; you count them by thousands; we are millions; yet in the counsels of Mr Wyndham the clamour of this handful of fanatics counts for more than the claims and needs of the whole nation. Yet Englishmen cannot understand the implacable feeling of the Irish heart that will never soften to them nor to their government.[86]

Rarely had a Chief Secretaryship promised so much and ended in so much disappointment. He had set out with an unique advantage. His mother had been born in Ireland and was a descendant of Lord Edward Fitzgerald, a leader of the 1798 insurrection. These grounds for popularity with the Catholic majority were increased by his liking for meeting people and visiting various parts of the country. To these were added literary ability, oratorical power, an able, driving personality, a sense of humour, and an enquiring mind; an acquaintance recalled an occasion after dinner when he 'put Fr Delany through a searching enquiry into the Society of Jesus, the power and functions of the General and provincials, on the status of everyone from the lay-brother to the top-dog'.[87] And he was clearly interested in benefiting the country. 'I want', he wrote in November 1901, 'to smash the agitation, introduce a land bill, get money for a harbour-fishing industry in the west, and float a Catholic university. After that anyone can be a minister who prefers missing all the joys of life'.[88] To these ends he introduced as his under-secretary, Sir Anthony MacDonnell, a Catholic and an Irishman, who had shown himself a forceful, independent-minded civil servant in the Indian service. MacDonnell sought to render British government in Ireland healing and efficient. It was a formidable task. Dublin Castle – in appearance 'a minor Kremlin half-screened by a curtain of business houses'[89] – enjoyed a sinister reputation in Irish history and the Irish executive was far from efficient. The whole system of government, Winston Churchill commented in 1905, 'was not democratic, autocratic, or even oligarchic. The land was hag-ridden by forty-one semi-independent boards, which overlapped in all directions'[90] and were financed from different sources. Their efforts to bring order into this relative chaos and to give Irishmen a larger opportunity to rule themselves, led Wyndham first, and later MacDonnell, into situations of conflict where they felt obliged to resign from office. Where the Chief Secretary was concerned, however, the turning point was the university question. Up to that it had been flowers all the way. His weakness on that issue marked a downturn in his popularity and the uprise of opposition to him.

Delany was one of a minority who showed sympathy and understanding towards him. To the provincial he commented that he was 'very sorry for him'. 'The very fact of the appointment of Sir Anthony', he said, 'shows how sympathetic and advanced in his views Wyndham was and what he really hoped and desired to see accomplished. That he has shown deplorable weakness is true, and his career is seriously damaged by it, but I cannot forget that he unquestionably brought to the Chief Secretary's office much more sympathetic and advanced views regarding Irish administration than we are likely to have from any Conservative who may take his place'. He wrote to Wyndham in the wake of the criticism which followed his retraction on the university issue. The Chief Secretary replied on 13 October expressing his thanks for 'words written in kindness and charity, of which there are not many'. It would be unreasonable, he wrote, 'to expect from Irish Catholics a full knowledge of the trend and resultants of political forces in England. We have not yet invented a political equivalent for steam, and must make the best of such winds as there are'. He had no doubt as to the destination he wished to reach and was impatient to find himself 'politically weather-bound'. He urged Delany to 'refrain from saying or writing words which might again raise false hopes of early accomplishment'. The disappointments of the past year had tended to confirm his original opinion that it was useless to patch up Irish education at secondary and primary level until the question of higher education was settled in principle.

On 30 October 1904 he wrote to Delany for the last time as Chief Secretary. Delany had written to congratulate him on his appointment of Professor Bertram Windle as president of Queen's College Cork. In reply he commented rather sadly:

> Until something effective can be done for higher education on a broad basis nothing better presents itself than to pursue the modest task of refuting the alleged dearth of eligible Catholics by a series of practical demonstrations. This is one of them. Prof. Windle is to have a seat in the senate. That was part of my plan.

The choice of Windle, in Delany's view, was an excellent one. He had been professor of anatomy and dean of the medical faculty at Birmingham University, and though the son of an English Protestant clergyman he became while still in England an active supporter of Home Rule, the Gaelic League and the Land League; and, after passing through a stage of agnosticism, he became also a Roman Catholic. He was to become an outstanding president of the Cork college.[91] On 7 November Delany invited Dr Walsh to dine with Windle and himself at University College. He had received splendid reports from England of Windle's work for Catholic education and learned that the new president had accepted Cork at a pecuniary loss in order 'to help forward the proper solution of the university question'. Windle's views on the 'proper solution' coincided with Delany's! He was to prove a strong support to him in the negotiations leading to the final settlement.

From Wyndham's statement in August 1904 until the replacement of the Tory government early in 1906 there was practically a complete silence in parliament on the university question, and an almost complete cessation of agitation in Ireland. Disillusionment with the political parties was widespread, but a greater unification in Catholic feeling and efforts was perceptible and a tendency to look inward for answers.

The disillusionment was voiced by Dr Francis R. Cruise in a perceptive contribution to the *Daily Chronicle* on 29 November 1905. He looked back on fifty years of unceasing struggle by Catholics for university education and the 'total failure' of it all, 'despite all the fair words and broken promises'. He was not a Home Ruler, but he was not surprised that so many Irish people were disaffected. The refusal to grant equality with others in higher education could not but render them disaffected and a danger to the union. Some politicians spoke of the loyalist minority in Ireland as compared to the majority. They omit to ask 'how long would the minority remain loyal if treated on the lines meted out to the majority?' So long as Ireland was ruled in the interest of the minority, to the crushing disadvantage of the majority, 'and its executive influenced by a band of Ulster extremists', it would continue 'to be largely disaffected, and to go from bad to worse' — if this were possible. 'The bane of English rule in Ireland', he concluded, 'seems to lie in unreasonable delay in conceding reasonable demands. Thus the psychological moment is lost wherein good might be done, gratitude earned, and solid peace secured. Under the existing regime all these are forfeited, and a prize set upon agitation and its dangerous consequences — the only means by which any concession is ever obtained'.

A manifestation of the trend towards greater unification was supplied by Dr Walsh's public change of attitude to University College. In March 1904 he accepted an invitation to attend a function of the college sodality. He presided at the mass for the occasion and subsequently, in the great hall, addressed the professors, officials, and about one hundred graduates and undergraduates. The audience was surprised and gratified by his words.

He had always been grateful to the Jesuit Fathers, he said, 'for the great work that has been done in this place'. As a bishop, anxious for the advancement of the work of higher education in

Ireland, he felt that it would not be possible for him to err by excess in any statement he could make 'of the magnitude of the service that has been rendered to the cause of Catholic higher education in Ireland by the brilliantly successful work done by the Jesuit fathers and by the staff of this University College'. And developing the Gospel's injunction to 'seek first the kingdom of God and his justice, and all these things shall be added to you', he assured his younger hearers that, quite apart from spiritual benefits, they were far from being losers in the educational sense by attending University College. The brilliant successes of its students were for all to see. Finally, he expressed the hope that 'when the long looked for measure of justice at length comes to us' there would be nothing in it to stand in the way of the Jesuit fathers continuing, 'under happier auspices', with resources and amidst appropriate surroundings, 'those great services as teachers' which they had been rendering the cause of Irish higher education for the past twenty years 'with such fidelity, such constancy, such undaunted courage and, in spite of every difficulty and every drawback, with unprecedented and unparalleled success'.

William Delany was visibly moved. Indeed for some seconds, unusual for him, he was at a loss for words. It was a moment of very special gratification. He responded to the address with considerable emotion. 'To myself and to my colleagues', he said, 'nothing possibly could be more cheering or more gratifying than such a testimony from such a source; and, on their part and on my own, I thank him from all my heart'. With reference to His Grace's kind words regarding the future position of the Jesuits in any change for the better that might be hoped for, he would say what he had said before the Robertson Commission, namely, that the new institution 'should be national in its constitution, and be governed by a body thoroughly representative of the whole Catholic people'; and for the Jesuits he asked only 'what should be given to everyone else — simple fair play for each individual on his own merits'.[92]

Serious differences on educational policy would arise again between him and the archbishop, but towards the college from this point on His Grace showed a much more positive spirit. To him, it was clear that the hope of a university settlement rested on its success. Delany's aim of 1883 had been fulfilled. The capacity of Catholic students for higher learning had been proved beyond a doubt. The college stood out as a first-rate university institution in all but legal status and material facilities. Its shabby building on the side of the street was a standing reproach to the politics which refused it money so lavishly bestowed on its less successful rivals. The policy on the fellows had been fully vindicated. Most helpful of all, perhaps, was the pride in their association with the college exhibited by some of the most influential and critical of the younger generation.

T.M. Kettle pointed out in his paper *The Nationist* on 21 September 1905 that 'the higher education of Catholics in Ireland is at present entirely financed out of the salaries of six Jesuits'. The critics, he continued, had often urged that the Jesuits wished to continue their system and retain their control. He believed, on the contrary, that they were 'quite honest' in declaring 'their willingness to hand over University College to a more representative government, and to ask no other recognition for their services in raising the college to its present position save facilities to establish halls of residence in connection with it'. As to the eminence of that 'present position' he had no doubt. On 2 November he wrote:

> Once again the honours list of the Royal University is mainly a record of the success of University College. The institution has now passed beyond possibility of competition, it occupies incontestably the position of *the* university college of Ireland.

A week later he paid striking tribute to its wider university characteristics, distancing it as far as possible from what he called 'the paper pomposity of Earlsfort Terrace', a conduit-pipe to transmit it 'a scandalously inadequate trickle of public money' and to hamper it with 'unintelligent programmes' and disfigure its students with certificates and degrees. University College, though miserably equipped, was 'a centre of vital thought and culture'. It counted on its staff, 'lecturers as brilliant as are to be found in any university in Europe'; its students lived 'in a climate of true university ideas', creating by their own efforts 'societies of every kind which give free play to the impact of mind on mind'. The Irish public 'must master and remember the gulf of difference between a man who is simply a graduate of the Royal University of Ireland and one who is a student of University College. The one has earned an exam. brand; and the latter has spent his college career under the stimulus of some of the finest minds in Ireland'. And what he said of the college, applied with equal force to the Medical School, Cecilia Street. The commission's condemnation of the Royal University did not apply in any particular to University College. 'The Royal must go, the college, with change of management and constitution, must remain'.

Kettle's pride in what had been accomplished, Dr Walsh's eulogy of the college, as well as Dr O'Dwyer's trenchant pamphlet on university education, were echoes of the new feeling abroad that what was to be achieved would come from the Catholic majority's own efforts, not from the generosity of the imperial parliament. The gospel of self-help had been preached for some time. It had three main versions, each dealing with a different order of ideas and breathing a different spirit, but each concurring in the principle that hope was to be placed in Irish effort alone. Sir Horace Plunkett had been arguing for years that co-operation was the one hope of economic salvation; Arthur Griffith had been pleading that the elected representatives of Ireland should exert their energies at home and not at Westminster; and Douglas Hyde had been crying out that if Ireland lost her language she would lose her soul for ever. The three versions were supported and stimulated by the advocacy of a journalist of rare ability, D.P. Moran of the *Leader*. Of the three, Hyde's was the more powerful and pervasive in the early years of the new century.

The Gaelic League movement, though academic and non-political in its profession and aims, directly stimulated the heart and brain of the nation, calling on it for fearless self-examination; reminding it of its distinctive history, traditions, customs, character, thoughts, duties; forcing it to examine what it really had to be proud of, what it should cling to, what faults had done it harm and needed correction. Within a short time, as has been seen, the movement had taken a powerful hold on the country. Thousands, irrespective of class or creed, expressing their new found pride in national identity, devoted time in evening and day-time gatherings to the study and practice of the Irish language. The new tide of feeling and thought created cross-currents which bedevilled Delany's final years at Stephen's Green. In 1905, however, the immediate spur to a policy of self-help in university affairs came from, ironically, Trinity College.

Ever since the middle of the previous century, Dublin University had become more and more removed from the majority population. Its Protestant Episcopalian tradition, and its association with unionism and the ascendancy class, had divorced it from sympathy with the land agitation of the rural population and the political struggle for Home Rule. The Catholic bishops, in their preoccupation with the Protestant crusade of the 1840s and 1850s,[93] their fear of proselytism and later of liberalism and secularism, had sealed the divorce not only by forbidding

Catholics to attend Trinity College but by representing it as an alien and hostile enemy to Irish Catholicism and the people's aspirations. Increasingly, therefore, as the century progressed, Catholicism and national aspirations tended to become identified; and the Protestant inhabitants were seen, by and large, as but an extension of the British garrison. Trinity, with its financial security, its long tradition, and its imposing buildings and facilities right in the heart of the capital city, became both an occasion of envy and a reminder of inequality; while, by contrast, the academic achievements of University College, in the face of all obstacles, stood out as a proud symbol of what Catholics could accomplish if given half a chance.

Dublin University's sense of isolation helped to provoke at times an aggressively arrogant reaction on the part of some of its distinguished fellows, which provided additional ammunition to its critics. Thus, in November 1903, the student magazine *TCD* had carried some verse, by Professor R.Y. Tyrell, directed expressly against 'the ill-considered zeal of the rank and file of an unscrupulous priesthood practising on the ignorance and superstition of an illiterate peasantry'. Delany inserted the offending piece in his pamphlet *A plea for fair play* with the comment that it was not easy 'to imagine a college in Oxford or Cambridge inviting Catholics to become resident students, whilst allowing one of its leading professors to lampoon Catholicism in the college magazine'.

In a letter to Dr Walsh, on 14 February 1905, he noted that Trinity College had been 'visibly going down in numbers, in educational status, in prestige, and in its power of dominance'. This was the explanation of its 'despairing efforts to bribe Catholics to come to bolster it up, and thus diminish the evidence — growing yearly more and more plain — that the best intellects of the country are keeping aloof from it and its congeners the Queen's Colleges'. The alleged 'bribe' was a scholarship scheme which Professor Tyrell announced on 28 January 1904. It consisted of twelve exhibitions of £40, and ten of £100, donated by Sir John Nutting, to boys and girls who had distinguished themselves at either the senior or middle grade Intermediate examinations each year and undertook to pursue their education at Trinity College. The scholarships, moreover, carried no obligation of college residence or even of attendance at a single lecture.

The scheme occasioned concern to those involved in providing Catholic university education, who had no funds to offer similar inducements. Feeling against Dublin University's privileged position intensified. The Catholic bishops responded with an appeal which reflected both the strength of feeling and the contemporary mode of issuing prohibitions to a submissive laity. It was read in all the churches on 5 February 1905. The congregations were reminded of Trinity's efforts over the previous three hundred years 'to wean away the Catholic youth of Ireland from their allegiance to their faith and their country' and were called on 'to spurn this new bribe as their fathers spurned similar bribes in the past'. No true Irish Catholic would accept the proffered scholarships; 'and those who may be weak enough to do so may rest assured that their fellow-countrymen will never forget their recreancy in this crisis of our struggle for educational equality'.[94]

A proposal for more positive action, to fight money with money, came from Dr O'Dwyer on 7 February 1905. He thought he saw his way to establishing 'a burse or scholarship for Limerick students in the university at least for the next five years'. The succeeding months brought evidence that public feeling against Dublin University was ripe to support a scholarship scheme to University College. The assembly of bishops on 14 June took up the idea of 'Catholic scholarships' with enthusiasm. To enable Catholic youths to obtain the higher education denied them by the government, they proposed scholarships to University College and to Loreto College, St Stephen's Green, or to the Dominican convent, Eccles Street, on the basis of the senior grade Intermediate examination results. The scholarships consisted of eight of £50 a year, and four of £25, tenable for three years. A broadly-based committee — including the Lord Mayor of Dublin, the president of the Gaelic League, and the chairman of the Dublin County Council — was set up to administer the scheme. Its leading spirits and chief workers, however, were Dr Walsh as chairman, William Delany as secretary, and Fr Murphy of the Catholic Headmasters' Association. The details were published in the press on 4 September 1905.

Delany awaited the outcome with some misgivings, which he expressed to Dr O'Dwyer. The latter, too, had his doubts, but felt that one thing had been gained, namely, 'the killing of Nutting's scheme'.[95] On 5 October he wrote to enclose his payment to the year's scholarship fund. The point had been made, he said, by calling 'mad-dog' after Nutting, and it was to be hoped that the name would 'have its proverbial efficacy and stop a rush to Trinity College'. The misgivings were allayed by the extent of the response. The prevailing mood of self-help was expressed by the fact that some counties formed committees to provide for their own students, while Wexford County Council gave a lead in founding a scholarship for that county. The General Council of County Councils commended the example to other counties. The considerable correspondence and the rush involved in computing scholarship results for the coming university term, on top of a host of other pressures, proved too much for a man of Delany's years. His letters on the scheme to Dr Walsh betrayed for the first time signs of forgetfulness and inaccuracy. On seven occasions between August and November he referred to mistakes he had made, mainly in regard to computations concerning scholarship awards.

The scholarships also gave rise to the problem of finding accommodation for the additional influx of students promised by the scheme. It was to be a continuing problem during the remaining years of Stephen's Green. The bishops at their June meeting granted Delany the use of the adjoining premises, nos. 82-84; and Dr Walsh at last made available the use of University Church for sodality meetings and mass. The archbishop also gave his approval to a proposal to acquire on lease a house in Donnybrook, with eleven acres attached, for a period of five or seven years, within which period it could be fairly hoped provision would 'have been made for university needs elsewhere'. It was characteristic of Delany that the 'house' he had in mind was Simmonscourt Castle, and that he envisaged its grounds as providing 'the recreations, football, cricket etc., to counteract the attractions of Trinity College in these matters that weigh so heavily with young men in these days'.[96] The proposal was still-born. The Jesuit provincial and his consultors appear to have considered it an excessive demand on resources already stretched in the interests of Irish university education.[97] The houses at 82-84 Stephen's Green also proved unavailable. The tenants' leases had not expired and they refused to vacate the premises. In October 1906, therefore, he obtained the archbishop's permission 'to erect on the grounds of the college a building of wood or iron' to house two or three small lecture rooms and two or more larger rooms — 'for scientific and chemical lectures' — now a particular need as the county councils were 'establishing local scholarships for higher scientific and technical instruction tenable in university situations'. The approval was availed of so rapidly that by the following May, the new buildings, known as the 'tin university' in allusion to some popular proposals of Fr Tom Finlay, were ready.

Fr Finlay's proposals reflected rather dramatically the mood of the time. In May 1905 he had asked: Why wait any longer for England to do something about university education? Begging was neither dignified nor profitable. Ireland would probably be deceived again as in the past. Why not help herself? Why not revive the old Catholic University? The causes which had brought about its failure in 1854 no longer existed. Catholics could now obtain degrees without any sacrifice of principle and there was an abundance of good secondary teachers and university professors who were Catholics. He set forth his scheme in considerable detail in the *New Ireland Review*. It would be financed mainly by parish contributions from which simple and unpretentious structures could be built on to University College.

The proposals of Fr Finlay were received with interest, and applied to the running of an autonomous national university. Shortly after the article appeared in the *Review*, Patrick Pearse spoke in its favour at a meeting organised by the Catholic Graduates and Under-Graduates Association. The principal speaker, Mrs Sophie Bryant, D.Sc., an English Protestant, singled it out as 'the most hopeful sign of the settlement of the university question' that had yet appeared. She was sure 'that if they went on insisting upon the national university and working their national university they would suddenly when they were not thinking of it produce the effect of making the British electorate turn round'. But she hoped that their national university would be democratic in the sense of being open to the son and daughter of the poor man as well as of the rich, and in the sense of not giving 'the education of the Catholic people of Ireland into the hands of the bishops or into the hands of the religious orders exclusively, but into the hands of the people of Ireland' (applause).[98] T.M. Kettle in *The Nationist*, from September 1905 to January 1906, pressed the merits of the scheme and urged, in the light of the response to the scholarships, that the cost of its implementation 'be met by lay generosity, whether on the part of public bodies or individuals'.

The challenge to further lay generosity was not made. A general election intervened with the possibility of a new government initiative. Delany, meanwhile, conscious of the unease felt by a better educated, more articulate and self-confident laity towards 'clerical influence', had been endeavouring to secure a representative governing body for University College. It was something he had first proposed as far back as 1885. Dr O'Dwyer encouraged the idea. He suggested, on 5 March 1904, that its members might be drawn from the Catholic senators of the Royal University, Delany's own teaching staff, and perhaps the Cecilia Street Medical School. The important thing was to have a body to which no exception could be taken and 'into whose hands we might ask parliament to entrust public funds'. Delany urged on the episcopal education committee 'the advisability of establishing a governing body predominantly lay and of a representative character for University College with the view of meeting the objections from various quarters based on the charge of undue clerical domination'. He was asked to draw up a draft scheme for the consideration of the bishops at their June meeting. This he did. The governing body he envisaged, was no mere rubber stamp. It would have extensive powers: managing the property and business of the college, sanctioning the graduation courses to be followed, appointing the president, having final approval on the appointment of professors, and being empowered to appoint a committee of its members and delegate to it such powers as it deemed expedient. The list of suggested members made for a prestigious combination. There were four senators, two graduates, one representative of the medical faculty, three from the Arts faculty, six clergymen, two businessmen, and eighteen other influential laymen. Among these last were the Lord Chief Justice, the Lord Chief Baron, the Lord Mayor, the president of the Gaelic League, John Redmond, M.P., leader of the Irish Party, and John Dillon, M.P.

The draft was considered by the hierarchy in June 1904 and, though warmly supported by some bishops, it was turned down. In October of the following year, Delany brought it forward once more. Again, it received much support but the opposition of Cardinal Logue was instrumental in its rejection.[99] A few weeks later the topicality of the question was underlined by a motion proposed at a meeting of the Catholic Graduates and Under-Graduates Association.[100] The proposer, Con Murphy, M.A., called for changes in the constitution of University College 'to allow for the direct representation of Irish Roman Catholic graduates and under-graduates on its governing body'. T.M. Kettle, according to the report in the *Irish Protestant*, 25 November 1905, put forward an amendment to the effect 'that the right which the president possessed of dismissing all members of the college council at his pleasure should be with-drawn'. Although the senior graduates present, including Professor Magennis, P.H. Pearse, Dr Donnelly and Arthur Clery, 'all threw in their weight on the side of clerical control', the incident became a talking point, and Delany felt it necessary to write in the *Freeman's Journal* to clarify and defuse the situation. He emphasised that he strongly supported the principle involved in Mr Kettle's amendment. Mr Murphy wrote in to say that the same principle was behind his original motion. Kettle, on 22 November, clarified the principle. The president of University College, he said, possessed the power 'of appointing and dismissing at his discretion the professors of the college by whose votes and from whose body the council is elected' and 'although in practice the liberal and progressive temper in which Dr Delany has always exercised it has given general satisfaction', the existence of such power was none the less 'at variance with the essential nature of representative institutions'.[101] The tragedy for Delany was that the establishment of such an effective and representative governing body as he had sought might have made it possible for 'the liberal and progressive temper' associated with his presidency to continue to the end of his time at University College.

Apart from the issue of a representative governing body, and his work on the scholarships for secondary pupils, he was also concerned during 1905 about the state of primary education. If a university were to have due influence on the educational life of the country it had, he believed, to 'establish direct relations with the general grades of teachers'. Hence, he gave notice of motion at the July meeting of the standing committee of the senate of the Royal University: 'that there be granted by this university a diploma or certificate for primary teachers' and 'that measures be taken to have the diploma or certificate obtained recognised as a teaching qualification by the Boards of Education in England and Ireland'.[102]

That same month Wilfrid Ward requested him to contribute to the *Dublin Review*. He would try to get the Maynooth man who 'has been advocating the capture of Trinity' to write, and he hoped that Delany would answer him in the same issue. The Maynooth man was the able and colourful Dr Walter McDonald, a well-known supporter of the Gaelic League. He had proposed at a debate in his college that Irish Catholics 'carry the war into the camp – into the very citadel – of the enemy' by attending Trinity College in large numbers and saturating it 'with the microbes of Irish nationality'. His speech earned an editorial in the *Times* of 26 June, which sought to dismiss it as a mixture of Roman Catholicism and Gaelic League spirit and used the opportunity to ask how Unionists wishing 'to preserve ties between the two kingdoms' could 'support a university plan which encourages nationalist agitation'. Although his views received little support, they were close to those cherished by Dr Walsh and they focused attention on Dublin University as a symbol of inequality. A month later, the archbishop launched a campaign against Trinity College which, it being an election year, was to have a considerable effect.

The previous February, before the Catholic scholarship scheme got under way, he had written to Delany on lines close to those of Dr McDonald. Delany had sent him an account of a Catholic student at Trinity who had complained to the provost about a professor who, during class time, had inveighed against the Catholic bishops' statement on the Nutting scholarships. The provost had insisted on the professor apologising to the young man. 'It all goes to sustain an old theory of mine', Dr Walsh replied on 13 February, 'that if our Catholic lads had been let loose on Trinity years ago, and set to storm the citadel . . . , there would be a different story to tell in Ireland today'. Now it was almost taken for granted 'that every young Catholic going in from Clongowes and elsewhere' was 'absorbed into the garrison'. He feared that the Nutting scholarships would attract 'the pick of the Christian Brothers boys' and every one of them, with some rare exceptions, would 'be absorbed as their pre-decessors (with equally rare exceptions)' had been.

Delany responded the following day, outlining in one long complex sentence, but in a more personal way than previously, the grounds of his opposition to Catholics attending Dublin University. The difference in outlook of the two men was shortly to be thrown into relief once more under a new govern-ment. 'There was a time', he wrote, 'when I too entertained the thought of trying "to storm the citadel"; but when I came to consider more closely the strength of their entrenchments in the constitution and powers of the governing body and the length of time that must elapse before we could set the smallest footing in it, and along with that an electoral body of 4,500, of whom 2,600 are parsons, and all strongly Protestant; and when on the other hand, I counted our forces — not alone as to their numbers, but as to their *resisting* and assaulting powers — and when I was made to realise more and more fully, in the atmosphere of fashionable Catholicity in this neighbourhood, the powers of absorption of TCD and the degree in which it transformed socially and politically, and to a large extent religiously, the Catholics who came under its influence until they became not infrequently more anti-Irish in their sympathies and more anti-clerical in their educational policy than many Protestants — when I came thus to estimate the chances of success I thought it absolutely hopeless, and that our only chance was to work on our own lines until little by little we could infuse into Catholics a spirit of self-reliance and self-respect, which year by year would place them in a position to hold their own in any combination that the future might bring with it'.

From July 1905 until well into the following year, Dr Walsh conducted a vigorous assault on Trinity College, making effective use of some severe strictures which the medical council had passed on the method of conducting examinations there. This, on top of popular feeling and pressures from the Irish Parliamentary Party and the senate of the Royal University, helped push the new Liberal government towards a royal commission to investigate the place held by Trinity College and Dublin University 'as organs of higher education in Ireland' and the steps to be taken 'to increase their usefulness to the country'.

Chapter XIII

THE WORST SOLUTION POSSIBLE: DIVIDED OPINIONS
1905-1907

The decision to set up a royal commission was announced in March 1906. Its members were appointed on 1 June, under Sir Edward Fry, Lord Justice of Appeal, as chairman. One of the members, Chief Baron Palles, sent a diplomatic letter to Delany three days later canvassing his support. He had made it a condition with the Chief Secretary, Mr James Bryce, when asked to act on the commission, that it would be within its powers to recommend a second college in the University of Dublin, with a 'consequent change in the governing body of the university' to make it more open to Catholics. Bryce had agreed to this. The archbishop of Dublin had told him that the bishops were prepared to accept the type of college sketched in the Robertson Commission report 'even though it be affiliated to the University of Dublin'. What he, Palles, feared were differences of opinion amongst Catholic witnesses before the commission. Should such occur the solution would 'be relegated to the Greek kalends'. Hence, he would like to know in confidence Delany's view on this 'limited question'.

Are you of the opinion [he asked] that by no means possible can the usefulness of the University of Dublin be increased? If not, what are the means which you would recommend to that end? ... If a person so influential as you are, and whose opinion would be regarded as conclusive, are of the opinion that by no change can a college in the university be made acceptable to Catholics, it would be better for me to throw up the sponge and retire from the commission.

Delany replied the following day. He had already come to the conclusion, on reading the names of the commissioners, that the chief outcome to be expected was 'a recommendation to establish a college acceptable to Catholics in a remodelled University of Dublin'. He would much prefer, 'from an educational, as well as from a religious point of view', the solution of a college within the Royal University as outlined by the Robertson Commission; 'but taking facts as they are' he was not now and never had been, prepared 'to say *non possumus* to every other alternative'. Hence, he assured Palles:

> If a college such as the Robertson Commission proposed, suitably established, equipped and endowed, and with the degree of autonomy there laid down, can be provided for Catholics in the University of Dublin re-fashioned as you suggest, I for one shall certainly not say or do anything to place difficulties in the way of such a result, or to give reason for the oft-repeated excuse for inaction to a luke-warm government: 'The Catholics are divided and do not know their own minds, and therefore we cannot do anything for them'.

Palles, he concluded, attached far too much importance to the views of 'an obscure person' like himself, but if the Chief Baron 'thought it of any use whatever' he was perfectly welcome, at his discretion, to make known what he had said.

Over the next year he was to be involved in negotiations and writing arising out of the Fry Commission. Indeed, during July and August, before the commission began its hearing of witnesses, and while it was waiting for the documents which it had demanded from the authorities of Trinity College and from various other bodies and persons, he found himself drawn into a lively and heated controversy which had developed in the press and through the country regarding what came to be called the Bonn proposal.

The controversy arose out of a recommendation from members of the Trinity College teaching staff that the constitution of the college be modified so as to make it acceptable to Catholics and enable Dublin University to 'become the National University of Ireland'. They suggested that Catholics should have a twenty-five per cent representation on the board of governors; that dual professorships be established in mental and moral science and in history; that a fully equal faculty of Catholic theology be set up; that there be available to students religious instruction from clergymen of their own churches; that a Catholic chapel be established within Trinity; and that a council be appointed to invigilate the safeguards for students in regard to religious faith and dogma. Their proposals, in short, envisaged not an autonomous Catholic college within the University of Dublin, but a remodelling of the constitution of Trinity so as to enable Catholics and Protestants to be educated there together. They were formulated during July with the co-operation of Fottrell and Synnott, two of the chief organisers of the Catholic Lay Committee of 1903.

Fottrell and Synnott, meanwhile, without any outward sign of their collaboration, conducted a parallel operation among Catholics. They drew up a statement for signatures which stated that Trinity College could not be accepted as the sole college of the National University unless certain requirements were guaranteed. The requirements were identical with the con-cessions to be proposed from Trinity. Having received four hundred signatures, the document, like that from the Trinity staff, was forwarded to the commission.[103] The aim was clear: to impress the commission with the agreement between what Trinity offered and educated Catholics sought, and thereby induce it to recommend a change in the constitution of Trinity College as the easiest solution to the university question.

The bishops would have nothing to do with his plan, Dr Walsh informed Fottrell, and even if they did favour it the Holy See would put them under an injunction to have nothing to do with it.[104] A few days later, on 31 July, he publicly condemned the Catholic Lay Committee's statement as a 'chimerical pro-duction embodying a senseless project' and ridiculed the idea, said to be contained in the Trinity proposals, that a twenty-five per cent representation on the governing body would be accept-ed by Catholics as a 'substantial representation of their interests'.[105] The Trinity scheme was published the following day. On 3 August 1906 the archbishop countered with the publication of a statement from the episcopal education com-mittee. It had been intended as a private document to the commission but he felt constrained to make it public following the publication against all precedent of the Trinity College proposals. The statement made it clear that the bishops would never 'accept any system of mixed education in Trinity College'. He added that Catholics did not seek entry to that establish-ment or any changes in its constitution for their sake. Many people, no doubt, 'set store by bringing the youth of Ireland together during the formative years of college life as a means of mitigating political and religious animosities and developing the feelings of comradeship in a common nationality which spring up naturally among fellow students', and, unquestionably,

such things were 'worth a great deal', but they were not to be
obtained 'by cramming the whole intellectual, religious and
political development of the best minds in Ireland within the
limits of one college'. It was an open question, he continued,
whether a country would be better educationally by being
reduced to one university, but it seemed preposterous 'to confine
it, as this scheme inevitably would, to one college'. Besides,
the scheme was unacceptable for other reasons. Trinity was not
popular. It had 'an anti-Catholic and anti-national tradition'.
And, 'under the most favourable circumstances, Catholics
could never hope to be more in Trinity College than a hopeless
minority'. Yet they were seventy-four per cent of the whole
population and had shown in the Royal University, by the
number, ability, and attainments of their students, their capacity for higher education. They had 'a right to a university
in harmony with their principles'. In summary, the standing
committee of the bishops felt they were safe 'in stating that the
Catholics of Ireland would be prepared to accept any of the
following solutions: 1) A university for Catholics; 2) A new
college of the University of Dublin; 3) A new college in the
Royal University. But they would on no account accept any
scheme of mixed education in Trinity College'.

In the *Freeman's Journal* the next day, Synnott defended
the Trinity plan. It at least was a definite proposal, whereas
the talk of a second college in Dublin University had not been
put forward by anyone and 'might mean anything from a
university in all but name, to a mere hostel'. At this point,
Delany joined in. Had Mr Synnott, he asked on 6 August, not
read the bishops' statement? They had promised their favourable
consideration to the Robertson proposal – a definite scheme,
surely. Hence, they had made plain what kind of college would
satisfy them, whether under the Royal or Dublin University.
On the other hand, the Trinity proposals had not been made
by the authorities of the college or by the authorities of the
Protestant body, while the recommendation of 'a twenty-
five per cent representation on the governing body, taking
chance of a stronger position afterwards', was ridiculously
insufficient.

During the controversy the hierarchy's attitude on 'mixed
eduation' was compared adversely to that of Catholic bishops
in England and Germany. Bonn University was used as an
example of similar religious conditions to those likely to exist
for Catholics in Trinity; and Catholics and Protestants were
said to work together at Bonn in harmonious unity. The Trinity

Lay Committee proposals became known as the Bonn proposal, or the Bonn scheme or plan. Where the Irish bishops were concerned, however, their objection to 'mixed education' had come to apply less to students of different religions working together and more, as Dr O'Dwyer informed the Robertson Commission, to a system in which teachers were appointed purely on academic qualifications, irrespective of their religious beliefs, and over whom ecclesiastical authorities had no control. They had no objection to Protestant professors for Catholic students, as witness the presence of one such at University College, provided they were in a minority and, as a result, constrained by the overall Catholic climate and management. This, clearly, would not prevail at Trinity College.

On 7 August Fottrell took up the argument with a hard-hitting letter. The archbishop, he complained, had condemned the Bonn scheme even before it was published. In thus denouncing a plan which he had not read he was carrying on the old tradition of the Irish bishops who had always prevented lay people discussing the important matter of their children's education. To illustrate this episcopal distrust of the laity, he referred to a letter written to him by Cardinal Newman some thirty years previously. In December 1873 Newman wrote of the absolute refusal which met his 'urgent representations' that 'the Catholic laity be allowed to cooperate with the archbishops' in the work of university education; and how he had come away from Ireland 'with the distressing fear that in that Catholic country . . . there was to be a gulf as time went on between the hierarchy and the educated classes'. He had assured Fottrell that he would be doing 'the greatest benefit to the Catholic cause all over the world' if he succeeded 'in making the university a middle station' at which clergy and laity could meet 'so as to learn to understand and to yield to each other, and from which, as from a common ground', they might 'act in union upon an age which is running headlong into infidelity'. Priests needed to learn that the deference which the laity owed to religion ought to be in keeping with reason.

Walsh, in reply, merely pointed out that it was not the bishops' function to interfere in educational matters except where the safeguarding of faith and morality was concerned. Delany on the same day, 9 August, sought to pare down the issue to two alternatives: Catholics either accepted the Bonn plan, by which they were offered mixed education within Trinity College, without equality of conditions; or any one of the plans which the bishops had declared to be consonant with Catholic principles and which gave Catholics equality of conditions with non-Catholics. He appealed to a wider forum, suggesting that public bodies and individual Catholics should speak out and show that Messrs Fottrell and Synnott did not represent the Catholic community. Shortly afterwards he moved from appeal to practice. He was involved in founding, on 24 August, the Catholic Defence Society, which was partly intended as a counter-weight to the Committee of Catholic Laymen, and which had as its objects: '1. To organise the Catholics of Ireland for the defence of Catholic interests', and '2. to propagate true Catholic intelligence, and to contradict the false reports which are daily spread with regard to Catholicity'. The society, which had the approval of Dr Walsh and many of the bishops, included amongst its members the lord mayor of Dublin, the Right Hon. Joseph Hutchinson, and was chaired by Patrick J. O'Neill, J.P., chairman of the Dublin County Council.

The controversy continued in the press during much of August. Lay Catholics made their views heard on both sides. On 11 August Archbishop Healy of Tuam declared that the Bonn scheme deserved no consideration because it was not a proposal from Trinity College, but merely 'from a certain number of the fellows and professors'. On the same day, in the *Irish Times*, the vice-provost of Dublin University, J.W. Barlow, agreed with Dr Healy's comment. His intervention was all the more significant in that he was the only member of the board of governors, indeed the only person connected with Trinity College, apart from the actual signatories to the scheme, who joined in the debate. The so-called Bonn plan, he said, was 'signed by a small number of junior fellows and a still smaller number of very junior professors', and was not 'a Trinity College plan'. The handful of junior fellows claiming to speak for the college were on par with the 'three tailors of Tooley Street' speaking of themselves as 'We, the people of England'.

This was a body-blow to the proposals. The *coup de grâce* was administered by what Mr Fottrell termed 'a splendid letter' from Fr Delany. The letter, which appeared in the *Freeman's Journal* on 18 August, drew attention to an article on Bonn University in the *New Ireland Review* of March 1905. He quoted from it to show that there was 'no analogy between the acceptance of Trinity by Irish Catholics and the acceptance of Bonn by their Rhenish coreligionists'; and that, in fact, there was a 'total dissimilarity of conditions in the two cases'. He noted that at Bonn twenty-five of the professors, or one quarter of the total number, were Catholics; whereas in Trinity under the proposed scheme there would be three out of seventy-five, or a mere four per cent. He had consulted the author, John Marcus O'Sullivan, who had been a student at Bonn, to enquire if he had modified his views in any way since writing the article. He had not. Moreover, O'Sullivan, in a letter which Delany quoted, stated that, far from a mixed university removing religious animosities, 'a fierce intolerance and hatred of religious views different from their own . . . seems to pervade all classes, and to be, if possible, more strongly marked in the case of the students'.

'Synnott and Fottrell have done good', wrote Dr O'Dwyer the following day. 'Their scheme is killed before the commission begins at all'.[106] His diagnosis was only partly correct. The supporters of the Bonn proposal received scant attention from the commissioners. On the other hand, the divisions unveiled during the controversy were confirmed in the submissions to the commission and made an unanimous recommendation from that body very unlikely. The submissions included support for an autonomous Catholic college, equal to Trinity, within Dublin University; for an autonomous college within the Royal University as outlined by the Robertson report; for a Dunraven-type scheme which would have Dublin as a federated university, with Trinity, the Queen's Colleges, and a Catholic institution as its constituent colleges; while there were arguments put forward by Trinity College, the authorities of the Protestant church, and the partisans of the Bonn proposal, for the retention of Dublin University as it stood without any widening to include an independent Catholic college or federated colleges. Delany's submission took issue with the Bonn proposal and with the idea of federating colleges in one university. The latter-type solution had not worked in other countries and was undesirable educationally. He was 'strongly in favour of separate universities suited to the character, religious convictions, national sentiment and social and economic conditions of the people amongst whom they are placed'.[107]

It was widely believed during the autumn of 1906 that Bryce was seeking a federal University of Ireland. This was the worst 'of all abominable ideas', Professor Windle wrote on 14 October, and Cork would 'fight it to the death'. He suggested that Delany and the presidents of the Queen's Colleges send a joint statement to the commission to the effect: 'We understand that one solution is this federal university. We desire to say we think this the worst possible solution of the difficulty. The colleges brought into it would be of different standings in age, equipment and income. Their interests would be vastly different. The result could not fail to be constant friction and an increasing struggle for supremacy on the part of the different constituents'. Similar results would not follow from the adoption of the scheme suggested by the Robertson Commission because the colleges concerned 'would be of very similar character' and had worked together for years 'with remarkable harmony, all things considered'. He had talked the matter over with the bishop of Limerick, who entirely agreed with him and suggested that the senate of the Royal University should issue a statement on the subject. He, being unwell, chose to leave the suggestion with Delany who was 'a far better hand at these things'. But, he concluded, 'let us act, for before we know where we are we shall be improved off the face of the earth'.

Delany was in full agreement. He had assured the Chief Baron that he would not say or do anything against a plan for a Catholic college within the University of Dublin. But it was to be an autonomous college equal to Trinity. In such an arrangement, he wrote later to Dr Healy, the Catholic institution might expect to enjoy a half-share with its neighbour. 'But when, along with Trinity we have the three Queen's Colleges, what chance will Catholics have of half?'[108] The federal solution was in the interests neither of education nor of the Catholic population. Hence, he persuaded his fellow senators on 23 October 1906, to pass unanimously the resolution: 'That in the judgement of the senate of the Royal University, it would be disastrous to the interests of education in Ireland to concentrate the control of higher education in one university'.

The commission commenced taking evidence three days later, and continued to do so till 2 January 1907. On 7 November Chief Baron Palles reminded Delany that he would probably be the only Catholic appearing before the commission and, consequently, 'the only opportunity of the true Catholic doctrine . . . being authoritatively stated before us'. He was particularly concerned that he make clear that, in the Catholic view, 'truth cannot contradict truth' and that, as a result, Catholics were not restricted by their religion from exploring any area of truth. Delany obliged in the course of his evidence before the commission on 12 November.

The thirty-two columns which his evidence occupied in the

First Report of the Fry Commission testify to why he was considered to be a key witness on the Catholic side. Once again, as before the Robertson Commission, his facts were abundant, his reasoning cogent, his views expressed in clear and forcible language, and he displayed breadth of mind and a thorough acquaintance with all aspects of university life. Not surprisingly, he underlined what had become a favourite theme. The solution of the university question must take account of the intense national feeling of the great mass of the Irish Catholics, and of not a few who were not Catholics, and which justly demanded:

> that as in England and Scotland no university scheme is forced upon the people against their will, and as the universities reflect and, in turn, nurture the national aspirations and desires, so in Ireland there should be for the great mass of the population a university in harmony with their national sentiments as well as suited to their economic needs and conditions.

In the past the government had ignored what was being sought. The policy appeared to be: 'Refuse Irishmen what they ask even though it seems reasonable enough; but give them something else they do not want and then complain to the world how unreasonable and ungrateful they are'.

Contrary to his usual style, he introduced an element of humour into the proceedings. He had not infrequently been at loggerheads with Dr Traill, the much taller and portly provost of Trinity. When, then, the chairman of the commission asked bluntly whether he thought the scheme whereby the University of Dublin would embrace the main university colleges was the worst solution possible, he softened his rejection with an incongruous image. 'The worst I can imagine. The word "embrace" would be very odd. I should like to know how we could "embrace". Dr Traill and I are friends, but we certainly should not embrace over the scheme'.[109]

The general trend of the oral evidence proved unfavourable to any form of Dublin University scheme. The hope, still shared by some, of an unanimous recommendation from the commission receded. The news in December of Bryce's imminent departure as British ambassador to Washington added to the general feeling of frustration, and gave rise to doleful rumours about his likely successor. 'If Winston Churchill comes here,' Professor Windle wrote to Dr O'Dwyer on 7 December, 'as it seems certain that he will before long, anything on earth may happen. Does it not sometimes seem to you that nothing but separation from England can save this country as a Christian country'?[110]

The commission issued its report on 12 January 1907. As expected, its members were divided. The Chief Baron, Sir Thomas Raleigh, Dr Douglas Hyde, Dr Dennis Coffey, and Professor Henry Jackson with reservations, were in favour of a federation of the five colleges under Dublin University. The chairman, Professor Butcher and Sir Arthur Rucker, declared for the Robertson scheme; and Mr S.B. Kelleher of Trinity College was opposed to both.

Although all, with one exception, had agreed on the need for a college acceptable to Catholics, their disagreement as to how to meet the need made it extremely unlikely that the government would take any action. Catholics, it was believed, could expect little sympathy from the Liberals. Surprise and relief was felt, therefore, when in the third week of January word spread that something might be salvaged; that Sir Anthony MacDonnell, irrespective of the commission's findings, had a bill drafted which would give effect to the proposals which the Chief Baron had appended to the report.

Delany was seriously alarmed, From his study of the Palles proposals for a federal solution it appeared that they would 'establish Protestant ascendancy in education for an indefinite time to come'. It was vitally important, he told Dr Healy on 21 January, 1907, that the hierarchy study the question and submit their judgement to the government before the government committed itself. Healy agreed that the Chief Baron's scheme was 'the worst of all proposals' and, in his view, the archbishop of Dublin was 'at the bottom of the business'. He could not speak out till the general body of bishops had discussed the plan, but there was nothing to prevent Delany, Dr Nixon, dean of the Medical School and vice-chancellor of the Royal University, and Dr Windle, reiterating their opinions 'in the very strongest manner'.[111]

Windle at this juncture became a leading figure in the opposition to the one-university scheme. In a caustic letter to Delany on 21 January, he was quite clear that legislation on the lines proposed by Palles could not succeed in face of Trinity opposition, the whole weight of evidence, the important note of Justice Fry (the chairman), Butcher and Rucker, 'probably the three best men of the commission', and Jackson's admission that while he approved the Dublin scheme he regarded it 'as impossible under the circumstances'. He could not understand the attitude of Douglas Hyde, president of the Gaelic League, or of Dr Denis Coffey, of the Catholic Medical School. To legislate on MacDonnell's lines could only lead to a complete setback of the settlement 'which might easily now be arranged on Robertson lines'. The bishops were suspicious of him. He asked Delany to impress on them that he was disinterested. He did not fear for Cork. It would fight its way out 'and into complete independence' before long. His advice was based on the view that the plan was 'educationally bad, impossible of carriage through parliament', and would result in 'a delay in a real settlement'. Each of the five colleges would have one-fifth representation on the governing body, but only one of the colleges would be represented entirely by Catholics. 'In other words', he said, 'you have a university with a permanent Protestant majority in its governing body'. He intended writing to Hamilton of Queen's College Belfast to see if its graduates' association might not take up the matter. He would also write to Gray of Dublin University and suggest 'that he should unlimber the Trinity guns and get their graduates into operation'. In Cork there was no association, and the men were 'so supine' that he could get them 'to do nothing except earn their living and sail boats and hunt'. It was 'the work of Sisyphus', he continued, to get anything done there, but 'a certain vein of stubbornness' made him go on and he would keep 'stirring up the people of Cork to insist on a university' in the hope that this would 'force the pace and complicate the settlement through Dublin'. He pointed out, however, that when the bill was introduced he and Hamilton would be tied as presidents of quasi-government institutions, and it would be up to Delany and Nixon to fight it.

A delay in the publication of the oral evidence before the commission caused disquiet. It was suspected that it was being held up by Sir Anthony MacDonnell because of its opposition to a Dublin University scheme. It was not published, in fact, until 1 February 1907; and by then Bryce had publicly committed the government to the introduction of an Irish university bill. The timing of his announcement evoked critical comment. He made it on 25 January, just two days before Augustine Birrell was sworn in as Chief Secretary, and when his own position was merely that of caretaker. 'He shouts "No surrender" at the top of his voice', Arthur Balfour declared, 'and he nails his flag to someone else's mast — a most felicitous picture of courage and discretion'.[112] But Bryce was determined that his scheme become law. He informed the House of Com-

mons that Dublin University was to be enlarged to a National
University which would include Trinity College, a new college
in Dublin, and the Queen's Colleges of Cork and Belfast. Other
colleges such as Galway and the Arts faculty of Maynooth,
could be affiliated and have, thereby, their lectures rank as
university lectures, but they would not have representation on
the university senate. The degree of autonomy to be enjoyed
by the colleges was left vague, but certain statements occasioned concern. The university was to provide teaching 'in advanced
subjects . . . in mathematics, physics, modern languages and
ancient languages . . . The new college would provide teaching
in less advanced subjects'. The scheme was acceptable, he said,
to 'the heads of the Roman Catholic Church in Ireland' and he
understood that 'the large majority of the Irish representatives'
were also prepared to accept it. He personally believed that it
was the only scheme 'politically possible under the conditions',
and, he added, 'I can hold out no hope that any other will be
proposed by the present government'.

Bewildered and incensed, Delany protested at length to
Dr O'Dwyer. 'Here we have at once', he wrote, *'mixed joint
education* under professors in whose appointment Catholics
will have little influence, and the Catholic college lowered to
the status of a mere preparatory institution'. Could it be possible
that any such scheme was laid before the bishops and that they
'expressed their willingness to accept it', as Bryce said? And if
this was so, 'what becomes of all the protests and condemnations
of pope and bishops for the past sixty years? And what becomes
of the demand for equality which was the main burden of all
Dr Walsh's many pronouncements?' If the bishops had not
expressed any such willingness to accept, what action did they
now intend to take after the publication in all the newspapers
of Mr Bryce's declaration? He asked O'Dwyer to advise him
for his own guidance on the senate of the Royal University
how matters stood. He added that he knew 'on excellent
authority' that Bryce's speech had no authority from the
cabinet and was not a final statement of their views. He felt
confident that were the bishops to inform the government
that they would prefer the Royal University scheme, the
government 'would give the fullest consideration to the suggestions that might be made'. He had written to the cardinal
on the subject, but he was not clear that His Eminence quite
realised the urgency of the situation.[113]

Sir John Ross of Bladensburg had a similar message for the
bishop. Bryce had acted 'with scarcely decent haste' and would

soon cease to be a member of the government. His action, therefore, could not be taken as binding on his successor. 'It looks like a *balloon d'essai* inflated by bluff'. He, Ross, could not see, in any event, how the new proposals could be made acceptable. The Catholics, under the Royal University, had had an equal vote in the senate and had made such good use of their position that they had achieved 'little short of an ascendancy'. Under the new proposals they would have to make their way with new colleagues and would have but a fifth of the votes. Thus, he declared, the proposals would entail irretrievable loss 'to our religious position and independence'. His regret was that the bishops had not taken a definite stance with regard to the Robertson scheme. Had they done so they would have 'put an end to all this intrigue and would have secured public opinion' which previously had never failed them. Their 'uncertain voice' had been disastrous. They were now in the sad position of having almost forced upon them a scheme which they did not like. Was it too late to act? He did not think so. If they now pressed for the Robertson plan, what could the government do? It dare not 'tell the truth — that the Robertson scheme is too favourable to the religion of the people'.[114]

But the bishops showed no inclination to commit themselves before the bill had been drafted. They appeared to accept Bryce's assertion that his was 'the only scheme politically possible' and that there was little hope of any alternative being offered by the government. 'The alternatives are this scheme or nothing', O'Dwyer replied on 27 January. He personally preferred the Robertson proposals, but he did not think there was sufficient 'difference of principle' between them and those of Bryce to justify him saying to the government 'give me my plan or nothing'. He agreed with Ross 'about the domination of a clique' in the entire proceedings, but the question had now passed beyond that stage. 'We have to accept or refuse a large and — for Liberals — generous proposal for a national settlement. We have to ask ourselves: if we refuse it what chance is there in our lifetime of getting better, indeed of getting anything at all?'

Sir John Ross passed on to Delany this unexpected evidence of war-weariness on the part of the bishop of Limerick. An equally discouraging reply came from Cardinal Logue. The bishops had made their views evident often enough, and not infrequently on tentative schemes 'which ended in a fiasco'. His Eminence's view was that the hierarchy should wait till they had something definite before them and some security that the proposers of the scheme were in earnest. Personally, he considered that Mr Bryce's scheme proposed 'the establishment of a fourth Queen's College in Dublin', but in the absence of definite details he believed that 'it would be dangerous to give an opinion one way or another'.

Delany's judgement of what was at stake, and of the motives of the chief promoters of the federal plan, were enunciated, in a surprisingly black-and-white analysis, to John Sweetman, chairman of the Meath Co. Council, chairman of the Committee of Lay Catholics who had pushed the Bonn proposals, and a former member of parliament for East Wicklow. Sweetman, despite his attainments, appears to have had a simplistic attitude to national and university affairs. In his opinion Bryce's scheme was aimed at obliging Catholics to give up University College which was 'becoming so powerful as to make England afraid'. Responding in similarly uncomplicated terms, Delany declared that the government had shirked putting the Robertson scheme into action because, seeing the position already achieved by University College within the Royal University, it seemed plain that as 'a great endowed Catholic college' it would dominate it altogether. And this was rendered more objectionable by the fact that 'along with being Catholic it would be intensely Irish'. Such an outcome 'was not regarded as desirable by a certain class even of Irish Catholics' and they, in consequence, preferred any scheme 'in which clerical and ultra-national views would be held in check'. The combination offered under the Bryce scheme gave 'ample security against such a danger', and 'hence the government found allies amongst Catholics for its own scheme of centralisation and for the abolition of the Royal University'. The anxiety about the junction of Catholic and 'intensely Irish' was mirrored in the eagerness with which the *Times* 'and the anti-Irish and anti-Catholic press in both countries' made capital out of the student demonstration at the Royal University in 1905. In the current crisis, he continued, he did not see his way as yet to any clear line of action. 'The promise of the endowed college' seemed 'to have neutralised all opposition, and blunted the judgement of those from whom criticism and condemnation might have been expected'.[115]

A lengthy letter to Chief Secretary Birrell, however, took a sophisticated line more adapted to hard political realities.[116] It would be advisable, he wrote, 'to ascertain confidentially' whether a majority of the Catholic bishops approved of the scheme. He then proceeded to outline reasons against the scheme on educational grounds, and compared it in parallel columns with the proposals of the Robertson Commission. Bryce's solution, he declared, was really that of Gladstone, which had been wrecked by concerted Protestant opposition. The same situation would materialise again. A proposal such as Bryce's 'would be made to seem destructive to Protestant interests on a large scale' and would add substance to 'the argument constantly pressed' that Home Rule, to which the government was dedicated, would mean 'the sacrifice of the loyal Protestant minority to the hostile will of "the rebellious papist majority"'. On such a thorny issue, it seemed to him 'a plain dictate of commonsense, as well as of political prudence', to opt for a solution which would involve the 'least disturbance of existing institutions and vested interests' and would be, at the same time, 'most in harmony with educational experience'. Such a solution had been suggested by the Robertson Commission.

The Protestant opposition, indeed, materialised quickly. On 31 January the scheme was condemned at a meeting of the Trinity College staff with the provost in the chair. A defence committee was organised. The previous day the Ulster Unionist Council, and on 1 February eleven of the thirteen Church of Ireland bishops, declared themselves opposed to it. Condemnations were issued by the senate of the University of Dublin on 4 February, and later by meetings of Trinity graduates. A reference to an Irish university bill in the king's speech of 13 February, and Birrell's subsequent notice of the introduction of such a measure, added momentum to the efforts of the defence committee. A memorial was sent to Balfour signed by up to four thousand graduates. A deputation visited the universities of Britain. As a result, protests were issued from Oxford and Cambridge, the universities of London, Birmingham, Liverpool, Sheffield and Bristol, the Scottish universities and the University of Wales, and also from two hundred and thirty-five fellows of the Royal Society.[117] On 20 March the general assembly of Irish Presbyterians admitted the principle of the proposal bill, but laid such emphasis on non-sectarianism as a condition of their approval as to ensure that no measure acceptable to them would be accepted by Catholics.

Catholic support for Bryce's proposals increased in proportion to the assertion of Protestant opposition. A range of professional bodies and a number of county councils passed resolutions calling for the immediate introduction of the 'proposed bill'. The *Freeman's Journal* consistently praised it, and in doing so was taken to be reflecting Archbishop Walsh's sentiments. Some bishops in their Lenten pastorals spoke well, if guardedly, of it. The leader of the Irish party, John Redmond, M.P., did likewise; and, according to Delany, a large majority of the teaching staff of University College 'publicly advocated the scheme without hindrance or discouragement' from him.[118]

Professor Windle and he occupied a different position. 'Nothing educationally could be worse than this present scheme', the Cork president wrote to him on 10 February, 1907, 'and nothing more abominable than the way in which it has been forced on the country by a little band of doctrinaires'. But he was not prepared to publicly condemn it since the government was unlikely to go any further and he did not wish 'to back Trinity in breaking the scheme'. Four other letters followed in the course of a week. 'I seem to do nothing from morning to night', he wrote on 18 February, 'but write letters about the university question' — a sentiment Delany could re-echo. He aimed to fight 'to the last ditch' but could not see how to do so effectively. If they supported at the next senate meeting a motion from Dr Nicholas condemning the Bryce proposals on educational grounds they would play into the hands of Trinity and give the government an opportunity of withdrawing from an awkward position; on the other hand, if they voted against the motion, and therefore for the proposals, they would be going against their own convictions and placing themselves in a position from which as Catholics they might wish to withdraw publicly afterwards. The delicacy of the situation was emphasised by notice from the two episcopal representatives that they would not be attending the senate meeting.

The dilemma was solved on the eve of the meeting. The Catholic senators 'put their heads together' at University College on 20 February and decided to draw up two new resolutions.[119] Delany framed them, and Sir Christopher Nixon, seconded by Dr Hamilton of Belfast, proposed them at the senate. They were passed unanimously. The first recalled the senate's previous resolution in October 'on the undesirability of a single rigid system of university education' and went on to state that now that the outline of the scheme had been put forward by the government, the senate did not 'deem it proper to take any course which might prevent the immediate removal of one of the greatest and most crying grievances under which the Irish people labour'. The second resolution read:

That in any scheme which would involve the establishment of one or more federal universities, it is essential in order to avoid the evils of one stereotyped system of higher education, that there should be granted to the federal colleges the largest possible amount of autonomy on the lines recommended by the Robertson Commission and with practical unanimity by the recent commission.

Shortly afterwards Chief Baron Palles sent a confidential communication to the Jesuit provincial that it was believed in certain quarters that 'the Jesuits' were offering opposition to the government's scheme, and that such an impression 'might operate to the disadvantage of the Society in any coming reconstruction of university conditions'. Delany replied at length on 5 March. Having thanked the Chief Baron for his 'friendly message', he pointed out that no Jesuit, except himself, had done anything which could be construed as opposition to the government's scheme. 'Probably the majority' of them, indeed, actively supported it.[120] He went on to explain his own and the senate's actions. The resolution which he had proposed at the October meeting had been seconded by Archbishop Healy who declared *that he was expressing the views of the Irish bishops — with one possible exception*'. The point of that resolution was not that the union of different colleges in one university would have injurious effects, but that the giving of the control of the over-all education to one central mixed body would be injurious. The whole force of the resolution 'lay in that word, *control*'. The autonomy of the colleges was being sacrificed. The recent senate resolution adhered to the need for autonomy, but made it clear that the senate 'did not intend to take an attitude of opposition to the government's proposals'. That too was his attitude. He had 'strongly deprecated any public criticism of Mr Bryce's scheme, or anything that would weaken the hands of the government'. Encouraged, however, by a happy phrase of Birrell against 'rigidity of outline', he had written confidentially to him, and had urged that the new Dublin college should 'be self-contained, both as regards staff and equipment, and that — whilst accepting the absence of [religious] tests — it should be educationally autonomous'. If these conditions were secured, 'the intrinsic question would be settled, and there would remain merely the tactical question: what solution is politically the easiest and best?' And on that question the government was 'in the best position to give the answer'. Meantime, he assured Palles, he would guide his action by that of the bishops.

The bishops' standing committee met on 16 April and issued a cordial but ambiguous declaration which had the hall-mark of Archbishop Walsh. It was quite possible, within the general outline of the government's plan, 'to meet substantially' the claims they had put forward. At the present, however, they could go no further than 'this expression in general terms' of their approval of the plan 'as the basis of a settlement'. When a detailed scheme had been fomulated they should be 'in a position to pronounce a definite opinion of its merits'. Despite this reserve, they wished to declare that the government's 'directness and frankness' should be met in Ireland by a most sympathetic spirit 'and with the amplest allowance for the difficulties which have to be overcome in dealing with a question of the kind'. They earnestly requested 'immediate action' from the government.

The 'difficulties' continued to be mobilised from Trinity College. Petitions were circulated appealing to old loyalties. A printed sheet, signed by 6,361 graduates, and by the vice-chancellor and vice-provost, was directed to the House of Commons. The members of parliament were reminded:

That the University of Trinity College was founded in Dublin by Queen Elizabeth in 1591, for the purpose of promoting education in Ireland, based on the principles of the Protestant religion; that for three centuries Trinity College has faithfully fulfilled the trust imposed on it by its founder and bene-factors, and has in consequence enjoyed the support of the Protestant people of Ireland.

The petitioners therefore humbly-prayed — 'that in any legis-lation affecting university education in Ireland, the Protestant constitution of the University of Dublin may be preserved unimpaired, and that the Protestant people of Ireland may not be deprived of privileges which they have enjoyed without interruption for three hundred years'.[121] Not surprisingly, given what E.H. Knox, M.P., termed 'the vast force of ancient prejudice',[122] conservative and non-conformist members rallied in opposition to the bill.

Dr Walsh meanwhile, in his labyrinthine way, found occasion to make public pronouncements critical of Trinity and its privileges and asserting the right of Catholics to full equality with it. 'The archbishop of Dublin by his tactics', Windle wrote to Delany on 11 April, had 'aided and abetted' the supporters of Trinity College in their opposition to the govern-

ment's plan. 'To constantly attack a place with which you want
to be connected and thus to embitter the feelings on both
sides is not the way to accomplish your object'.

Gradually, however, other political concerns were taking
over from the university question. The large Liberal majority
in the 1906 election had raised expectations to an exaggerated
level, even though the legislative veto of the House of Lords
still remained to block any notable progress towards Irish
self-government. 'A comprehensive measure of Home Rule',
Tom Kettle declared in a celebrated public address on 'The
philosophy of politics', might not be regarded as a 'final'
settlement. 'Life is growth, growth is change. It may have
bivouacs but no barracks'.[123] The Liberals' actual response
was but a new version of the old Tory devolution scheme.
The government's Irish Council Bill, announced in January
1907, envisaged the setting up of an Irish council, composed
mainly of elected members, which would have control over
eight departments of the Irish administration, including education, local government, agriculture and technical instruction.
The Lord Lieutenant would retain wide powers of veto; and
beyond him again there remained the overriding authority of
the cabinet and, ultimately, of the imperial parliament. The
main architect of the proposed measure was Sir Anthony
MacDonnell who, as noticed earlier, had been brought to Ireland by Wyndham, and had been assured of more freedom to
initiate policy than was customary for an Under-Secretary.[124]
He took up office in October 1902 with three main reforms
in mind: the solution of the land question on the basis of
voluntary sale; the establishment of a university college in
Dublin acceptable to Catholics; and the coordination of the
mass of semi-independent boards which made up the Irish
government without alienating nationalist opinion. The land
question proved amenable to a quick solution at the expense
of the British treasury; but in the other two areas there was no
such convenient aid to consensus. He sought a solution by
appeal to moderate middle opinion. Believing that there was
in Ireland 'a large body of moderate opinion, Catholic and
Protestant,' to which expression was not being given 'owing
to party organisation',[125] he hoped to obviate the domination
of the 'extremists' — the Irish nationalist party and the Ulster
unionist party — by establishing a council of moderate and
responsible 'men of business' who would be independent of
the landlords and tenants, as well as of clerical pressures of any
kind.[126] To forestall possible nationalist opposition to his

plans, he talked vaguely of the high hopes of Irishmen being shortly realised: talk which further increased popular expectations.

The actual Council Bill, as a result, met with widespread condemnation as a meagre pittance. It was, as the prime minister, Henry Campbell-Bannerman, conceded, 'a little, modest, shy, humble effort to give administrative powers to the Irish people.'[127] Redmond and Dillon rightly saw the proposed measure as an attack on the Irish party, but they hesitated to condemn it outright, hoping to salvage something for Irish self-government by a range of amendments. Many churchmen expressed open dissatisfaction at the projected take-over of education. What troubles the clergy, D.M. Moriarty informed Redmond on 17 May, is 'the bogey of Irish Clemenceaus taking education out of their hands'.[128] Bryce, indeed, seemed to believe that the opposition of the clergy was the rock on which the bill eventually perished. What was essential, he wrote to Goldwin Smith on 31 May, was 'getting the schools out of the hands of clerics, whether Roman Catholics or Protestant. It was because the bishops and priests feared this that they gave such vehement and successful opposition to the bill'.[129] John Dillon was quite clear, however, that the great weight of lay opinion was the important factor, On 29 May, in a letter to Redmond, he scorned 'the ridiculous impression that the Council Bill was killed by the priests'.[130] The decisive step was Redmond's. At an irate national convention of the Irish parliamentary party on 21 May, attended by over three thousand delegates, he publicly denounced the measure in an effort to preserve at all costs the unity of his supporters.

Birrell had introduced the Council Bill on 6 May. He did not view it as 'something intrinsically valuable',[131] thought MacDonnell mulish and deluded in his trust in a large body of moderate opinion,[132] and was determined not to permit him the relatively free hand he had enjoyed under Bryce. He set himself the task of winning over nationalist support for the bill. Following the bill's rejection by the national convention, however, Campbell-Bannerman seized the opportunity to announce, on 3 June, that his cabinet had abandoned both the Council Bill and the university scheme. It was the political death knell for Sir Anthony MacDonnell. His influence came to an end at the close of the summer. He had become a political liability: abused by such as John Burns, M.P., as a 'sun-dried bureaucrat',[133] and managing to unite in common hostility both nationalists and unionists.

Campbell-Bannerman's abandonment of the Council Bill and the university scheme, and his government's handling of both issues, greatly added to the prevailing mood of dissatisfaction and unrest. The tide of impatience with the imperial parliament and its governments was rising on widely different shores. The Irish party leaders found themselves accused by their party organisation, the United Irish League, of being too compliant; and its younger members, the Young Ireland branch of the League, which had among its most vocal representatives students from University College, were particularly critical. Discontent was such, indeed, that a section of followers actively advocated withdrawal from Westminister; and one member of parliament resigned his seat and then successfully contested it on a platform of abstention as a Sinn Fein candidate. The unrest flowed over into the following year. Agrarian agitation broke out in Galway and Roscommon, and, after the defeat of a Home Rule resolution from Redmond in the House of Commons, Belfast experienced serious riots. The victims there included two relatives of Edward Carson, M.P. for Dublin University. In considerable anger he told the government that if they were not willing to govern the country according to the ordinary conditions of civilization, they should 'go out of Ireland and leave us to govern ourselves'.[134] The *leitmotif* of self-reliance, mixed with deep dissatisfaction, was in different forms influencing every sector of Irish life.

As might be expected the general malaise communicated itself in an acute fashion to the student body at Stephen's Green. Encouraged to view themselves as the future leaders of a Home Rule Ireland, they resonated to the national feelings of the moment. From 1903, indeed, a blend of nationalist impatience towards British rule and of resentment towards authority generally had been evident amongst them and had provided mounting problems for Delany. Where university education itself was concerned many experienced a sense of grievance at being condemned, as they saw it, to the degrees of a second class institution by reason of the bias and ineptitude of the government. The sudden abandonment of the Bryce scheme served to confirm their suspicion that a just treatment of Irish affairs could not be hoped for from British governments. Hence, when, in the autumn of 1907, Augustine Birrell, in deference to Delany, spoke at a public meeting of the Literary and Historical Society on his plans for university education in Ireland, and pledged himself to do all in his power to solve the question in the next session of parliament, he was, to Delany's great embarrassment, scorned and ridiculed by his audience. It seemed but another instance of fair promises by an English politician.

Delany had managed to steer the college through four years of unrest without any weakening in academic achievement, but he had forfeited in the process the popularity which he had long enjoyed with the student body. The occasions and course of his conflict with them left bitter feelings which were to obscure for their generation the extent of his achievement, and to cloud for some the memory of 'the golden years at 86'.

Chapter XIV

STUDENT UNREST: A REPUTATION TARNISHED

It has been remarked that former students of the college
tended to look back on the years from 1897 to 1908 as a very
special period in their lives. To Felix E. Hackett (professor of
physics), Dublin then seemed a city of peripatetic discourse.
Its boundaries were the Royal and Grand Canals, within which
the majority of the students lived, an easy walking distance to
the college. The motoring age had not arrived; only two tram-
lines were electrified. The streets sank to silence early; and
'talk, merging into discussions of the problem of the day or
of the theatre or of the more abstract topics of the lecture-
room, went on easily, walking across St Stephen's Green or
homeward from the L. and H. debates or from the closing of
the National Library'.[135] Arthur Clery, professor of law, wrote
of 'the brilliant and varied life that existed behind the shabby
exterior of the Stephen's Green buildings', and how the Gaelic
League movement gave students an ideal, 'raised the tone of our
lives, and an exceptionally high moral standard prevailed amongst
us'; and pointing to outstanding names among the student
body, he insisted that Joyce, in his *Portrait of the Artist as a
Young Man,* had given 'a wrong impression of the whole' by
'confining himself to a small knot of medical students'.[136]
Hugh Kennedy, first attorney-general and chief justice of the
Irish Free State, spoke, like many others, of the liberal education
that was provided with 'the contact of minds and the play of
intellect, with the personal intercourse between professor and
student, which is regarded as constituting the ideal values of
university education'.[137]
The memorable intensity of those years owed much, as has
been noted, to the political, cultural and social developments of
the time, and to the college's special position as the standing
argument in favour of an endowed university for the majority
population. At the L. and H. debates from 1900 to 1905,

according to Thomas F. Bacon, nephew to Delany, auditor of the society, and later a distinguished barrister, 'a definite and lasting discontent with political methods' was in evidence. 'A new and more keenly critical outlook on national affairs had awakened among the younger generation of educated Irishmen'.[138] It has been noticed, too, how this discontent manifested itself with regard to the university question, particularly after the strictures on the Royal at the time of the Robertson Commission; and how T.M. Kettle's articles drew a careful distinction between *the* university college of Ireland' at Stephen's Green and the mere examining body of the Royal University at Earlsfort Terrace. At that address the Royal had its large examination hall, which was also used for orchestral concerts and a variety of other purposes. There each year it conferred its certificates and degrees, disfiguring its students, in Kettle's phrase, by its 'paper pomposity'. The irreverence of Kettle, capturing the prevailing mood, was matched by a current anecdote of the antics of Oliver St John Gogarty. Knocking at the great door of Earlsfort Terrace, he enquired of Peter the porter: 'Is this the Royal University?' Peter, red-faced and irate, and knowing his man, said, 'You know right well it is'. 'I don't know', said Gogarty, 'last time I passed this way it was a flower show'.[139]

Impatience with the continuance of the Royal and with government procrastination found particular expression on that occasion each year when the senate of the university conferred its degrees on successful students; and, again, a few weeks later, at the annual inaugural meeting of the Literary and Historical Society.

For a number of years, indeed, there had been a great deal of electric tension at the conferring ceremony in the great hall at Earlsfort Terrace. The presence of a large number of northern students added an explosive dimension to the occasions. The chancellor, the Earl of Meath, for his part, seemed to consider it his duty to emphasise the gratitude the university should feel to the English parliament, and the loyalty the students should have to the monarch. From 1899 on, in particular, the speeches met with a running commentary of quips and sarcastic interruptions; and proceedings ended with students singing *God Save Ireland* when the organ took up *God Save the King*. In 1900 a jingoistic speech in support of the Boer War caused something of a disturbance. Still, up to 1903, the interruptions were generally the doing of a small minority. In that year the senate made the mistake of introducing a large force of police into the hall to ensure greater solemnity. The Robertson Report had

been published. There was platform activity in every part of
Ireland in support of a just settlement to the university question.
Disturbance was feared at the conferring. The senate's action,
however, served as an irritant rather than a contribution to
peace, and resulted in a general uproar. In 1904, after all the
talk of the justice of Catholic claims, Wyndham declared that
the government would do nothing and had never pledged itself
to do anything. Delany, at that juncture, wrote his open letter
to the Lord Lieutenant, later incorporated into his *A plea for
fair play*, in which he suggested that the government's response,
'after fifty years waiting', was 'tantamount to a declaration that
Ireland could not expect justice from Westminster'. A stormy
conferring ceremony on 27 October was expected, and further
precautionary measures were taken without success.

That evening T.M. Kettle and Frank Sheehy-Skeffington,
M.A., wrote to the *Freeman's Journal* to express their opinions
on happenings past and present. They condemned the authorities
of the Royal University, senators and officials, 'who provoked
today's scene'. Until recently the uproar at the proceedings had
been the work 'of a small knot of irresponsible undergraduates
and was discountenanced by the more responsible of the
students'. But the authorities, it would seem, were determined
to coerce the students into silence, instead of treating the matter
humorously. 'Last year they introduced large bodies of police
into the building — with the result that the noise was worse
than ever'. This year they sought to pack the audience: denying
tickets to undergraduates who had a legal right to be present
and even to some graduates. The senate, Kettle wrote, 'based its
refusal on a statement which lacks the savour of truth, namely,
that "an exceptionally large number of candidates were to
receive degrees", and, to crown all, this liberal and progressive
senate, which has so long shut its fellowship against women,
repenting profitably, opened its arms to receive them yesterday,
and swamped the candidates with a spring-tide of ladies' tickets'.
The natural result, in Sheehy-Skeffington's words, 'was that all
the graduates and undergraduates were united by a common
grievance', and even those who — like himself — had 'hitherto
opposed the disturbance as discreditable to the student body,
were delighted at the vigorous and effective protest which was
made today, against the action of the authorities'. He hoped
that they learned the lesson 'that any attempt at coercion only
aggravates the evil which it aims at suppressing'. Neither writer
wished to condone the attitude of the students, but they condemned that of the authorities in not understanding 'the

psychology of the undergraduates in meeting assembled'.

Year to year seemed to send a message and challenge. Despite even greater precautions, the demonstration in 1905 brought the senate of the Royal to the brink of dissolution. The senate's minutes recorded that towards the close of proceedings 'a number of persons' took 'possession of the organist's seat and the approaches thereto' and 'prevented the organist from playing the national anthem, as it has been the practice to do at such functions. During the course of the disorder members of the crowd shouted out that they came for the purpose of preventing the playing of *God Save the King'*. The *Freeman's Journal*, of 28 October, noted that when the organ gallery was occupied some students shouted out 'God Save Ireland', which was then sung while the conferring continued and was sung again as the senators left the building. The *Evening Mail*, on 19 November, under the heading 'Disloyalty at the Royal University', added that loyalist members of the senate were hissed on leaving Earlsfort Terrace. It called for the punishment of 'important offenders'.

Several newspapers carried accounts of the incidents and commented on them. An article appeared in the *Times* on 2 November which was both sanctimonious and sharply pointed. It described the students' behaviour as an affront to the king, and to the Protestants of Ulster, and queried was this 'a foretaste of what the Protestant youth of Ireland would have to endure in the new university' demanded by the Irish Catholic bishops. 'If the able Jesuit Father', it continued, 'who is at the head of the Roman Catholic college in St Stephen's Green, cannot keep the rowdy and intolerant members of his present flock under control, or, apparently, identify them when they "break bounds" in this outrageous fashion, it may well be asked whether he would be likely to be capable of securing fair treatment for unionists and Protestants in an independent university financed by the state but placed under his government?' The paper saw the influence of the anti-English Gaelic League at work in the outrage.

To this dangerously loaded attack, Delany replied with a letter to the editor on 4 November. Quoting the section just given, he presented such information about the college as met the innuendoes and provided grounds for counter-attack. It was twenty-two years, he wrote, since the Catholic bishops of Ireland entrusted the college to himself and his colleagues, and during that time they had 'never interfered, directly or indirectly', with the management of it. The college was mainly non-residential, and had 'an average attendance of about 180 extern students, of whom during the last session thirty-one were women'. During its twenty-two years it had 'been open to students of all denominations', and there had always been, 'amongst the women students as amongst the men, a considerable percentage of non-Catholics — Protestants, Presbyterians, Methodists, Jews — attending its lectures'. Amongst the professors there had always been 'one or more Protestants', and currently on the college's governing council there was a Presbyterian. 'All shades of political opinion from extreme unionist to extreme nationalist' had been represented 'both amongst the students and the professors', and found 'free expression in the debating societies of the college'. And yet, he said, there had never been, in the whole twenty-two years, 'a word of complaint that any individual has had to suffer insult or disrespect on account of his religious belief or his political opinions'.

Hence, he made bold to assert, 'that the manifestations at the Royal University was not due to the "intolerance" of the students of University College'. What, then, was the cause of it? It was not far to seek. 'Injustice always and everywhere' bred discontent; 'and in colleges and universities as amongst nations discontent is the fertile mother of disorder, culminating often, especially in youth, in words and acts of open disrespect to the authorities who are held responsible for the injustice. And amongst Irish Catholic students' there was 'discontent, universal, profound, bitter discontent,' for there was 'grievous injustice'.

The students who took part in the recent manifestation 'repudiated the charge that there was intended . . . any act of personal disloyalty or disrespect to the king. Their protest, they declared, was not against the king, but against the king's present government — the government, whose prime minister again and again publicly acknowledged the grievous educational injustice under which Catholics labour in Ireland, and who yet never lifted a finger to remove it, and who', they complained, 'in this, as in other Irish questions', governed Ireland at present 'entirely at the bidding of Ulster orangemen'. They objected, they said, to the playing of *God Save the King*, not from any personal disrespect to the king, 'but because in Ireland the party of ascendancy, who claimed a monopoly of loyalty, as they did of everything else, had made the people at large look on that air as a party tune clearly akin to that of *Croppies, Lie Down*; and under that aspect these students objected to having it forced on them as a matter of course on such an occasion as the general meeting of the university'.

Personally, he did not share that view, and deeply regretted the whole incident, but he thought it just that the students' explanation should be heard, and he asked 'thinking Englishmen to consider the matter in all its bearings' and whether the best way of treating it was that 'of magnifying it into an act of grievous disloyalty, and of intensifying discontent by vindictive punishment, whilst the grievances (which caused the discontent) remain unredressed'.

A special standing committee meeting of the senate was called to discover means of dealing with the guilty parties and to discuss measures against the repetition of such happenings in the future. It was held on 3 November and the chairman, the Earl of Meath, who had summoned the meeting, delivered a strongly-worded speech which, contrary to usage, was published in the press. He represented the 'outrage' as 'a distinct and successful effort made by a body of students to repudiate all allegiance to the gracious sovereign who since his accession to the throne [had] shown himself a model constitutional ruler'. Two senators, he said, had expressed their intention of resigning unless steps were taken 'to prevent a recurrence of such a disgraceful scene'. Four culprits were named at the meeting – Thomas Kettle, a graduate, J.E. Kennedy and Sarsfield Kerrigan, undergraduates, and Thomas Madden, a medical student, who had no connection with University College. The secretaries were asked to summon all four to a meeting of the standing committee in four days time.

The Earl of Meath, already unpopular with the students for his unionist views, had not helped the situation by his speech being made public. The *Leader*, the favourite paper of many of the students, made a strong attack on him under the heading 'England's faithful senate', and was particularly critical of a part of his address in which he spoke of the Royal's £20,000 a year being withdrawn if the people of Britain got it into their heads that the money was spent 'on the training of Irish students in sentiments of disloyalty'. Moreover, a memorial signed by 150 students, endorsing the protest against the anthem, was sent to the standing committee. 'We protest', it said, 'against the wasteful, unjust and inefficient government of which that air is a symbol'. About the steps of 86 St Stephen's Green students gathered to inveigh against 'the shameful manner in which the Catholics of this country are defrauded of their right to higher education' and to assure 'the Earlsfort Terrace institution that its attempt to masquerade as a university will not be successful'.

The special senate meeting of 7 November was marked by

elements of high drama and of farce. The *Freeman's Journal*, of the following day, noted that a large body of police were in position at Earlsfort Terrace at eleven o'clock that morning. Some sixty or seventy students had gathered on the entrance steps. The first senator to arrive, Sir Christopher Nixon was 'boohed', but not loudly. Inspector Grant asked the young men not to stand in front of the door. The other members of the committee passed through in silence or with good humoured cheers. The Earl of Meath, however, went in by another entrance. When the meeting assembled it was found that all four candidates for possible censure had refused to attend. Tom Kettle had pointed out that he had not been present at the conferring, and both he and Thomas Madden, who belonged to the College of Surgeons and not to the Royal University, threatened legal proceedings. Kettle, moreover, with his instinct for the attention-catching gesture and phrase, had publicly denounced the university authorities and declared his intention of burning his degree. The two under-graduates, Kennedy and Kerrigan, questioned the powers of the senate to summon them or judge them. Decision was deferred to a further meeting.

In the meantime, further outside support for the students' protest was not lacking. The annual convention of the Gaelic League at the Mansion House, Dublin, passed a resolution heartily congratulating 'the nationalist undergraduates of the Royal University on their spirited protest against the identification of higher education with flunkyism and disloyalty to Ireland'.[140] Copies of the resolution were sent to the press, the senate, 'and in particular to the Rt Hon the Earl of Meath', the Very Rev Dr Delany, S.J., and Dr M.J. Cox. Support from the League and the *Leader* was not unexpected; from the *Irish Catholic* it was. On 11 November its editorial commented favourably on Delany's reply to the *Times*, but concluded with the comment that the actions of the few students had done more than the members of parliament over the previous session to make the British public realise the present anomalous situation affecting university education in Ireland. It was the kind of comment that added to Delany's difficulties. There were a number of students only too ready to believe that such a protest was the most effective means of getting Britain's two reluctant parliamentary parties to commit themselves to solving the university question. One of the actual participants in the 'organ raid', Patrick J. Little, destined to become a minister in successive Fianna Fáil governments, wrote in after years:[141]

We were all proud of our achievement and believed that we did stir the British politicians into speeding up the long delayed measure of establishing the National University.... Afterwards I intensely disliked 'rags' at conferring as disorderly and unintelligent and as a degrading caricature of our own conduct!

Delany, as his letter to the *Times* indicated, sought to make the best of the situation, availing of the student disorder to give added strength to his arguments for a university settlement. So much so, indeed, that Sheehy-Skeffington felt obliged to point out in the *Irish Protestant* that the college authorities did not know about or support the disorders, but took advantage of them to present their case after the event.[142] Delany feared correctly, however, that the inaugural meeting of the Literary and Historical Society, fixed for 8 November, might provoke further 'outrages'. The subject on which the auditor, Thomas F. Bacon, B.A., was to read a paper was 'Higher Education and National Life'. Delany sent him word, through Fr Darlington, that the great hall would not be available for the occasion and suggested the postponement of the meeting to a later date. 'In the present state of inflamed feeling over the organ situation and the senate's reaction', he wrote, 'the L and H meeting might lead to disturbances which would be gladly availed of by the unionist press and by the enemies in parliament of the Irish university campaign. Besides, the case of the 'organ raiders' was still *sub judice* in the senate and disturbances might not help the case of the students involved'.[143] Bacon agreed. As it became evident, a little later, that the senate was making no immediate judgement, and that the atmosphere had cooled, Delany suggested 22 November for the inaugural. Two of the visiting speakers declared themselves unavailable, Stephen Gwynn because of another engagement and Dr Mahaffy of Trinity College because he did not wish to speak in a rival college where the students were at loggerheads with the authorities. M. McDonnell Bodkin, K.C., and Thomas P. Moloney, K.C., stood in and with T.M. Healy, K.C., M.P., and Sir Christopher Nixon, M.D., of the senate of the university, constituted the guest speakers for the evening.[144]

In the course of his reported speech, Nixon paid a glowing tribute to Delany. There was a singular appropriateness, he said, in discussing the higher education question within the walls of that college which, when the history of the university struggle was written, 'must exact the wonder and admiration of its keenest competitors', whilst it could claim that, 'more than its most favoured rivals', it had 'stimulated the growth of an intellectual life, and brought higher education within reach of those who needed it most'. When the final stage of the struggle was reached, he hoped at no distant date, three names of those who 'climbed the steep, where Fame's proud temple shines afar' would be long remembered, 'Newman, Molloy and Delany — names inseparably connected with the Catholic University and University College'. Turning to Delany, he expressed the hope that he would be spared to enjoy the fruition of his labours and his triumphs, 'triumphs which you predicted would follow from the development of the wealth of intellect which lay dormant and hidden in Catholic Ireland'. He felt he was expressing the feelings of Catholics towards the religious order of which Fr Delany was such a distinguished member when he echoed the archbishop's wish of the previous year that its members would continue their great services in the new university to come. He concluded with the words: 'I hope that those gentlemen at the back of the hall are as satisfied with the part they have taken in these proceedings as I am with mine'.[145]

Unfortunately, he had been subjected to almost continual loud interruption of a disrespectful nature: 'Why did you send your son to Trinity?' 'Good old Christy'. 'Sit down, Sir Christy'. Delany, mortified and furious, made an unscheduled interjection. The *Irish Times*, of 23 November, reported his words:

> The educational work of this establishment is intended for gentlemen. The conduct witnessed here tonight is not that of gentlemen; and therefore those young men who have made this disturbance here and rendered it impossible to hear the speaker whom we invited, I repudiate, and I trust that very few of them, if any, belong to me. I want to say more than that, that the continuance of the debate in this establishment shall not take place if again such conduct is repeated, for I shall not subject ladies and gentlemen to come here and be treated by blackguards in that fashion. (Loud applause)

'I have one more word to say', he continued, 'that I have for twenty years been a colleague of Sir Christopher Nixon in educational work, and during that time a stauncher colleague I could not have in the defence of Catholic interests. He has been at all times ready to do all that lay in his power, at great professional sacrifices, to advance university education in Ireland, and above all to advance and promote in every way the interest of the establishment of which he is the dean of faculty' (applause). 'And if there are Catholic Medical School men making that noise (A voice — 'There are') — I deplore their action, and am ashamed of it, and so are their colleagues, and I am sure their colleagues will make them feel it when they go out of this hall' (applause). The auditor, writing of the occasion much later, considered that the interruptions were excessive 'and merited the strong reproof administered by the president when, at the end of Sir Christopher's speech, he apologised on behalf of the college'. This, he thought, was 'recognised by the interrupters themselves, if one might judge by the applause which the back of the hall gave to the president after his closing address'.[146]

As he rose to speak, also, the president was greeted with applause. Of his platform appearance, it was said, that 'his spare figure easily assumed the stance of the orator, his hand holding his gown as the folds of a toga. His speech had substance and point, and he used to full advantage the resources of a well-modulated voice; but he relied for his effect not on its charm but on his complete, persuasive lucidity'.[147] He relied, too, in common with all successful public speakers, on the instincts of an actor, playing on the emotions of the moment as his text required. On this occasion, as if sensing the chastened but difficult mood of his audience, he blended emotion and reason to evoke both the easy cheer and solid applause; availing of the opportunity to give vent to some personal desires regarding a university settlement and to defend the Royal at the expense of Trinity College, then particularly unpopular because of the scholarship controversy.

He did not subscribe, he said, to the description of the Royal as a mere examining university. All who had gone out from University College had been directly or indirectly taught by the Royal. Trinity College and Dublin University had no such connection. The University of Dublin, apart from Trinity, was a sham. There was nothing in the world like it. In the Royal the programme of teaching was in the hands of a very learned body. Its professors had had the benefit of training in some of the leading universities of Europe. There was 'a wider culture applied in the teaching and examinations of the Royal' than there was in Trinity. The latter had 'one type of educational culture. The students went to the schools that fed Trinity College. They then went to Trinity College and ended in Trinity College'. Hence, 'when people spoke to him of the prestige of Trinity College, he denied it, he despised it' (applause).[148] He felt it due to his colleagues, he declared, to make that statement.

The term 'national university' was being used as embracing Trinity College. The word 'national', he believed, was doing infinite harm with regard to education in Ireland. He would not touch Trinity. The Protestants of Ireland were strictly entitled to a place in which they could have confidence – a teaching institution in harmony with their political and racial instincts, and much good might it do them. He would not interefere with it. But he would say that the majority should have at least equal rights with the minority, and what the government had given to the minority they should give to the majority. He honoured the words of Dr Traill when he said, in deprecating the removal of the divinity school from Trinity, that the college was founded 'to be a place of learning and religion'. It would be a bad time for Ireland when religion was separated from learning (Hear, hear). Their first duty was to God, and, secondly and closest to it, was the duty they owed to their country, to their traditions, and to those who went before them; and they should try to be worthy of them and to tread in their footsteps, to love their land and its traditions, and do all they could to be worthy sons of such fathers (applause). In conclusion, he asked his hearers to protest against any system in which they were not to be taught anything about God or religion, and to be given all other degrees, but no degrees in theology (Hear, hear). He held that there was no true education that ignored a man's soul or which did not enable them to be at once true christians and true Irishmen (applause).

Such rhetoric, filtered through the abridged newspaper report of another age, has a jaded, hollow ring for the modern reader. The disillusion of hindsight, and a mental recoil from years of inflated 'patriotic' eloquence, present obstacles to appreciating the enthusiasm of a generation directly experiencing the birth of a nation.

The *United Irishman* of 2 December 1905, Arthur Griffith's separatist newspaper, published a letter from the students who had been called 'blackguards'. They had intended no personal insult to Sir Christopher Nixon. Their protest was against the anomaly of 'one who accepted honours and emoluments from the government' protesting 'against the government's policy and parsimony'. The paper, not surprisingly, saw Delany's defence of Nixon on the one hand, and his attack on Trinity on the other, and then his defence of the Royal, when he did not speak up for it before the royal commission, as 'paradoxical'. It also took him to task for his views on a national university. 'When he openly shows that he does not desire and is not aiming at a university for the Irish nation, we think it time to point out to Fr Delany that if he does not want a national university the nation does not want Fr Delany'. Yet the writer declared himself puzzled because he had recently heard Fr Delany speak in favour of a national university at a public meeting in connection with the School of Irish Learning.

The writer's puzzlement echoed that wider confusion, previously noticed, as to what was signified by the Irish 'nation', by 'national' and 'nationalist'. The terms were used with different applications by the same people from one occasion to another. Hence, in the university context, Bryce's scheme, which included the Church of Ireland and Presbyterian institutions of Trinity College, Dublin, and Queen's College, Belfast, was spoken of as a scheme for a national university; while Augustine Birrell was to actually establish a National University which excluded both colleges. In the first instance, 'national' was applied geographically, embracing the inhabitants of the entire island irrespective of creed or political differences; in the second, its application was largely limited to the Catholic majority. Irish politicians and journalists tended to apply it now the one way and now the other. The leaders of the parliamentary party (also called the nationalist party, to add to the confusion) and men of a more radical persuasion, such as Arthur Griffith, the leaders of republican opinion, and D.P. Moran of the *Leader*, frequently made believe that there were no deep-seated religious and political differences between unionists and the Catholic majority, that all were part of the 'national' population or the Irish 'nation'; yet when they came up against the stern reality of Irish unionist intransigence and hostility towards self-government, or even towards the establishment of an endowed university for the majority, they instinctively spoke of the majority as the true Irish 'nation' and their cause as the 'national' one. The unionists were seen as Irish with a difference. They were 'West Britons' determined to preserve their minority dominance at the expense of the 'Irish people'. Trinity College, with its proud Protestant traditions, its imposing presence and comparative wealth, was the particular symbol of this ascendancy and different allegiance: desiring to be English, as W.B. Yeats wrote in 1899, setting herself 'against the national genius' and teaching her children 'to imitate alien styles and choose out alien themes'.[149]

The famous religious question in Ireland, therefore, had scarcely anything to do with theology. Catholics and Protestants, Arthur Clery noted,[150] just found themselves separated, socially apart in Dublin as much as in the north, with their *casus belli* commonly an economic one: the benefits of industry, commerce and government patronage being mainly enjoyed by the Protestant minority, and this, in turn, begetting different political and cultural allegiances. To the minority, naturally jealous of these privileges and fearful of the papist majority, the granting of increased power and influence to the Catholic population seemed foolish and dangerous. Hence, both British and Irish unionists believed, or affected to believe, that Home Rule meant Rome rule, evoking the fires of Smithfield, and that the spending of public money to endow a Catholic university was a suicidal exercise. The unionist press, in consequence, was only too ready to highlight signs of disorder in what was termed the Roman Catholic University College and to pillory them as marks of intolerance, disloyalty, and the Irish Catholics' inability to govern themselves. In short, the university question was at bottom not merely an educational question, but a political and economic one; and to William Delany, close to the coalface, the views he had expressed about Trinity College in 1886 were still pertinent twenty years later. He could not see it as part of the authentic 'national' tradition, or contributing anything constructive to a 'national' university.

The senate of the Royal University, in its subsequent meetings regarding the 1905 disturbances, found itself divided. The vice-chancellor, Dr Molloy, presiding in the absence of the chancellor, gave it as his opinion, that while the senate could take action to prevent disorderly conduct in future, it had no powers to punish or try its graduates or undergraduates. Its functions were purely academical. Charles Doyle — who had had such a remarkable run of successes in the first Intermediate examinations and subsequently a distinguished career at the bar before being appointed county court judge — was called in as legal adviser. His judgement was in accord with the views of Dr Molloy. When the matter was put, however, to the law-officers of the crown, they, strongly supported by the Earl of Meath, pressed for the punishment of the offenders. At a special meeting on 15 December, a letter from the leading legal authority, Chief Baron Palles, decided the issue. Unable to attend this or some previous meetings of the senate, he wrote to convey his views. He sided with Mr Doyle's opinion. His letter concluded with a firmness which both discomfited the chancellor and virtually determined the senate's decision.

I regret to be obliged to add [he wrote] that in my opinion

the address of the chancellor on 3 November, which although delivered at a meeting of the standing committee (the proceedings of which have, up to this, been deemed private and confidential) was widely circulated through the public press, had prejudged a material part of the matter to be now judically decided, and that any award of punishment to which he may be a party will be liable to be quashed by the King's Bench *a certiorari.*

As it is impossible that the senate can dissociate itself from its respected head, my opinion is that the proceedings should be allowed to terminate. Certainly, I for one, decline to take the responsibility of being a party to their further continuance.

The senate decided to take no further action beyond making arrangements to prevent future disturbances. Judge Shaw resigned, as a result, on 18 December. It was thought for a while that many other resignations would follow. The Earl of Meath sought to persuade the Chief Secretary to move on the matter. This failing, he sent in his resignation in March 1906. The chancellorship was not filled until twelve months later, when Lord Castletown was appointed.

Up to this William Delany's standing was high with the students. None of the opposition was directed against him personally. There is some evidence that he knew the names of those who had taken part in the seizure of the organ, namely, Francis Cruise O'Brien, John E. Kennedy, Eugene Sheehy, Patrick Little, and Thomas Madden from the College of Surgeons.[151] A year later he was to write to John Sweetman:[152]

I had reason to believe that the students knew that I defended in the senate and saved from any penalty those who had taken part in the raid last year; that I was not in favour of having *God Save the King* played; and that I hoped to succeed in getting it omitted as it is not played on such occasions elsewhere. O'Brien, especially, who became prominent afterwards, knew all this perfectly well.

Cruise O'Brien's prominence in 1906 was to prove a rock on which Delany's popularity perished. He was both the auditor of the Literary and Historical Society and the editor of *St Stephen's,* a college magazine. A member of the Young Ireland branch of the United Irish League, he became – in the words of his celebrated son, Conor – 'one of the most obnoxious of the new intellectuals in the (Irish parliamentary) party organisation, critical of the party leadership, and rich in, if little else, the power to say wounding things in a memorable manner'.[153]

Delany had been deeply upset by the 1905 incidents. Apart from his personal embarrassment in his dual rôle as senator and president of the unruly students, the near dissolution of the senate and the unionist reaction underlined the danger to the fifty-year quest for an endowed Catholic university. In his seventy-first year, he was finding it increasingly difficult to sit lightly to student unrest. He determined that in 1906 there would be no grounds for complaint. Unfortunately, he made a serious misjudgement which reaped increased trouble. His action, he told John Sweetman, was explained by his anxiety to avoid as far as he could 'a repetition of such escapades this year in circumstances which could be used by our enemies to justify charges of rebellious disloyalty, "insult to the king" and all the rest of the farrago of last year's abuse'.

The senate took particular precautions to ensure that proceedings at the conferring would be uninterrupted. Great care was taken in the distribution of admission tickets. The secretary had a cornet-player standing by to play *God Save the King* in the event of the organ being put out of commission. Police surveillance was increased.

On 26 October, on his way to the conferring, Delany was informed by some students that they intended to hold an indignation meeting against the limitation on admission tickets and the police precautions. They planned to hold it opposite the Royal University building or, if prevented there, at University College. He instructed them not to have their meeting in the college or on the college steps. He had no objection to their holding it opposite the college or anywhere else. At the university, he asked the superintendent of police to prevent any meeting in the college or on its steps 'but to allow the students to hold their meeting if they wished opposite the college or anywhere else they might choose'.[154]

The conferring, according to newspaper reports, went fairly quietly at Earlsfort Terrace. As the crowd was dispersing, however, what appeared to be 'a black bomb' was thrown from the steps of Alexandria College opposite the university. The crowd scattered excitedly. One student gave the object a kick and disclosed 'a wooden shell filled with lime'. The police kept the crowd moving and prevented any further scenes in the vicinity. Subsequently a body of student demonstrators made for University College. Delany, who had just returned home and was in his room, was told that a large number of them were trying to make their way into the college hall. In the process one of them, according to Francis Cruise O'Brien, was 'ill used by a constable'. The president came down and addressed them. Just as he could not permit a minority who differed from them to hold a party meeting in the college, so he could not allow them to hold their meeting in the building. To do so would be to identify the college with their words and actions. Hence, he was obliged to request them to hold their meeting elsewhere.

Deterred from proceeding with their demonstration by the presence of a strong force of police, and discomfited by heavy rain, the students stood around for some minutes, 'during which they unbosomed themselves of a vast amount of strong language', and then marched, four deep, 'over the western side of Stephen's Green and down Grafton Street, singing *God Save Ireland*, the police following close behind'. As they passed down Grafton Street 'the demonstrators raised their voices to a tremendous pitch, and jostled those whom they met in a most reprehensible fashion. At the corner of Nassau Street a cyclist was pushed off his machine'. They eventually finished their journey at the Cecilia Street Medical School where they had determined to hold a protest meeting.

The unfortunate thing, from the point of view of Delany's relations with the student body, was that he had not relied solely on his noted powers of persuasion. The students' grievance against the senate was almost forgotten in their fury at the use of police against them. It placed Delany, in their view, on the side of the despised ascendancy. Their meeting, as reported in the *Daily Express* was attended by large numbers of students, both from University College and the Medical School, and was punctuated by denunciations of him. The first speaker, Mr A. McCarthy, set the tone. They were denied their right that day to be present at the conferring of degrees and, 'without any justification whatsoever, a force of police had been brought to the university buildings for the purpose of preventing them from expressing their nationalist sentiments' (Cheers). They had succeeded in drowning *God Save the King*, which would make some of the senators of the Royal University feel very uncomfortable. 'But they had hardly expected to receive from a man whom they had previously believed to be of their way of thinking such treatment as was meted out to them by Fr Delany (Hisses). He had actually ordered the police to clear the steps of the University College, which had been recognised from time immemorial as the students' meeting place; and he had even threatened them with arrest when they attempted to hold a meeting inside' (Renewed hissing). Hence, he proposed for the meeting a resolution, which had been drafted for him by Mr Sheehy-Skeffington: 'That we censure the conduct of the president of the University College in allying himself with the police for the purpose of preventing the expression of our nationalist views' (Applause).

Sheehy-Skeffington, a former registrar of the college, a graduate of some years standing and, therefore, much older than the majority of those present, supported the resolution. He urged them to continue their protests against the anthem until it was done away with entirely. Fr Delany by his conduct on this occasion 'had shown that University College refused to associate itself with the principle of nationality'. The authorities of Cecilia Street, by comparison, 'were not ashamed or afraid to allow a nationalist demonstration to be held on their premises' (Cheers). 'After today they recognised no difference between Fr Delany and the provost of Trinity College, except that the former gentleman's anti-nationalist policy was more harsh than the other's'. Mr F. Sheehan of the Medical School said he had never been deceived by Fr Delany, unlike a great many others. But the time had come 'when they were bound to repudiate that rev. gentleman, heart and soul' (Applause). He proposed that they should form a strong, nationalist students' club, and provide themselves with proper quarters in the city. A feeling of betrayal was marked among many students: the feeling that they had been 'betrayed by their own president who had called on the myrmidons of the English government to keep them out of their own college'. He had sided with the ascendancy against them. Hence, the resolution was amended to read: 'That we censure the conduct of the president of the University College in allying himself with the ascendancy party, and calling in the police for the purpose of preventing the free expression of our nationalist views'.

Supporting the resolution, Cruise O'Brien — a frail figure with long black hair and jutting chin[155] — declared that he too had not been fooled by Fr Delany, 'because he always knew him as an old Whig, trying to pass himself off as a nationalist when he wanted to please that party, and posing as a unionist when the other side was to be conciliated. Most of them, he suspected, had a pretty accurate idea of the type of man Fr Delany was; and they were also aware that half the men on the senate of the Royal University were of the same class'. Fr Delany 'had never tired telling him in the past that no other university had to suffer the same anthem being foisted upon the students'. He was pleased to see 'how unanimous the two Catholic colleges were in repudiating Fr Delany's action' (Applause).

The chairman, J.F. Byrne, B.A., in putting the resolution to the meeting, said 'it was not the exclusion of the students from the function that they wanted to fight against so much as the ascendancy party which was at the back of it' (Hear, hear). What the students of University College wanted was –

A voice – To get rid of the Jesuits (Applause).

Another voice – Fr Delany is not a Jesuit (Laughter).

The chairman then concluded by expressing the hope that on degree day next year they would be able to make a still more vigorous and affective stand (Applause). The resolution was then carried unanimously.

The accounts of the affair which appeared, in large headlines, in the papers that evening and on the next day, caused concern to some parents of students and others connected with the college. They sent copies of the *Daily Express* of 27 October to Delany, expressing the view that the speeches amounted to acts of public insubordination which called for correction in the interests of collegiate discipline. He, however, as he wrote later, 'regarded them as the hasty utterances of a moment of excitement, natural enough in the special circumstances, and determined therefore to take no notice of them'; although, as he informed John Sweetman, 'very erroneous accounts' of what had taken place were given by Cruise O'Brien and others.[156] He would not concede, then or later, that his calling in of the police was a mistake. The Dublin Metropolitan Police were to his mind the guardians of the public order. They had never been, unlike the Royal Irish Constabulary, identified with the repression of national feeling. He underestimated the spirit of rebellion that was abroad and failed to appreciate that any government police force was seen as hostile to national aspirations. He also underestimated the pertinacity of Cruise O'Brien, Timothy Mangan and others once they had experienced a feeling of power. The subsequent actions of O'Brien as auditor, and of some other committee members of the Literary and Historical Society, forced his hand.

The previous year the committee had summoned an extraordinary meeting at which a resolution was passed 'cordially endorsing the action of the students who prevented the playing of the national anthem at the recent conferring of degrees'. Delany declared the resolution out of order on the grounds that the society was not a political one, and as *ex-officio* president he had ordered it to be expunged from the minute book. The honorary secretaries, Francis Cruise O'Brien and John Kennedy, refused to carry out the order. After deliberation, however, the resolution was expunged.

It is relevant to recall that the society had been revived by Delany in 1884; and that he had drawn up its code of rules, which laid down that the president of the college was *ex-officio* president of the society, that its meetings were to be held in the college, that the work was to be carried out by an auditor and a committee of seven, and that the list of subjects for debate was first to be submitted to the president for approval.

For 1906-1907 the committee was constituted as follows: auditor, F. Cruise O'Brien; T.F. Bacon, B.A., ex-auditor; Thomas Bodkin, A.E. Cox, Maurice Healy, T.A. Mangan, G. O'Byrne, J.A. Ronayne. During the year Bodkin resigned. Cruise O'Brien and his supporters, according to Delany, co-opted in his place O'Connell Sullivan, a medical student not connected with University College. On 28 October, two days after the indignation meeting at Cecilia Street, a meeting of the committee was called. Present were Messrs O'Brien, Mangan, Cox, Ronayne and O'Byrne. The minutes of the meeting show that Mangan proposed, and Ronayne seconded a resolution that: 'We, the committee of the L.H.S. condemn the action of the president in exposing students to insulting treatment at the hands of the police, especially having regard to the fact that no previous intimation of his objection to a meeting was afforded through the ordinary channels of information'. The resolution was carried, and the secretary, A.E. Cox, was instructed to forward it to Fr Delany. The latter learned from the secretary that Messrs Bacon and Healy, who were absent, had received no notice that any such motion was to be proposed at the meeting; but that the auditor, notwithstanding, had ruled that it was in order to proceed with it.

Apart from the irregularity involved, the action of the auditor and his committee in accepting, passing and sending a resolution of censure to the president of the college raised at once, in Delany's view, a serious question of collegiate discipline. He had no objection, he stated subsequently, to four or five students of the college expressing disapproval of his action, but a formal vote of censure from the same students, as constituting the committee of the college debating society, was a very different matter. It implied a claim on the part of the committee to sit in judgement on the administrative acts of the head of the college and to censure him as they saw fit. To accept such a resolution would imply a recognition of the committee's claim and 'establish a precedent for similar votes of censure on any number of future presidents'. Accordingly, he conceived it his duty to return the resolution. He replied very calmly to the secretary's letter, making it clear that he viewed the question as 'one of constitutional discipline, and not of personal discourtesy'.

The secretary was asked to point out to the committee that their functions, as a committee, referred solely to the carrying out of the work of the Literary and Historical Society. They had no authority to deal with anything else. The previous year when the committee expressed dissent from his action in postponing the inaugural meeting, they were dealing with a matter relating to the society, and their resolution, in consequence, was not out of order. The present resolution, however, had nothing to do with the work of the society. 'It was plainly *ultra vires* for the committee, and ought to have been so ruled by your chairman'. He could not accept it, therefore, and must request that it be expunged from the minutes, 'expressly on the ground that it deals with a matter which does not come within the functions of the committee'.

He had no objection, he continued, to receiving it as an expression of the views of individual members on the action which he felt it his duty as president to take, 'after grave reflection and with much reluctance, for the interests not of the college alone, but of Catholic education in Ireland'. They were quite entitled to such views. In the students' position they were natural enough. They spoke and acted 'from the feelings of the moment' and had no responsibility for anything beyond it. He could not, and did not expect them 'to realise the crushing weight of responsibility' that rested on him, as president of the college 'at this most critical moment, in the interests of Catholic education'. He only asked, 'on the strength of a life-time spent in working for Catholic education' that where they thought him mistaken they would give him credit for acting according to his conscience and to the very best of his lights.

Dissident students are seldom impressed by appeals to experience and past services. The committee considered the president's instructions and plea the following day, Tuesday, 30 October. Six members attended, apart from the auditor. O'Byrne, having examinations in London, had resigned. Cox proposed, and Healy seconded, that the resolution be rescinded as *ultra vires*. The auditor declared the proposal out of order. A motion to discuss the question was similarly treated. A further proposal that the resolution be rescinded on the grounds that the committee could not speak for the society on the matter, and that it was passed without due consideration, was defeated by four votes to three. The resolution, therefore, remained in the minutes of the committee and a formal notification of this was sent to the president. He made no reply. He reserved the matter for the next meeting of the college council, whose function it was to deal with questions of misconduct or of insubordination. In his view the main fault lay with Cruise O'Brien. Apart from him the committee was equally divided; and he had ruled out of order even a motion to discuss the question, though it was supported by three out of six members, two of whom had been absent at the previous meeting.

Delany wrote to him to give him notice that his recent conduct outside and inside the college was coming before the college council on 5 November, and that if he wished to present himself and make a statement he should ask the council that he might be heard. The committee of the L. and H. responded at a special meeting on 2 November by supporting Cruise O'Brien, and asserting their 'unquestionable right . . . to be considered the legitimate channel of expression of student opinion'. At the college council the question of O'Brien's behaviour inside the college was considered in detail, the president having requested that no cognisance be taken of occurrences outside the college. Before a decision was reached, he informed the council that he had promised O'Brien that he would ask for a hearing for him and that O'Brien was in attendance. The council declined to see him on the grounds that the case rested on the official minutes which they had before them, and that nothing he might say could explain those away. O'Brien was informed that the council would be writing to him.

The registrar wrote the following day on behalf of the president and council of the college. 'The council had under consideration the minutes of the dates 28 October, 30 October and 2 November', and regarded the action taken by him as chairman 'as grossly irregular throughout, and in its reference to the governing authority of the college as distinctly insubordinate'. They were unanimous that the least penalty his conduct merited, in the interests of college discipline, was his rustication for the session 1906-1907. He was thereby informed that he was rusticated for that period of time 'and excluded from all participation in any function of the college'. The recipient was thus deprived — the hardest blow for him — of the opportunity of delivering his inaugural address as auditor of the L. and H. Shortly afterwards, Delany announced the postponement of the inaugural meeting.

On 9 November Cruise O'Brien asked for and obtained an interview with the president. He complained of the injustice done him by the sentence of rustication. He had acted in the belief, which he still held, that he and his committee owed obedience only to the society which had elected them, and that the president and council had no authority to supervise or deal with their actions as a committee. Delany pointed out that it was he who had established the society, that he had power also to dissolve it, 'and that Mr O'Brien's contention would establish an authority superior to that of the president and council, and therefore plainly subversive of authority and insubordinate; but Mr O'Brien held to his position, and nothing came of the interview'. The following day the president went to England for a ten day break.

In the meantime, the Literary and Historical Society met and letters were sent to the college council from O'Brien appealing against his sentence, and from Mr Healy, as one of the honorary secretaries, asking reconsideration of the sentence. The council held an extraordinary meeting on 12 November, which Cruise O'Brien attended and at which Healy's request was considered. O'Brien made a statement to the effect that he should not be singled out for punishment, that the committee of the L. and H. shared responsibility equally with him. After he had left, the council weighed the matter and saw no grounds for reversing their decision. He had refused to permit the committee of the society to discuss a formal instruction from the governing authority of the college. They wrote to him to this effect.

The registrar was instructed to write also to the secretary of the L. and H. to inform him that by virtue of O'Brien's rustication he ceased *ipso facto* to be a member of the society; and that the college council could not accept the committee's claim of 2 November to have an 'unquestionable right ... to be considered the legitimate channel of expression of student opinion', particularly on such questions as the general government of the college, and hence 'must insist that the authority of the president and council be acknowledged by the L. and H. Society as well as by all other college departments'.[157]

On the same day on which the correspondence secretary, Maurice Healy, received the letter from the council, there was also sent to him a requisition signed by six members of the L. and H. requesting him to call an extraordinary general meeting 'to consider the president's postponement of the inaugural address and to discuss what action should be taken by the society in the matter'. He called the meeting for the first legal date, Saturday, 17 November. The newspapers, meanwhile, carried reports of the council's rustication of Cruise O'Brien, and of letters of censure being sent to Messrs T. Mangan and J.A. Ronayne.

As the date of the meeting approached, it became known that O'Brien proposed to take the chair on the grounds that he was auditor and that no sentence of the college council could have the effect of removing him from his position. The secretaries and other members sought to persuade him to refrain from this extreme course, and he consented to stand down in favour of an agreed chairman. When the latter, however, proved unable to act, O'Brien returned to his former decision. He installed himself in the chair. The correspondence secretary proposed an alternative chairman, and was seconded by A.E. Cox, the records secretary. O'Brien 'ruled the motion out of order'. Several members then rose to protest that by the decision of the college council O'Brien had lost any right to preside, that if his contention were correct that the council did not have authority to remove him the society had expressed no opinion on the matter, that he should have the good taste to absent himself so that the meeting might discuss freely a question which affected him personally, and that he was stultifying the proceedings of the society in as much as the council could not recognise a meeting at which he took the chair in defiance of their express instruction. The chairman ruled them out of order. Thereafter, it appears that most of those opposed to his action remained silent out of protest.

Cruise O'Brien made a statement as to his position, and read the correspondence between himself and the authorities of the college. A resolution was then proposed by a Mr McCarthy, and supported by Mr Flood: 'That this meeting declines to recognise that the council of the college has any authority in virtue of which it can expel a member from the society or deprive him of any function vested in him by the society'. The resolution was supported by Messrs J. O'Byrne, Ronayne, Mangan and R.J. Sheehy; and Messrs D. Carroll, F. McCormack, and Rory O'Connor, speaking under protest, opposed it. Feelings ran very high. Apart from two clearly opposed groups, there were, according to one participant, quite a number of students who were 'not fully in sympathy with O'Brien', but still 'shared the pretty general feeling that the college council (which was only Fr Delany writ large) . . . was high-handedly exceeding its powers' in removing him from office.[158] When the time for division came, the objectors refused to vote on the ground that the meeting was wholly irregular. There being in consequence no opposition, the resolution was declared carried unanimously. A large number then withdrew from the meeting as a protest. It has been suggested that some sixty members were in favour. Looking back on the occasion in later years, Cruise O'Brien commented: 'Those observers who talk about Ireland being priest-ridden might have had some food for reflection had they been there'.[159]

Among those who left the meeting were the two honorary secretaries. Their record of what followed in their absence was drawn from those who remained and from accounts in the press. The meeting, following the withdrawal, decided to send a deputation to the president asking permission to have the inaugural address delivered in the college. In the event of a refusal, the committee were instructed to arrange for the holding of the inaugural meeting outside the college. Three days later, 20 November, an account of the proceedings appeared in the *Irish Independent*. The secretaries immediately wrote to the paper repudiating the account as unofficial and incorrect. A note in the *Independent* stated that Cruise O'Brien had personally furnished the account and guaranteed it official. O'Brien then wrote acknowledging the report to be from him and pledging his word for its accuracy. He described himself as 'auditor of the Literary and Historical Society'. Messrs O'Connor and McCormack wrote to the paper to protest that their remarks had been misrepresented. The society had clearly split in two; the split became official when the president refused the use of any room in University College to a society under the auditorship of O'Brien. He and his followers went to the Medical School in Cecilia Street, and subsequently to a club in Dawson Street, for their meetings.

Throughout the controversy, Cruise O'Brien made use of the press to proclaim his opposition and to embarrass the university authorities. With reference to the motives of his action he gave a special interview to a reporter from the *Irish Independent* some days after the extraordinary meeting of 17 November. He had acted in the interest of 'the simple rights of students'. Because of 'the paucity of our numbers', he said, 'and the anomalous position of our college, the authorities try to exercise much more jurisdiction than they would in a university whose student body was efficiently organised'. The present dispute was 'the culmination of a long-standing difference on the vitally important matter of student liberty. We do not want anarchy; all we ask is that discipline be restrained within the bounds of reason, and that students be treated as responsible beings'. In University College the student as a factor was 'utterly ignored'. The root-cause of this was the college's connection with the Royal University — an institution 'regarded with loathing by the student body, not only on the grounds of nationalism', but because it was 'academically a failure', and was a clog on the students both in their purely academic life and in their relation to national life. Yet this institution was regarded as sacrosanct 'by a section of the governing body of the college', and any attempt to give utterance to student opinion regarding it was 'closured'. He concluded, speaking as if for the great body of students:

> We are anxious that the public should clearly see our position, and attribute it, not to hostility or insubordination, above all, not to anti-clericalism, but to a simple, and I hope, reasonable desire to obtain the same measure of academic freedom for ourselves as is enjoyed by the students of other universities.

The president of University College might comment on Cruise O'Brien's distortion of facts, his fellow-students who opposed him on 17 November might be cynical about 'Crusoe's' concern for 'student liberty', but there was no denying his general ability, his influence over others, his self-confidence, and his capacity to express himself both with sweet reasonableness and in short biting phrases. His irreverent description of Delany as 'a decaying old Whig' became celebrated amongst his contemporaries. Excluded from the college, he determined to make the occasion of his inaugural address a memorable one. He hired the hall of Dublin's Antient Concert Rooms for the meeting. The theme was 'Democracy and Education'; the guest speakers were Arthur Griffith, William McGrath, K.C., Lindsay Crawford, and Edward Little. The majority of the students, however, seem to have felt at this stage that matters had gone too far or far enough. The meeting was not well attended.[160] It was for O'Brien a disappointing ending to a year which had promised so much. The president and college council had formally removed him from auditorship of the L. and H., and previously they had closed down *St Stephen's* magazine because of a 'usurpation of power' and a 'manifest violation of ordinary collegiate courtesy' by him and his editorial committee. The course he had pursued as editor foreshadowed, indeed, his performance as auditor.

Successive editors of *St Stephen's*, which ran from June 1901 to June 1906, paid tribute to the support shown it by Delany. An occasion of conflict arose in November 1905, however, when he refused permission to the editor, John Kennedy, to report an extraordinary meeting of the Literary and Historical Society on 6 November, in which outspoken comments were made about the senate of the Royal University and strong exception was expressed to the president's postponement of the forthcoming inaugural address because of its proximity to the disturbances on degree day. The meeting had been reported in the public press, but Delany argued that a report in the college magazine would appear to support 'the groundless and false' impression created by certain outside parties 'that the government of the college' was 'not in harmony with the national feeling both of the bulk of the students or of the country generally'.[161] His cautious censorship caused considerable ill-feeling.

This came to a head the following year when *St Stephen's* representative council had Cruise O'Brien as editor, two Arts and two Medical School students as sub-editors, and P.J. Little as manager. The magazine began to tend towards open disaffection. There were vague references to 'the authorities' of the college, but the main target was members of the senate of the university. In the words of P.J. Little, the paper expressed the nationalist viewpoint 'in attacks on people like the Earl of Meath and Sir James Creed Meredith, who was the Protestant and unionist joint-secretary of the old Royal University. . . . These attacks were apparently too strong meat for the college authorities and were regarded as impugning authority and, I suppose, as getting too much into politics, and so *St Stephen's* was suppressed, about the same time as the rustication of Cruise O'Brien'.[162]

The impugning of authority, however, did not stop at articles in the magazine. Early in March 1906, Delany learned that O'Brien had instructed the printer to remove the medallion on the cover and to substitute for 'Magazine of University College', a new title, 'Magazine of the Catholic University of Ireland'. Moreover, envelopes and letter-headings with the new title had already been printed. He wrote to the manager of the representative council that this was not in order: that the Catholic University still had a legal existence, and that University College had no right to usurp its name on its publications.[163] He informed the printer that the medallion was not to be removed and that all proofs were to be initialled by him. This drew a letter from the manager, P.J. Little, and the honorary secretary, Joseph Brennan, objecting to his countermanding their express order to the printer without reference to them; and they pointed out, that under the 1903 constitution of *St Stephen's*, its council 'was appointed the supreme governing body of the magazine' and that, therefore, 'no intervention from outside, however well considered and well-intentioned', could be allowed by them while they had the honour to constitute the council. The president and college council, considering the matter on 22 March, pronounced on lines similar to those they were to pursue in the L. and H. controversy the following autumn. The magazine was the property of the college, it had been founded by the president, and its control, as that of all other collegiate property, rested with the governing body of the college; no body of students was competent to confer its supreme control upon a student council; and, therefore, the action of the members of that body in taking on themselves, without reference to the president, to give directions for the removal of the medallion of University College from the cover 'was a usurpation of power that they were not entitled to, and a manifest violation of the just rights of University College, as well as of ordinary collegiate courtesy'. The president, on the advice of the council, felt precluded 'from any further recognition of a council of *St Stephen's* holding that attitude'.[164]

A month later, on 24 April, the printer informed Delany that Messrs O'Brien and Little, instead of bringing back to him proofs initialled by the president, had brought the proofs directly into the works and had them run off. Two days later, the honorary secretary of the magazine's representative council sent a resolution to the registrar, proposed by Mangan and seconded by O'Brien: 'That we consider the insinuation of the college council that we have committed a breach of collegiate courtesy entirely unfounded, and that it proceeds from a complete misunderstanding of the facts of the case'. The 'impugning of authority' led inevitably to the suppression mentioned by P.J. Little.

On the lapse of *St Stephen's*, a new magazine, *Hermes*, succeeded it. It was run by Thomas Bodkin and Maurice Healy. When Cruise O'Brien as auditor led the L. and H. Society out of University College, the society was reconstituted within the college with Maurice Healy as auditor and Bodkin as one of his committee. It seems more than a coincidence. Caher Davitt was to write years later, in the *History of the Literary and Historical Society*, that as a young student he had the impression that rivalry existed between those, like Healy, Bodkin and others, who were resident at 86 St Stephen's Green, and the general body of non-residents, including such as Cruise O'Brien and John Ronayne, and that this rivalry was partly responsible for the development of two parties within the society.[165] The residents, usually numbering about twelve, were mainly ex-Clongownians and, according to another contemporary, tended to be influential in the L. and H. 'because of their calibre and the fact that they were on the spot for meetings'.[166] As against this view, some of the residents actually supported O'Brien; and one has to keep reminding oneself that, despite the brilliance of the generation, the total number of students at University College scarcely exceeded one hundred and eighty, and of these only a handful were regularly involved in student activities, so that those actively engaged knew each other well and, in the intense emotional atmosphere of the time and the encouragement to see themselves as future leaders, they found ample scope for rivalry and difference.

Political attitudes and allegiances provided a further strand in the web of disharmony within the college, occasioning division not only with the authorities, but also with fellow students. John Sweetman in his letter of January 1907, queried Delany:

> Why did you make yourself unpopular with Young Ireland by calling the English police to prevent a few young students from making a speech on the steps of the University College against that party tune *God save the king?*

The Young Ireland branch ('the Yibs') of the United Irish League, the official organ of the Irish parliamentary party, had been founded over a year previously with T.M. Kettle as its natural leader. Its members, who included Sheehy-Skeffington, Eugene and Richard Sheehy, Cruise O'Brien and Rory O'Connor, were largely drawn from the L. and H. Society, and were 'undiluted if unorthodox supporters' of John Dillon, M.P.[167] They urged concentration on Home Rule to the exclusion of all ameliorative measures, not even excepting, save in unforeseen circumstances, the long awaited university bill. It was not a doctrine to find favour with William Delany. P.J. Little, indeed, recalled that:[168]

> The university question was a very live one in our domestic college life, because there was a definite conflict between Fr Delany and the college authorities and the Nationalist

party headed by John Dillon and strongly supported by the Cecilia Street Medical School.

An undoubted coolness in relations between University College and the Medical school was perceptible after about 1904; and it seems significant that medical students were prominent during those years in disruptive scenes at the conferring ceremony and in the L. and H., that Cruise O'Brien found active support among them, that it was to Cecilia Street the protestors marched when dispersed from the steps of 86, and that it was thither, also, that the L. and H. repaired when refused a room in the college. But 'the Yibs' were to some extent, too, a source of friction within the student body itself, not only in relation to those who were not members, but even on occasion among themselves when emotional issues were involved such as the Irish Council Bill of 1907, and later the question of Irish as a compulsory subject for matriculation.

It all made for a tangled, troubled scene sufficient to tax the talents of a young and vigorous president. Delany was now in his seventy-second year, and was also anxiously engaged in negotiating and writing about the proposed federal solution to the university question, and immersed in the scholarship scheme and in building extensions. Little wonder that he experienced 'a crushing weight of responsibility' for the future of Catholic education; and that in trying to walk a middle line between various conflicting interests he showed signs of losing one of his chief strengths, his self-confidence and sureness of touch. It might be argued, indeed, that, apart from one instance, he acted with great coolness in not allowing himself to over-react to persistent provocation; but that one instance of recourse to the police was the kind of mistake that students neither forgive nor forget. It damaged trust and respect, and undermined much of what he had accomplished for them and with them.

The Literary and Historical Society was continued within the college by what was termed 'the conservative party'. Its members included Thomas Bacon, Healy, Bodkin, Cox, Rory O'Connor and J.J. (Ginger) O'Connell. 'Many of us felt', wrote Bacon, 'that the society, which had owed its revival in 1897, and a great measure of its success as a factor in our university education, to the continued interest and encouragement of Fr Delany, would be guilty of something more than ingratitude if, in the end, it turned its back upon him because of a severe exercise of his presidential authority in a matter of college discipline'. [169] Healy was elected auditor, and it was decided to press ahead with their own inaugural meeting in the great hall of the college. The auditor gave his address on 'Irish Industrial Development'. Fr Finlay, rather than Delany, presided, perhaps for political reasons, perhaps because of the theme of the address. The immediate storm had passed, but a spirit of criticism and revolt was to continue in the college for the remainder of its days.

The following year, subsequent to the agitation over the Council Bill and the government's withdrawal from a university measure, political feeling was once again very intense. Delany determined to avail of the tensions of the moment to have the provocative anthem discontinued at the conferring ceremony. Through the new chancellor, Lord Castletown, an assurance was obtained from Lord Aberdeen, the Lord Lieutenant, that its discontinuance would not be taken amiss by the king. He then proposed to the standing committee of the senate:

> That it is expedient for many reasons that the conferring of degrees in this university should be confined to the purely academic ceremonial, as it is in the University of Dublin and elsewhere.

The motion was carried with but one dissenting voice, and at the senate meeting on 31 October it was passed by eleven votes to five.[170] This move ensured relative peace at the conferring ceremony, but not at the L. and H. inaugural address a short time later.

The 1907 inaugural was a special one for Delany. It was to be graced, as has been seen, by the new Chief Secretary, Augustine Birrell. It proved less than a success. In the same class as Chesterton, Belloc, Max Beerbohm, and Bernard Shaw as a conversationalist, Birrell, as a public speaker, had a captivating, unaffected manner, with a capacity for the wittiest observations without the suspicion of a smile.[171] At the L. and H. his historic speech conveyed his sympathy for the frustrations of the past and his firm intentions for the future. 'I believe', he said, 'that this question ought to be and, please God, will be solved in the next session'. There was no cause in which he would more willingly 'suffer political extinction than the cause of securing for the Irish people that higher education which justice demands they should have'. He pledged himself to do the very best that mortal man could do in the next session of parliament.

He was to abide by his pledge. To many of his audience, however, it seemed like the old familiar record playing the old familiar tune. Arthur Clery, noted for his graceful, suave manner and polished speech during his student days, but now in the words of C.P. Curran, bitten by 'the Gaelic bug', gone 'Irish-Ireland' and sporting a shaggy beard, led the attack on the Chief Secretary's speech, ridiculing his promises, and deriding his nonconformist conscience and all his liberal gods.[172] Delany was deeply upset at the reception; but his sense of humiliation was made complete when, during his own address, a band of students — many of them seemingly not from the college — created such an uproar, punctuated by cries of 'police', 'police', that he had to desist from speaking.[173]

The year ended with a further note of challenge and change from the Literary and Historical Society. For some time motions on the eligibility of women for membership had been brought forward at the society's meetings and defeated. A few weeks after the 1907 inaugural, two extraordinary general meetings of the L. and H. considered the question again and voted by sixteen votes to twelve for an amendment in the rules of the society, whereby 'students' would henceforth 'be interpreted to mean both male and female students'.[174] To the president there must have seemed no end to occasions of conflict. It was his misfortune, on top of all else, to face the agitation for women's full share in higher education as it reached its climax. His instinct, training, and increasing cautiousness, placed him at odds with the degree of change being demanded by many younger men.

University College, 86 St Stephen's Green

Professors and students '86'. James Joyce is second from left, back row.

Fr A. Finlay

Fr Darlington

Thomas Kettle

Augustine Birrell

Contemporary cartoon: '*Taking his little pig to market* : Quot porculi, tot sententiae : Mr. Birrell's Education Bill Task'.

John Dillon

John Redmond

Chapter XV

THE ISSUE OF WOMEN'S RIGHTS

It was not that he was opposed to equal rights for women in higher education: quite the contrary, he would claim. It had not been possible for him to accommodate them at University College, during his first term as president, due to shortage of space for his male students and the lay-out of the college buildings; but, as has been seen, he arranged in 1886 for some of the fellows to be available for lectures in the Royal University buildings, and for tutors to lecture at the new educational establishments opened for Catholic women students — St Mary's, Dominican College, founded in 1886, and Loreto College, in 1893. As the century drew to a close, however, an increasing number of girls were entering for the Royal University examinations and seeking entry to the lectures of the fellows at University College. The Medical School, Cecilia Street, responded to the new demand by accepting women students in 1896. Thus, when Delany returned to Stephen's Green the following year he found a body of students, led by the redoubtable Francis Sheehy-Skeffington, M.A., in a vocal mood on the discrimination being exercised against women.

Sheehy-Skeffington, 'bearded and in knickerbockers, and quick firing in speech', was both a pacifist and a militant feminist. 'He loved argument', one of his contemporaries wrote, 'and had a neat opinion on every point of human behaviour. . . . His every opinion was a principle for which he was ready to die. . . . No one agreed with him, but we all loved him for his courage, his Cato-like intransigence, and his unquenchable good humour'.[175] Delany reorganised the great hall of the college, the only space available, to provide opportunity for women students to attend lectures by the fellows. Sheehy-Skeffington became college registrar.

First year students were not catered for in these arrangements. The next year, 1902, the Irish Association of Women Graduates and Candidate Graduates was founded with, as one of its aims, the securing of equal advantage with men in university education. At this stage, degrees were still not being given to women in the older English universities, nor were lectures fully open to them. Cambridge, indeed, was to defer admission to degrees until 1921, and admission to full membership of the university until 1948. In Ireland, the three Queen's Colleges had admitted women students practically on par with men by the turn of the century; in 1903 Dublin University permitted women to avail of its lectures, examinations and degrees in Arts and in the Medical School, and the Robertson Commission recommended that in any scheme for a new university college in Dublin women should be placed on an equal footing with men. These factors combined to revive feelings of discrimination in regard to University College. In 1904 the Women's Graduates' Association — believing that Delany had indicated on a previous occasion that were Trinity College to open its doors to women, his college would feel obliged to act likewise — addressed a memorial to the president of University College seeking full entry to the lectures of all the fellows in the Arts faculty.[176] He passed it on to the college's academic council, and all members agreed that no more could be done than had been done three years previously when the great hall had been reorganised for the benefit of the women students.[177] In the prevailing circumstances, the council could envisage no possible arrangement by which women could be placed in a position of full equality with men, particularly in regard to laboratory work. A further memorial was prepared and presented to the senate of the Royal University regarding the exclusion of women (first years) from lectures given by fellows of the university.

Shortly after this, a fact came to light which added to the president's embarrassment. It turned out that the registrar of the college, Sheehy-Skeffington, had not only drafted the memorial to the senate but had obtained signatures for it both within and outside the college. In May, Delany sent him 'a friendly admonition' pointing out that as an officer of the college he ought not publicly advocate schemes which were in opposition to the policy of the college. Sheehy-Skeffington replied that he could see no inconsistency in acting as he had, because no definite policy had been formulated by the college authorities within his official knowledge, and he considered that the admission of women to Trinity College had intensified the need for University College, for its own prestige, to show itself no less progressive. But, since he wished to be free for the future, he gave six months notice of his resignation of the registrarship.[178] He did not take correction easily when 'a principle' was involved. Although he later remarked that he could not see how the president could have acted otherwise in the circumstances, their disagreement was part of the background to his subsequent denunciation of Delany at the Medical School meeting in November 1906. It also provided fuel to those who wished to misconstrue the president's policy. The *Leader* joined his critics in July 1905.

The surest way to offend Delany was to accuse him of being unfair. Where the women students were concerned he believed that he had done everything possible for them. Hence, when Moran of the *Leader* raised the matter with him during 1905, he discussed his position frankly and brought him on a tour of the college to see for himself its over-crowded condition. He was furious, therefore, when there appeared in the *Leader* on 16 July, by an anonymous correspondent, the statement:

> One is forced to believe, no matter what the alleged reason may be, that the real reason, though not avowed, for the exclusion of women students from fellows' lectures is to secure to the regular students at University College a monopoly of those lectures.

His sense of fair play outraged, he wrote an indignant private letter to the editor. The anonymous correspondent's statement, he declared, was 'offensive in its form' and 'absolutely without foundation in fact', as he had previously demonstrated to him (Moran). He had given him a list of the thirty-one women students, 'seventeen per cent of our whole number', who attended lectures at University College. Two were candidates for fellowships; four for the M.A. degree; sixteen for the B.A.; eight for second Arts; and one attending lectures in political economy only. This disposed of the charge that women were 'excluded' from lectures 'in order to secure a monopoly' for the other students. He had explained that the only area they were not admitted to was first Arts classes, and this was simply because the only room which would accommodate women in addition to men students was the great hall, and he had shown him the other rooms which were already over-crowded with the men students. He had pointed out, moreover, 'that several of the fellows', with his 'cordial approval and permission', lectured at Loreto College 'in the subjects not taught in the great hall — including first Arts subjects'. Hence, he had personally given Moran 'absolutely convincing evidence' that the statement, which he had permitted to be published in the *Leader*, was 'entirely without foundation'; and his paper, therefore, 'had been made the vehicle of a false charge against a public educational institution and against the Catholic priests who were responsible for it'. It rested with him, the editor, who permitted the publication, to decide how 'to deal with an anonymous writer in such circumstances'. The uncharacteristic outburst argued a high degree of exasperation with attacks on college affairs. The *Leader*'s popularity, besides, with the members of the L. and H. and the fact that some, like Cruise O'Brien, wrote for it were not likely to commend it to him. Still, it was not the wisest or most politic reaction to so relentless and powerful a publicist as D.P. Moran.

Pressures on the women's front eased somewhat, however, with the onset of the Fry Commission. The Women's Graduates' Association was granted permission to appear before the commission. It was represented by Miss Agnes O'Farrelly, M.A., of University College, and Miss Hannan, B.A., of Trinity. Their case for equal rights in a coeducational situation was weakened by Miss White, the lady principal of Alexandra College (catering for Protestant women students) seeking recognition for her institution as a constituent college in the University of Dublin. She impressed the chairman and Chief Baron Palles by her assertion that a large proportion of parents would prefer their children remaining at Alexandra College and taking the pass lectures there rather than attending Trinity in common with the men students. The commissioners in their report recommended that the governing body of Trinity be empowered to recognise teachers in any colleges for women within thirty miles of the college. They also expressed the belief that many parents would prefer education for their daughters in colleges exclusively for women; and they recommended that these parents be consulted.[179]

Within a year or two of the Fry Report extra room was provided at University College by the building of the garden classrooms, the temporary contraption known as 'Fr Finlay's tin university', and this made it possible to cater for a fuller entrance of women to the college.

Quite apart, however, from difficulties about accommodation, Delany, like the Fry commissioners, had misgivings about the whole idea of the joint education of men and women. The strident character of much of the feminist agitation at the time, reflecting the views of merely a-minority of women, did little to persuade him. Like most of his male contemporaries, it required the demands of a world war — then unthinkable — to make him accept the notion of a woman doing a man's work. He had an exalted protective regard for women which reflected, perhaps, a blending of the Victorian tradition in which he had lived for sixty years, his clerical celibate training, and his personal innate sense of chivalry. After the introduction of the National University Bill in 1908, he was to write to Archbishop Walsh that experience at University College had shown, what had already been noted in Chicago, that the work of a co-educational system tended 'to diminish refinement amongst women students, and to lessen markedly in the men students the love of courtesy and consideration for women'. Of course, he added, there were 'other and nearer considerations' into which he need not enter.[180]

His own 'love of courtesy and consideration for women' was quite remarkable if one were to accept as accurate an illustration handed down happily by caricaturing colleagues. Returning to Stephen's Green after dining at the Viceregal Lodge, he informed the Fathers at recreation:

There was a most upsetting happening. After lunch, in the course of discussion, someone wondered where Queen Victoria was now. Was she in heaven?

—'Not among the teetotallers in any event', responded one young man.

I should not have minded that remark in the smoking-room, [Delany continued] , but there were ladies present.

This almost exaggerated sense of respect, protectiveness, and discretion with regard to women, joined to a more down to earth and moralistic attitude, were reflected in his response to the resolution from the L. and H.; and the committee of that body, no less than his younger Jesuit colleagues, found therein material for caricature. He rejected the resolution of 17 December, 1907, changing the interpretation of 'student' in the society's rules to mean 'male and female students'. When approached by a student deputation, he informed them that he did so, not as president of the L. and H., but as president of the college, 'who had every right to interfere in important matters which directly concerned the college'. He then went on to give reasons for his decision which touched on those 'other and nearer considerations' of which he had made mention to Dr Walsh. According to the deputation's clever report, he spoke of 'the great dangers which would result from the ladies being out late at night and having to cross the city on their return home'; and he pointed out 'the gravity of the situation for the male students, whose morality would be or might be jeopardised through intercourse with the lady students in the Literary and Historical Soceity, as well as the possibility of undesirable or unhappy marriages which such an arrangement would bring about'.[181]

Their president's old fashioned outlook might provoke in his students and his junior colleagues a mixture of annoyance and mirth; but he was determined to avoid any development which might possibly damage the reputation of the college and delay the university settlement, and his outlook in fact was not that much out of step with middle class attitudes in the Dublin of his day. Discretion and reserve in relations between the sexes was expected. Moreover, women, despite the feminist agitation, were still placed on a romantic pedestal, so that a gentleman watched his words in their presence and it was inconceivable that a respectable woman would use an indelicate word in the presence of a man. Hence, the audience at Synge's *The Playboy of the Western World*, according to Lady Gregory's well-known cable to W.B. Yeats, 'broke up in disorder at the word *shift*'.

The L. and H., besides, on later reflection, was not all that sure that it was a good idea to allow in women. When their entry was permitted under a later administration, several motions were defeated before they were finally accepted by the slender margin of nineteen votes to seventeen. Thomas Bodkin, a former auditor and staunch oppositionist, still maintained the opposition argument years afterwards. The debating unions of Oxford and Cambridge, and the Historical Society of Trinity College, he pointed, out, had not admitted them. They 'provided distraction from serious business'![182]

The final comment on relations between the students and the college authorities during the last years in Stephen's Green, came on 14 April 1908 in a very frank letter from Maurice Healy, president of the student council and auditor of the L. and H. He told Dr Delany that his decision regarding the lady students had been very unpopular. A further dispute, he remarked, now seemed likely to break out, this time regarding the constitution of the student representative council. A draft had been approved by J.A. Ronayne as 'representative of the left', but as he was rusticated and not strictly a student the whole question of the validity of the constitution was at stake. The issue might be an occasion of expressing support for Ronayne. But, Healy went on, 'I think all this is only a little skirmish in the warfare against the college authorities that seems to have commenced in Tom Kettle's time, and to have been handed down through Skeffington to Cruise O'Brien and Ronayne'.

He himself had not hesitated to differ with the president on a number of occasions while making it clear that though he did not accept his views he did accept his authority. But, it had not been 'an easy thing to support the authorities in college. They have always been unpopular, and I am afraid now they are likely to remain so until they change their sphere to a larger institution'. In the year or two left, he appealed for an expression of confidence from the authorities in the Literary and Historical Society. Its governing body had shown itself particularly responsible over the previous year. He concluded:

> For this letter I am inclined to apologise. To you who have lived nearly four times what I have lived once it is, I am sure, a not unfamiliar product of great self-confidence. But I much prefer to damage myself a little than to leave unsaid what you might not otherwise have heard — and I am encouraged by the unvarying kindness you have shown me in all student (and personal) affairs.

Delany replied with characteristic civility. He outlined Ronayne's position and pointed out that while the college council had decreed that he be formally excluded from the college as a student, he (Delany) had asked that the matter be left in his hands. As a result, he had told Ronayne that he could obtain permission to re-enter the college after a while. He suggested that Healy and the student council send a request to the college council for Ronayne's reinstatement; and he worded the request for them.

It was instances of such urbanity that made even Cruise O'Brien — for all his strong feelings of having been ill used and his many severe strictures on 'the Jesuits' and the president of the college — leave on record that he cherished 'kindly memories of Dr Delany. We used to call him Dr Delany in order to draw from him his invariable retort: "Don't call me Doctor, sir. I am not an apothecary"! He always fought with steel like a gentleman, nor, I think, did he have any wish to fight at all if he could have avoided it'.[183]

In recounting at some length the occasions of conflict between students and president there is the danger of presenting an unbalanced picture of life at the college; and of making straight the paths of 'the odd mentality to which all Catholic education appears an obscurantist tyranny'.[184] One thing, however, it does make clear, namely, how inaccurate was James Joyce's depiction in *Stephen Hero*, and in the *Portrait of the Artist*, of a 'shivering society' of servile youths living contentedly under an authoritarian regime and, in the interests of future employment, seeking to ingratiate themselves into the good graces of the authorities. Certainly – as Joyce's friend and contemporary, C.P. Curran, pointed out[185] – a measure of discipline and docility was demanded in the classrooms; and why not? Did not students attend to be taught? And nobody more than Joyce used his notebook and his professor's definitions to greater advantage. But outside class the picture of general subservience depicted in *Stephen Hero* was 'grotesquely unreal'. Curran continued:

> *I have known no institution of its kind where authority was so lightly exercised.* There were, to be sure, examinations to be passed. But for students like Joyce or myself there was obligatory attendance at nothing; no chores; whatever was done was done voluntarily. Professors and students worked on cordial terms and in an unforced relationship. Authority in the college, as I knew it, ran no risk of being corrupted by subservience and I do not think that many students went far out of their way in the interests of future jobs, as Stephen says, to insinuate themselves into the good graces of the authorities.[186]

A similar testimony was provided by 'John Eglinton' (William Kirkpatrick Magee) who, as assistant librarian of the National Library where so many of the students studied in the absence of a college library, had ample opportunity to observe the 'servile youths'. In his *Irish literary portraits* he represented Joyce as 'one of a group of lively, eagerminded young men in University College who were interested in everything new in literature and philosophy (and) in this respect far surpassed the students of Trinity College'.[187] Turning to the slightly

later period of 1905, when the Literary and Historical Society
was divided and 'many of the students were still cross with their
president', C.P. Curran still failed to find any notable alteration.
He recalled being present at a function in the great hall, and
how when Cruise O'Brien entered the students gathered about,
'chaired' him with no great difficulty 'and proceeded in cro-
codile around the hall and up the staircase, still singing *God
save Ireland*, to deposit him at length at the door of the president's chamber'. Here, he commented, 'was no great care on
anyone's part for expedient graces'.

> The political atmosphere had sharpened; the university
> situation had grown more acute; but the temper of the
> students had not essentially changed. The young cocks were
> crowing as of old. The tune came from no 'shivering society'.

The lull in the political life of Ireland, Yeats wrote in the
Daily Chronicle in January 1899, 'has been followed among the
few by an intellectual excitement . . . and among the many by
that strong sense of something about to happen which has
always in all countries given the few their opportunity'.[188]
That excitement coursed through the veins of the student
population of University College. It was William Delaney's
unwelcome task to apply a brake when it threatened to spill
over into open insubordination, or into political manifestations
which endangered his primary obligation to the future of Irish
university education; but he was no more 'authoritarian' than
the students of the L. and H. were 'servile'. 'A very democratic
assembly, by no means very docile and by no means humble',[189]
was how Birrell described them, speaking from experience!
   At the time Maurice Healy wrote to the president, the
settlement of the university question was at last in sight. Birrell
had kept his promise. The bill for a National University was
going through parliament, its widespread acceptance a tribute
to the Chief Secretary's patience and negotiating skill.

Chapter XVI

MR BIRRELL AND THE FINAL SOLUTION

Augustine Birrell, tall, burly, and wearing glasses, was fifty-seven years of age when appointed Chief Secretary in 1907. Born in Liverpool of Scottish and Northumbrian parents, he was the son of a Baptist minister. He described himself as theologically-minded but unorthodox. The prime minister, Campbell-Bannerman, considered that he had most of the requisite qualities for his new post. He told the king that Birrell did not make enemies and was blessed with 'literary sense and knowledge, sympathy, good-nature, humour and breadth of view'.[190] In keeping with Edmund Burke's dictum that 'the temper of the people amongst whom he presides ought to be first study of a statesman', he was well-read on Irish history, interested himself in the Anglo-Irish literary revival, and was committed to the idea of Home Rule. Indeed, in his first speech as Chief Secretary in the House of Commons, he captured the sympathy of the Irish majority by an appeal to Ulstermen to cease troubling the dry bones of an outdated bigotry.[191]

His first months in Ireland, nevertheless, did not augur well. The opposition to the Council Bill and the university scheme which he had championed, and the government's subsequent withdrawal of both measures, damaged his credibility in the eyes of the general public. Undismayed, he clarified his objectives in the area of higher education and on how best to woo support for them. He had never been happy with the Bryce proposals. Hence, when Redmond wrote to him on 25 May, 1907, pointing out that his (Redmond's) position with the electorate had been weakened by the controversy over the Council Bill, and urging him to press forward with a university measure embracing Trinity College — since the college was in a 'blue funk' and might be persuaded to negotiate now, but not later when the immediate danger had passed — [192] the Chief Secretary told him firmly that he was not interested in a scheme including

Trinity. A bill interfering with it stood no chance of becoming law. He had plans of his own and intended to make them clear to 'everybody in Ireland'.[193] At the same time he informed the prime minister that Redmond's position had become very difficult. In face of accusations that he was permitting Home Rule to be snowed under, he would be obliged to make a definite move for or against the government next session. If his support were to be kept, the government would have to offer him something 'too good to be lost'. He (Birrell) recommended two things which were due in justice to Ireland, namely, a university bill and land reform.[194] On 3 July he was in a position to reassure the Irish members in the House of Commons that 'he would strive during the coming August to discover a means which would enable the vast majority of the Irish youth to obtain education in a university to which parents and priest could send them with perfect confidence that nothing would be taught them destructive of their religious beliefs'.[195]

The treatment accorded his Education Bill by the House of Lords during his short time as president of the Board of Education, 1906, had taught him to proceed cautiously, consult widely, and to measure support and opposition before openly advocating any particular scheme; while the futility of trying to obtain northern and southern agreement on a common university, had turned his thoughts towards a revival of Haldane's proposals of 1898. The concept of two separate universities had been acceptable then to many Liberals and Conservatives. It might have a greater chance of success nine years later. Neither institution, however, could be openly denominational. The Liberal party's commitments and the state of British public opinion would not permit such. Religious groups, *qua* religious groups, could not receive official recognition.

During the autumn of 1907 he won over Redmond and John Dillon, the latter of whom he described as 'very anti-clerical', to the general idea of two universities, one centred on Dublin, the other in Belfast.[196] He consulted with Dr Traill, now provost of Trinity College, and, having assured him that the college would be left untouched in any new university bill, gained his cooperation.[197] The Catholic bishops presented a particular problem. Although episcopal opposition to 'mixed education' had abated, and both Dr Walsh and Dr O'Dwyer had argued the Catholic case not on religious grounds but as a claim in justice for the deprived majority, and the bishops as a body had waived exclusive claims, yet Walsh was known to be strongly committed to a college within Dublin University. Birrell decided to make his appeal through the archbishop; but before doing so he consulted Delany. He knew where the latter stood with regard to Trinity; he had learned much about him from Haldane; and within a short time of his arrival in Dublin had established friendly relations with him. During October he discussed his plans with him. On 9 November they dined together at the Viceregal Lodge. Nine days later he sought an appointment with Dr Walsh. He explained to the archbishop his reservations about interfering with Dublin University and felt that he had convinced him that the time was not opportune for one national university. Dr Walsh, it appears, agreed to cooperate with him in a scheme where all reference to Trinity College would be omitted.[198]

During December Birrell flattered Delany and enlisted his active assistance by discussing further with him his plans and difficulties. The two universities would be undenominational, but would have governing bodies so constituted as to suit the people for whom they were intended. The scheme had a much better chance of being accepted than when Haldane proposed it. Trinity College had been frightened by the extent of the support for the Bryce plan, especially among non-Catholics, and was prepared to welcome almost any proposal which would leave it untouched. The authorities of the Belfast college had come to realise that changes were inevitable, and he hoped that they would agree that their college would gain more by being transformed into a university than by being joined in any federal arrangement. How to go about persuading opponents was the problem.

Delany addressed himself to the question on 16 December. He had pondered on their conversation, he wrote, and, in his view, a great deal turned on the mode of procedure. 'The central knot of the triangle is this: how to persuade a non-conformist and low church Protestant House of Commons to establish and endow a university for Roman Catholics?' Begin, he suggested, by dealing with the easiest part and in the easist way. 'It is part of your plan to establish a university in Belfast. Begin with that separate item. Let Belfast do, as Leeds did and Liverpool: petition the king to grant them a charter'. The petition, as in those other cases, would be referred to the king's council whose judgement would be based 'on academic grounds'. In this way there would be no scope for anti-Catholic issues to arise; and with the granting of the charter the House of Commons battle would be 'more than half over beforehand'. It would no longer be a question of establishing a university for Catholics. A charter to Belfast would leave the Royal University, by that very fact, to the Catholics. The withdrawal of the northern senators would leave its senate still a mixed undenominational body, like Belfast, but the preponderance would be Catholic in one case, and non-Catholic in the other. The question before parliament would then become: 'How to remodel that existing university controlled by the Catholic majority so as to make it more effective and its government more academic and representative? . . .. The question would have been reduced from what might fairly appear to them a question of *principle* to a question of *practical details*'.

Between this and then, he continued, it would be opportune for one of the Liberal newspapers to bring before the British public 'the crying anomalies of the present distribution of public educational funds, the gross inconsistency, from the *present nonconformist point of view*, of telling the Catholics of Dublin and of Ireland — three-fourths of the population — that if they want higher education they must seek it in Trinity College, in a Protestant institution, from Protestant teachers — in an institution which is, and has been, the very stronghold of Toryism and is entirely out of sympathy with the political and national sentiments of the mass of Irish Catholics as well as being unsuited to them socially and economically in their educational needs'. Given a series of articles in January in a leading Liberal paper and an article in some monthly for February, 'the battle in the House of Commons would be won before going into the field'. The writer might also compare the examination results of the Queen's Colleges with those of University College and ask how the Chief Secretary was justified in spending £35,000 a year on those institutions. Such comparison would add to the argument in favour of change.

By the close of December the Chief Secretary had the framework of his plan ready for the cabinet. The latter gave it their tentative approval. It was printed as an official confidential document and sent to a small number of people for examination before being submitted to the treasury. The select group of recipients included: Cardinal Logue, Dr Walsh, Dr Healy of Tuam, Dr Mannix of Maynooth, Delany, and somewhat later John Redmond and John Dillon. The three bishops' approval was a prerequisite to that of the treasury. Birrell's letter to the archbishop of Dublin on 31 December accompanying his 'Heads of proposals for new universities and colleges', stated that he wished to be sure that he had a scheme which 'would receive general support in Ireland'. And with a facility for prudent disclosures, he commented that 'unhappily nobody in England *really* cares a straw about the university question in Ireland except a fanatic crowd who, terrified by the neo-Catholicism of the Church of England, see popery writ large over the whole subject'. In his own constituency in Bristol he was thought 'a visionary and a bit of a fool for taking so much trouble about so *sentimental* (!) a grievance'.[199]

His covering letter to Delany referred to a number of suggestions made by him. He (Birrell) favoured 'a smallish senate' for the new university. He did not agree that some bishops should be appointed *ex-officio*. It would be strongly objected to by the House of Commons and the House of Lords, and as the bishops would in any event be on the senate 'as nominees and afterwards (doubtless) by election — why stir the mud?' To Delany's indirect advocacy of the Royal University, he made it clear that his plans involved 'the removal of the Royal and the substitution of another in its place'. A really new start, 'freed from the former *examining tradition*', was necessary if the position was to be carried by storm; and if we don't so carry it, he added, 'we shan't carry it at all'. He emphasised that the enclosed printed memorandum was for Delany's 'private eye alone', and that nobody else had seen it apart from Cardinal Logue, Archbishops Walsh and Healy, and Dr Mannix. He emphasised once more his anxiety about the whole issue. His hands were tied by the House of Commons and 'a wreck' was easy. His wife joined him in sending her regards.

During January 1908, Delany and Dr Walsh exchanged a number of letters on the new scheme. The archbishop informed the Chief Secretary on 6 January that all sorts of irresponsible people in Dublin had some knowledge of the project. In his view, he continued, the scheme was better than any other he could think of, 'excepting, of course, one that would give us equality with Trinity College Dublin in *point of university status*, e.g. a *second* college in the University of Dublin, or a scheme such as Mr Bryce's'. But supposing, he added, that as regards academic status 'we have to succumb to our fate as representatives of a conquered and subject race . . . are we to have *equality* in anything in this scheme?' Would the Catholics get as much money 'as the two great Protestant colleges and universities all get?'[200]

The Chief Secretary's plan envisaged Queen's College, Belfast, becoming Queen's University, and serving the northern, particularly the unionist, population; and the Queen's Colleges of

Cork and Galway joining with a new Dublin college as the colleges of a further university, catering mainly for the majority population. He envisaged two senates, with governing bodies for each college. The members of the senates were to be nominated at first, but elected after a fixed time. On the Dublin-based body there were to be the three college presidents, representatives of the three governing bodies, delegates of convocation, some nominees, and some co-opted members. The Belfast senate was to be on similar lines. The governing bodies of the colleges at Dublin, Cork and Galway, were to consist of the president, some members appointed by the senate, and the representatives of the faculties and of local bodies. His tentative membership list of the Dublin-based senate was confined to twenty-five members.

Delany, who had been away for some days' complete rest, replied to Birrell's letter on 8 January. He agreed that it was desirable 'to establish a new university — under a new name' and that the senate should be 'of moderate dimensions', but he had serious misgivings about limiting membership to twenty-five persons and about the choice of members. He pointed out that the senate of the Royal University had thirty-six members but that the average attendance between 1887 and 1906 was only 16.8, and twice there was just a bare quorum of seven. As to the membership of the body, he believed that the list would not 'evoke any widespread interest or support' since the public bodies in Ireland were not consulted in the selection, and many of the names were not known outside Dublin and there only to educationalists. He recommended a senate of fifty members constituted as follows: nine *ex officio* members — the Catholic and Protestant Archbishops of Dublin, the local head of the Presbyterians, the Lord Mayor of Dublin; the lord chancellor or another judge named by him, the chairman of Dublin Co. Council, the president of the Dublin, Cork and Galway colleges; six members appointed by the Lord Lieutenant; twenty-nine elected members; and six members coopted by the senate. The elected members would be distributed thus: five from the Dublin college, two each from Cork and Galway, four from convocation, six members of parliament representative of Leinster, Munster and Connacht, two from Dublin Corporation, one each from the Cork and Galway corporations, the Intermediate Board, and the Board of Agriculture, and four from the General Council of County Councils.

Membership of the body, therefore, would follow the lines of the new English universities and be based 'not on denominational reasons but on broad democratic principles'. The *ex officio* appointments of the bishops would be on the same grounds as that of the lord mayor and the chairman of the county council, namely, that they were 'highly important local personages'. He noted, finally, that 'by connecting the local elective representative bodies with the university, its hold on the country would be enormously increased beyond any that could be expected from the suggested scheme; and thereby, too, it might be more confidently expected that the local bodies would help by funding local scholarships and otherwise the financial support of the university'. He hoped that in any event the new act would 'give powers to the county councils and municipal bodies (similar to those given in England by recent acts) to make some local provision in furtherance of higher education'. The following day he wrote to say that he had meant to include a plea for representation for 'the modern faculties — engineering, commerce, agriculture — and also law'. He was at pains to emphasise that his views had no higher authority than that of personal opinion. The archbishop of Dublin, by contrast, in his letter of 6 January, had adopted a different line on the question of representation. His view was that representation on the governing bodies of the new colleges should be as 'purely academic' as possible, and that the proportion of local government representatives suggested by Birrell was too high and might 'open the door to all sorts of jobbery'.

Replying to Delany's two letters, the Chief Secretary emphasised that while his list of senators was only provisional he did wish to make it clear that he did not want 'a large board nor an academic body, nor a *social* body of nobles and landlords, but a working body'. Subject to this proviso, he was prepared to admit the force of the criticism that the list was 'not sufficiently representative' and was, therefore, perhaps, too short.[201] Some days later he wrote again. He commented at length on the financial aspects of the scheme, and then asked for 'a list of persons, not offices'. Delany's list of officers would 'be hotly opposed by the advocates of a purely electoral body representing the university and no outsiders'. He thought that the nonconformists might not object to the archbishop of Dublin being *elected* by the graduates and constituent colleges for the time being, as distinct from he being appointed *ex officio*.[202]

The next day, 20 January, Birrell asked Dr Walsh for the general views of the hierarchy without 'any commital'. He undertook to discuss the proposals with Redmond and Dillon. Then, having outlined for His Grace the plans for the different colleges, he added, with unconscious irony: 'apart from this outline my correspondence with your Fr Delany (to whom I wrote a long letter yesterday — which he is quite at liberty to show you) will let you know the lines on which I am proceeding'.[203] On the same day, in fact, and hence before Dr Walsh received the Chief Secretary's letter, Delany informed the archbishop of the communication he had received and of Birrell's wish for 'a list of names'. On 21 January he wrote to say that he had written to Birrell withdrawing his suggestion about 'following the lines of the new English universities' and referring him to His Grace 'for the additional names he wants to make his list fuller and more representative'. 'Our list of educationalists', Delany continued, 'is as yet a very short one and, when we go outside the educationalists, it is not easy to hit upon a principle of choosing' which is 'at once satisfactory to our side and Mr Birrell's who does not like "personages" in any number'.

The Chief Secretary had his way too with the leaders of the Irish party. On 22 January he informed John Redmond of his intentions and progress.[204] The party were anxious to avoid any serious difference with the Liberals, already embarked on a course of conflict with the House of Lords which would break eventually its veto on Home Rule. On that day also, Dr Walsh brought Birrell's proposals before the body of bishops. They accepted the general framework of the scheme. Their criticism was concentrated on the number of members on the senate, the composition of the governing body of the Dublin college, and the issue of affiliation. Much of their discussion centred around Maynooth's place in the affiliation plans, namely, how it might be included 'not as a constituent college but in some other way so that the students could obtain degrees under conditions prescribed by the university'.[205] To ensure, however, that the Chief Secretary's bill would not be held up by lengthy discussions on a building programme for the new Dublin college, they suggested that existing halls and residences might be used, and also that public bodies might be empowered to grant and establish scholarships.

Thus, Birrell's powers of persuasion appeared to be surmounting all obstacles, and an acceptable solution to the university question seemed at last in sight. By the end of the month, nevertheless, Delany was beginning to have misgivings. A very unfriendly article on Irish university education had appeared in the Protestant *Christian World*. It was written by a Mr Horne, a friend of the Chief Secretary, who had come to visit different

Irish colleges and whom Delany thought, when he called on him, to be quite sympathetic. The critical tone of his article brought to mind the many times in the past when hopes of a settlement had been raised only to be wrecked on the shoals of prejudice and nonconformist opposition. Was it about to happen all over again? 'If these are the ideas of a friend and *quasi*-agent of Mr Birrell', Delany wrote to the archbishop, 'do they not seem to portend that the scheme will be drawn so as to free the poor enslaved Catholic laity from the tyranny of the clergy, and to give them a university that make true patriots like "Pat" in abundance? I confess I have great misgivings. But, we will see'. It seemed to presage a plan of campaign drawn on familiar lines: 'Work upon anti-clerical feeling among English Protestants; and then tell the Irish bishops and clergy how sorry you are, but you are driven by the nonconformists and we, therefore, must take and be thankful for whatever may be offered to us'.[206] For a short time at this stage he seemed to have been almost of one mind with Bishop O'Dwyer who, according to Birrell, was 'honestly convinced that the bill was a nonconformist conspiracy to obtain control of the education of the Catholic laity'.[207] He did not permit his suspicions, however, to interfere with his friendly relations with the Chief Secretary.

Birrell planned to introduce his bill on 31 March, just before Easter. Knowing of the opposition of Dr O'Dwyer and of Dr Sheehan of Waterford, he avoided pressing its advantages with the body of bishops. His negotiations were conducted entirely through Archbishop Walsh. Due to influenza, he was unable to send the confidential preliminary draft charter for the new university and a copy of the draft bill to the archbishop until 20 March. The draft allowed for the affiliation of other colleges to the university. Dr Walsh, on 28 March, saw the references of affiliation as too wide. They might lead to pressure in support of such intermediate colleges as Castleknock, Clongowes, and others, thereby leading to a 'dragging down of the academic worth of the degree to a very low level'.[208] Birrell, on the following day, agreed that a more severe wording was required, but that Maynooth and Magee colleges must be allowed in through some 'general permission clause'.[209]

The bill was introduced in the House of Commons on 31 March 1908. Speaking of the senate of the new university in Dublin, the Chief Secretary announced that it would consist of the chancellor and vice-chancellor; the three presidents of the constituent colleges; some persons — one at least a woman — nominated by the crown; fourteen persons representing the colleges; five elected by convocation; and six co-opted. 'Our object', he said, 'is to make it an academic body, and to present anything like an *ex officio* representation appearing on it, in order that the university graduates and professors hereafter may have full power of representing themselves'. Professors were to be appointed and dismissed by the senate. Those of Cork and Galway would continue in their positions; their places when vacated being filled by the senate.

With regard to colleges affiliated to the universities, he did not approve of the idea generally but expected that the senate would affiliate Magee College and Maynooth. With regard to finance, Belfast was to get £28,000 a year, the Dublin college £32,000, Cork £18,000, and Galway £12,000. In addition, £60,000 would be given to increase the size of the Belfast institution, and £150,000 was to be found for the building of the Dublin college. The latter sum, in conjunction with the available Royal University buildings, was sufficient to build a worthy edifice. No money was to be supplied for the provision or maintenance of any chapel or other place of religious observance, or for the provision of theological or religious teaching. The bill was clearly weighted to mollify nonconformist opinion and to entice the orange opposition of northern Ireland by means of favourable provision for Belfast's university.

In the course of his very measured and conciliatory speech, Mr Birrell managed to lay the blame for the abandonment of the federal university on the opposition offered by Trinity College.[210] Taking up this point, Mr Massie, M.P. for Wiltshire, observed that the price to be paid for 'hands off Trinity' was three denominational universities, 'one practically Protestant, one practically Presbyterian, and one practically Roman Catholic', instead of one great national university. He was not sure that Trinity College would not live to repent its decision, 'because it was now standing aloof from the great stream of national life, and its lot might yet be that of the pool which was proud to stand still while the great river rushed by'.[211]

Remarkably, considering the occasion and his desire to win wide support for his bill, Mr Birrell singled out William Delany for special mention a number of times in the course of his speech. Even allowing for an element of diplomatic valediction, it was an eloquent indication of the impact made by University College's successes and of its president's standing in Irish education. Speaking of university facilities in Ireland, the Chief Secretary referred to the colleges of the Royal University: 'the three Queen's Colleges at Belfast, Cork and Galway, and the Catholic University College in Dublin, so long and so honourably associated with the name of Dr Delany, and with which the famous medical college in Cecilia Street is closely allied. It may be said', he observed at the expense of accuracy, 'to form a medical faculty and a medical school under the headship of Dr Delany'. His further comments regarding University College referred to it as 'Dr Delany's College'. Coming to the delicate question of a president for the new Dublin college, he paid a notable tribute:

> An important question arises as to the president of this new college in Dublin; and I need scarcely say it is a very important subject. The first man who would occur to us is Dr Delany, whom I have already mentioned and who has for many years devoted himself with great success and with the utmost industry to the education of Catholic youths in University College. But there are objections to that course which he appreciates himself, and he has written to me to say that he feels that those objections prevail — *he is seventy-six years of age* — but his one desire is that this scheme should be a great success and he wishes, before he dies, to see a university in Dublin.
>
> There are some objections to starting with a clergyman, and there may be in some minds objection to starting with a Jesuit. I am bound to say that any Chief Secretary who has enjoyed the acquaintance of Dr Delany will not feel that, but it will be felt in certain quarters, and I do think that until tradition grows up it is rather desirable that the head of this new college should be a layman, in order that the tradition should not spring up that the president has to be a clergyman. We all know how in our colleges of Oxford and Cambridge a tradition grows up and is preserved.
>
> Therefore, while I tender my thanks to Dr Delany for his patriotism in this matter, I think it would be better that the president of this new college should be a layman — a Catholic layman and a younger man — in order that it should secure a good start under energetic and sympathetic rule. That is all I have to say on the subject.[212]

Apart from the opposition of a number of unionists, mainly

from Ulster, the bill was well received. Leave was given to introduce it by 307 votes to 24, and it was then given its first reading.

Outside parliament, reaction to the bill was very mixed both amongst Catholics and nonconformists. Birrell carefully played each off against the other — letting the nonconformists know of his problems in persuading Catholic acceptance, and informing Catholics of his difficulties with government and nonconformist opposition. Thus, on 2 April, he wrote to Delany, then in London, regretting that he had missed seeing him, saying that he sought 'a good long and highly confidential talk', and inviting him to dine with himself and his wife and to name the day. He hinted at some of his problems. 'The people who have been so noble and self-oblivious and patriotic, suddenly reveal unsuspected depths of personal ends and aims and jealousies. Then there is the *money* and the deep rooted suspicion of everything *Irish* in the British treasury. I shall be rife', he added, 'for a *retreat* with some *bookish* monks 'ere long, so keep an eye upon me. I hope we shan't quarrel 'ere the job is through'.

Six days later Delany wrote Dr Walsh a 'confidential' letter regarding his evening with the Birrells and the discussion that took place. He was delighted to learn from the Chief Secretary that His Grace had accepted a place on the senate. This settled his own misgivings about that body with its constitution which, according to Birrell, was to allow 'unlimited *licence* of teaching'. With regard to the name of the new university, there appeared to be two possibilities, namely, St Patrick's or the University of Ireland. Both Birrell and he inclined to the latter title as being broadly national, conveying 'no suggestion of creed or party', and placing the institution on a higher plane than any other name, associated with Dublin, Cork or Belfast, would carry. As to the name of the Dublin college, Mr Birrell saw no reason to change from University College, Dublin. He had agreed. 'It would seem to have more of *continuity* for Newman's and the Catholic Bishops' College than any other which I could suggest'. He had impressed on the Chief Secretary the desirability of giving to Irish local bodies — as was done in England — the power of establishing local scholarships; and he had advised that the Royal University buildings be utilised as soon as possible 'for the purposes of the new college'.

Birrell had spoken of the presidency of University College. Dr M.J. Cox had declined the position. The only remaining names were those of Dr Denis J. Coffey, dean of the Medical

School, and Joseph McGrath, secretary of the Royal University,[213] 'with a strong preponderance of influence in favour of Coffey'. Delany had told him that he had made it a rule for himself not to speak in favour of anyone, and hence had abstained from recommending McGrath; but that, 'as to fitness and administrative capacity', he was in his personal judgement 'more suited' for the position. Delaney went on to advocate McGrath's case with the archbishop. Professor Butcher had told him that on the Fry Commission 'Coffey had seemed very weak and second rate'. This coincided with his own conviction. His impression was that Birrell was still open to representation. 'He seemed to think Coffey not the more suitable, but the man most pressed on him by (John) Dillon'. Hence, if His Grace agreed with him regarding Dr Coffey's 'lesser fitness' — at a time when there was the necessity 'not merely of carrying on an institution already working, but of organising from the bottom a wholly new and complex one' — he felt sure that a frank expression of view from His Grace would carry great weight with the Chief Secretary.

He then took up a 'serious point' which he had omitted to raise in his talk with Birrell, but which he wished Dr Walsh and the bishops to examine, namely, the question of 'joint education for young men and young women'. As has been seen, he had serious reservations about co-education. In America, he wrote, 'where co-education grew up and flourished', there were already 'grave doubts about the wisdom of maintaining it', and hence it was important, 'before committing ourselves finally to it here, to weigh the matter duly and make up our minds'. There was an urgency about making a decision, because if there was not to be joint education 'it would be necessary to make suitable provision for the separate education of women, which would of course entail additional expense'.

On 10 April he returned to the question of the presidency of the new college. He had been approached, quite independently, by Dr Adeney, curator of the Royal University, and Dr McClelland of University College to arrange for an interview with His Grace. They seemed 'filled with dismay at the prospect of Coffey's appointment'. Adeney, he added, was 'a very competent man, an Englishman and a Protestant. McClelland was also most competent, a north of Ireland Presbyterian'. The archbishop refused to become involved. He asked Delany to inform the two men that he had nothing to do with the appointment to the presidency, that he had not been consulted about it 'directly or indirectly', and that it would be altogether out of place for him to tender an opinion unless it was asked for.

Shortly afterwards the Chief Secretary arrived in Dublin. Dr Adeney called on him; Delany left a letter at Dublin Castle for him; and Dr Walsh seems to have expressed some support for McGrath. Birrell sent a messenger to Delany with a reply. He had not directly consulted the archbishop, but he was given to understand that he considered Coffey to be 'in every way a good second' to Dr Cox. He regretted if his information on the point was 'untrustworthy'. He did not know 'that any third candidate of any pretension existed' until Dr Adeney turned up. He wished that he had known 'a little sooner'.[214] This, Delany remarked, despite the fact that he had mentioned to him in London that McGrath was the superior candidate for the post. Birrell continued that he was going to England the following day, but would be back in a week's time and would seek an appointment with him. He concluded with a diplomatic reminder: 'The sea of troubles is already choppy and I am by no means confident of success. For in England nobody cares a filbert what happens to the bill'. Delany, who relayed the content of the letter to Dr Walsh, considered the comment to be a bad sign 'at this stage after the triumph of the first reading'. It seemed plain to him 'from Mr Birrell's expressions' that he had 'already appointed Coffey'.

The last word in their correspondence on the appointment of the new president came from the archbishop on 17 April. The Chief Secretary was 'quite mistaken' in supposing that he had 'expressed, or even formed, any opinion about second-bests'. Indeed, the only reference he had made to the question of an appointment was to suggest 'that nothing should be done in the present state of the case'. When Birrell had mentioned two names, 'saying that one was no longer in the field, so that the other was now the only one before him', he had replied that he could not see how he 'could expect to have names before him, so long as there was question of a non-existent office, with no information before the public either as to salary, or as to *tenure*, or to any of the conditions of appointment'. He concluded:

To me the idea of appointing *anyone* in such circumstances is simply ridiculous, and the only conceivable explanation of it is that the people who misled him so lamentably on the Council Bill of last year, are now misleading him again for purposes of their own.

These indications pointed to John Dillon, M.P., who Birrell had told Delany was pushing Coffey's case, and to whom, as will appear, the Chief Secretary had reason to feel obligated.

Dr Denis Coffey, in fact, proved to be a very successful president of the new college. Delaney's judgement as to his 'lesser fitness' compared to McGrath, who was later appointed registrar of the university and a member of the senate, was probably less objective than he believed. There were certainly sufficient aspects to the comparison to distort perspective. Joseph McGrath had been a brilliant pupil of his at Tullabeg, he had taught at University College, and his family was distantly connected with the Delanys. His appointment would maintain continuity with the Stephen's Green college, its standards and traditions. Dr Coffey, on the other hand, whom he wrongly judged to be 'second rate', was dean of the Cecilia Street Medical School with which relations had been strained for some time. Delany had a low estimation of the general cultural level of students from the Medical School; and had frequently stated that the education of medical students was too confined: they needed exposure to the humanistic dimensions of an Arts course. Hence, one of his fears with regard to Coffey's appointment, if P.J. Little's information is accurate, was that it might be detrimental to wider university learning. He is alleged to have said that University College under Dr Coffey would prove 'an apothecary's hall'. And then there were the distracting political undertones associated with the Young Ireland Branch of the United Irish League: the conflict, noted by P.J. Little, between Delany and the college authorities and the nationalist party headed by John Dillon and supported by the Medical School. In Little's view: 'the appointment of Coffey indicated where the greater influence operated'.[215]

The severest setback Delany experienced, however, in regard to appointments arising out of the university bill, related to his friend and colleague, Fr Tom Finlay. During the first week of May he had received three letters from Birrell's secretary seeking his advice and conveying information regarding membership of the governing body of University College. On 9 May the names of the members of the governing bodies of the three colleges of the university were announced. Finlay's name was not among them. Delany was shocked. The omission, indeed, occasioned widespread surprise. As an educationalist, and as one of the best known figures in the country, his inclusion had been taken for granted. Rumour and suspicion of back-door influence by a member or members of the Irish party circulated in Dublin. The party, and particularly John Dillon, was known to be hostile, as noted earlier, to the Irish agricultural co-operative movement of which Finlay was a leading member, on the ground that it was a 'red herring' drawn across the trail of Home Rule.[216] And, of course, there was the memory of his opposition to Parnell, and Dillon's view of him as an 'intriguer'. Deeply upset, Delany wrote to John Redmond on 16 May:

> It is widely current in Dublin that the exclusion of Fr Finlay's name from the list of members of the governing bodies of the new university and college in Dublin is due entirely to the intervention of a member of the Irish party, who is said to have strongly urged his exclusion on Mr Birrell . . . .. Seeing that the very existence of this college is due entirely to the fact that Fr Finlay, with my other Jesuit colleagues, has devoted to its support and development, not merely what remained over beyond his personal maintenance of his salary from the Royal University, but all the gifts and *honoraria* which he received as a priest, and that he made himself jointly with me, responsible to the National Bank for a debt of £6,000 incurred in the early part of our administration — a debt of which £1,500 still remains — you can understand that I feel it a duty to my valued friend and colleague, and a duty also to the Catholic public, many of whom are shocked by such a rumour, to ask you frankly and simply, as leader of the Irish party, whether any such action has taken place to your knowledge and with your approval, or with the knowledge and approval of the Irish party? And if so, on what grounds?

What he hoped to achieve by the letter, beyond registering a protest, is not clear. A political leader was scarcely likely to admit in writing to back-door manoeuvring, least of all to so formidable a dialectician as Delany. Redmond replied three days later that he knew 'nothing whatever about the matter'. He took no part 'in the preparation of the list of members', he never objected to anyone, nor was he consulted. 'The Irish party took no action either'; and he knew of 'no action on the part of any member of the party', such as Delany had suggested, 'directed against Fr Finlay'.

A further dimension to the exclusion was indicated some weeks later, in a letter from Birrell to Dr Walsh concerning the senate of the new university. He wrote on 8 July that the names of Nicholas Synott and Fr Finlay had been pressed on him. 'The latter gentleman', he wrote, was 'an able man'; but he had 'no personal desire to see him on the senate' though 'Butcher and Delany would like to see him there'. What did His Grace think? Dr Walsh's reply is not available. On 20 July, however, Edmund Talbot, M.P., wrote to Delany from the House of Commons:

> I have not left Birrell alone about Fr Finlay, though he is still very obdurate. He makes out high ecclesiastical authority is the chief opposition, and wants to know why I am such a jesuit!! I am afraid I have not much hope. But he has promised me he will have another try.

Finlay was appointed to neither the governing body nor the senate.

On the morrow of the signing of the university bill, Birrell acknowledged Delany's disappointment at the treatment accorded one of his closest colleagues.

> This was a painful business, and perhaps I ought to have been more adamantine than I was; but I was frightened at the beginning of the controversy of the letters S.J.; perhaps I need not have been so, but one never knows what a Protestant will shy at. Then again, I had to conciliate certain high potentates, so that my path was perilous, and it was hard to say which of the perils were real perils, and which phantasms of the brain. To put it plainly, I am sorry that Fr F. was excluded, but I could not see my way to act otherwise.[217]

Despite the failure of some of his hopes and expectations, Delany remained a staunch supporter of the bill in the months it was under discussion. The country generally was not enthusiastic. Many saw it as a victory for the unionist supporters of Trinity's privileges. The church bodies, other than the Church of Ireland, were critical. The Presbyterian General Assembly came out against it. On the Catholic side, the hierarchy at their general meeting on 23 April found fault with a number of aspects of the bill, and expressed great annoyance that Archbishop Walsh had negotiated so extensively with Birrell without keeping them regularly informed. They sought two permanent seats on the senate of the new university, and written guarantees as to the position of Maynooth.[218] Their criticisms and misgivings, however, were not made public. Dr O'Dwyer alone spoke out against Birrell's measure. In the *Irish Educational Review,* May 1908, he attacked it for making no provision for religion. Its constitution was as applicable to a Mohammedan country as to a Catholic one: it was not the type of university at all that the English people were careful to give themselves. He considered the representation in the senate quite unsatisfactory, as also the absence of provision for orthodoxy among the professors in any subject. By and large, it was a case of *'fiat experimentum in corpore vili'.*[219]

Birrell, fearing that O'Dwyer was engaged in 'dangerous machinations' to have the bill condemned from Rome, found an antidote in an unlikely quarter. The 'very anti-clerical' John Dillon introduced him to his brother, Fr Nicholas (Henry) Dillon, the guardian, or superior, of the Franciscan Friary at Limerick. Fr Dillon, in Birrell's words, 'kept the Vatican well informed both as to the actualities and potentialities of this theologically harmless measure'. Through him, the Chief Secretary was assured that Rome did not intend to condemn his university project.[220]

During the month of June, Dr Walsh persuaded the body of bishops to give guarded support to the bill as it stood.[221] In that month's issue of the *New Ireland Review,* however, one of the most influential theologians in the country denounced the measure as ruinous to both religion and education. Fr Peter Finlay, S.J., rector of Miltown Park theological college, and brother to Fr Tom Finlay, attacked on a number of fronts. The bill caused great hardship and injustice by discontinuing the extern degrees. It degraded the higher education of women and made that of religious sisters impossible. Mr Birrell's university was more 'godless' than the Queen's Colleges had been; and his animus against priests was very evident. How else explain that among the representatives of University College on the senate, not one of the six priests among the fellows had been chosen; that the three Queen's Colleges were allowed keep their professors while University College was not; that the Jesuits, whose devotion and heavy pecuniary sacrifices had made University College a brilliant success and thus done most to render necessary a settlement of the university question, had been ignominiously dismissed. The bill enshrined a secularist institution, conceived chiefly to safeguard Trinity College and perpetuate Protestant ascendancy. It should, therefore, be rejected; for half a loaf — when poisoned — was worse than no bread!

Delany clung to the belief that the bill, in spite of all contrary prognostications, would prove generally satisfactory. Its constitution was such, in his opinion, that the Catholic instinct of the people could work on it and mould it in accordance with Catholic principles. Hence, he confined his endeavours almost entirely to influencing certain decisions arising from the measure. His interventions on the presidency of University College and on behalf of Fr Tom Finlay, as has been seen, proved ineffective. A similar fate met his persistent efforts to preserve the granting of degrees to extern students. On 11 May, as the second reading of the bill was introduced, he wrote to *The Times,* pointing out that Trinity College and London University made provision for extern students and pleading that the new university 'continue the democratic practice of giving degrees to poor students in the country'. Those genuinely seeking degrees, such as teachers in schools throughout the land who could not attend normal lectures, were being particularly penalised by the exclusion. Letters to the public press, and the raising of the matter in parliament, all proved fruitless.

In supporting one other modification, however, where his advocacy was joined to that of the bishops, he experienced success. This was the question of Maynooth's affiliation to the new National University, as it was now called. Birrell, in the early stages, had believed that the bill stood no chance if it included Maynooth as an affiliated college.[222] Delany, for his part, was convinced that if affiliation was ruled out, or allowed subject to conditions unacceptable to the hierarchy, the bill would be seriously defective as a settlement, and might even be condemned by the bishops and be abandoned by the government. He argued trenchantly in favour of Maynooth's recognition in a letter to *The Times* on 1 June, quoting in the process long passages from the constitutions and charters of the universities of Liverpool, Manchester and Birmingham. The combined reminders of the bishops and of those, like Delany, who urged affiliation, persuaded the Chief Secretary to make provision for it. Maynooth was allowed to be affiliated by the senate as 'a recognised college' of the university, as distinct fom the constituent colleges. When subsequently an amendment was brought forward in parliament refusing to the senate of the National University the right to affiliate colleges, and thereby seriously threatening Maynooth's position, Delany supplied John Redmond with copious notes and arguments to make a successful intervention on the issue. Speaking on 24 July 1908, the Irish party leader based his argument on the grounds that the same trust and power to affiliate which was given to the universities of Leeds, Liverpool, Birmingham, and Sheffield — and he quoted from their charters — should be given to the senate of the Irish university; to act otherwise was to treat the Irish people as if 'they were not to be trusted' and could lead to a situation which might seriously undermine the whole project. The amendment was defeated by 216 votes to 75. In the margin of his personal volume of *Hansard,* alongside Redmond's speech, [223] Delany wrote: 'The whole of this argument and the charters were forwarded to Mr Redmond by Fr Delany'.

In the House of Commons on 11 May, during the important second reading, critical attitudes to the bill manifested a very different emphasis to that expressed by its Irish Catholic detractors. Birrell's scheme was compared unfavourably with that of Bryce by a number of speakers. Dr Hazel of West Bromwich for example, himself a graduate of Trinity College, deeply regretted the dropping of Bryce's plan for a national university with Trinity College at its head, and trenchantly assailed Trinity's opposition to it. 'The distinguished advocates who represented Dublin University', he declared, 'carried the fiery cross round the combination rooms of Cambridge University and the common rooms of Oxford, and raised a considerable academic uproar . . . with the result that they appear to have frightened the present Chief Secretary into giving up the Bryce scheme. They said: "Trinity is saved". But saved from what? And saved for what? Saved from the possibility of being a great national university; saved for the use of the ascendancy party and the Episcopalian Church! That might be a victory, but from the general standpoint of education in Ireland it was not a victory to be proud of'. He hoped the Chief Secretary would carry out 'the recommendations of the commission in regard to Trinity College. It called for reform at every turn'.[224]

A more familiar line of opposition was followed by northern unionist speakers and by one of Trinity's representatives; and was met by sharp rejoinders from members of the Irish party. James Campbell of Dublin University dismissed Birrell's university as 'a glorified seminary';[225] and William Moore, Armagh North, described the bill as 'a scheme to satisfy the bishops' who had no right to state money.[226] Captain S.L. Gwynn of Galway reminded Mr Campbell that there were 'three Protestant professors' in the University College conducted by the Jesuits, but received the ambiguous reply that Campbell was 'speaking of the Roman Catholic bishops, not of Jesuits'.[227] John McKean, Monaghan South, heatedly asked Moore, 'What was state money? Where did it come from? Was the "state" superior to the people? Was it not the people of Ireland who constituted the state of

Ireland? Yet, three million, three hundred thousand people, who paid taxes far beyond their proper proportion were not to be allowed education such as they wanted. Such a thing was unconstitutional, it was unjust'.[228]

Moore was probably the most vociferous of the hostile critics. He shifted ground as it suited his argument. Thus, having talked of Birrell's project as 'a scheme to satisfy the bishops', he went on to protest 'against the way the bill is being pushed through . . . because of the advice of Dr Delany who has been the Chief Secretary's adviser throughout'. To Birrell's denial, the response was: 'Then it is the one solitary occasion on which Dr Delany's advice has not been taken'.

A major contribution to the debate was made by Haldane, the Secretary of State for War and a father-figure to Birrell's scheme. Sensitive to the House's ambiguous attitude to denominational education, he emphasised the expedient nature of the bill.[229] Its aim was to deal with the 'altogether inadequate provision for higher education in Ireland'. In the process 'denominational difficulties' had to be faced and dealt with. The principle underlying the bill, he said, was to seek 'to put the educational case first, and then to reduce the denominational element to the very smallest we can possibly encompass'. In many English and Scottish universities 'a denominational atmosphere' pervaded everything 'but not in an offensive and mischievous way'. Such things could not be eliminated altogether. What could be done, however, was to ensure that they did 'not interfere with education' and made 'no special demands on the funds of the state'. In Peel's and Gladstone's day the religious question had preponderated over education. Today in Ireland there was evidence that the 'educational question' held preponderance. There had been 'a tendency to give up extreme claims . . . and to accept things which twenty-five years ago would not have been accepted'. One of the most notable signs of this advance and that upon which the bill was based, was the declaration of the Catholic bishops at Maynooth in June 1899. He enumerated the four claims which they had waived. A further advance had been the report of the Committee on Higher Education in that same year advocating that whatever self-government be accorded to the Roman Catholic university should be granted also to the proposed northern university. The committee had stated that the 'question of atmosphere' was of great importance. This, indeed, in Haldane's view, was 'the root of the whole matter'. What was being asked for by both the Catholics and the Presbyterians in Ireland was that the students who went to the university 'should not be exposed to influences which would directly militate against their religious faith'. They did not seek to have their own religion taught there, nor to have state funds for denominational teaching, merely 'some security against their young men having their minds influenced by teaching of a kind which' was 'directly hostile to the religious teaching in which they had been brought up'; and they were content that the governing body, appointed by the crown for the first five years, be composed of people who would be trusted to see that the students' religious faith was not subjected to such an attack.

After this manifestation of 'sweet reasonableness', he turned to the advocates of the Bryce scheme for a federal examining university. Such a project, he declared, had been condemned by the 'strongest educational tribunal which ever sat in this country'; the special committee of the privy council, which sat in 1892 on Liverpool's request for a separate charter from the federal Victoria University and recommended the government to turn from the federal system and 'concentrate itself upon the principle of the teaching university, with close association between the teacher and the examiner'. In Ireland there was a tradition of teaching university colleges. He mentioned Cork and Galway and added: 'Besides that, there is the little University College in Dublin which has a most honourable record, and which has kept its standard high against great and almost overwhelming difficulties, the college over which Dr Delany has presided with great ability'.

He had been astonished to hear Hazel, the member for West Bromwich, speak well of Bryce's scheme. Quite apart from the question of its educational merit, it was, after all, 'denominationalism writ large', with a Catholic college, and an Anglican and a Presbyterian college; and it involved meddling with existing institutions, which was a mistake in Ireland. Trinity College had had 'a great and honourable record', and it was 'one of the bodies most dangerous to meddle with. The English statesman who lays his hand on that ark of the covenant shall surely perish'. Hence, he concluded, the government's plan stood as a plan without a rival; and he asked for a vote in its favour 'in the name of education, of expediency, and of justice to Ireland'.

Both Redmond and Dillon devoted much of their attention to the charge of a 'denominational university' which had been levelled against the scheme. Redmond, referring to Trinity's 'undenominational' status, quoted 'a very eminent Presbyterian', Judge Shaw, who had written to him: 'The undenominational system is all right, it appears, as long as it is worked by a majority of Protestants, but all wrong when it is worked by a majority of Catholics'.[230] Dillon struck the same note. During the first reading he had made much of 'the unconscious hypocrisy' in the House and in the country. There was talk of denominationalism and clerical control in the new university; but for one hundred years Trinity College, and Queen's College, Belfast, since its foundation, had insisted on having a Protestant clergyman as provost, whereas the new university college was being started 'under the presidency of a layman'. Again, the Queen's University, which was held up to the House 'as a free institution and as a sample of free teaching' required a written promise of its lectures and professors to abstain from teaching or advancing any doctrine or statement derogatory to the truths of revealed religion or disrespectful to the religious convictions of any portions of their classes; yet the new university, which was being criticised, was to be perfectly free, and its professors not to be called upon to sign any undertaking. On 11 May he returned to this point, comparing the declarations demanded of the Queen's University professors to the college, 'formerly Dr Newman's, now the college of Dr Delany', at which 'no declaration of any sort or kind is required', and emphasising that Dublin University was surely 'a denominational institution' – since during a hundred years all its provosts, prior to Dr Traill, had been Anglican clergymen, and it had had only two Catholic fellows. He concluded with an affirmation of Haldane's point about an appropriate atmosphere and with an equation of Catholics' needs with those of the Irish nation. What the Catholics of Ireland wanted, he declared, was a college which their sons could attend without being subjected to an atmosphere which, at every turn, would be hostile 'to the faith in which they had been brought up and to the national creed . . . of their fathers'. This was 'not a Catholic but a national claim'.[231]

Birrell's university acknowledged, in fact, the reality of the political and religious divisions in the country. William Delany, conscious of this aspect of the bill, as an Irishman regretted it. It is indicative that one of the comments which he underlined in his own copy of Hansard was that of Mr Hutton, M.P. for Yorkshire West Riding: 'By this bill they were making the universities a dividing and not a unifying force and that was a deplorable result'.[232]

The most significant and unexpected intervention during the

second reading was that of the highly influential senior member for Dublin University, Edward Carson, the solicitor-general. If the new university was denominational, he stated, then so too was Trinity College. Indeed, he appreciated why Catholics sought a college of their own rather than enter the Protestant atmosphere of Trinity. 'So far as I am concerned', he said, 'I have no fear of my Roman Catholic fellow-countrymen, but I prefer them educated and highly educated to uneducated'. Hence, he saw it as the duty of all Irishmen to wish the scheme God-speed and he hoped that the new university might prove 'a step forward in the union of all classes and religions in Ireland for the progress of our country and its education'.[233]

Birrell, greatly heartened, expressed the view that, given Carson's speech, the bill was now likely to pass. He then turned on those opponents of his measure who spoke from a narrow sectarian viewpoint:

We, Protestants, who have succeeded to Roman Catholic institutions, and enjoyed our education in colleges founded by William of Wykeham, and Lady Margaret and other devout Roman Catholic persons, have banged the doors of these institutions for centuries in the faces of people belonging to the same faith as their founders. We, who have benefited by their education, enjoyed their literature, being brought up, many of us, in some places still under their influence, have the audicity to pretend that a university will be endangered and not be a true seat of learning because it may well be that Roman Catholics may have a predominant influence in it. I repudiate this from the bottom of my heart.

Leave for a second reading was granted by a majority of 344 to 31. The bill went before the standing committee on 20 May. Fifteen days were devoted to its discussion between that date and 8 July.

In the intervening weeks, Delany pressed the case for the two issues which he considered of great importance. On 1 June he had a letter in *The Times* in support of the affiliation of Maynooth. He feared that its rejection at this stage might result in an episcopal condemnation of the entire bill. On 17 June he wrote on the granting of degrees to external students. During the third reading, 23 and 24 July, Sir William Collins proposed an amendment in favour of the external students. Both Redmond and Carson opposed it; the Chief Secretary declared that he could not possibly accept it; and it was rejected by 263 votes to

38. Redmond's speech regarding Maynooth, and the defeat of the amendment against the senate's right to affiliate, have been mentioned; but a further amendment, supported by some prominent members of the Irish party, came near to undermining the measure. It required Maynooth students to attend a constituent college of the university for two years before being deemed eligible for a degree. A particularly astute speech from Birrell was necessary to encompass its rejection. These issues apart, the debate on the third reading proved uneventful.

The bill's passage in the House of Lords was marked by an interesting, if rather confused supporting comment from Lord Robertson of the 1902 commission. The question at issue, he declared, was not one of handing over the youth of Ireland to Roman Catholic bishops and clergy. They were already in their hands. Rather was it a question of parliament affording an opportunity

> of having infused into the domain of higher education in Ireland those humanising and liberalising influences which the Roman Catholic Church — to give it its due — knew so well how to use, as was illustrated by the signal success of the Jesuits in education, and he was sure that their lordships would agree with him in saying that that distinguished man, Dr Delany, was a worthy representative of these traditions and achievements.[234]

It was a fitting epitaph to Delany's showing before an unfriendly chairman in 1902. He seldom made an enemy.

The bill was signed on 1 August 1908. As a conclusion to a long struggle it was received with relief at home, and was favourably commented on abroad. The *Freeman's Journal* saluted it. John Dillon described it as 'one of the greatest services to the Irish nation which it has ever been given to an English statesman to render'.[235] And *L'Univers* was of the opinion that 'nothing more important or happier had happened to the sister-isle since the Act of Union'!![236] William Delany looked on it as a special triumph of Birrell's. Many years later, in 1916, the year which marred the Chief Secretary's political career, he recalled a visit he had made to John Morley's house on 20 November 1898. Morley spoke of discussing the Irish university question with Arthur Balfour and of the latter's admission that, despite his own keenness for the proposed measure, it was opposed by the radicals and had few supporters among the Tories generally. When Morley asked the Liberal whip how many of his party would vote for it, the answer had been seven at the outside. Yet, Delany added, 'ten years later, Birrell, son of a nonconformist minister, and a decided radical, carried his National University Bill by 344 - 31, 2nd reading, and 207 to 19 on the 3rd reading'.

It is not inappropriate at this point to pause, as on a pinnacle, to survey what had been effected by the bill.[237] With the passing of the Irish Universities Act an 'examining university', the Royal, was replaced by two new teaching universities, at Belfast and Dublin. The former was to succeed to the property and endowments of Queen's College, Belfast. The latter was to have three constituent colleges — two former Queen's Colleges, which became University College Cork and University College Galway, together with a new institution which would retain the name University College Dublin. It was further allowed to affiliate 'such institutions as have a standard deemed satisfactory by the university', an arrangement which permitted the entry of Maynooth. 'No test whatever of religious belief' was to be permitted for any appointment in either of the universities; while a greatly increased participation of local initiative in higher education was ensured by empowering the Intermediate Board and local authorities to give scholarships and grants-in-aid to matriculated students. Continuity between the old University College and the new was preserved by the provision that all former graduates were to belong to the body corporate of the new university, and by the continuance in office of most of the former teaching staff. The power to make all appointments in the new institutions was vested in two distinct statutory commissions, one for Dublin and one for Belfast.

Delany, who had been nominated to the senate of the new National University and been made a member of the governing body of the new University College, soon found himself actively involved in preparing the draft statutes of both institutions for submission to the statutory commissioners. By October 1909 the final appointments to professorships were made, and the new college began its academic life in the old university house on Stephen's Green. In the immediate aftermath of the act, however, the staff on the Green continued to function under their old president; while he and Birrell exchanged letters of explanation and congratulation, and the old University College, most appropriately, celebrated its silver jubilee.

Chapter XVII

THE AFTERGLOW OF THE ACT; EXPLANATIONS, CONGRATULATIONS, AND A SILVER JUBILEE

On 3 August the Chief Secretary wrote about the university, its charter, and the question of student halls. The following day, having heard from Delany, he wrote again. His letter and Delany's reply were indicative of the close relationship which had developed between them, Birrell consciously playing up to the much older man, but always with a blend of humour and respect.

I must send a line, [he wrote], from the man and from the minister to thank you for all your great kindness and tender paternal (as towards an erring son) interest extended to me through these strenuous months. I know that on one or two points you are disappointed: (1) You are a shameless, invincibly ignorant extern. There I could hold no quarter with you. Sometimes, even as I was binding you to the stake and heaping the faggots around you, I was assailed by horrid doubts whether I was right after all. But I cried *retro me Satanas*,[238] and applied the match. (2) The treatment of some members of your college.

He went on to excuse his exclusion of Fr Tom Finlay, and then concluded:

The Maynooth amendment was an ugly incident and, as nearly as possible, wrecked the ship. The Catholic members of the committee . . . made it plain to their Protestant colleagues that they thought it a good amendment and a blow for freedom, as I dare say it was. . . . The only thing I am fairly proud of is my speech in the House on this amendment during the report stage. I still shiver when I think of the rock.

Now I trust good will come out of all this work and labour . . .

314

Despite the Chief Secretary's rather implausible explanations of his stance with regard to the extern students and Fr Finlay, Delany replied in a similarly light and friendly vein. Characteristically, he was already looking ahead and availed himself of the occasion to direct Birrell's attention obliquely towards Home Rule. He wrote on 6 August:

Many, very many thanks to the man — and absolution with a plenary indulgence to the minister with whom in his difficulties I feel much sympathy, even when lecturing him as befits my profession.

I congratulate you most cordially on your splendid success, all the more remarkable as it was distinctly 'off your own bat' — the victory of the man much more than of the minister or of the party, which he had to drag after him, and many of whom in their heart of hearts would not have been sorry to see him bowled out. Deeply interested as I was in the success of the bill, my interest was much intensified in watching the progress of the struggle, and the manner in which against heavy odds your good-humoured firmness sweetened by tact and ready wit, carried you successfully through many trying encounters where the ordinary Anglo-Saxon minister, even though solid and capable, might most easily have come to grief.

I hope you will enjoy your well-earned holiday, and that you may take courage from this success to tackle, and I hope with equal success, some of the other big problems which make the Chief Secretaryship so burdensome a post. . . .

About the same time, Delany sent an account of the bill to Rome. His letter reflected his resilient tendency to fix on the positive aspects of a situation and its prospects for growth. In a sense he was justifying himself. He wrote:

In its general lines the scheme is what I have always advocated as the best for Catholic interests, namely a *separate* university for Catholics, as against a common university in which Catholics and Protestants would be joined together, and in which the history and philosophy could not be controlled by Catholics, and the Catholic students would be enticed to attend the lectures of the Trinity professors, many of whom are known to be agnostics.

In the new university, he continued, the three constituent colleges were to be controlled by a body of thirty-five or thirty-six members, of whom twenty-eight were Catholics, including the archbishops of Dublin and Tuam, a Limerick priest (Fr Andrew Murphy) and himself. There were eight Protestants, but nearly all were known to be friendly to Catholic education. The governing body of the Dublin college was on similar lines but with fewer Protestants represented and with two bishops and himself amongst its members.

Having outlined the financial provision, he remarked that while they were, of course, grumbling that this was not enough, it did constitute a 'huge difference' compared to present conditions. The main blot on the bill, as he saw it, was that all the members of the governing bodies, except the college presidents, had to go out of office every three or five years. The government could not have obtained agreement for *ex officio* positions for members of the Catholic hierarchy, but he felt confident that, if not elected, the bishops would either be appointed by the crown or coopted by the new governing bodies.

With regard to the absorption of the University College fellows in the new institution, he expected that most of them would be carried over. 'There was surprise', he said, 'at the omission of Fr T. Finlay's name from the list of professors chosen for the governing body'. He then added to the mystery surrounding the identity of his opponents:

I remonstrated over and over again with Mr Birrell about this, and I have reason to think that personally he would have liked to include Fr Finlay, but some of the Irish Catholic members objected to him strongly on political grounds and an article in the *New Ireland Review*, strongly criticising the new university, was attributed to him, so that I did not succeed in having his name inserted.

He did, however, have good hopes of having him named as professor, 'as the majority of the commissioners with whom it will rest are very friendly to me'. He concluded rather cryptically that if he could obtain 'the reappointment of three or four Jesuit fellows' it would secure an income of at least £1,200 to £1,600 'for carrying on here or elsewhere an institution of our own'. It was hoped 'to find a suitable place near the new college', the site of which was still uncertain.

The National University Legislation coincided, very fittingly, with the silver jubilee of the Jesuits' links with University College,

St Stephen's Green. There was occasion, as a result, for a dual celebration which William Delany determined to make a memorable occasion. On 15 October he wrote to Dr Walsh inviting him to 'a college dinner . . . on Thursday the 29th in modest celebration of the twenty-fifth anniversary of our taking charge of the college in 1883'. It would be considered a great favour if His Grace were to attend. The archbishop replied instantly. The following day Delany wrote thanking him for his letter and his kind reference to the celebration, but expressing the great disappointment of all that they would not be favoured by His Grace's presence. The note of disappointment seeped into his further comment that he could understand 'how in present circumstances' in His Grace's 'important and responsible position' considerations might present themselves of a nature which would prevent them enjoying that privilege.

Chief Baron Palles, too, regretted that he would not be able to attend. But he captured the atmosphere of the occasion with the remark that it must be a proud moment for Delany to look back on the work which, under his 'auspices and guidance', the college had accomplished. He had achieved the goal at which, during all that time, he had aimed. 'It is undoubted that but for the work done by University College the recent Act would not have been passed'. The celebration, indeed, in Delany's eyes, commemorated the efforts of a quarter of a century, and proclaimed their successful issue. Approximately two hundred guests assembled for the 'modest celebration' at the college. The three toasts of the evening were: 'The bishops', 'The Royal University of Ireland Senate', and 'The professors and students of the college'. Each toast, in turn, was proposed by the president.

The success of the college was the *motif* running through the evening's speeches, but Delany's share in that success was adverted to repeatedly. It was first emphasised in a letter read from Cardinal Logue regretting his inability to be present. 'You have kept the flag flying', he wrote, 'during the darkest and most hopeless period of the ostracism to which the Catholic youth of Ireland have been subjected'; and far from merely marking time, had 'by the triumphant successes of University College . . . forced the most determined opponents of higher education in Ireland to acknowledge that our young people needed only the opportunity and facilities to take a leading place in the intellectual progress of the country'. The present settlement, such as it was, had 'been largely due to the object lesson which University College' had 'kept before the eyes of the country during the past twenty-five years'.

Dr Healy answered the toast to the hierarchy in the absence of Dr Walsh. Having joined with Delany in paying tribute to the work of the bishops in bringing about the new education act, he went on to praise the efforts of Birrell, Balfour, and the members of the Irish parliamentary party. Then turning to his 'friend, Dr Delany', he stated that the sentiments of the cardinal were re-echoed by the bishops of Ireland generally. It was his conviction that the university settlement had been accomplished as a result of the achievements of University College and of the services of Delany 'by his voice and pen'. He recalled his evidence before the Robertson Commission and how, in face of so many early drawbacks, 'he set about his work like a man, and by zeal, energy and support, and his own great heart, he succeeded in climbing the great hill before him, and making the University College what they had seen it to be in competition with other colleges in Ireland'.

The archbishop then went on to pay tribute to the Royal University, the quality of its degrees, its contributions to the higher education of women, and the general impetus given to higher education 'from the remote hills of Antrim to the valleys of Kerry'. The speech, as reported in the press, closed with a diapason appropriate to the adulatory spirit of the evening:

> This was a new era; a new dawn was opening up before them. He hoped that a brighter day would open up over the hills of Ireland, and he prayed to God that the dawn would usher in a brighter day to all, without distinction of politics or religion. He took the liberty also of saying that when that day came, he hoped that neither the present nor a future generation, nor the historians of this new university, would ever forget the labours of the man who had led that forlorn hope, so to speak, through the desert, through so many toils and troubles, and brought his people to take possession of that happy land for which they had worked so hard and laboured so zealously.[239]

The toast of the senate gave Delany an opportunity to pay a special tribute. For the first time he disclosed in public how, within a month of his coming to the college, the leading members of the senate, Catholics and Protestants, came to him to assure him of their help in making University College a success 'so that it might pave the way for a settlement of the Irish university question'. That assurance had been 'most honourably fulfilled'. It was thanks to the senate's unfailing support in the fellowship scheme, that the college was able to keep open and that 'little by little its most brilliant students became its brilliant professors'. Thus the survival and success of the college was 'due directly to the help given by the senate of the university'.

Lord Castletown returned thanks on behalf of the senate; and Delany then paid eulogistic tribute to 'the professors and students of the college'. His words were couched in rhetoric of a kind which, one surmises, he had used from time to time to stir staff and students towards greater achievement.

> To our professors I only say, with absolute confidence, that they would be an honour to any college in any university in the world; that they have brought to their work here in Dublin, the knowledge and experience gained in the most illustrious universities of Europe.

He named the great centres of learning — Oxford, Cambridge, Dublin, Paris, Prague, Rome, Berlin, Bonn and Heidelberg — and pointed out that, as a result, neither professors nor students had been 'confined to one stereotyped phase of intellectual formation'. Turning to the spirit and climate of the college, he declared:

> Such has been the oneness of purpose, and the unity of heart in our work here, that from the day I came here, twenty-five years ago until today, never once has there been a shadow of disagreement, never once have I had to utter a word of censure or of reproval on any one of that body of professors. And of my students I can simply add, that the list of our professors and tutors, makes manifest that our professors and tutors are in the large majority themselves the pupils of the college, and thus bear the same testimony of what the spirit and working of the college have been in their formation. It is the students of old and the students of today, trained on the same lines, that have made the college what you see it.[240]

The element of rodomontade is seldom absent on such occasions, indeed it is even expected. But the president's words about his staff were so hyperbolic, and his reference to the students so guarded, as to give his final speech a particularly unconvincing ring. That there was substantial unity and agreement between professors and president is undoubted. His quality as an educationalist came out in his choice of men and in his capacity to work with them, on the whole, smoothly. But to say that there had 'never once been a shadow of disagreement' nor need of reproof, when in more recent years many of his staff clearly disagreed with him on the Bryce proposals and on his handling of some of the student protests, was to take credulity beyond breaking point. It was, however, in his delicate and oblique reference to the students that his attribution of 'oneness of purpose and unity of heart' appeared most clearly as protective dressing. The students were his Achilles' heel. Their restless and critical spirit was the ghost at the banquet.

It seems likely, nevertheless, that old wounds would have healed and grounds of grievance been submerged by his acknowledged part in the achieving of the National University and by the accolades of the silver jubilee, had not his handling of a new and more explosive issue made him 'an enemy of the people'. He made the mistake – in terms of popularity and posthumous regard – of frankly opposing Irish as an obligatory subject for entry to the new university. It reaped a harvest of denigratory criticism proportioned to his suspected influence in the moulding of the new institution; and it resulted – on the presumption that language and national identity were inseparably intertwined – in charges of being unpatriotic, and in a cavalier dismissal of all past services both to the university settlement and to the language revival. A few years previously, Sir Horace Plunkett, noted for his sharp eye for moral cowardice,[241] remarked to Bishop O'Dwyer on 'the splendid moral courage of that man', meaning Delany.[242] The attribute was to be severely tested as Delany experienced the intellectual cruelty of his own countrymen: 'the bitterness of speech', which Yeats wrote of, 'burning in fires of a slanderous tongue'. It commenced within a few weeks of the passing of the Act.

Chapter XVIII

THE COMPULSORY IRISH CAMPAIGN

'We are left alone with our day, and time is short and
 History to the defeated
May say Alas but cannot help or pardon'.
 W.H. Auden, 'Spain 1937' in *Collected shorter poems, 1930-1944*
 (London, 1950), p. 189.

The Gaelic League's promotion of the Irish language received
a notable boost in 1900, when the Intermediate Education
Commission agreed to Irish being given an important place in
the intermediate examinations. This success, achieved through
the advocacy of Dr Douglas Hyde, supported by John MacNeill
of University College and Dr Hickey of Maynooth — in face of
strong opposition from three Trinity College scholars, Drs
Mahaffy, Atkinson, and Edward Gwynn — gave new status to
the language and increased confidence to its promoters.[243] They
determined that a knowledge of Irish should be a necessary condition of entry to the new university.

A public meeting to this end was called for the Rotunda Hall
in Dublin on 7 December, 1908. Patrick O'Daly, secretary of the
League, wrote to Delany on 23 November, inviting him to
attend. He replied two days later. He regretted that he would be
unable to be present. Even were he able to attend, however, he
would have considered it better to decline the invitation since
he could not support the resolution before the meeting. He
continued:

> I am a member of the Gaelic League, in great sympathy with
> it and delighted to do all I can to help its work and especially
> to foster and promote the study of Irish both inside and out-
> side the university. But the proposal to make, in present
> circumstances, the Irish language an essential subject for
> admission into the university I should feel it my duty to
> oppose most strenuously for many very good reasons which
> could not fit within the limits of a letter.

321

He expressed this disagreement most reluctantly because he appreciated and admired 'the zeal and enthusiasm for the old land and the old language' which had inspired the action of those who originated the resolution; but it was one of the dangers accompanying zeal and enthusiasm that they tended 'to concentrate attention on one aspect of a problem to the disregard, partial or total, of other aspects no less important for a satisfactory solution'. He would continue, nevertheless, to give the whole subject his most serious attention, 'and entirely from the point of view of the best interests of true Irish education as well as of education in Ireland'. O'Daly, acknowledging his letter, expressed appreciation of 'the courtesy and candour' with which he had explained his views regarding 'the position of Irish in the new university'. But there was a far less restrained reaction when his 'candour' received public notice. This occurred as a result of a meeting of the Gaelic Society of University College on 27 November. The society had been established in the college the previous year, 1907, to further Irish studies, and some twenty students had joined it.

Delany left explanatory notes of his stance throughout the essential Irish controversy. They include a detailed account of the historic inaugural meeting of the society on 27 November, 1908. He had made the great hall available for the occasion, provided tea for the speakers, and contributed towards the expenses. Having brought the speakers to the hall, he was about to leave, since the meeting was to be conducted through Irish, when Miss Agnes O'Farrelly, M.A., 'pressed him to stay and encourage them by his presence even though he took no part in the proceedings'. A paper was read on 'The status of Irish in the new universities'. It was written in Irish by T.P. O'Nowlan, M.A. A number of people spoke to it. The chairman, John MacNeill, B.A., who privately knew Delany's views,[244] asked him if he wished to contribute. He replied that he had not been able to follow the discussion as he knew no Irish, 'but that if Mr O'Nowlan's paper put forward the demand for compulsory Irish at matriculation he felt it his duty to express his dissent as otherwise, being present, he would be taken as assenting by those who would read the account of the proceedings'. MacNeill stated that O'Nowlan had put forward such a demand. Delany then felt obliged to express the reasons for his dissent. The *Freeman's Journal* of 28 November gave a detailed report of the meeting. In the process the main arguments used in the subsequent controversy were encapsulated, and Delany was shown in opposition to two men whom he regarded as friends and who were to become leaders of the new emerging Ireland, John MacNeill and Padraig H. Pearse.

O'Nowlan's paper dwelt at some length on the richness of Gaelic literature and on the educational value of the Irish language. Turning to the new universities, he argued that Irish and Irish history should be given their proper place in them. If the Irish language did not get its proper place, he said, it would not live, and Irish literature would not thrive in the time that was coming. Hence, 'Irish should be taught to every student of the new universities, whether they liked it or not'. Dr S.P. MacEnri, speaking to the paper, argued 'that if Irish were obligatory in the university it would be taught in every secondary school in the country'; while P. O'Daly stated that the League wanted Irish to be 'made obligatory on every student at entrance to the university', that this was as practicable 'as it was to have Latin and natural philosophy' so, but that the League might be prepared to do things gradually and 'be satisfied if it was decided that Irish should be made obligatory at the end of four years'.

Delany, in his unscripted response, strung his arguments together as he spoke. He was received with applause. He regarded himself, he said, as holding a trust. In his capacity as a senator of the new university and a governor of the new college, as well as in his capacity of educationalist of long standing, 'it was his duty to weigh the *pros* and *cons* of every proposal that affected the welfare of the university and that affected education in Ireland'. He would define his position this way. Some twenty-three years ago, when there was question of a university settlement, he had argued for a separate university for Catholics and had written to a friend (Dr Kavanagh) that: 'In a new university, such as Catholics want, the Irish language and Irish history and Irish archaeology, as Catholic Irishmen understand them, would evidently hold an honoured place in the curriculum and be duly honoured in the honours list' (Applause). And he had also written that such a national university, 'thoroughly Catholic and thoroughly Irish under Catholic and Irish control', would speedily draw to it Irish Catholics from all lands, as well as Catholics from other nations who had no such purely Catholic university at home, so that it was not unreasonable to expect 'that such a university would become before many years one of the foremost Catholic intellectual centres of the world, its degrees a symbol of sound Catholic teaching as well as of the best intellectual training' (Applause). 'That,' he said, 'was his position twenty-three years ago; that had been his position ever since; for that he laboured and worked, and that was his position today' (Applause).

The remainder of his speech met with little enthusiasm. He was with them entirely, he declared, in holding 'that the university ought to do all it could to develop and encourage the Irish language, Irish history and Irish archaeology', but he was not with them in advocating that the language should be essential for entry to the university.

He wanted the university to be national, and, therefore, not for any section or portion of the people, but for all the people. There were a great many people who did not care enough about Irish to have it taught to their children, and if they were to make Irish essential, they would have a university of a handful instead of a National University.

He would demonstrate this by figures. That year out of 1,098 students who presented themselves for matriculation examinations in the Royal University, only fifty-eight entered for Irish. One-nineteenth of the whole number! See, he said, the kind of university there would be if only those who knew Irish were admitted! The students were not prepared for such a regulation. Again, it took time to train teachers. A teacher was not capable because he knew Irish. Classical and mathematical teachers had taken years of work in universities to become what they were. To teach Irish properly, 'not the Irish of the fair or market, but the Irish of scholars', it was necessary to have trained men, 'trained with the time and labour of years'. He hoped those teachers would come, and it should be the work of the university to produce them by having the Irish language, Irish history and archaeology on its programme, and by inducing men to put their hearts into it, and not by telling them, 'You will be kicked out unless you do it'.

What, he went on, would be the position of bishops or priests connected with the university if a man came to them thoroughly trained but not knowing Irish? Were they to say: 'We cannot take you in here and make you a Catholic and nationalist Irishman; you must go to Trinity College and become a Trinity College Irishman'? And what of Irishmen in America and Australia who supported self-government for Ireland and wanted to send their sons to the new university? Hence, 'taking into account all the effects that would follow, he could not as a priest and a Catholic consent to make Irish essential..The time might come when it would be in part the language of the country, and then it might come in as an essential part, but not till then'. At present, what instruments of learning Irish had they? In the case of every other subject in the university course, 'all the intellects of Europe had been working at it for centuries. There were commentaries and dictionaries, and a standard of taste and language had been fixed. Would anyone say that there was a standard of language in Irish? He saw men criticise one another very severely (Laughter). They disagreed with each other on small elements of grammar'. It was necessary to train scholars in the language, in middle Irish and ancient Irish, and in dealing with manuscripts, and they would gradually produce dictionaries and commentaries. He hoped this would be done, and that the university would do everything to assist it, and that books would be brought out. But it all had to be done, he concluded, 'before Irish could be used as an instrument of culture; and he deplored any urgency which made it seem that the Gaelic League tried to get hold of the university'.

P.H. Pearse, B.A., B.L., following up this frank statement of views, acknowledged 'the good work' done for Irish by the previous speaker, but said that 'Fr Delany's speech showed that there was a fight before them. He was sorry Fr Delany was against them; but perhaps he would come back to them again, as Dr Mahaffy had come round'. People complained of 'the hardship of having Irish obligatory, but nobody complained of the hardship of having Latin . . . and other subjects obligatory'. John MacNeill, as chairman, summed up the Gaelic League's position in the light of the evening's discussion. 'Fr Delany', he said, 'refused assent to that part of the paper which said Irish should be an essential subject'. Delany interjected: 'an essential subject, and that now. Everything else I am heartily with'. The chairman, continuing, stated that 'he looked upon a good and cultivated knowledge of the Irish language and Irish history as being now an essential part of a liberal education for almost every Irishman' (Applause).

Delany: 'So do I'.

The chairman then said that he could not agree that because the university was a national one catering for all elements in the nation 'that exceptions should be made in regard to the knowledge of the Irish language. He and other speakers for the Gaelic League had for years maintained that they could not regard any form of education for Ireland as national which did not embody the teaching of the Irish language'.

Delany: 'Certainly'.

The chairman declared that with regard to students coming from overseas, nothing would be easier than to make an exception for them. As regards Fr Delany's figures, he did not accept them as conclusive. In the intermediate examinations 'the number who presented themselves in Irish was something like four thousand —'

Delany: 'Five thousand, and I am very glad of it'.

These figures were far more significant, MacNeill continued. 'These students were the material from which the students of the future university would be drawn'. On the question of books, it was clear to him that in Ireland 'there was no modern language which was now so fully and so copiously provided with books and apparatus of instruction as the Irish language was', and on that point he would quote the testimony of the archbishop of Dublin at the Leinster College: 'that the teaching of Irish was the best teaching of any modern language now to be had in the country'. With regard to the philological teaching of Irish, almost incalculable strides had been made in the last two or three years. Switching to Irish, MacNeill concluded that 'he did not think that the Gaelic League would be satisfied with the time limit mentioned (four or five years), though they might be forced to accept that. Therefore, it should not go out that the Gaelic League would be satisfied with anything except what it had stated before the public already' (Applause).

Delany, writing of the occasion later, remarked that he felt obliged 'in common candour' to express his dissent 'on that one point' even though it might not be well received. 'I realised at the time that my action would have been unpopular, that it would bring me a great deal of obloquy and misunderstanding'. Just how much he could not foresee. Even at the meeting he appears to have been taken aback by the audience's reaction. His interjections during MacNeill's address underlined his agreement with the Gaelic League's aims. He was clearly anxious to avoid a parting of the ways with people he valued as friends. With the publication of the proceedings in the newspapers, however, he found himself pilloried to a degree which appalled him. Due to his position and acknowledged influence, his speech was taken to forecast the view to be taken by the majority of the new senate. If he who was considered to be well disposed towards the language thought thus, what hope was there of most of the other senators? His speech was taken up, therefore, by the Gaelic League as a challenge to battle. And almost inevitably in such a confrontation, issues were over-simplified and opponents became villains.

He received many letters of congratulation and support, of which a number were devoted to attacking the credentials of the pro-Irish champions: 'Mr X has a son in Trinity'; 'Mr Y has sent his boy to England for education'; 'Mr Z has never hitherto been noted for any nationalist tendencies'. On the other hand, many communications to the press, as well as private letters, were marked by opprobrium and personal attacks; and among the common run of Gaelic League supporters one query from his lengthy address had been singled out, twisted, and spotlighted with furious indignation – whether the uneducated language of the peasant was to be a test for university education?[245] And, inevitably, there were hate-spiels from anonymous cranks. One such has survived and testifies to the depths of emotion and venom which the issue had aroused. It ran:

> Reverend Father, is it not delightful how the movement is shaping in the new university? There is one invariable law of history: whenever nationalism is opposed by clericalism (in the absence of external protection) clericalism goes to the wall. Of course, Irish studies will be absolutely deadly to your ascendancy. The history of Irish land and language is a constant record of clerical hate of Ireland. Priests cursed Tara and destroyed the national unity. Priests fastened the English yoke on the Irish neck, and gave the clanlands to the Norman adventurers. Priests sold the parliament. Priests killed the language and preached in English – such preaching! – to Gaelic congregations. Priests killed Parnell. Yes, you do well to fight against Irish studies. But the jewel of the business now is that *now* you must fight in the *open*. No getting behind the Castle now. . . . It is you alone who have to operate the whole show in your own pious university, now that you have it. Heaven bless it! In the open. In the open.

In the light of so much criticism in the newspapers during the week 30 November to 6 December, Delany decided to write to the *Freeman's Journal* in self-defence. His letter appeared on 7 December, the date on which the Gaelic League were scheduled to hold their meeting in the Rotunda Hall. He who so recently, at home and at Westminster, had been hailed for his contribution to Irish university education, now found himself in the position of having to justify his right to be considered an 'Irishman'. In the public correspondence on Irish in the universities he found himself credited, he wrote, with holding a position exactly opposite to what he did hold, and with advocating views which he utterly repudiated.

I am described as a West Briton, as sneering at the Irish language, and hostile to its being taught, and as wishing to assist it to an inferior position in the new National University of Ireland.

For these and any similar statements there was not any shadow of foundation. They were one and all 'baseless slanders'. He continued:

> To begin with, by birth and education and character and sentiment, I am an Irishman of the Irish, proud of my country and in most heartfelt sympathy with her people in their national aspirations. For well nigh fifty years I have worked to the best of my power in the service of Ireland and of the Irish people. In my long educational career, next to the discharge of my duty to God, and as a part of that duty, the stimulus that cheered me to toil on through any and all difficulties was the hope of contributing, even in a humble way, to the establishment in Ireland of an Irish national university, such as Newman once described, a university governed by Irish Catholics, and, therefore, in harmony not only with their religious convictions, but also with their national sentiments as Irishmen.

In this spirit, from the very outset of his coming to University College and of his connection with the senate of the Royal University, he had made it his first object 'to help towards the resuscitation of Irish studies by the establishment in competent hands of a professorship of Irish at the university'. A special statute had to be obtained for the purpose, but in 1887 Fr Edmund Hogan had been appointed, and he thought that it would 'hardly be questioned that that appointment, and its results in producing accomplished and enthusiastic Irish scholars, contributed in no small degree to paving the way of the Gaelic League'. Of that body he was himself a member. From the outset, he had been in cordial sympathy with it. He agreed with it 'in desiring that Irish should be known in every home in Ireland, and should be taught — well and adequately taught — in every educational institution in Ireland from the elementary school to the university, and that in the university Irish studies should hold a foremost place'. Seeing the strange misunderstanding of his position in certain quarters, he hoped he would be pardoned for showing that his sympathy with the work for the Gaelic League was not one of mere words. In the past four years, out of the slender means at his disposal, he had spent over £150 'on this one subject of promoting Irish language and Irish history' through supporting the *Feis ceoil* and the *Oireachtas*, and the School of Irish Learning in lectures on Irish history and special classes in the Irish language. So much, therefore, for the charge that he was, or ever had been, hostile to the study of Irish.

Where, then, did he differ from the Gaelic League? 'On one point alone': the proposal that Irish be made an essential subject for matriculation in the new university. It would have been pleasant for him to agree with the proposal; it would have saved him 'much misrepresentation and unfriendly criticism', but he could only have done so in opposition to his 'clear convictions and sense of duty as a senator and an Irish Catholic'. He did not propose to enter now on 'this thorny question'. Later, in calmer moments, he might have an opportunity to explain the reasons which dictated his line of action. For the present, he desired merely to make perfectly clear his position with regard to the study of the Irish language.

In further letters, prepared for the senate of the university and for the bishops' standing committee, he elaborated on the reasons dictating his line of action.[246] Although it is unlikely that he seriously contemplated the possibility of Irish becoming the living language of the country, he was conscious that few had done as much for its promotion as he; and, hence, to make clear to his readers that he could not be accused of being out of sympathy with it, he prefaced his argument with further instances of his work on its behalf. Long before the Gaelic League was founded, he said, he had encouraged the language at Tullabeg, 'and so effectively that in one year seven boys, who won senior grade exhibitions, obtained honours in Irish'. In 1896 he had secured 'the placing of Irish on the programme of modern language scholarships which 'till then had been limited to French and German'. He had also helped to create the fellowship in Irish at University College; and John MacNeill, in recognition of his encouragement to the language, had invited him, in 1901, to be an honorary member of the Gaelic League. Thus, he 'approached the question from a most friendly point of view', but was forced to the conclusion that he could not in conscience or honour support the proposition.

He gave four reasons: 1. that the university was meant to be national, 'in the ordinary broad sense of that word'. Consequently, he felt 'bound in justice to all Irish students not to shut them out by imposing a new and hitherto unheard of test, which many of them, without fault of their own, would be unable to satisfy'. Further, he held himself 'bound in justice to the university' to bring into it the largest possible number of students whose personal character and intellectual acquirements were of the proper standard.

> The larger the number the greater the probability of turning out scholars eminent in the various departments of literature and science, who will at once do credit to the university and render good service to the country in their manifold walks of life.

2. He submitted tables of figures, and the registrar's report from University College, to show that Irish received preferential treatment at the college in the number of lectures and exhibitions available, and yet only a very small proportion of students opted for it. 'With all the enthusiasm for Irish that has been created in many parts of the country', he wrote, 'over ninety per cent of university-going students, for one reason or another, choose to offer another language in preference to Irish'. Hence, for the senate to make it compulsory 'would mean, in present circumstances, to enforce on a reluctant majority of over ninety per cent the views of a minority of less than ten per cent'. In his letter to the bishops, he added the experience of the public lectures at the college. John MacNeill had lectured in Irish history during the session 1905-6, and P.H. Pearse on elementary and advanced Irish. The lectures were excellent but 'attendance was very unsatisfactory and considerable expense was incurred'. In the session 1906-7, he had arranged for another series of lectures in Irish history by John MacNeill, and again the attendance was most unsatisfactory though the lectures were well advertised. These varied experiences made him feel that the Gaelic League's insistence on obligatory Irish was unrealistic, that it did not reflect any deep commitment on the part of the majority of the population, and that to give way to the demand was both to damage the scholarly status of Irish in the university and to permit the Gaelic League to dictate university policy.

3. He considered the proposition 'injurious to religion'. The Catholic body had for fifty years been demanding a university controlled by Catholics. Now that it had been granted, Catholic students, however well qualified, were to be refused admission unless they passed an examination, oral and written, in the Irish language. Should they fail they would be compelled to go to Trinity College or to Belfast. In other words, the senate were being asked to hold 'that it is more important to foster the

Irish language than to preserve and foster Catholicity among Irish Catholic students'.

4. Finally, he pointed to the additional burden thrown upon ecclesiastical students, wishing to learn Greek for professional purposes, 'if they be deprived of the option of substituting it for a modern language and forced to add Irish to a course already heavy enough'.

The Gaelic League, meanwhile, held its meeting on 7 December. John MacNeill spoke sharply of making things more disagreeable for those opposed to them. The real orator of the evening, however, and a dominating figure in those years, was Dr Douglas Hyde. In line with League policy, and in reverse of George Canning, he called the old world into existence to redress the balance of the new. 'There will be a fight', he announced, 'as there was a fight in the days of the Confederation of Kilkenny between the old Irish and the new Irish . . . I shall be on the side of Owen Roe (O'Neill)'. From that moment, one of his biographers wrote:[247]

> The supporters of the League threw all their energy into the fight; so fierce was the struggle, so intense the spirit which animated the protagonists, that many of the League's most devoted members seriously injured their physical health by the labours and exertions they undertook. . . . Controversy ran riot through the land.

The struggle for essential Irish took on the lineaments of the old struggle against the old enemy — with whom the opponents of compulsion were now, somehow, identified.

Branches of the Gaelic League began to mushroom at home and overseas. On 9 December the League in London, and on 11 December the Cork County Council, passed resolutions, supplied by League representatives, 'that the Irish language, both oral and written, be made an essential subject for matriculation, and up to the point where specialisation begins in the new universities. . . .' Prior, indeed, to the Rotunda meeting, Very Rev Canon Ryan, parish priest and vicar general, had enlisted public pressure by means of a large assembly in Tipperary on 3 December which called for Irish language and history to be compulsory 'in the new Dublin university'. He was intolerant of opposition. Writing to Delany after his letter in the *Freeman's Journal*, he did not mince his words:

With elementary Irish, and more advanced Irish history, as

essentials for matriculation, the new university would have the Irish stamp and would receive enthusiastic Irish support. *Without that stamp I'm afraid it will come in for stamping of another kind.*[248]

It is distinctive of the Irish and Scots, unlike the English, Chesterton observed, to think in terms of family and to damn a man through his ancestors.[249] Some of those who opposed essential Irish experienced the effects of this trait. John MacNeill in his preface to his *Irish in the National University of Ireland*, which appeared early in 1909, felt obliged to remind his readers that instead of various questions, criticisms, and 'researches into the nationality of Fr Delany and Mr P.J. O'Neill', chairman of Dublin County Council, the question should be, since Irish was an essential part of Irish higher education, 'what sort of National University we are going to have?' He refused to believe that there was any radical difference on the matter between his friends, Delany, O'Neill, and himself. 'We start from the same premises. The same conclusion awaits us'. A number of other members of the essential Irish lobby also deeply regretted the bitter criticism to which Delany was being subjected. T.P. O'Nowlan and Dr George Sigerson protested in public letters. The question ought to be argued on its merits. Personalities should be avoided. Some regard should be had for conscientious conviction and past service, and the latter should be occasions, not for greater bitterness but for stronger argument. Archbishop Walsh, though anxious to avoid open conflict with the League, had doubts about the legitimacy of 'the popular feeling' that was being roused. He told MacNeill that he had been alienated by 'the shocking, vulgar abuse . . . and the utterly irrelevant arguments' brought forward. He saw in the agitation 'a vicious attempt to intimidate and terrorise'.[250]

Replying to him on 14 December, MacNeill was regretful but unyielding. 'I regret', he wrote, 'the acrimony that has accompanied part of the discussion', and continued:

I regarded Fr Delany's speech as strongly, if not immediately, leading up to the accomplishment of my own views. His interspersed remarks during my reply tended even more clearly in that direction. But I could hardly explain to Your Grace how intense and bitter was the disappointment that Fr Delany's statement produced outside. I have been doing my best ever since to spread a sounder and cooler view.

The newspaper report of his speech at the Rotunda, he went on, was condensed and conveyed a desire on his part 'that things might be made more disagreeable for those who might be opposed to me'. This did not refer at all to those within the university who differed on the question, 'but to the intolerant opposition of an extreme section to the language movement in all its aspects'. Nothing, indeed, was farther from his mind 'than to employ the engine of unpopularity as a substitute for reasonable discussion in the university'. He was convinced, however, that the Gaelic League would not abate the principle and that the national interest was with them. He had the responsibility to stand by the League in public, though it was most disagreeable to Dr Hyde and himself 'to have to appeal at once to the outside public and to our colleagues in the senate'. He wished to emphasise to His Grace the need to have the resolution on essential Irish accepted by the senate. If the senators adopted it they would lift the university 'out of the common category of English provincial universities'. They would give it 'a distinct standing before the world' and, perhaps more important, secure for it 'the affection and pride of Irish people at home and abroad'. This, to his mind, was 'the truest expediency, and the only effective substitute for the prestige of time and great names that belong to other universities'.[251]

While this storm was blowing about him, Delany was almost submerged in diverse activities. Apart from his work at the college, and the operation of the scholarship scheme, he was engaged towards the close of 1908 in negotiations to ensure that Dr Walsh would be appointed the first chancellor of the National University; and early in 1909 he was faced with a series of meetings regarding the statutes for the governing body of the new University College, and the appointment of professors and lecturers and their 'schedule of salaries'. He was also concerned about the provision of college buildings, and about the position of the Jesuits living at Stephen's Green and the possible need of obtaining alternative accommodation for them. All sorts of problems and requests seemed to find their way to his desk. And this trend was further increased with his appointment as acting-provincial of the Irish Jesuits in February 1909, due to the illness of the provincial, Fr Conmee. The appointment placed him in a particular predicament with regard to the Irish language controversy. A number of his subjects represented to him that his views might wrongly be taken to reflect those of the province generally; and they sought leave to join in the debate on the pro-Irish side. He refused. Common sense and the interests of education, he claimed, were too plainly on the 'non-essential' side; and he felt, besides, that the issue was being used to give vent to anti-clerical and anti-Jesuit prejudices.[252]

One of the petitioners, Fr Edmund Cahill, later well-known as an author and a man of strong Irish-Ireland sympathies, wrote to him on 6 January that he found it impossible to believe that there was 'any unfair anti-clerical or anti-Jesuit bias' involved; 'although in the heat of jarring opinions unfair and very unjust things may have been said'. It was a mistake to commit the members of the Order 'to the anti-compulsory view'. It would tell a great deal with the clergy, and with men whose opinion would go far 'in moulding the decisions of the local bodies throughout the country'; which bodies, he took it, could, if substantially united, 'ultimately force the acceptance of their wishes'. In the circumstances, he would 'have thought it only fair to the side of truth (on whichever side truth lies), and to the Society itself, and to the members of the Society who hold the compulsory view, to have the fact clearly stated that opinions in the Society are, in fact, much divided'.

The bishop's standing committee met at University College on 19 January 1909, and issued a carefully worded statement. The framing of the university curriculum, they declared, was a matter for the university senate; and they noted with pain that the senate was receiving, at the hands of the public press, treatment which was 'neither creditable nor serviceable to the nation'. Whether, in fact, it was good for the Irish language movement, and good for the new university, to make Irish compulsory was a question for 'fair argument'. They, for their part, looked forward to the day when the Irish language would again be spoken throughout the country, and would in consequence become largely the medium of instruction in the constituent colleges. But to reach that stage by far the best means, in their judgement, was 'to set up in the (constituent) colleges bright centres of Gaelic study' that would 'by their light and by their rewards, attract young Irishmen within the sphere of their Irish influence'. The progress of Irish in the seminaries and in a number of the intermediate schools of the country, 'so far from being an argument for compulsion', showed what the voluntary system had hitherto done, and what no doubt it would do still more successfully in the colleges of the new university. It was possible, they added:

> that in existing circumstances, compulsion, instead of being a help, would be a hindrance to the language movement. It

certainly would drive away from the university not a few students who, if once brought under the influence of the gaelic school of a constituent college, would grow up good Irishmen.

Because they entertained these views, their lordships concluded, and were 'deeply concerned alike for the revival of our national language and for the success of the National University', they deemed it right 'to put them on record for the information of our own people'.

To the Gaelic League the general drift of the statement was irrelevant. They concentrated on the assertion that the question of compulsory Irish was one for 'fair argument' and proclaimed, in consequence, the absence of any disagreement between themselves and the bishops.[253] In fact, the issue had gone way beyond the bounds of 'fair argument'. The League, with its eight hundred branches, aided by various nationalist groups, had set in train a powerful agitation in which considerations of common sense and education, as proclaimed by Delany, had become as driftwood in a flood of emotion and idealism inundating the country. The movement by now had infiltrated most of the county and urban councils, and was receiving backing from Irish societies in the United States and Australia, as well as in England. Already on 6 January, the Monaghan rural district council charted the way forward with a call to its county council 'to refuse to strike a rate for scholarships to the new National University unless the national language gets a place of honour within its walls'.[254] The bishops' statement had little chance of an attentive hearing. Ears were closed to counterargument. There was only one acceptable solution. Speeches, writings and resolutions supporting essential Irish continued to hammer away at the senate, and particularly at those like William Delany who were known to be opposed to compulsion.

A special effort was made to win over the Irish nationalist or parliamentary party. Hitherto it had not committed itself. Its members were divided. Some were frightened off by 'the atmosphere of anti-clericalism that hung around those who were for Irish; others, from genuine conviction, were in favour of purely optional Irish'.[255] Of the latter, John Dillon was the leader. The League organised well for the parliamentary party's national convention which was to be held at the Mansion House, Dublin, on 10 February. John Boland of the Irish party had an appropriate motion on the agenda: 'That this convention approves of the inclusion of the Irish language among the compulsory subjects for matriculation in the National University of Ireland'.[256] On the eve of the convention, bodies of students marched with bands, torches, and banners inscribed 'No Irish, No Students, No University', to the Gaelic League office in Sackville Street (now O'Connell Street) where an open-air meeting was held. The demonstration was organised by the University Club,[257] which had been associated with the defiant elements in University College and had been nurtured by John Dillon.

The following day, however, Dillon made a public stand against essential Irish. In line for once with Delany's sentiments, he displayed as always the courage of an attack on his convictions. Repeatedly interrupted by a hostile audience, he persisted in his argument. He deprecated the tactics of those who represented the quarrel as one between *pro* and *anti*-national factions. Both sides desired a place of honour for Irish studies. But it was not logical to claim that without compulsory Irish the National University would not be a truly Irish University. Compulsory Latin did not make a Latin university, anymore than compulsory arithmetic made an arithmetic university. 'Take care', he warned prophetically:

> that in making Irish compulsory you may not take the fine edge off the enthusiasm of the Gaelic revival, and bring down the study of Irish to the level of the study of Latin.

He feared that any attempt to force compulsory Irish on the Protestant schools, or on the universities of Belfast and Dublin, would prove intolerable and check the movement in favour of the Gaelic revival, which had been progressing slowly among the Protestants of Ireland. He also saw such an attempt as having wider and deeper implications. Those with ears to hear were but a third of the audience. He estimated that he was defeated two to one in the vote.[258]

Delany, meanwhile, was continuing to find means of fostering Irish within the university, while opposing it as a compulsory subject. In a letter to Dr Walsh on 31 January, he noted that it was obligatory on medical students in first Arts to pass in French or German. In his view, Irish should be an alternative option in this case, as it was for matriculation. He was surprised that such 'strong Irish advocates' as Drs Cox and Coffey had ignored the point. He observed, however, that in the lists of medical students from 1902 to 1906, fully half were from Belfast and of the remainder 'many were preparing for the army . . . and for English appointments'. Hence, if left optional, he felt sure there would not be 'an average of a dozen offering Irish'. This fitted in with his own experience at University College, and with what nearly all headmasters he met told him, namely, that:

> The great *mass of students*, left to themselves, would *not* take Irish, though of course they like to pose as most out and out nationalists.

His observation touched the nub of the controversy. Many of the supporters of Irish appear to have been devoid of any appreciation of the language as such or of a desire to speak it. Its appeal was that it was *not* English and, in consequence, a symbol of national difference. Therein lay a partial explanation, at least, of the movement's zeal and intolerance, qualities which were fired by the impassioned eloquence of the co-founder and leading spokesman of the League, Douglas Hyde. Himself a Protestant, he had seen in the Irish language a means towards a national regeneration embracing men of all origins, creeds and classes. Sadly and ironically, his over-all aim was lost sight of in the fevered agitation which he personally had done so much to create. His powerfully emotive oratory at the Thomond Feis in Limerick on 5 June, 1909, was, perhaps, the high-water mark in his divisive demagogy. The meeting was chaired by Canon Ryan of Tipperary who, at this juncture, according to the *Clare Advocate*, was being lionised by the Gaelic League following a recent speech of his.

The *Munster News* reported on 7 June that an address was presented to the president of the League from Limerick County Council, a body which had already supported the cause of compulsory Irish. Hyde, in reply, stated that he saw the county councils as 'the voice of Ireland', its only free representation at home. He continued:

> The real question that is at stake under the cloak of (compulsory) Irish in the new university — the real question that is at stake is this — is Ireland going to be Ireland or is it going to be Irelandshire (Hear, hear), or is it going to become a poor little miserable imitation third-rate English county? (Cheers). The fact is universally admitted — I have never met anyone to gainsay it — that now has been put into the hands of the Irish people, for the first time in three hundred years, the power of *saving their national life* through the new uni-

versity (Cheers). By making Irish essential or compulsory, you will be impressing upon it — marked and stamped upon it — the hall-mark that every nation loves to impress upon what is nearest and dearest to it (Cheers). The university should lay down the law that nobody can enjoy its privileges except the man who proves he is an Irishman having learnt the language of his native country. . . .

Nobody could deny, he stated, that the Gaelic League could save the Irish language through the new university. Why, then, wasn't it done? Why all the outcry made against it? He was not going to tell the real reason. 'Ah! the real reasons have never been put upon paper at all' (Cheers). A lot of other reasons had been given — sham reasons — bogus reasons.

> There was a reason that it would be unfair to the poor Protes-
> tants of Ireland (Laughter): the university was not intended
> for the Protestants of Ireland. It would be very unfair on the
> poor civil servants of England: the university was not intended
> for the poor civil servants in England but for the Irish people
> (Cheers). It would be very unfair to the American Irish —
> well every national society in America has passed a resolution
> saying: 'We will never go to that university unless it is an Irish
> university' (Cheers). It would be very unfair to the 'genteel'
> schools in Ireland (Laughter). Well the 'genteel' schools do
> what others do, and more than that they never did (Hear,
> hear). It would be very unfair to some diocesan colleges: Ha!
> it would be pretty hard on some of them, but they must do it
> (Cheers).

It is said, he declared, that the Irish people did not want compulsory Irish. Was that, then, why he was made a freeman of
Limerick? Was that why nineteen county councils had followed
the lead of Limerick County Council. Why had 130 out of 170
district and urban councils done the same thing? Why had the
great convention that met in Dublin last February passed the
League's resolution? Above all, why did the general council of
county councils pass that resolution and decide to send a
deputation to the senate of the new university to insist that
Irish should be a compulsory subject? (Applause).
    He wished to avail of the occasion to impress on Limerick
County Council, and all the county councils, the need to act
at once. The new senate, when elected, would 'be deadly hostile
to the Irish language'. There would be 'the three presidents of

the three colleges'; and, as they knew, 'one of them had already voted against Irish' and he did not think the others would vote for it. There would be fourteen college professors elected by the fellows and not too friendly to the resolution. 'The new senate', he went on:

> will have no representative of the people upon it, no representative of public opinion whatsoever. It can afford to snap its fingers at every county council in Ireland. I am neither approving nor disapproving of it — a university ought to be academically governed — but I say the present senate, which is not an academic senate, but a senate which is deliberately appointed to represent the people of Ireland ... have the power of placing that university in the groove ... that the people of Ireland desire (Cheers). Unless you get Irish made an essential subject by the present senate, you will never get it, in my opinion, from the senate that will succeed them.

Hence, he concluded, the business must be settled soon while the present senate was 'in its heyday of power', and before that power was handed over 'to this absolutely irresponsible body of professors' (Cheers).

Delany, writing to Dr Walsh, pointed to a strange irony in Hyde's words:[259]

> Apparently his only hope is in the nominated British senate — the *elected academic body*, he thinks, would have none of his compulsory Irish — so we are compelled to tie their hands in advance.

Dr Windle of University College, Cork, himself a former active propagandist for the Gaelic League,[260] felt bitterly aggrieved at the League's tactics. In a letter to the archbishop on 15 July, regarding a notice of motion on compulsory Irish put forward by Hyde for the next senate meeting, he declared that he thought 'all this trickery on the part of the Gaelic League ... more than disgusting. They look upon the unfortunate university in no other light than as a thing which may be used to forward their narrow and selfish ends, and to accomplish them they are ready to wreck the whole higher education of Catholics by driving boys and girls wholesale into Trinity and Belfast'.[261]

Hyde and MacNeill had on their side, however, the ultimate

argument — the backing of the county councils. The final pressure on the senate was well orchestrated. In September 1909 a massive procession was staged in Dublin. Swelled by several thousand children, many of them from the Christian Brothers' schools, it took three hours to pass a given place. Pointed little dramas enacted on lorries, and placards and banners, urged spectators to support the cause of the native language. Platforms were erected at various places along the route so as to reach all the listeners; and on the platforms, significantly, were representatives from nearly all the county councils.[262] Subsequently, the deputation from the general council of county councils, mentioned by Dr Hyde, called on the senate to announce that their granting of money for scholarships was dependent upon Irish being an obligatory subject for matriculation. The senate, seeking to stave off the inevitable, informed the deputation that the university courses would have to be discussed by the academic councils and the general board of studies, which were not yet in existence.

It was not, therefore, until April 1910 that the struggle began in earnest within the university. By that date each college had its academic council, composed of all the professors of the college; and the university's representative body, the general board of studies, which dealt with university studies and courses, had been established. The deliberations of these bodies — as seen through the correspondence of Windle, Delany and Dr Walsh — were intricate and marked by disagreement. Put very briefly and generally, the progression was as follows. The board of studies, having examined the question, recommended an open programme for matriculation, no subject being obligatory. Windle, in an effort to placate the Gaelic lobby, made a further recommendation, which was passed: 'that for students who, at matriculation, did not pass in Irish language and history, instruction in this subject shall be provided in the colleges of the university, of which instruction students shall be obliged to avail themselves'. The board's recommendation, which was to hold for the academic year 1911-12, was then submitted to the academic councils of the three colleges of the National University. Those of Cork and Galway accepted the board's open scheme, without reference to Windle's proposal. Dublin, however, voted to make mathematics a compulsory subject for everybody and Latin for almost everybody and failed, only by a casting vote, to pass a resolution making Irish obligatory for the session 1911-12. Dublin also adapted Windle's proposal to cover not just students who did not pass Irish at matriculation but those who did not *take* Irish at matriculation, and required them 'to attend a course in Irish language, literature and history, to the satisfaction of the professors of those subjects during the early part of their course of study for degrees'.[263] The senate, meeting on 5 May 1910, adopted the stance of the Dublin academic council both with reference to mathematics and Latin and with regard to subsequent instruction in Irish; and thereby, in Windle's view, threw open the doors to compulsory Irish. His annoyance was bluntly expressed to Dr Walsh, as chancellor, on 26 May.[264]

> The only logical alternative to compulsory Irish was the open scheme. The scheme was approved by a large majority, by the board of studies and by two out of three colleges, i.e. by three out of the four bodies which the senate had to consult. In spite of this they fell in with the views of one-quarter of the bodies consulted and made mathematics compulsory on everybody . . . and Latin on almost everybody. Those who did this must take the consequence of their action and also accept, with such grace as maybe, Irish as compulsory. I am sorry, for I think we might fairly have stood on the entirely non-compulsory platform, but there it is.

Hyde, indeed, had read the signs and proposed to the senate at that meeting that Irish be essential from 1913 on. The proposal was ruled out of order, and referred back to the board of studies. That body at its next meeting adopted Irish as an obligatory subject from 1913. The Dublin academic council, in turn, signified its approval of the board's decision by a large majority, but Cork and Galway held out for the original open scheme. The final decision rested with the senate at its meeting of 23 June 1910.

Ignoring the unpopularity involved, Delany canvassed strongly against essential Irish. He emphasised that the interests not merely of education, but of religion, were at stake. It was a fruitless exercise. The motion proposed by Hyde was carried by twenty-one votes to twelve. Some of the supporters of the motion could hardly have been called champions of the Irish language; while opponents such as Dr Healy, Dr Pye and W.F. Butler, were certainly not anti-Irish in any ordinary sense of the term. The question for the senate, however, as has been noticed, was not between Irish and no Irish, but rather between the prospects of the university with and without *essential* Irish.

As a postscript to the story, the principal protagonists were afforded the opportunity of launching Irish studies in the new university. John MacNeill became an outstanding professor of early Irish history at University College, Dublin; while Douglas Hyde proved a genial, if unexacting, professor of modern Irish at the same college. Many years later, in 1938, he received the supreme acknowledgement of his work for the promotion of the language with his appointment as first president of Ireland. His biographer in that year, Diarmid Coffey, recalled the struggle for essential Irish and gave unwitting testimony to one of its unfortunate effects.

> The establishment of Irish as a compulsory subject in the National University was the crowning achievement of the Gaelic League. It was in the course of its campaign for compulsory Irish that the numbers and strength of the branches reached its maximum. It had obtained great influence not only in the county councils, but also in the parliamentary party. As a political but still non-party organisation, it was in some ways the strongest body in Ireland. *Its success might be measured by the fact that, except for some professed unionists, it was rare to find even a convinced opponent of the idea of reviving Irish as a spoken language brave enough to express his opinions in public.*[265]

Truly, it had been a strange controversy. At the start the majority of people, as individuals, seemed indifferent or hostile to the idea of compulsory Irish. Even many of those who strongly supported the cry for it, knew no Irish, did not intend to learn it, and did not have their children taught it. Archbishop Walsh, as has been seen, had doubts about 'the legitimacy of the popular feeling'. Nevertheless — whether by 'intimidation' as he suggested, or by conviction, or a mixture of both — it became evident during 1909 that there was majority support for the teaching of Irish to the younger generation; and the country's representative bodies, most significantly a preponderance of county councils, ranging themselves in support, carried the day. The senate's decision, therefore, might be said to have reflected the majority feeling of the country; or, more accurately, of that part of it that was concerned with sending its children to the National University. And there, perhaps, was the most significant blind spot in the policy of agitation. 'The university was not intended for the Protestants of Ireland', Douglas Hyde declared in one breath; while in another he identified being Irish with support for his campaign for essential Gaelic and Irish history.

In a word, only one historical tradition and culture was acknowledged as authentically Irish. The effect was to isolate as outsiders many who were proud of Ireland as their country and had devoted much of their lives to its development. One such was A.E. George Russell, who gave expression to his reaction in the much quoted poem — 'On behalf of some Irishmen not followers of tradition'.[266] To him the goal ahead was more important than 'the tale of what had been'. He wrote:

> They call us aliens, we are told
> Because our wayward visions stray
> From that dim banner they unfold,
> The dreams of worn-out yesterday.
> . . . .
> . . . .
> We would no Irish sign efface,
> But yet our lips would gladlier hail
> The first born of the coming race
> Than the last splendour of the Gael.

And yet this considerable section of the population was expected to welcome or acquiesce in a Home Rule Ireland, a country markedly Gaelic and Catholic.[267]

Few appeared to advert to what was ultimately at stake. Those like Dillon and Delany who, in somewhat different contexts, pointed to the narrowing of the meaning of 'national' and to its divisive implications, were shouted down. It was as if the Catholic majority had found a badge of distinctiveness, which they were determined to wave in defiance of the government and, in particular, of the orange minority which had swayed government policies for so long. In the process, the possible long term effects went unregarded; and then, as later, the mistake was made of presuming that the orange drum because it was big and loud was also hollow. Time was to show, in Kettle's phrase, that 'a bucketful of Boyne water' could 'put the sunrise out'.

The policy of compulsory Irish was to survive for some sixty years; and was to receive a special boost with the establishment of an Irish state of twenty-six counties. Eventually, following years of mounting discontent, it was removed from matriculation requirements. The change occasioned scarcely a protest. Delany, however, had swum against the popular tide of his day and forfeited his public prestige. He became identified in the public mind with the 'Castle Catholics', and was dismissed as a 'West British' Irishman.

Some thirteen years later, in one of those minor twists of history, John MacNeill, who had nudged him into the firing line, paid an overdue tribute. By then, MacNeill himself had experienced the pain of public obloquy — the misrepresentation which followed his attempt, as president of the Irish Volunteers, to cancel the insurrection of 1916. He wrote in the preface to his *Celtic Ireland*:[268]

> About eighteen years ago, a great Irishman, great and Irish in his zeal for learning and education and in his love for Ireland, the late Dr William Delany, S.J., rector of University College, offered me an unexpected honour, inviting me, an outsider, to give a special course of lectures in the college on early Irish history . . . Dr Delany's request was to me more than a call, it was a calling.

Nevertheless, later again, when *A page of Irish history: the story of University College, 1883-1909* was published, the extreme republican newspaper, *An Phoblacht*, of 17 May 1930, still nurtured an unforgiving image of Delany. 'On three occasions', it declared, 'the authorities of University College came up against the students and public opinion; and on all three, after a hard and bitter battle, they suffered defeat. One was upon the question of the British national anthem. . . . The second was concerning the admission of women. . . . The third was upon the question of essential Irish. . . . On all three fronts the then president of University College took the side that lost, and posterity judges accordingly'.

For Delany, however, as the contest over compulsory Irish raged and drew to a close, there were other pressing matters to distract his attention from the experience of unpopularity and defeat. A host of issues regarding the new college and university, and his remarkable appointment as Jesuit provincial on 31 July 1909 — 'remarkable' considering his age — were filling his horizon. Moreover, far from being intimidated by the aggression unleashed against him on the Irish question, he courted further unpopularity by a public defence of the Royal University and its senate.

Chapter XIX

DEFENDING THE OLD, EQUIPPING THE NEW

The occasion of his public defence of the Royal was a series of denigratory articles in the *Catholic Young Man* during 1908. The advent of the new university had sharpened the criticisms of the Royal and its senate which had been in evidence ever since the Robertson Commission. Now, as if to exalt the new institution, its predecessor was dismissed and ridiculed as a 'sham' university. This he deemed a complete distortion. It offended his highly developed sense of justice and fair play; and belittled his own work as a senator. He replied with articles of his own.

He praised the quality of the Royal's degrees, compared its buildings not unfavourably with those of certain celebrated European universities, pointed out that being residential was something peculiar to English universities, and defended the work of the senate. Having thus supported it in its more vulnerable aspects, he went on to emphasise that in the number of its students it was greater than Trinity College or the Queen's University, and that it gave something which the new National University would not provide, namely, degrees to external students. In no way, therefore, was it correct or fair to term it a 'sham' university. In the emotional atmosphere of the day such reasoned championing of an institution associated with 'national' subordination provided further ammunition to his critics.

The incongruity of the situation was not lost on him. He had had a hand in the establishment of the Royal, but no one had done more to overthrow it with a view to having it replaced by a superior institution. Yet he was now assailed for speaking well of it. He had striven to build up University College to be a worthy centre of learning, and was now attacked for not praising it sufficiently to the detriment of the Royal. Again, he was attacked for defending the senate, which was accused of being imperialistic in many of its members. That aspect of it was better known to him than to any of his critics, and he had sought over many years to moderate the provocative imperialism of certain senators; but he felt obliged, in fairness to that body, to give credit for its efforts to raise up University College to secure the successes which would bring about the senate's own dissolution. Subtly grateful acknowledgements, however, evoked little appreciation in a polarised society.

He had more success in a strictly practical venture – the election of Dr Walsh to the chancellorship of the new university. On 12 December 1908, he informed the archbishop that he had written confidentially in his favour 'to several of the most important members of the senate'. He was meeting those of his professors who were senators the following day, but he knew they would be with him. He had asked Dr Coffey of the Medical School 'to have a talk with his men', and he had no doubt about the result. He had written also to Belfast and Galway. Hence, he felt that he could safely undertake to say that His Grace's election 'would be most cordially welcomed by the whole senate'. Walsh, however, remained quite circumspect. He did not wish to be involved in a contest for position, or to be 'a party to a continuous election'. He had heard rumours that the Gaelic League was putting Dr Hyde forward, and he had no wish to be placed in opposition to that organisation; and privately he seemed to be under the impression that Delany might himself have ambitions for the position.[269]

Delany wrote to him again on 13 December, with reference to the rumours about Hyde. He did not anticipate the likelihood of his 'being started as a candidate' when it was known that the great mass of the senate was about to propose His Grace. 'It would be too distinctly proving beyond yea and nay', he wrote,

that the Gaelic League want to capture the university, and that they don't hesitate to propose a Protestant as head of the university meant specially for Catholics against the archbishop of Dublin. A more glaring example and proof of anticlerical spirit out of mindless presumption could hardly be imagined. It would open the eyes of the great mass of moderate leaguers to see in what direction they are being held.

But he could not imagine them 'being such fools'. Two days later, following a meeting with Chief Baron Palles, he wrote to say that he had sent a letter to Hugh MacNeill, brother of John MacNeill, to find out if there was any substance to the rumour. John MacNeill informed his brother 'that it was the first he had

heard of it, and that there was no foundation to the story'.
The final communication preliminary to Dr Walsh going forward was made the same day, 15 December, by the Chief Baron.
He told the archbishop:[270]

> I was loyal to the wish you expressed to me. To the last it
> was not 'till I knew from Windle that Fr Delany was bent
> upon Your Grace standing that I worked for you. . . . I saw
> Fr Delany last night . . . and arranged with him to ascertain
> from MacNeill or some one else would Hyde be put forward.
> He wired me this morning that he finds there is no foundation for the rumour, and that he is with Your Grace. Thus, I
> hope the sole difficulty in Your Grace's way has been removed.

It had. He was elected without contest, and the appointment
was for life. It was Delany's last senatorial success of any note.
In the senate of the new university his influence was to be very
much less than in the old. It receded in the face of advancing
years, a fading memory, and the hard fact that he was no longer
a major luminary in university matters now that the university
question was solved; he was retired, and his own lay Catholic
fellow-countrymen were in control.

His Grace's appointment proved of little benefit to Delany
and his colleagues. On the contrary, there was a virtual dismantling of direct Jesuit links with the college, beginning with a
physical displacement. Delany was not clear at first whether
the community house at Stephen's Green would be required
for the new institution. He suspected that it would, but hoped
the community would be left and not have to seek alternative
accommodation. After all, the former tenants had remained
when he moved to Stephen's Green in 1883. He wrote to the
archbishop on 5 August 1909, requesting an interview 'to learn
his mind and that of the bishops' on the matter. Dr Walsh replied
by letter that he could not speak for the bishops, and hence
could not say, 'even in a friendly way, what view might be
taken of any course proposed'. Besides, from the beginning he
had 'abstained from anything to do with the Dublin college'.
He recommended that he consult Bishops O'Donnell and Foley
who were on the governing body.

Some days later, Delany wrote again. He would write to the
two bishops, but one matter more immediately concerned His
Grace. If the occupancy were to be handed over, he would have
'to find a home for the community and for the resident students'. When the site of the university was chosen he hoped to

build a hostel nearby, but meanwhile, for the next two or three years, it might be necessary to take a large house near Stephen's Green, and for this he sought His Grace's approval. Dr Walsh does not appear to have answered, probably because of absence on holidays. Thus, when Delany was informed on 27 September by the governing body of the new University College that they were applying for the use of the premises at 86 Stephen's Green for a period of three years from November of that year (1909), he had to reply that he was not in a position to give a definite answer until he had ascertained the wishes of His Grace regarding the community's transfer 'to other temporary premises within the city', and those of the bishops whose tenant he was. He would endeavour to discover the mind of the bishops and of His Grace, though the latter was away at the moment, and give a definite and, he hoped, satisfactory answer. The delay helped foment a rumour that he was trying to hold on to the buildings for some ulterior motive, perhaps even the founding of a rival Jesuit college![271]

The following day he sent a letter to the archbishop to await his return. 'I am naturally attached to this place', he wrote, 'with which my work has so long been identified'. He was disposed to continue there if that seemed more desirable to His Grace and the bishops, but he saw the college's predicament and was quite prepared to move, with His Grace's approval, to temporary accommodation where he could set up a hall of residence for students. The decision to move was finally conveyed to him in mid-October. He replied happily to Dr Walsh on the 15th.

> I have been happy here and at my age I like the *vias antiquas*, but I recognise most fully the advantage of having a new institution begin its existence in the old home of Newman's Catholic University, and this helps me to go not merely with resignation but with positive gladness.

But it was not just a matter of change of residence. His Grace was also anxious that some members of the Jesuit teaching staff sever their connection with University College. Chief Baron Palles, writing to him on 28 September, noted that apart from Dr Hogan, S.J., who had not applied for reappointment, 'all the other Stephen's Green fellows, and all the Cecilia Street fellows, should be appointed to the new offices equivalent to their own'. He had difficulty 'about Fr Darlington and Fr Browne, but only in consequence of what Your Grace mentioned from time to time'. Under the Act they ought to be appointed, unless it could be 'affirmatively shown' that they were not competent. This was a most unpleasant task to undertake and he was not prepared to decide it affirmatively. 'They are amongst the actual teachers whose teaching produced the results of the Stephen's Green College — which was one of the effective causes of the new university'. He observed that Dr Coffey was 'quite determined to vote for Browne and Darlington'.[272]

Over a week later, on 6 October, the Chief Baron was able to inform Dr Walsh that he had smoothed the way by inducing 'the candidature of Fr Darlington to be withdrawn'; and hence, relieved of the legal difficulty arising from the Act, he was prepared to vote with His Grace 'on the three philosophical chairs in Dublin and on the philosophical lectureship in Cork'. In urging the propriety of Fr Darlington's withdrawal, however, he had stated that he considered the Rev Mr T. Corcoran, S.J., to be 'the most eligible candidate for the professorship of education' and that he intended to vote for him.[273]

Strange things, indeed, were happening with regard to university appointments. Local politics, influence, and acute rivalry between candidates, were marring the beginnings of the new enterprise. Delany's nephew, John Bacon, M.A., who had held the chair of English with much success for nine years and was a fellow of the Royal, was not appointed. Delany wrote to the Joint Board of Commissioners[274] on 19 November to point out that he was 'thoroughly competent and qualified for the position' and 'an efficient teacher'. He was at a loss, he said, as to why the commissioners 'witheld the recommendation from him and him alone, without any word of explanation, which they gave to all other fellows of University College who had applied for reappointment'. Bacon appealed without success; and Robert Donovan, a controversial choice, was eventually appointed in his place on 10 April, 1910.

An instance of an even more unusual appointment occurred in the history faculty. The Chief Baron, in his letter of 6 October, had remarked that, next to philosophy, the most important professorships, 'from a political and religious point of view', were in history, and that the standard of applicants was not high. One of those applying for the professorship of early Irish history was John MacNeill. Despite their disagreement over essential Irish, he wrote to Delany on 17 August, 1909, for a reference. 'The principle teaching work' he had done in early history had been done under Delany at University College and at his invitation. 'I owe you a debt of gratitude', he continued, 'for that opportunity, and I ask you to increase the obligation by giving me a testimonial in support of my application'. It was given willingly. He was appointed, much to the regret of Mrs Alice Stopford Green who was writing regularly to Delany regarding historical studies in the new college. 'I am afraid history fares very badly', she wrote on 28 October. 'Irish history seems to me lost for the present, and the chances do not seem to me very good for general history. This I look on as a great misfortune, for I look on history as one of the first necessities for Irish students now'. In effect, history fared well. MacNeill, as has been noted, proved a very able professor. His appointment, however, was not unexpected; whereas that of John Marcus O'Sullivan to general modern history was completely unexpected, even to himself.

He did not have a degree in history. A graduate in philosophy from Heidelberg University with a doctorate thesis on 'Pragmatism', he was not considered sufficiently orthodox, it seems, for a chair in philosophy. Disappointed, he went to discuss his predicament with the ever approachable and optimistic Fr Darlington. According to a well-attested story,[275] the ensuing dialogue — which bears the hallmark of Darlington's staccato speech and eager goodwill — took place.

> Darlington. 'Let me see now. Let me see. Have you any other subject?'
>
> O'Sullivan. 'Well, I did history in my first year.'
>
> Darlington. 'By jove, you did history. Capital, capital. You apply for history.'
>
> O'Sullivan. 'But I know very little history.'
>
> Darlington. 'It does not matter. Philosophy, history, a good combination. Teach them philosophy. What the young men are interested in is ideas. Apply for history.'

He did, and gained the professorship — helped no doubt by the dearth of quality candidates! He proved an outstanding success.

Fr Darlington, whose unconventional, independent ways did not endear him to Dr Walsh, was succeeded in the chair of metaphysics by Professor W. Magennis, in whom Delany, strangely, expressed 'little confidence'. He informed the archbishop that he was 'strongly anti-clerical'. He wished 'he had some post outside the university'.[276] He expressed much the same fears, however, about Kuno Meyer, after he had recommended him for a lectureship in Celtic studies.[277] At this juncture he seemed pre-

IRISH UNIVERSITY EDUCATION

FACTS AND FIGURES

𝔸 Plea for
Fair Play

By William Delany, s.j.
President of University College, Dublin.

Third Edition

LONDON
JOHN MURRAY, ALBEMARLE STREET, W.
1904

Delany's pamphlet

Douglas Hyde

Eoin MacNeill

disposed to such interpretations. The aggressive tone of the Gaelic League agitation, his desire to see Birrell's undenominational university fully Catholic in practice, together with strained nerves and physical exhaustion, had induced an attitude of suspicion and excessive caution with regard to appointments. The year 1909 had been, in fact, the most taxing in his career. Towards the end of it he was laid up for several weeks. When he wrote to the Joint Board of Commissioners in support of John Bacon, on 19 November, he did so from hospital. His work as chairman of the managing committee of the scholarship fund, and his work on a sub-committee of the senate and of the governing body of the Dublin college, on top of other commitments, proved too great a burden.

The Catholic scholarship committee consumed time and energy. After the payment of the final instalments for 1906 and 1907 he had been immersed in the operation of the 1908 scheme with its intricate claims, and in the complex winding up process of the entire scholarship programme as the Royal University was dissolved. Into 1910 he was in regular contact with the bishops with regard to its final operations and only in May of that year was he in a position to settle the last payments and submit the balance sheet to them. It was a measure of his concern for accuracy, and his personal sense of accountability for the administration of the fund, that scrupulous worries about his performance were to recur to disturb his declining years.

With respect to his work on the sub-committees, the early months of 1909 were particularly demanding. The pace of meetings was such in the preparation of draft-statutes that the completed drafts for the college were submitted to the statutory commission in February, and those for the university in April. As secretary to the sub-committee of the governing body, he had the task of preparing its memorandum for a meeting with the commissioners on 26 April; and on the same day he appeared before the commissioners again as the chief spokesman of a deputation from the trustees of the School of Irish Learning[278] seeking 'the institution of a professorship of early Irish in the university and the appointment of a professor thereto'.[279] He was requested 'to forward in writing to the secretary of the commission a statement of the views of the trustees'. In the midst of so many calls on his time, he was appointed acting-provincial, in February 1909, and then, six months later, was made provincial.[280] The almost inevitable result was physical collapse. The appointment testified, however, to the regard in which he was held at Rome and among his colleagues at home.

Many of the latter, indeed, had paid open tribute to him as a man and a religious on the occasion of his golden jubilee as a Jesuit only a few years previously.

Part IV

From Provincial to obscurity: 'the propaganda of silence'

And I have asked to be
Where no storms come,
Where the green swell is in the havens dumb,
And out of the swell of the sea.
From 'Heaven-Haven' in W.H. Gardiner (ed.) *Poems and prose of Gerard Manley Hopkins* (London, 1953), p. 5.

As we grow older
The world becomes stranger, the patterns more complicated of dead and living . . .
. . . . .
. . . . .
We must be still and still moving
Into another intensity
For a further union, a deeper communion.
T.S. Eliot, 'East Coker', v, in *Four Quartets* (London, 1959), p. 31.

It is this we learn after so many failures,
The building of castles in sand, of queens in snow,
That we cannot make any corner in life or in life's beauty,
That no river is a river which does now flow.
Louis MacNeice, 'Autumn Journal', 1, in *Collected poems, 1925-48* (London, 1949), p. 122.

Chapter XX

THE MAN, THE PROVINCIAL, THE EDUCATIONALIST IN DECLINE, 1909-1912

He was fifty years a Jesuit in 1906. His fellow-Jesuits' expressions of appreciation were conveyed in many letters of congratulation. Two of these indicate the esteem in which he was held at this time among the older and younger members of the province, and of the reasons why he was so highly regarded. The first came from a priest of the older generation. He wrote:

I take this opportunity of offering you very frankly and very sincerely my most cordial congratulations and good wishes.

There has been no one for very many years — and probably not even before many years — who has been such an honour to the Society in Ireland as Your Reverence. You were the first to lift our education out of the old rut, and you are now the first representative of a real undertaking as to what education actually is and what it ought to be. You have met with such opposition, and often from quarters where you might naturally have expected friendliness, and yet the opinion of the whole province is that we have never had so broad-minded and capable a superior, or so genial and edifying a member of a community. No one has ever known you to do an unkind deed or speak an unkind word.

Excuse me for speaking so plainly, but I think it is an occasion when you ought to know the high esteem in which you are held by everyone in the province and indeed by everyone whose opinion is worth anything in Ireland.

The letter from the younger man was equally revealing, but carried a more personal emphasis. 'I feel', he said, 'that, though others naturally rejoice with you because of all the blessings that have been yours in all these years, I have quite other and personal grounds for sending you my good wishes'.

The time I spent under your rectorship on the Green was meant, of course, to perfect my academic education; but far more important to me was the insight which I then obtained into the Jesuit ideal by living with Your Reverence.

Some of the lessons I had from you were formal ones — ones that you will recall; but of more value far, as I already know by experience, was the lesson I learned simply from being in contact with you. I know the meaning of one of St Paul's words 'magnanimity'. I think I learnt from Your Reverence that it means tolerance, so wide that the breath of petty or uncharitable opposition cannot ruffle it, and that it is the patience of the Christian combined with the self-control of a gentleman. I think I learned from Your Reverence, too, the secret that most work is done if it is done unhurringly, and another lesson you often taught — that there is always plenty of time for saying one's prayers.

At the dinner to celebrate the occasion, Professor George

O'Neill, S.J., a former pupil of Tullabeg, produced some inflated verse, which reviewed in rhyme Delany's career from the time he left home 'till the years he pleaded 'a nation's claim'

With flashing word, with zeal aflame,
Bearing aloft the banner Newman flew
To the clear heights of Newman's noble aim.[1]

The letters he received from members of a province not noted for its readiness to dispense praise, meant more to Delany than any amount of public recognition and acclaim. That his standing with his colleagues continued at a high level, in spite of the controversy surrounding the subsequent years, is indicated by the unpublished memoirs[2] of a former Jesuit, John Bithrey, who had been fourteen years in the Order and later became an inspector of classics for secondary schools. Bithrey recalled vividly the 3rd day of December 1908 when he visited Delany, then acting provincial, to request his letters of departure from the Society of Jesus. He supplemented his account with a somewhat romanticised pen-picture of the personality and career of the president of University College which, as the sole extant attempt at a portrait, is worth quoting at length, despite its aura of hero worship. Bithrey did not dispense praise lavishly. His memoirs are far from being a paean to the Jesuits he had known. He found Delany

in his room, in the second storey of his house in St Stephen's Green, a room to which one climbed by many much worn steps of stone. It was a wide and lofty room with two fine windows looking south. It was littered with books and papers, and was untidy, as all rooms are that never feel the magic of a woman's hand; nor was there anything in it to support comfort, except a big armchair, over the back of which lay a warm-looking, heavy rug. One thing, and only one, seemed in good order, the priedieu, with its thick cushion for the knees, its ledge containing missal and breviary, the gold and purple stole that lay folded on its upper surface, and the crucifix, a cross of polished ebony, with the figure of Christ in alabaster. . . . If the rest of the room was a wilderness, here, one felt, was a centre from which light and healing and warmth were diffused.

In response to his knock, Fr Delany said 'come in'

with the martial, incisive voice characteristic of him; for he was a man with a military manner. He had the soldier's incisiveness of speech; there was a tang, a genial asperity, an authoritative tone in his utterance, suggesting that the speaker could not brook either contradiction or delay. It was the utterance of a man who makes up his mind quickly, who expresses himself clearly, and is accustomed to issue orders and be obeyed.

Bithrey had met him more than once. As a student sitting the yearly examinations, he had had his mid-day meal from time to time at Delany's table and 'had listened to him holding forth in his assured and aristocratic way'. But he had never come to close quarters with him, being 'much too shy ever to draw near to one so superb and so magnificent'. To him Delany 'always seemed a kind of deity upon a pedestal, to be approached with reverence and awe. For he was a man of the most courtly manners and his princeliness of demeanour made a deep impression on all who met him, even on those of the very highest rank, such as the Viceroys and the Chief Secretaries whom he counted among his friends. He seemed to have acquired, as a sort of second nature, the grandeur of a Roman cardinal and the stateliness of a Spanish hidalgo'. This dignity, Bithrey conjectured, dated from Delany's time in Rome. 'Before he left Rome he had become in mind and manner a prince of the church; and a prince of the church, in mind and manner, he remained to the end; though no distinction of any kind was ever conferred upon him and he was never anything but a simple Jesuit priest'.

Bithrey went on to present a somewhat inaccurate version of Delany's career and to declare that 'the solution of the Catholic university question was due more to him than to any other man'. The term which described him most completely and most truthfully, he thought, was 'magnificent'.

He was magnificent in conception, magnificent in utterance, and magnificent in execution. As a public speaker, such was his eloquence and such his intensity of conviction, that the ablest and most practised parliamentarians were thrown into the shade by him. When they appeared on the same platform with him, they gave the impression of being disenchanted with life; whereas he spoke like a man who, having never lost or lowered his ideals, was animated by the zeal and fervour of his youthful days. And yet this priest, who in public life

was so splendid . . . was of comparatively humble origin . . .
and was, in private life, as simple and humble as a child.

The last named characteristics were particularly evident in his
dealings with his religious superiors. He submitted so fully to
directives, of which perhaps he disapproved, and executed them
so loyally, that they might have been thought to be of his own
devising. 'But he knew his rights as a Jesuit and he asserted them
fearlessly'. One of those rights was freedom of speech at provincial congregations. He once said publicly, at a provincial
congregation, that the rectors of the Irish houses and the provincial of the Irish province were rapidly turning themselves into
'mere beadles'; that they were degrading the authority of their
offices by referring everything to Rome and, thereby, acting
contrary to the wishes of the founder of the Order. It was a
criticism, Bithrey remarked, that gave great offence, 'and a well
known provincial was heard to say: "William Delany, because of
this utterance, is down and will never be up again."'

'Perhaps his chief quality, in the eyes of those who knew him
intimately,' the pen-picture concludes, 'was his religious fervour.
He was, above and before all other things, a man of prayer.'
His daily mass was said with great devotion and hours were
spent each day in meditation. 'It is true that in business matters
he impressed all competent judges as a man with a master mind;
but it was the intensity of his religious fervour, the strength and
certainty of his supernatural conviction, that most impressed
those who came in contact with him.'

Bithrey, in fact, was taken aback by Delany's reception of
him on that 3 December, 1908. He was met with the detached
incisiveness of which he was to write later. 'How do you propose to make your living? Have you made any arrangements?'
When he replied that he had made none, he was told, to his
surprise, that that was very foolish of him, that the whole
object in delaying his letters of release was that he might make
suitable arrangements. Some time later, however, he experienced
a different side to Delany: one which disposed him to view the
acting-provincial, and his achievements, in a warm light. He recalled that he was summoned to collect his letters the following June.

Fr Delany was a very different man this time. He was warm
and friendly and almost affectionate. He spoke words of
regret and paternal warning and, when I knelt down to get
his blessing, there was a significant break in his voice. . . .

Laying his hands upon my head he let them rest there long and lingeringly, with a pressure that spoke a world of fatherly tenderness.

Although Delany's stance with regard to student opposition and the essential Irish question lost him some sympathy, it was generally appreciated by his colleagues that his resistance on those issues was true to his character and ideals as was his stubborn persistence in the cause of higher education. Hence, when it became evident that Fr Conmee's health made it impossible for him to continue as provincial, the province consultors had no hesitation in recommending Fr Delany as their first choice to succeed him.[3] He wrote to the General to say that he would accept whatever he (the General) decided, but that, in his own view, he was unsuited to the position because of his age, his health, and his lack of knowledge of the members of the province, and because he was, besides, involved in demanding occupations in preparation for the establishment of the new university. He enclosed a letter from his physician, Sir Francis Cruise. The assistant-general, Fr Walmesly, replied on 18 February 1909. The matter should be referred back to the province consultors. Meanwhile, he could draw much consolation 'from the implicit confidence' which the fathers of the province, 'together with the General and his assistants, manifestly reposed' in him. After the province consultors put forward suggestions to meet Delany's objections, the General decided to make no appointment till the summer. On 14 June he announced 'that Fr Delany should act as full vice-provincial till 31 July and then be proclaimed provincial'.

In some respects he was a most suitable man for the post. Apart from his educational achievements, he had been a superior for much of the previous forty years, had represented the province at two general congregations of the Order, in Spain in 1892 and at Rome in 1899, had been a consultor to the provincial since 1900, and had experience as acting-provincial. Besides, as has been indicated, he was appreciated for his affability, approachableness, and deep spirituality. On the other hand, his reasons against his appointment were well-founded. In his seventy-fourth year and in failing health, he was little suited to the government of the whole province. Since 1883, except for his time at Gardiner Street, he had lived at St Stephen's Green in a small community, engaged in a rather specialised work. Absorbing himself completely in his work, as was his wont, and taking little beyond a theoretical interest in the activities of other houses, his acquaintance with most of the priests of the province was slight, and he knew the younger ones only in a passing way. Hence, he felt that the detailed mastery of the complicated conditions, material and personal, under which the works of the province were being conducted, was beyond his power. His estimation appears to have been largely accurate. Fr Cyril Power, interviewed in 1974 and still brightly alert at the age of eighty-nine, remembered him as 'a medium-sized, thin, and very dignified man, affable and charming to speak to, but too old to be an effective provincial. He knew very few people. The province met very few of the university staff'.

With his inadequate knowledge of the younger priests and of those not yet ordained, he found it difficult to assign to the various posts in the province the persons whose qualities were best suited to them. His faulty knowledge of his subjects became something of a by-word and led him into some embarrassing situations. There was the saintly and elderly brother in Limerick who was reprimanded in mistake for a rather wayward companion and who, being a saintly man, accepted the reprimand in silent puzzlement as 'the will of God'! And on another occasion, it is said that the provincial, misled by the names on the province catalogue, appointed to a particular position a man some time dead! He was too shrewd and experienced, however, to make many serious mistakes. Given his limited knowledge, he avoided pitfalls by adopting the principle of making as few changes as possible. For the good administration of the separate houses, he trusted almost entirely to the judgement of the local superiors and interfered only in exceptional cases.[4] His exhortations to the various communities during his annual visitations were marked by a note of Christian joy, encouragement, and hope;[5] and at all times he appears to have shown himself paternal, kindly and urbane in his dealings with individuals.

His provincialate, nevertheless, was not a mere holding operation. In some ways he was more enterprising than many of his predecessors. A number of key decisions had to be made following the establishment of the National University. Alternative accommodation was required for the Stephen's Green community, and for the resident students. The practice of providing a hostel for students went back to Newman's time, and he was determined to continue it, especially for those coming from country areas. There was also a need to provide a house of studies for Jesuit scholastics seeking university degrees. Prior to this they had been located at Tullabeg, with their own Jesuit lecturers, taking their qualifications from the Royal University. Now that attendance was necessary at a constituent college, and foreseeing that before long a special qualification in education would be a requirement for all secondary school teachers, he viewed the acquisition of a suitable dwelling in the Dublin area as a priority.[6] Due to the deferring of decision by his ailing predecessor, and the resulting scarcity of time, his options were limited to the purchasing and adapting of an already existing property.

His immediate problem was shortage of money. The Irish province had never been wealthy. This had hitherto never seemed to worry him. At Stephen's Green, it used be said that the smallest unit he thought of was a hundred pounds. 'Give him £100', was the president's regular response to a request for financial assistance in educational projects.[7] Such was the folk-lore. It was greatly exaggerated but, as has been seen, he had a name for extravagance in the Order. When over-all authority became his, however, he was obliged to take a closer look at the province's financial position. As a result, he became involved almost immediately in a minor confrontation with members of the hierarchy.

Payment was due from their lordships for improvements to the buildings at Stephen's Green and for the additions made to them in recent years. The archbishop's solicitor informed him on 3 February 1909 that he had come to an arrangement with Fr Delany for the sum of £2,213. 6s.[8] Eight months later, when Delany was provincial, the money was still outstanding, an answer had not been received about evacuating the houses, and permission had not been forthcoming for the alternative accommodation he had 'temporarily engaged . . . pending selection of the site of the new university'.[9] On 28 September he wrote Dr Walsh that he was informing the governing body of University College, regarding the occupancy of the Stephen's Green buildings, that he could not give a final answer 'till he had ascertained the wishes of His Grace and those of the episcopal body.

At the meeting of the governing body in mid-October, embarrassed at appearing to be holding up the work of the new college, he explained his financial predicament. The matter was referred to the finance committee of the university. The episcopal representatives, Drs O'Donnell and Foley, were upset. The last named wrote to him on 25 October expressing his surprise that he had raised the question at the meeting of the governing body, since it was really something for the bishops to settle. He suggested that he discuss it with Bishop O'Donnell before the matter went to the finance committee. He was sure that the bishops, who had dealt so generously with the requirements of the governing body in respect of the Stephen's Green buildings, had no desire 'to treat in a different spirit the man and the Order that took in hand the cause of Catholic higher education when it was in a helpless condition and raised it to the proud position which it has held during the past twenty years'. Delany contacted the Bishop of Raphoe, withdrew the subject from the finance committee, and wrote to Bishop Foley. The bishop in reply remarked that it should have been possible by arrangement with Dr O'Donnell to have avoided 'the very awkward and unpleasant situation . . . at the meeting of the governing body'. He would write again to the Bishop of Raphoe to expedite matters. [10] One week later, on 4 November, Lord O'Hagan contacted the archbishop seeking a cheque for the Jesuit fathers, who were due to sign the deed of surrender that day. [11] The money was paid after the community and students had moved to their new premises at 35 Lower Leeson Street, and Winton House, Winton Road (off Leeson park), respectively.

Delany had informed the archbishop on 15 October that he was unable to obtain a suitable single premises, that the Jesuits likely to be appointed professors would stay at Leeson Street, 'and Fr Darlington with one or two others at Winton House with the resident students'. For the present he himself would remain at Leeson Street to help as well as he could 'in starting the new university and the new college'. He asked His Grace's approval and blessing on the new start. He was glad, as noted earlier, to see the new college 'begin its existence in the old home of Newman's Catholic University'. It would be 'the fitting complement' of His Grace's chancellorship 'in stamping Birrell's "unsectarian" university as a distinctly papist establishment'.

The new accommodation was regarded as distinctly 'temporary'. He planned to move community and students close to the new site of University College when that was chosen.[12] He was in no doubt that the new institution should make a fresh and impressive start in spacious surroundings. At the senate he argued strongly that it should be located outside the confines of the city in order to provide better facilities for the physical and moral well-being of the students. He was almost alone in his views, which were considered impracticable.[13] Fifty years were to pass before a later president gave body to them.[14] At the time it was thought best to keep the college within the city as a rival to Trinity, and for the convenience of the medical professors and students. In 1910 the decision was made to transfer it to the former, much abused, Royal University premises at Earlsfort Terrace. Adapting to the new arrangement, Delany set about purchasing a site closer to Leeson Street for a permanent student hostel. A large amount of money had been willed to the province which could be used to this purpose. Unfortunately for his peace of mind, the validity of the will was publicly contested.

The original sum involved came to £50,000. It was left to the Society in 1908 by a wealthy Dublin merchant, Charles Kennedy, who had no immediate family and who had verbally expressed an interest in providing a hostel for students.[15] A nephew, Frank Kennedy, entered a *caveat* against the will. The then provincial, Fr Conmee — wishing to avoid a lawsuit — sought an arrangement. The nephew agreed to accept £25,000 as a settlement. Delany, in 1910, used the remaining half of the money to purchase a site at Hatch Street which provided easy access to the Leeson Street residence. He had in mind the construction of an imposing building appropriate to students of the long awaited Catholic college. To his disappointment, he found that, when legacy duties and expenses were paid, the estate brought in only £12,000. Rather than alter his plans, whatever else was required was drawn from province funds intended for the maintenance and education of Jesuit scholastics and the support of the missions. It was afterwards questioned whether this application of province funds was strictly regular. He and his consultors, at all events, thought it so; and it was in the tradition of his life to build on a grand scale. The rather over-powering structure, now known as University Hall, Hatch Street, was the result. It was completed at a cost of twenty thousand pounds.[16]

Before the building commenced, however, Frank Kennedy, against family advice,[17] decided to contest the will. Believing that a bluff was being employed, Delany pressed ahead with the construction. To his surprise, the matter came to court in June 1911. The plaintiff's case was based, in part, on the declaration of the Catholic Emancipation Act of 1829 that the Society of Jesus was an illegal organisation. As such, he contended, its members could not be beneficiaries of his uncle's will.[18] The suit received much public attention. Considerable sympathy was expressed for the plaintiff at the expense of the religious order. Dr Walsh had advised Delany the previous year, when seeking approval for a house for Jesuit scholastics, to try to amalgamate holdings rather than expand into new ones. 'We are living in critical times', he wrote. 'Religious institutions in a neighbourhood are not always looked upon with a favourable eye by the neighbours'. There was no more stern critic, he added, 'than our friend the Chief Baron himself of the system which has, as he puts it, constructed a ring of "mortmain" around the northern suburbs of the city'.[19] The case was dismissed by the court, and so promptly as to provide little opportunity for the dispelling of the atmosphere of criticism.

In May 1910 Delany entered into negotiations to buy Rathfarnham Castle, some four miles from the city centre, and fifty acres of surrounding land, as a house of studies for the students from Tullabeg.[20] The negotiations broke down. The following year, after unforeseen delays and having viewed alternative possibilities, he yielded to a sense of urgency and bought a residence and estate, without prior consultation with the General or Archbishop Walsh. He declared it suitable for his purpose and also — a novel idea in Ireland at the time — as a place for conducting workingmen's retreats. The property, however, was situated a mile further out than Rathfarnham. The General was not happy with the purchase. Among other things, he judged it too far from the city.[21] In 1912, therefore, Delany reopened negotiations for Rathfarnham Castle. He ceased to be provincial during that year; and it was left to his successor, Fr T.V. Nolan, to complete the transaction. The Rathfarnham house of studies and the country's first residence for 'workingmen's retreats' were to continue as such for over sixty years.

In the midst of his preoccupations as provincial he remained very concerned about the provision of a university education adapted to the needs of the country. At the end of his pamphlet *A plea for fair-play* published in 1904, he had italicised the need for a university *'suitable to the social conditions, and to the manifold, urgent industrial needs of the Irish Catholic population'*. On 13 July 1910, he wrote at great length to his friend, P.J. O'Neill, chairman of Dublin County Council, advocating as a principle that the funds devoted to higher education by the county councils, 'be employed, primarily, for the furtherance of such education as the present economic conditions of Ireland show to be *absolutely necessary* for the welfare of the people'. The principle, once established, how was it to be embodied in a practical form? The answer, he declared, was 'an education dealing with agriculture, industries, and commerce'. He went on for several pages to detail how these areas might be developed within the university, and how the county council scholarships might be applied to them.

His recommendations included the scientific study of agriculture at university level, the programme for the subject being drawn up by an advisory committee composed of skilled agriculturalists and of university science professors, and having among its aims the training of teachers in agricultural affairs with a view to setting up an agricultural centre in each county to advise on the cultivation of land, and on how to deal with diseases to crops and cattle. Travelling scholarships would be made available in this whole area, and scholarships would also be available to the University of Nancy for the study of forestry 'with the view of utilising our waste lands'. By means of such a programme and such scholarships, he believed that professorships, fellowships, and scholarships in Agriculture would become as highly regarded as in Medicine, Arts, and other academic subjects in the university. What he advocated for agriculture ought also be applied to commerce: forming appropriate bodies to advise, drawing up detailed schemes adapted to each area, and embracing along with purely commercial branches of knowledge 'such cognate questions as industrial and commercial economics, finance, banking, the philosophy of history in relation to trade and commerce and the like, which being largely scientific in their treatment, would raise the study to a level comparable with that of other professional studies, which universities have hitherto provided for'. In the long term he hoped that in each county there would be established 'properly equipped centres' for the furtherance of both agricultural and industrial knowledge, 'thereby increasing the productivity of the country'.[22]

As with his proposal to move University College to spacious grounds outside the city, so his plans for agricultural and industrial development were ahead of his time. To the senate of the university and the governing body of University College the immediate problem was how to get the new institution safely under way. There was little time or money for wide-ranging schemes. Given his own record of responding to challenges and making do on slender means, it is not unreasonable to surmise that Delany, envisaging himself in control and perhaps twenty years younger, welcomed such opportunities of meeting 'the urgent needs of the Irish Catholic population'. As matters stood, he felt increasingly out of tune with the members of the controlling bodies. That same year, an embarrassing incident occurred which appears to have convinced him that his usefulness and influence were irretrievably impaired.

At a meeting of the governing body of University College the question arose why the sum allocated to the institution had not been fixed at a higher figure than £32,000. Sir Christopher Nixon stated that when he was in London negotiating on the matter he had written to Fr Delany asking whether that amount would be sufficient. Fr Delany had wired him to say that £32,000 or £30,000 would be ample; and hence he had not held out for the larger sum of £45,000 of which there had been question. Delany declared that he had no recollection of sending such a message. Sir Christopher, however, was able to produce conclusive evidence.[23]

After this, he attended the meetings only on rare occasions. The break was forced upon him initially by the fact that for six months, from 4 December 1910 to 5 May 1911, he was seriously ill and could attempt no work of any kind.[24] Apart from this, his slip of memory had brought sharply home to him his declining powers. He now seemed to feel that his mistake had seriously undermined his standing with the governing body. Hence, when it went out of office in October 1913 he did not seek re-election. He had the consolation, however, of seeing Fr John Gwynne, on behalf of the students, and his old colleague, Fr Tom Finlay, coopted to the new body.

There was one issue, nevertheless, which did occasion his attendance at meetings. From 1909 to 1912 he actively supported in the senate and on the governing body the claims of Loreto College, St Stephen's Green, and of the Dominican university college, St Mary's, Eccles Street, for full recognition as affiliated colleges of the university. Both colleges had done well in the examinations of the Royal University. They sought recognition, particularly for courses in Arts, up to master's standard, and in Education. Loreto College applied to the senate on 27 January 1910, calling attention to its list of impressive results, and pointing out that its closing would be a special hardship to the many 'who held strong views in favour of separate education for women'.[25] St Mary's College, in turn, emphasised that it was founded 'to afford Irish Catholic women an opportunity of separate university study'; and it respectfully submitted to the senate that the sentiment in favour of such separate training was still very widespread in Ireland, and that it would be unwise, and might work serious injustice, not to recognise its existence. It was to be presumed, the submission stated, 'that the authors of the University Act did not mean to exclude from the degrees of the university all educated Irishwomen, except those who themselves, or whose parents, approve of and are prepared to accept, the system of coeducation'.[26] Memorials in favour of recognition, signed by more than three thousand people, were forwarded in support.

The case was a strong one. The Teachers' Guild of Great Britain, however, and the Irish Association of Women Graduates sent in counter-memorials. The last named body argued that teaching in separate, unendowed women's colleges must necessarily be inferior. They sought mixed education in the sense of common attendance of men and women at lectures and laboratory work. 'Such attendance', they continued, doubtless to Delany's wry amusement, as had 'been in operation for many years at Cecilia Street School of Medicine . . . and at University College under the management of the Jesuit fathers, from 1905 up to the dissolution of the Royal University'. They sought for women students 'the same advantages and the same profit from the state endowment' as were enjoyed by men students.[27]

The question came before the governing body on 19 April 1910. Delany took the lead in the matter and proposed, being seconded by Dr O'Donnell, that both colleges be recognised. The proposal was defeated by five votes. A subsequent motion for the recognition of the Arts courses in the colleges was also defeated, but by a much smaller majority. When in the following month the request came before the senate decision was deferred. Early in the next year, 1911, the episcopal standing committee asked Loreto College to revise its scheme for affiliation and, this being done, gave it, in April, their full approval.[28] The senate, on 12 May, sent the new submission back to the University College governing body for consideration. The latter declared in favour of recognition for a period of three years. The Dominican college then renewed its application, and this too was approved on 15 July. Both decisions were sent on to the board of studies. Whatever chance there was of final recognition for one applicant, the possibility of two being accepted was remote. Dr Windle, writing to Archbishop Walsh, announced that while Cork was loathe to oppose 'the wishes of a sister college' if they could be assured of the legality of the action, he very much feared that the whole thing was 'tending to the break-up of the National University as a teaching institution'.[29] Eventually, after much fluctuation and a conflict of legal opinion, the senate refused the applications on 30 October, 1912.

Delany's earnest advocacy, which was almost certainly based on his dislike of coeducation and his feeling for the justice of the case of the two colleges, was attributed by some to a disingenuous desire to avail of the precedent thus established to develop the projected and imposing Jesuit hostel into a recognised college, and also, perhaps, to apply it to the Order's

Mungret College. There was no evidence to give colour to the suspicion, but it had its effect in strengthening the senate in its decision. His almost legendary, and rather unfair, reputation for over-subtlety worked against him now that there was no longer a struggle to be waged with orange adversaries or with the government.

In June 1912 Fr Tom Finlay was appointed superior of the Leeson Street residence and of University Hall[30] — completed in October of the following year. By then, Delany had ceased to be provincial. In May 1912 he informed his consultors that, as from the succeeding August, the General, in view of his health, 'had determined to free him from the cares of office'.[31] That October a thoughtful letter came from the assistant-general, Fr Walmesly, congratulating him on his 'release from a burthen which, under years that are not quite as they were, must have sometimes come near the intolerable, but which had been borne with immense edification, really intense satisfaction, and very great benefit to the province'.[32] The end of his term as provincial marked also the end of his effective participation in university or, indeed, in any other public affairs.

Chapter XXI

THE FINAL YEARS: 'OUT OF THE SWELL OF THE SEA'

No memory of having starred
Atones for later disregard or
Keeps the end from being hard.

> Robert Frost, 'Provide, Provide' in *The poetry of Robert Frost* (London, 1971)

His health broke down once again before the end of 1912, and never fully recovered. He lived on, however, for a further twelve years. They were to be amongst the most tumultuous and significant in his country's history; but his grasp of events had deteriorated and he was increasingly out of joint with the times.

The previous decade had been the prologue. Even then, as has been seen, he had been out of step, marching to the beat of a different drum. The country had undergone, indeed, a dramatic transformation, a transformation more evident to the perceptive visitor than to the participants. Hilaire Belloc had perceived it in 1909. Writing to Fr Matthew Russell, on 1 January 1910, of his 'run through Ireland', he noted how the country had become richer, and commented that soon people across the Irish Sea would 'wake up to find Ireland transformed'.

It will be interesting to see how the professional English politician at Westminister will take the change; at any rate it is too late to stop it now they have lost competence even to misgovern Ireland, and they must let her take her own course.[33]

The new century had ushered in the change. Considerable economic and social improvement followed Wyndham's Land Act of 1903. Money was advanced to the tenants to buy their holdings and the landlord class, as a result, lost much of their

370

power and influence, except in Protestant Ulster. A better off and more independent farming community became a vehicle of dissent against the government and of support for Home Rule; and their sense of identity was channelled by the Gaelic Athletic Association, the Gaelic League, and the spreading 'Irish-Ireland' movement, which, as noted earlier, tended to identify national and Gaelic with Catholic Irish and to inculcate, in effect, an anti-British, separatist spirit.

A further factor for significant change in Catholic Ireland and in the demeanour of Irish Catholics was the operation of the new system of local government introduced in 1898 which transferred power to locally elected bodies, such as the county councils and the urban and rural district councils, and gave them — as the essential Irish controversy demonstrated — a significant voice in the affairs of the country. Largely dominated by the Catholic majority, who found in them an invaluable training-ground for self-government, they marked that shift in control and influence, which Dr O'Dwyer had stressed before the Robertson Commission,[34] from the educated landlord ascendancy class to a 'democracy' of farmers, shopkeepers, and publicans.

Before the close of the first decade of the new century, 'the battle of two civilisations', in D.P. Moran's phrase,[35] had been joined: the continuation, in mainly cultural form, of the old struggle between Ireland and England. Gaelicism, linked to Catholicism, was nourishing a nationalism which, as Professor F.S.L. Lyons has observed, was 'reacting primarily against England — English manners and morals, English influences, English Protestantism, English rule'.[36] No resting place was being admitted 'between the rejection of the English culture and the restoration of the Gaelic culture';[37] and the Anglo-Irish, in consequence, became incidental casualties. By the time of Belloc's visit, therefore, the area of middle ground was fast receding. There was little room for such as Delany who shared no hostility for Britain or things English, and who mingled a regard for the crown, for English friends, language and literature, with a deep love of his own country, its language, its progress, its self-government, and saw no contradiction. Increasingly, others did. And the bell was tolling, too, for such as Redmond, and even Dillon, and all on the narrow middle path between the jarring loyalties: 'only ghosts can live between two fires'.[38]

As the country 'took her own course', William Delany, in progressive retirement, seldom going out of doors or reading a newspaper, lost touch with the younger generation and lived, in political sympathy, in the world he knew best, the world which aspired to Home Rule within the empire. For some years he busied himself on a book designed to confute certain contemporary forms of unbelief. His special lectures to students at University College had shown an unusual grasp of knowledge in the fields of modern science, philosophy, and psychology, and an ability to relate it positively to areas of faith and morals. He had also shown, over many years, an attraction to newspaper controversies, and had participated in several with considerable success. Even while seriously over-worked as provincial, he had taken a leading part in two disputations of an apologetic nature which excited much contemporary interest.

The first, in the *Irish Times* during 1910, brought him into opposition to the Rev J.E. Moffett, Grand Master of the Orange Society, who alleged that all the Jesuits took an oath 'to extirpate the heretical Protestants' doctrine, and to destroy all their pretended power, legal or otherwise'. Delany denied the existence of any such oath, and challenged Dr Moffett to produce any evidence for it. On the same day he wrote two letters to the *Express* on the same subject, pointing out that eight years previously in that paper he had successfully challenged the 'same calumny'; and he went on to give the history of the fabrication. The controversy produced many letters from Protestants, and soon it had expanded into various aspects of Catholic teaching, especially the declaration that 'outside the Church there is no salvation'. Delany's lengthy replies, exhibiting a rare blend of theological learning and clear, apposite expression, won him, from his most able adversary, Dr J.W. Tristram, warm praise and, to his amusement, doubt about his orthodoxy.

The second controversy commenced shortly afterwards, November 1911, in the pages of the *Irish Independent*. This time the adversary was Sir Edward Fry, of the Fry Commission, who, in a published pamphlet, had accused the Jesuits of teaching and adopting the principle that 'the end justifies the means'. Challenging him to produce evidence, and showing that the 'abominable slander' had been dismissed by official courts in Germany as without foundation, Delany offered to pay £50 to any public charity if the charge could be substantiated. Sir Edward replied to the *Irish Times*. The two sources he referred to were the *Lettres Provinciales* of Pascal, and a definition of a Jesuit in certain dictionaries written by Protestants for

a Protestant public. Such argumentation from a lawyer of such
great authority was quite extraordinary, Delany replied; and,
with question upon question he pin-pointed the weakness of
Edward's case:-

> If he were on the bench trying a case involving personal
> character, would he accept such evidence as conclusive?
> Would he accept as trustworthy witnesses to a man's character,
> his well-known bitter enemies? Or those who had no personal
> knowledge of him? And who were reared in strong personal
> prejudices against him? Or would he not rather attach more
> weight to the witness of those who had life-long intimate
> relations with him, and who knew him thoroughly, and of
> whose personal trustworthiness the judge could have fullest
> assurance?

Among Dublin Catholics, he said, there were scores of men,
'in the front rank of their professions', who were in that position
towards the Jesuits and could give him the required information;
and he named in particular Chief Baron Palles, the Lord Chief
Justice O'Brien, and the Attorney General.[39]

He showed no wish, however, to push his opponent into a
posture of abject submission. When W.F. Dennehy of the *Irish
Catholic* sought to give 'Sir Edward Fry no alternative but to
apologise or take an action' in defence of his 'scandalous libels',
and planned to send copies of the paper to the leading members
of the Society of Friends, of which Fry was a member, Delany
informed him that his 'zeal outran his discretion', and asked him
to desist. Dennehy replied that his (Delany's) 'tenderness of
feeling for Fry and his friends was characteristic, and fresh
evidence of kindliness of heart'.[40]

A work of apologetic intent was, therefore, in the context
of his attitudes and practice, an attractive proposition to Delany.
Gradually, however, the amount of reading and research involved,
his own exacting standards and his failing powers, combined
to make him abandon the project. The remainder of his days were
mainly devoted to religious duties, to some work as a priest in
nearby convents and hospitals, to occasional letters to the newspapers, letters to friends and visits from friends.

He maintained a regular correspondence with Dr Walsh, for
whom he continued to have great reverence as his archbishop and
a mixture of special regard and resentment as a person.[41] He
wrote from time to time to old friends such as John Morley,
Sir John Ross of Bladensburg, Lord and Lady Aberdeen, and

Augustine Birrell. The letters were frequently occasioned by some misfortune which had befallen the recipients or their families, and only seldom related to public affairs.

The war years brought suffering to the Aberdeens. In April 1915, Lord Aberdeen wrote to thank him for his long letter on a bereavement, and 'especially for the concluding sentence, in which you gave me an assurance that you remembered us in your prayers'. He thanked him also for his letter to the 'noble young wife' of their mutual friend, Roger Bellingham, assisting her 'to bravely accept her loss'. His letter mentioned that Lady Aberdeen was in Ireland. Delany wrote to her that same day, 15 April. He had been so occupied with work which interested him greatly, he said, that he never looked at a news-paper and hardly ever went out. Hence, he had only now learned in a letter from Lord Aberdeen that she was in Dublin. He extended 'a most cordial welcome'. He hoped that her interest in good works for Irish people would not have been lessened by 'recent regrettable events'. The country's 'political and religious history', he continued, had so profoundly affected the social conditions of the people, 'and created so wide a gulf between those few who abound, and the many who are in need', that it was good to welcome a viceroyalty which had as its predominant characteristics — not political influence, or special functions, but 'to promote the well-being of the *whole* people, but more especially to help the poor, the sick, and the suffering, who form a large part of our Irish people'.

The previous year, 1914, he had written to Birrell to support the application of a candidate for a better position and to enquire after his wife who was ill. The Chief Secretary, replying from London on 16 July, related that his wife was 'still very ill' and that she still remembered Delany, and he would pass on his message to her. He then touched on the current disagreement regarding the Home Rule Bill between northern unionists and the Irish parliamentary party.

It is indeed a *nemesis* for dishonesty and ill-usage in the past to see both English parties in the hands of their *Irish* supporters, trying hard to understand what it is the two *Irish* parties are quarrelling about, and completely failing to *measure* the situation.

Two years later, after Birrell himself had failed 'to measure the situation' and was surprised by the 1916 insurrection, and then recalled to England, Delany wrote to him in sympathy. Like the majority of the Irish population at the time, he regarded the Easter rising as fruitless and irresponsible. Birrell replied on 10 May:

> It is always agreeable to be in any measure supported by those who *know* — if indeed anybody knows Ireland or can say beforehand what is likely to happen within her boundaries. In looking back over nine years I am fully alive to many mistakes, and could I live through the years again I would behave differently on many occasions — but *generally* the policy, though of necessity open to the charge of weakness, was, I am sure, right. In Ireland under the present constitution it is *easier* for an English Chief Secretary to play the part of a *strong* man, than of a *weak* one. None the less, the circumstances of my departure are melancholy enough, and I am grateful to the Almighty for having removed my wife from the earth before the blow fell. Alone I find it easier to bear.
>
> That good may come out of it is always the prayer of fallen man. What else could it come out of?
>
> I trust your accident was not serious. I shall always remember you with pleasure and profit.

A few days later, on 20 May, Delany's sympathy flowed out to John Redmond who, because of the public reaction against General Maxwell's reprisals, was being accused of not speaking out and, hence, of condoning the execution of the revolutionary leaders. He told him that he remembered him, his 'anxieties and burdens', each day in his mass and prayers. He then offered a suggestion which had been in his mind 'since the outbreak of this insane attempt at rebellion'. It was that all the messages Redmond had received, from inside and outside Ireland, repudiating the rising should be put together in pamphlet form as a permanent record. This would make it clear, he said, that 'the so-called rebellion was not an *Irish* rebellion and had not the approval of the Irish race', that the Irish race warmly endorsed his policy and leadership; and that the desire for entire separation was not the leading idea of the mass of Irishmen. Furthermore, it would tell powerfully with the recruits whom Redmond's powerful advocacy sent to the front, showing that 'all thoughtful and experienced Irishmen' were with him, and that those who had *Home Rule within the empire* considered it well worth having and fighting for. Besides, he felt that such a pamphlet would be 'most useful permanently as a warning to thoughtless young men against the danger of secret societies and risking one's life at the bidding of unknown nobodies against the clearly expressed judgement of the whole people'.

To Dr Walsh, he wrote mainly on minor matters. From time to time he wrote seeking permission to say mass in his niece's house at Rahney where he went to recuperate. Anxiety about the disposal of the scholarship funds seemed to grow on him with the years. In 1911, as secretary of the Catholic scholarship committee, he made the final report to Dr Walsh, acting for the bishops. There was a surplus remaining of £550 which, he thought, 'might be invested to provide an annual scholarship of £20 for a yearly essay'.[42] The money was lodged in the bank. As time passed and he felt his own final accounting approach, he became quite worried about the sum of money. In January 1918 he wondered if His Grace knew about the 'surplus balance'. Old age, he said, had been dulling not only his memory but his judgement. In April of the following year it was troubling him again. The sum now came to £608. He was quite at a loss what to do and wished 'very much to be free of such a responsibility' at his age. He asked His Grace what course he should take. Three days later he thanked him for his advice and counsel.[43] In September 1920 he sent the deposit receipt to him in order 'to bring to a close' his responsibility, and he hoped that His Grace would dispose of it as he thought fit. Rather pathetically he wrote again on the 17th of the month:

As my years have been mounting up: eighty-five on 4 June last, and wintry weather forces me to keep the house, though otherwise, thank God, enjoying good health, I thought it prudent to place secretaryship in Your Grace's hands.

Only two letters to Dr Walsh during those years had any bearing on public affairs. In both instances as from a haven, 'out of the swell of the sea', he reasoned in terms of earlier certainties about events happening outside his door and occasioning suffering and deep emotion. The first concerned the great strike of 1913; and James Larkin, defying accepted ways, was the inevitable target. He wrote on 1 December 1913, to congratulate the archbishop on a letter he had published about the strike. The main difficulty, in Delany's view, was the false notion held in England, and to some extent in Ireland, that 'the Transport Union of Ireland is a trade union in any true sense, and that opposition to it means opposition to trade unionism, which, of course, the whole body of trade unions are bound to resist and to fight against to the last'. The Irish Transport Union, he continued, was not a union working on trade union lines and principles. It was 'absolutely controlled' by Larkin, who made no secret that he condemned trade unions, that he was a socialist, was 'out for rebellion', had 'a divine message for creating discontent', that his object was to 'do away with employers', and that 'the damnedst of curses is labour'. He called William Martin Murphy, the leader on the employers' side, a murderer, used the 'tainted goods' cry, and depended on the sympathetic strike. Referring to a recent issue of the workers' paper, Delany noted that Larkin spoke of a childhood vision he had experienced and of the mission he had got 'to transform the world'. It seemed to him that Larkin was 'on the high road to the lunatic asylum'.

Delany's letter underlined how recent an arrival on the public stage was the working class movement and the awareness of an urban problem. The popular interpretation of history focused attention upon political rather than social and economic factors, and the 'social question', up to the early years of the new century, was taken by most people in Ireland to refer to the rural problem rather than the urban one. It was only after 1907, when the rumblings of socialist egalitarianism seemed to herald social anarchy, that the urgency of the situation impinged on the majority of clergy and people. There had been general sympathy and support among churchmen for the trade union movement, but in the new century this attitude underwent a change with the growth of strike action and the fear that Irish trade unionists being members of British-based unions were being contaminated by socialist and irreligious sentiments. 'Socialism', in a confused way, stood for anarchy and a threat to the *status quo*. It was one of the most obscure words in the English language, Shane Leslie told a Dublin audience in 1910, covering 'many opposites, a great many controversies, and sometimes a multitude of sins'.[44] Attacked by Bishop O'Dwyer in 1906 and by Cardinal Logue in 1908, what it stood for in the eyes of most clergy was indicated by the cardinal's lenten pastoral of 1912, namely, the subversion of religion, morality, human rights, the peace and well-being of the community, and the profession of atheism and the renunciation of marriage and the family. Not surprisingly, active Irish labour leaders tended to be identified with socialists, so portrayed, and to be attacked accordingly.

William Delany had a deep-felt sympathy with the victims of the appalling slum conditions, and he saw the new university and a Home Rule Ireland as having a major responsibility to combat poverty by developing the economy of the country; but, in common with most of the Irish clergy, his social attitudes were largely determined by the surrounding social, political and economic ideas of the time which, by and large, favoured a static conception of society and of the Church and looked with suspicion on any ideas or actions that might threaten the value system of Catholic Ireland. Hence, Larkin's extravagant statements apart, his criticism of him for his abuse of trade unionism and for being a socialist. He himself had lost touch with the thinking of that small but important body of priests, which included his younger colleagues, Tom Finlay, Lambert McKenna and Michael Phelan, who had seriously attempted to analyse socialism and to distinguish the reality from the myth. While his vision remained part of an older, more stable world, they were arguing for social change, distinguishing between the practical aims of socialism and the theoretical principles on which it was based, and maintaining that strong labour and employers' organisations were essential to the well-being of society. Their grasp of what was involved helped to keep some channels open between the Church and the militant labour leaders: James Connolly, the representative figure of Irish socialism, complimented Finlay, indeed, as early as 15 July 1899 (*Workers' Republic*), for his understanding of Marxism.[45]

Delany's second letter to the archbishop came many years later — when 'the John Bull of the good old days', in Auden's words, with

His acres of self-confidence for sale,
Had passed away at Ypres and Passchendaele;[46]

when widespread revolt was in course in Ireland against British government; and when, in Chesterton's estimation, over the hills and valleys of Ireland its word was wind, and its bond was waste paper.[47] Delany could not come to grips with it all. His sympathies were split. So many people he knew were on the side of the revolution; yet since his days at Rome, at least, he had a horror of armed rebellion, and he could not see how a clandestine organisation could be justified in the light of traditional church teaching. The cold-blooded reprisals of Michael Collins's 'squad', in particular, he found impossible to accept. His rather wandering letter was written on 27 November 1920.

He wondered how University Hall had escaped being raided, since he was pretty certain that many of the students were 'not deeply attached to the present government'. Personally, he felt that 'the powers that be' were absolutely unfit 'to govern any country', and the general outlook was saddening 'beyond anything in living memory'. It was especially sad to realise that there was 'a controlling inner gang', who were 'the authors of these abominable assassinations that were furnishing our enemies with such arguments of our unfitness for self-government'. He spoke of a young man, 'a respectable solicitor', who had been 'sworn in by a leading Sinn Feiner — sworn to obey orders from *unknown chiefs* and carry them out as directed without question'. This, if true, would bring those who recognised the inner gang under the excommunication of the bull *Apostolicae Sedis*, as the Fenians came under it in 1870. The recent arrest of John MacNeill and Arthur Griffith made him anxious about one of the fathers 'who made himself conspicuous in championing Mac Neill'. Finally, he congratulated His Grace on his restoration to 'health and vigor', especially just then when the public welfare was 'in such pressing need of his influence'.

The seemingly indestructible archbishop died in April 1921, at the age of eighty. William Delany lived on through the divisions of the civil war to the emergence of a new Irish state. 'In continuous communion with God', wrote Fr Tom Finlay in hagiographical terms, 'he waited through the evening of life for the Master's summons'.[48] It came on 17 February 1924, at the age of eighty-nine.

His old friend from Tullabeg days, Judge Bodkin, wrote after his death that up to the end he 'always looked at least twenty years younger than his age'. Moreover, 'to the very last his brilliancy of conversation, his indescribable fascination of manner, ranging from grave to gay, from serious to serene, was maintained . . . even after he was confined to his room at Leeson Street'.[49] The obituarist in the *Clongownian* of 1924 noted that 'to many, many people the death of this old man was the loss of an intimate friend'. Fr William Stephenson and Fr Cyril Power, among the few remaining links with those years when this book was being written, remembered the elderly Delany, respectively, as 'gentlemanly, suave and welcoming — though rather distant'; and 'friendly, chatty and talkative' to the young Jesuits who visited Leeson Street from University College. He had a rather 'grand manner' but great charm, Fr Power added. 'He could talk and would talk to everyone, but he liked to associate with the gentry, especially the Protestant gentry. Like all the old fathers, he was very conservative in such ways!'

Whatever about his domestic image, William Delany as a public figure was virtually forgotten. He had been by-passed by the accumulation of events: events engineered to a considerable extent by men of his college on the Green, his professors, lecturers, or students. He was remembered, if at all, by the public as an old Whig who had been hostile to Young Ireland and the Irish language. 'Most of us are posthumous and ought to be buried long ago', George Russell (A.E.) wrote to Sir Hugh Lane, of whom he made an exception, on 22 February 1908.[50] The judgement had a particular application to William Delany. He was such a forgotten figure before the end of his life, that John MacNeill in the preface to *Celtic Ireland*, already quoted, which was published in 1920, spoke of 'the late Dr Delany'; and a national newspaper made a similar reference. His fellow Jesuits had to take special care to conceal the allusions from the old man. By the time of his death, and for some years before it, he was, in Fr Power's apt summary: 'a great man who had outlived his reputation'.[51]

Chapter XXII

AN APPRAISAL: 'IN THE GALLERY OF NATION-BUILDERS'

The late Professor T. Corcoran, in his *Clongowes Record, 1814-1932*, remarked of William Delany's venture at Tullabeg that 'the whole concept of conducting a complete course of studies leading to external university degrees, attached to and conditioned so largely by the working of a secondary school of moderate size, and placed far away from any important urban centre, was always of doubtful validity'.[52] The implication that Delany's judgement was clouded by extravagant ambitions for St Stanislaus College might be seen, in the context of Professor Corcoran's study, to be a justification of the amalgamation of Tullabeg with Clongowes, did it not reflect, to some degree, certain traits shown forth in Delany's career. His tendency to become wrapt-up in his work of the moment and to see it, for the time, as the most important work in the province, was one of a number of those personal characteristics for which he was to suffer.

Excessive expenditure led to his demotion at Tullabeg. He suffered many disappointments because of an over-trustfulness in political friends. He displayed a rather cerebral, insistent, almost unimaginative, approach to people and problems which led him to underestimate national feeling and, as a result, into head-on clashes with the student body and with the leaders of the essential Irish lobby. Although basically a very straight man with a strong sense of duty, his character was such a blend of simplicity and astuteness, that his motives were sometimes questioned and his decisions and actions misunderstood. Again, though he would have denied it stoutly, he not infrequently 'used' people, however nicely, for the 'greater' ends he had in view. This was perhaps an almost necessary fact of life; but his distancing of himself, physically and psychologically, from the immediate work committed to him was a rather personal characteristic. It involved him in frequent absences from Tullabeg, and earned him the reputation at University College of 'ruling from beyond the clouds'. Joined to his practice of not consulting others in making decisions, it occasioned much criticism. Finally, still in a critical vein, it must be kept in mind when measuring his undoubted success as an administrator and leader, that neither at St Stanislaus College nor at St Stephen's Green did his students number more than two hundred nor his teaching staff more than twenty-two — the equivalent, in other words, of a small modern school.

Notwithstanding such criticism, it might be argued that his financial extravagance was but an excess of a virtue often ascribed to him, magnanimity; and that it was justified in that it transformed Tullabeg from a remote country school into a college which helped give new life to Irish Catholic education, and brought University College from virtual extinction to the position of the leading university institution. Magnanimity and vision, indeed, were two characteristics which went a long way towards explaining his success and influence. And if he was absent a great deal in his later years at St Stanislaus College and seemed distant to students at University College, the remarkable thing was that neither establishment appeared to suffer as a result. He had the capacity both to establish clear lines of administration, which kept an organisation moving smoothly, and to inspire people to work for the ideal he had in view. The trustfulness which he exhibited to politicians with mixed success was exhibited in larger measure to staff and students with more positive results. Putting people 'on their honour', however indirectly or even unconsciously, expecting high standards, was part of William Delany's approach, and the fact that in large part it was responded to tells something of his personality.

Some words of Edmund Burke, in his speech on 'The French Revolution', are particularly relevant to much of Delany's outlook and philosophy. 'Nothing is more certain', he said

> than that our manners, our civilization, . . . have . . . depended for ages upon two principles, and were, indeed, the result of both combined: I mean the spirit of a gentleman, and the spirit of religion.

Delany's gentlemanly qualities were remarked on again and again. Urbanity, respect for others, calmness, tolerance and the absence of vindictiveness, were all traits noticeable in his dealings; and were joined to decisiveness, moral courage, and a patient, and, at times, courageously stubborn persistence. His fellow Jesuits, in different words, singled out 'his charity' as 'his greatest quality'.[53]

If one facet above others were to be chosen, however, it probably would be the controlled energy which appeared in his enormous capacity for work, while yet finding time for the regular observance of his religious duties and prayer. Although only a part of his vast correspondence remains, the evidence of what is extant leaves the researcher with a sense of awe. Letter after letter, memorandum after memorandum, flowed from his pen without any secretarial help, and all were carefully expressed, almost all contributed to the educational discussion, few were light weight or gave the impression of hackneyed thinking. In them, as in his evidence before two royal commissions, one has the feeling of a man who was widely read, had tested his reading against experience, had a sharp, incisive mind, and a distinctive capacity to marshal his arguments. If leadership is marked primarily by an energy above average and a capacity to inspire others, he had the required attributes.

He would also fulfil some of the other requirements of latter-day diagnosticians of 'leadership' in that he was an 'encourager' and 'suggester'. Professors and lecturers at Stephen's Green experienced a backing and freedom in their work, student societies were fostered and flourished, an easy relationship existed between teacher and student; and college life was marked by a ferment of thought and self-expression. But his was not a 'leadership that distributes leadership', in keeping with a democratic system.[54] He ran mainly a 'one man show', with a style moulded in earlier, more stable times.

As he grew older, and youth responded to a new climate of independence and change, his style no longer seemed appropriate. And he was unfortunate in having to face in close succession the three powerfully emotive issues of feminism, nationalism, and compulsory Irish. But, by and large, despite some blunders and breakdowns in health, he met them with a disciplined calmness, and with integrity towards what he conceived to be his duty as an educationalist and a priest. If like most men he played many parts, the parts of educationalist and priest were most real to him. The single-mindedness with which he tried to fulfil those combined rôles was both a strength and a weakness. It led to denigration and obloquy at the hands of those whose primary concern was to assert national difference by defying symbols of government or by insisting on essential Irish; but it did not prevent him achieving his life's goal. He had not been appointed president to promote Home Rule, still less national independence; nor was it his function to impose Irish on future students. His obligation, as he saw it, was — by advocacy, negotiation, and examination successes — to assist in bringing about a just university settlement. From that point of view, it was almost immaterial whether Home Rule was achieved or not, and equally irrelevant which British party was in power. He was prepared to work and negotiate with each of them for the end in view, and to seek to curb such student activities as seemed likely to jeopardise a satisfactory solution. That his efforts had a distinct bearing on the achievement of the National University was widely acknowledged, as has been seen, by contemporaries of different allegiances. Posthumously, that verdict was strongly affirmed by many of those who knew him and had worked with him.

The editor of the *Clongownian*, as part of an obituary notice, attempted to sum up Delany's contribution to Irish education in a concise appraisal. He was, he wrote:[55]

the soul of that hard fight for that fair play in university studies which was the ambition of all far-seeing Catholics. That that fight was won so triumphantly is due in part to him. The policy which he followed for forty years was ever much the same. He took whatever material he could obtain, first the small school of Tullabeg, then the limited numbers of University College, and he showed that, handicapped for funds, equipment, and even staff, these students of his could meet and overcome the far more numerous and more favoured sons of Protestant institutions.

It was an ambitious and difficult talk. It depended on never failing success, on inspiring generation after generation of students, on commanding the absolute devotion of generation after generation of helpers. This Fr Delany did. Step by step, now using the London matriculation, now the Intermediate system, now the Royal University, he made good his proposition, that Irish Catholics were capable of profiting by and desirous of the best education possible. It had been considered an absurdity; in forty years Fr Delany made it an axiom.

It was Judge Bodkin's verdict that to William Delany 'more than any other man alive or dead, Ireland owes the National University'; and he went on to draw attention to one source of his friend's influence. He recalled an occasion when, as a young man, he had been of assistance to Delany by means of some articles in the *Fortnightly Review* setting out 'the overwhelming successes of University College in the examinations of the Royal University'. Fr Delany 'showed as much interest and enthusiasm about my "inspired" controversial articles as if they were the main machinery of his scheme, and not a mere detail. It was thus', Bodkin concluded, 'that he could command every man's best work'.[56]

A fuller appreciation, from an equally well-disposed source, appeared six years later with the publication of *A page of Irish history: the story of University College Dublin, 1883-1909.* The highly critical comment of the reviewer in *An Phoblacht* has been noted. Another reviewer, however, and one much better qualified to speak on the subject, found fault with the book for different reasons. William Magennis, one of the most distinguished links between the old college and the new, wrote in *The National Student* magazine that 'the cold austerity of the historian's polished periods' left the reader without a proper sense of the real magnitude of what had been achieved, and of 'its importance in the re-shaping of modern Ireland'. 'In the twenty years that followed 1883', he said, 'Fr Delany, aided by Fr T.A. Finlay, and with slender resources, but with inextinguishable faith in his mission and indomitable resolution, carried almost to completion a noble work of construction for Catholic Ireland'. In the historian's stark account, however, written without a feeling of enthusiasm, 'the grandeur of Fr Delany's undertaking is dwarfed, and the glory of it eludes the imagination.'

Professor Magennis had had his differences with the former president of University College while cherishing, nevertheless, the latter's untiring efforts. He concluded his review with a laudatory backward glance.

> I join with the compiler in his desire to remove from Fr Delany's renown as an educator the cloud which for some unaccountable reason has, of late years, overhung it. He spent himself (and the fortunes of his Order) in untiring efforts for the promotion of Catholic education. As a pioneer educationalist he blazed the trail for lesser men to follow: and we are all immeasurably indebted to him. Retrospectively, I see him in truer proportions — a grander and finer figure in the gallery of nation-builders — than when he was leading us. The passage of time instead of dimming my reverence for his peerless service to education, augments it.[57]

The cloud was to linger. In the renewed Irish-Ireland atmosphere of the nineteen-thirties, there was little desire to hear of one who had been friendly with Tory cabinet ministers and had opposed compulsory Irish. Arthur E. Clery, another celebrated link with the past and a devoted Gaelic Leaguer, giving his impressions of the same book in the same review, did not mention Delany. He spoke of the work as 'a record of the golden glorious days of troubled lives', when Pearse was teaching, and Kettle learning at '86'. It recalled, apart from those who became world famous, Thomas MacDonagh lecturing in English, who had as his successor Austin Clarke, the poet, and 'a long procession of successful efforts, interesting people', including 'many judges, ministers, and politicians, successful and unsuccessful'. And he gave notice that 'being Catholic and Irish', the memory of nearly all would be blotted out 'in fifty years or less': for 'the punishment of oblivion awaits the great men, as the holy men of our country. The propaganda of silence is the most powerful propaganda of all'.[58]

The silence was pierced again, however, twenty-four years on when the centenary of the Catholic University was celebrated;[59] and again two years later, 1956, when, in tribute to the work of Delany and his colleagues, the National University marked the fourth centenary of St Ignatius Loyola by conferring the degree of Doctor of Laws (*honoris causa*) on the then 'head of the Irish province of the Society of Jesus'. The vice-chancellor of the university and president of University College, Dublin, Professor Michael Tierney, declared the conferring to be a small recognition of the great debt owed by the National University, and continued:[60]

It is no more than the simple truth to say, that without the help of the Irish Jesuit fathers, University College, Dublin, and with it the National University of Ireland, would never have come into existence. It was they who took up Newman's work when it seemed to have reached the final point of failure, and who, by their learning, their administration and teaching ability and their characteristic devotion, made it shine with fresh lustre and kept its brightness undimmed until the historical moment came for its full expansion.

The work of Delany, of the Finlay brothers and of the three remarkable Englishmen, Fr Gerard Hopkins, Fr Henry Browne and Fr Joseph Darlington, will always remain an inspiration to those responsible for the direction of university education in Ireland. It was probably due to Fr Delany in particular more than to any other single man that the National University was given its present form.

One of the 'remarkable Englishmen', Joseph Darlington, died in 1939. Writing of his career in *Studies*, Professor John Howley inevitably spoke too of Delany. He had been a student during his presidency and, like others who only knew him officially, 'thought him imposing in a wrong sort of way'. He had 'a very impressive appearance and a very remarkable voice . . . a platform voice, very clear and resonant'. They classed him as 'a good speaker, but commonplace'. They knew nothing about 'his real work, his battles by letters, on committees and conferences'. They did not realise, he continued: 'what a corkscrew road we were travelling and how our president, in his efforts to build up a new college and secure its future, had to deal not alone with our natural enemies but with false brethren. Again and again that future was nearly wrecked. He had not merely Irish politicians to consider, but the Castle. . . . Fr Delany had to walk warily, and often Fr Darlington had to check our youthful enthusiasm. Naturally, their caution was unpopular. . . . It was years after the event that I realised how very short-sighted we had all been and how unjust'. William Delany, to Professor Howley's mind, 'embodied the college', and in his view also, 'he, more than any other Irishman was the creator of the National University'. Besides, he concluded, 'he built up University College Dublin — not in stone, that was left to his successor — but in mind and spirit. . . . We will not know his real magnitude until the Society of Jesus sees fit to publish his full-length "Life and Letters" '.[61]

Time is the great leveller, the master of perspective. As it passes and the noise of far-off battles recedes, it begins to seem that he whom John MacNeill described as 'great and Irish in his zeal for learning and education and in his love for Ireland'[62] may at last take his place, warts and all, 'in the gallery of nation-builders'. What he has accomplished, Fr Tom Finlay remarked, 'has profoundly affected . . . all the secondary schools of Ireland. . . . He was a notable figure in that movement for reform in education which has resulted in so many changes and the force of which is not yet spent'.[63]

NOTES TO THE TEXT

(See page 414 for list of abbreviations)

PREFACE

1. In P.J. Joyce, *John Healy, Archbishop of Tuam* (Dublin, 1931), p. 187.
2. From 'text of introductory address' in *Irish Jesuit year book, 1956*, pp 31 ff.
3. Letter to Delany, 15 June 1904, in I.J.A.
4. *Clongownian*, 1924, p. 18.
5. From Delany's address to Catholic headmasters given in *Printed report of conference of Catholic headmasters* (Dublin, 1883), p. 12.
6. Quoted in *A page of Irish history: story of University College, Dublin, 1883-1909* (Dublin, 1930), compiled by Fathers of the Society of Jesus, p. 548.
7. In W.H. Gardiner (ed.), *Poems and prose of Gerard Manley Hopkins* (London, 1954), pp 195-6.

PART ONE

Chapters I, II, III

Chapter I

1. *F.Jn.*, 7 Dec. 1908.
2. Pigot, *Directory of Ireland, 1824*, p. 165; Samuel Lewis, *A topographical dictionary of Ireland*, (2 vols. London, 1837), ii, pp 250-1,

3. Much of the background to the early years is taken from the uncompleted MS 'Fr William Delany and his work for Irish education' (I.J.A.), by the late Professor Lambert McKenna, S.J., who entered University College in 1903, later became a member of staff, and collected information and letters from relations and contemporaries of Delany in preparation for the proposed biography.
4. M. McDonnell Bodkin, K.C., in the *Clongownian*, 1924, p. 16.
5. Peadar MacSuibhne, *Paul Cullen and his contemporaries, with their letters from 1820-1902* (Naas, 1977), vol. v, p. 163.
6. W.B. Yeats to Russell, 31 Jan. 1888 (I.J.A., Russell papers).
7. Darlington MS, 'The history of the Catholic University of Ireland and the policy of Fr William Delany, president of University College' (I.J.A.).
8. John Bithrey, unpublished memoirs, specimen pages, book 9, p. 5 (I.J.A.): Bithrey had been a Jesuit for fourteen years when he left the Order in 1908; he subsequently became an inspector in the Department of Education.
9. I.J.A.
10. C.W.C.A. The section on Tullabeg contains ministers' journals, prefects of studies books, college calendars, programmes, conspectus, school rules, Delany's marking book, some letters, and notes on the

388

history of the college. For a fuller treatment of Tullabeg, see T.J. Morrissey, 'Some Jesuit contributions to Irish education' (2 vols, unpublished Ph.D. thesis, N.U.I. 1975), i, pp 263-358, ii, pp 359-501.
11. S. Farragher, C.S.S.P., 'Fr Joseph Edouard Reffé, dean of studies, 1864-88' in *Blackrock College annual: centenary year, 1860-1960*, p. 59.
12. Fr Beckx to Delany, 27 Sept. 1875 (I.J.A.).
13. *Clongownian*, 1924, p. 16.
14. C.W.C.A.: school rules of Tullabeg.
15. P. Sexton, S.J., 'Irish secondary teachers and their struggle for status' (M.Ed. thesis, Univ. Birmingham, 1974), 'synopsis' and pp 24, 26.
16. In Delany's reply to Tuite's letter of 31 Aug. 1880 Fr Tuite, in common with many contemporaries, held the lay teachers of the day in low esteem. He instructed Delany, with reference to school concerts and dramatic productions, not 'to put the names of those extern masters on any tableau in the college on which are to be found the names of our people. We must respect ourselves if we wish to be respected by others' (I.J.A.).
17. 'The report of Messrs D.H. Dale and T.A. Stephens, H.M.I. of schools, on intermediate education in Ireland' in *Report from commissioners, inspectors and others: education (Ireland)*, H.C., 1905, xxvii.
18. *Clongownian*, 1910, pp 220 ff.
19. McKenna MS, ch. v.
20. To Lord Emly, 8 July 1875 (N.L.I., Monsell papers, MS 8317).
21. M. McDonnell Bodkin, *Clongownian*, 1924, p. 17; see also Bodkin, *Recollections of an Irish judge: press, bar and parliament* (London, 1914), pp 20 ff.
22. McKenna MS.
23. R.F. Foster, *Lord Randolph Churchill* (Oxford, 1981), ch. 2, p. 39; but note the confusion with the bishop of Cork, also William Delany (1803-86).
24. See Foster, *op. cit.* pp 38-42 and 56.
25. Italics mine.

Chapter II

26. Edmund Dease, M.P., to Delany, 12 Mar. 1873; and see Desmond Bowen, *The Protestant crusade in Ireland, 1800-70* (Dublin, 1978), pp xi, xii; and R.C.K. Ensor, *England 1870-1914* (Oxford, 1936), pp 137 ff.
27. Leman to Wm. Monsell (Ld. Emly), 11 Dec. 1874 (N.L.I., Monsell papers, MS 8318(14)); see, too, E. Howley, *The universities and secondary schools of Ireland, with proposals for their improvement* (Dublin, 1871).
28. Churchill, *Intermediate education in Ireland: a letter to Sir Bernard Burke, C.B., Ulster, from Lord Randolph Churchill, M.P.* (Dublin, 1878).
29. Bodkin, *Recollections of an Irish judge..*, pp 24-5.
30. June 1878 (I.J.A.).
31. John V. Cassidy to Del. 22 June 1878, enclosing a letter from Fitzgibbon (I.J.A.); Cassidy, commissioner for intermediate education, conveyed Delany's views to Fitzgibbon and others, and was very anxious generally to be of assistance. According to R.F. Foster, *Lord Randolph Churchill*, the Duchess of Marlborough 'was much involved in the choosing of personnel for the Intermediate Education Commission, and was closely advised by Dr Delany' (p. 39).
32. The O'Conor Don to Del., Oct. 1878 (I.J.A.); day not given.
33. 23 Nov. 1879 (I.J.A.).
34. *Printed report of conference of Catholic headmasters* (Dublin, 1883), p. 12.
35. See Fergal McGrath, *Newman's university: idea and reality* (Dublin, 1950), pp 98 ff.

36. Quoted by Myles W. O'Reilly in pamphlet, *Two articles in education* (London, 1863).

37. William Kirby Sullivan to Monsell, 13 Apr. 1886 (Monsell papers, MS 8318(5)).

38. *Hansard's parliamentary debates, 4th series*, vol. 187, p. 338.

39. P. MacSuibhne, *Paul Cullen and his contemporaries* (Naas, 1962), ii: Cullen to Alderman Boylan, pp 85-6; Cullen to Catholic Association, 29 Jan. 1852, p. 119.

40. 'Address of the Catholic University committee to the clergy and laity of England', quoted Mac Suibhne, *op. cit.* p. 82.

41. Fergal McGrath, 'The university question' in P.J. Corish (ed.), *A history of Irish Catholicism* (Dublin, 1971), vi, p. 104; and see N. Atkinson, *Irish education* (Dublin, 1969), pp 137 ff.

42. Dease to Del., 12 Mar. 1873 (I.J.A.).

43. Sullivan to Monsell, 16 June 1873 (Monsell MS 8318(6)).

44. Diary entry, 1872 (C.W.C.A.).

45. *A page of Irish history..*, p. 18.

46. Monsell MS 8316(6).

47. 'Some notes on the Irish university question and the position of the Jesuit fathers in relation to it' (I.J.A.), p. 4; Marlborough had spoken out on the matter at Drogheda.

48. Churchill to Del., 19 Nov. 1879 (I.J.A.).

49. Del. to Kavanagh, 26 May 1879 (I.J.A.).

50. Del. to O'Conor Don, Mar. 1879 (I.J.A.), no day given.

51. R. Carton to Del., 21 May (I.J.A.).

52. Richard Assheton, first Viscount Cross (1823-1914), M.P. for Lancashire, Home Secretary (1874-80 and 1885-6), chairman of the royal commission on the Elementary Education Acts (Cross report of 1888).

53. Little to Del. 29 June (I.J.A.).

54. *Ibid.*, 20 July.

55. Langdale told a relation of his,

Edmund Dease, M.P., who published it almost twenty years later in the *Spectator*, 31 Dec. 1898. Dease, who lived not far from Tullabeg may have provided his friend, Delany, with an early insight into Disraeli's intention.

56. Mitchel Henry to Judge Little (5 Aug.) who sent a copy to Delany (I.J.A.).

57. Exceeding his powers or authority.

58. In 'Some notes on the university question. . .', pp 10-11 (I.J.A.).

59. Related in Dr M. Tierney (ed.), *Struggle with fortune: a centenary miscellany for Catholic University of Ireland 1854, University College Dublin 1954* (Dublin, 1954), p. 6.

60. 'Some notes on the university question . . .', p. 11 (I.J.A.).

61. Walsh to Del., 23 Jan. 1881 (I.J.A.): he had used those words, he told Delany, in dissuading Dr Woodlock, Bishop of Ardagh, from any form of recognition of the Queen's Colleges.

62. W.E. Forster, M.P. for Bradford, vice-president of the education department; he had a keen interest in education, was married to the daughter of Dr Thomas Arnold of Rugby, and was responsible for the Elementary Education Act of 1870.

63. McKenna MS, ch. viii.

64. Delany's 'Memorandum on the fellowship controversy' (I.J.A.): unfortunately, the 'private understanding' was not in writing. It may be noted, however, that Dr Henry Neville, rector of the Catholic University, in a memorandum for the bishops in October 1882, recorded that the episcopal education committee, chaired by the cardinal, decided on 2 October 'that all the fellowships allotted to Catholics at present should be centralised in the Catholic University College, St Stephen's Green' (D.D.A., McCabe papers, f 215/9).

Chapter III

65. Tuite to Del., 31 Aug. 1880, quoting the General's letter (I.J.A.).
66. McCabe to Tuite, 13 Jan. 1882; see also McCabe to Del. 16 Jan. (both in I.J.A. and D.D.A., McCabe papers, f 49/1).
67. Fr Walsh, S.J., to Tuite, 15 Jan. 1882 (I.J.A.); and Del. to Tuite, c. 19 Jan., notes 'that strong influences must be at work' because when he personally visited Dr McCabe the latter had said: 'Do nothing at present, let matters stand' — apart from taking steps to reissue the public notice 'in such terms as would meet His Grace's wishes' (I.J.A.).
68. G. Porter to Del., 9 Mar. (I.J.A.): Porter had been prefect of studies at Stonyhurst College, England (1857-8), and in 1879 was appointed to Rome; in June 1881 he was made rector of Farm Street church, London; but in October was called to Rome to act as General's assistant in the absence of Fr Weld on world visitation; in 1886 he was appointed archbishop of Bombay, where he died on 28 Sept. 1889.
69. McCabe to Tuite, 18 Jan. (I.J.A.); also McCabe's diary, 1881-84 (D.D.A., f 5/17).
70. Undated reports (D.D.A., f 45/9); but on 11 Feb. 1882, Tuite to Dr Moran, Bishop of Ossory, mentions that he is enclosing Delany's report (I.J.A.).
71. Tuite to Del., 17 Mar. (I.J.A.).
72. Porter to Del., 12 June (I.J.A.).
73. Printed memorandum for bishops' perusal, by Dr Neville (D.D.A., McCabe papers, f 45/9).
74. Porter to Del., 11 Oct. (I.J.A.); he also sought to dissuade him from his 'dream of a missionary career'.
75. *Ibid.*, 5 Nov. (I.J.A.).
76. Del. to Egan, 28 Nov. 1882 (I.J.A.).
77. 'University papers, 1882-84' (D.D.A., f 45/8): 'Case with respect to the legal obligations of the fellows of the Royal University', 1882.

78. 30 Nov. 1882 (D.D.A., f 45/8).
79. 2 Dec. (D.D.A., f 49/1).
80. Del. to Tuite, and Del. to Walsh (I.J.A.).
81. Michael J. O'Dwyer had a distinguished career, becoming lieutenant-governor of the Punjab and receiving a knighthood.
82. Porter to Del., 1 March 1883; but on 20 Dec. 1881 — when he was assured of the General's interest in his work and of his support for it, and also quietly reminded to 'try not to raise the whirlwind about his ears by a careless financial administration' — and again on 1 Mar., 27 Mar., 25 Apr., 11 Oct., and 14 Dec. 1882, he was prompted by Porter and promised support in face of 'enemies and the indifference' of many Jesuits (I.J.A.).
83. Oct. 1883 (I.J.A.).
84. 3 Sept. 1883 (I.J.A.).
85. Del. to provincial, Fr Browne, Oct. 1883 (I.J.A.).
86. *Ibid.*, 28 Oct. 1883.

PART TWO

Chapter IV

1. 'Memorandum of the agreement entered into this day, 26 October 1883, between the trustees of the Catholic University of Ireland and the Jesuit fathers' (I.J.A.).
2. This had been the practice: see the memorandum for the bishops presented by Dr Neville, Oct. 1882 (D.D.A., f 45/9); and it had been the reason given by Fr Egan and Archbishop McCabe against Dr Casey teaching at Temple Street.
3. Dr Molloy to McCabe (D.D.A., f 45/9), and A. O'Connor (solicitor) to McCabe, 1 Dec. (D.D.A., f 360/2).
4. The Bishop of Down and Connor was quoted in the press in Nov. 1884 as stating that the bishops had severed their connection with

University College: 'The institution is now the private concern of the Jesuits, who have taken a lease of the place, and conduct it at their own risk and peril' (D.D.A., f 147/1).

5. *Prospere procede ... esta perpetua*: every success and may the work be lasting.

6. Del. to Fr Browne, new provincial, Nov. 1883 (I.J.A.).

7. D.D.A., f 16 (section on N.U.I.).

8. Quoted McKenna MS, ch. ix.

9. D.D.A., f 16.

10. Del. to Walsh, 26 Jan. 1884 (I.J.A.).

11. Dr Gillooly to Fr Browne, 4 and 7 Feb. (I.J.A.).

12. *Blackrock College Annual*: centenary issue, 1960; p. 92.

13. *Ibid.*, p. 91.

14. McKenna MS.

15. Dr McCabe to Dr Woodlock, 23 Jan. 1882, and latter's reply; McCabe to Lord O'Hagan, 28 Jan.; to the bishops, 31 Jan., and their reply (D.D.A., f 45/8).

16. Del. to Fr Whitty, asssitant-General, 26 Dec. 1885 (I.J.A.).

17. D.D.A., f 17.

18. McKenna MS, ch. ix.

19. Minute book of the Royal University, 1880-86, vol. i, p. 217 (at offices of National University of Ireland, Dublin): the royal warrant was read at the senate meeting on 21 October.

20. Papers relating to Bishop Butler, Nov. 1884 (L.D.A.).

Chapter V

21. Del. to Butler, 22 Nov. (I.J.A.).

22. Walsh to Del., 5 Dec. (I.J.A.).

23. 'Dr Delany's memorandum on the public correspondence on the fellowships which appeared in the *Tablet* and *Freeman's Journal* in Dec. 1884': Delany's own summary so entitled (I.J.A.).

24. Del. to Ld. Emly, 12 Dec. 1884 (Monsell MS 8318(14)).

Chapter VI

25. Much of this account follows that of McKenna MS.

26. Del. to Emly, 12 Dec. 1884 (Monsell MS).

27. Del. to Emly, Jan. 1885, no day (I.J.A.).

28. Quoted in Christopher Hollis, *Newman and the Modern World* (London, 1967), p. 133.

29. Min. book. of Royal Univ., i, p. 361: the meeting of 3 July 1885.

30. Dr Walsh, *Memorandum on the Irish education question* (Dublin, 1887), p. 74.

31. 2 May 1885 (D.D.A., f 368/2).

32. Del. to Kirby, 5 May 1885, in Kirby papers, P.J. Corish (ed.), *Archivium Hibernicum*, xxxii, p. 3.

33. Fr Arnellini to Del., 3 Aug. 1885 (I.J.A.).

34. *F.Jn.* 11 Aug.

35. *Addresses of Most Rev Dr Walsh, Archbishop of Dublin* (Dublin, 1886), pp 153-4.

36. No date given, but clearly refers to late Sept. 1885 (I.J.A.).

37. Dec. 1884; no day (I.J.A.).

38. Del. to Emly, 12 Dec. 1884 (I.J.A.).

39. Del. to McCabe, 12 Dec. 1884 (D.D.A., f 45/8: 'University 1882-4').

40. In his summary notes on the business, Delany remarked that he had 'placed the whole matter unreservedly in the hands of Mr Parnell and his party' (I.J.A.).

41. McCarthy to Del., 10 June: he had fixed on 3 July 'for a debate on the Royal University and the Queen's Colleges. I trust to you', he continued, 'lending me a helping hand' (I.J.A.).

42. Walsh to Del., 14 May 1885, remarked that Parnell had told him of 'a most useful letter from Fr Delany' which he would turn to good account (I.J.A.).

43. Lord Carnarvon to Del., 3 July (I.J.A.): his feeling concurred with much of what Delany had said and he hoped before long to have 'the opportunity of making personal

acquaintance with one of whom I have heard so much'.
44. Del. to Salisbury, 25 July 1885 (I.J.A.).
45. Del. to Birrell, 9 June 1908 (I.J.A.); also in Delany's private memo entitled 'An episode in the history of the Irish university question', p. 1. See, too, *Hansard 3*, CCC (28 July 1885).
46. Letter of 5 Oct. in a private memo entitled 'Correspondence re. grant-in-aid sought for by the Irish party on behalf of University College' (I.J.A.) which related his intentions, his meeting with Parnell, and correspondence with Dr Walsh.
47. Walsh to Del., 5 Oct. 1885 (I.J.A.).
48. Del. to Walsh, 6 Oct. (D.D.A., 402/2).
49. Delany's memo 'Correspondence re. grant-in-aid . . .'.
50. *Ibid.*; and Walsh to Del., 9 Oct. (D.D.A., f 402/2).
51. Del. to Walsh, 10 Oct. (D.D.A. *ibid.*).
52. Memo of 'Correspond. re. grant-in-aid . . .', post-script; and Del. to Whitty, 26 Dec., no year (I.J.A.).
53. 3 Oct. 1885 (I.J.A.).
54. McKenna MS, ch. x.

Chapter VII

55. O'Dwyer papers (L.D.A.): Delany writing to Dr O'Dwyer, undated letter, states that prior to his (Delany's) long letter to Dr Kavanagh on 14 Jan. 1886, 'Lord Carnarvon, in two long conversations, had given me clearly to understand that in the opinion of the government amalgamation with Trinity presented insuperable difficulties; but that the government were favourably disposed, he himself strongly, to giving the Catholics an independent Catholic university — with the Cork and Galway colleges made Catholic, and a great central Catholic college in Dublin suitably equipped and endowed as compared with Trinity

College'; see R.F. Foster, *Lord Randolph Churchill* pp 230-32, on the government's serious interest in bringing in an acceptable university bill.
56. From 'An episode in the history of the Irish university question', a private account which Delany put together after the 1908 Act and which linked Birrell's successful scheme with that of 1886 and noted the part played by Dr Walsh in both (I.J.A.).
57. The printed copy, which was widely circulated, ran to eight pages of more than quarto size.
58. See Dr Walsh, *Letters and addresses on the Irish university question* (Dublin, 1897), pp 87-8.

Chapter VIII

59. He died on 3 Feb. 1886.
60. Croke to Del., 11 Dec. 1886 (I.J.A.).
61. O'Dwyer papers (L.D.A.): an incomplete letter from an unnamed member of the Irish party to Dr O'Dwyer, 21 Jan. 1899, stating that some ten years previously Parnell had told him that 'he would not accept the bill on any terms; firstly, because he thought that if the priests got their university they might not continue to be such good Home Rulers, and secondly because it proposed to take the funds required from the church fund, which latter he himself desired to draw upon for other purposes connected with the land question'.
62. D.D.A., f 402/4.
63. Healy to O'Dwyer, 25 Oct. 1886 (L.D.A.).
64. O'Dwyer to Walsh, 2 Nov., and 3 and 24 Nov. (D.D.A., f 402/5).
65. *Ibid.* (24 Nov.), and O'Dwyer papers (L.D.A.).
66. O'Dwyer papers (L.D.A.); the announcement of the appointment appeared in the *Irish Times* and *Cork Examiner*.
67. At the bishops' meeting he had

promised to resign because he was given to understand that there were meant to be two episcopal representatives on the senate, representatives chosen by the bishops, and that the government had failed to approach their lordships for their nominations (L.D.A.).

68. Healy to O'Dwyer, no date (L.D.A.).

69. Healy to O'Dwyer, no date (L.D.A.): Healy mentions that a letter had been sent to Rome complaining about O'Dwyer not retiring from the senate.

70. 10 Dec. (D.D.A., f 402/5) and 11 Dec. (D.D.A., f 347/7).

71. Walsh to O'Dwyer, and O'Dwyer to Walsh, 4 Jan. 1887 (D.D.A., f 402/6).

72. O'Dwyer to Walsh, 8 Jan. 1887 (D.D.A., f 402/6).

73. 9 Jan. (L.D.A.).

74. Keating to O'Dwyer, 25 Oct. 1886 (L.D.A.).

75. Del. to O'Dwyer, no date (L.D.A.).

76. Croke to Walsh, 28 Jan. 1888 (D.D.A., f 403/4).

77. Quoted in Maisie Ward, *Insurrection versus resurrection* (London, 1937), p. 54.

78. Croke to Walsh, 28 Jan. 1888 (D.D.A., f 403/4): the government 'has not left us a vestige of liberty. Every day reveals some fresh excess of despotism'. And on 7 Jan. he had written that 'trials and imprisonments, and releases from prison, and rejoicings thereat, are the order of the day'.

79. Russell papers (I.J.A.).

80. This was scarcely thanks to Dr Croke who, according to his letter to Dr Walsh, 12 Jan. 1888, had told Persico that 'he distrusted everyone and everything Roman', that he feared English influence at Rome against Irish nationality, and that 'if the pope sought to check substantially the action of either priests or bishops in Ireland, the Irish race over the world would resent such interference and disregard it', and

he himself would resign the see of Cashel. He was disappointed that the papal envoy had been impressed by Dr O'Dwyer 'as honest and honourable, though somewhat conceited and imprudent' (D.D.A., f 403/4).

81. Croke to Dr Murphy (assistant to Dr Walsh), 13 June (D.D.A., f 403/4).

82. Croke to Walsh, 14 June (*ibid.*).

83. Whitty to Del., 3 July 1886 (I.J.A.).

84. Del. to Whitty, 29 June 1887; Whitty to Del., 17 Aug. 1887 (I.J.A.).

85. Private memo of Delany re. Klein, 1892 (I.J.A.).

86. Instruction from Fr Fulton, official visitor from the General, 31 Mar. (Province consultor's minute book, 1887).

87. Del. to Purbrick, Aug. 1887 (I.J.A.): first italics mine, second as in text.

88. Letters of 18, 25, 26 Oct. 1887 (I.J.A.).

89. 3 May 1904 (I.J.A.).

90. Walsh to Browne, 18 Oct.; Browne to Walsh, 20 Oct. 1887 (Folder entitled 'Precis of letters 1850-1903', I.J.A.).

91. *A memorandum on the Irish education question* (Dublin, 1887), pp 67-74 (D.D.A., 62/2).

92. Province consultors minute book, 27 March 1888 (I.J.A.)

Chapter IX

93. 27 Jan. 1887 (I.J.A.), Arnold writing to Delany.

94. Darlington MS 'Hist. of Cath. Univ. and policy of Fr Wm. Delany', p. 3 (I.J.A.).

95. McKenna MS, ch. ix.

96. Aubrey Gwynn, 'The Jesuits and University College' in Dr M. Tierney (ed.), *Struggle with fortune*, pp 44-5.

97. See n. 4 (Part Two), statement of Bishop of Down and Connor (D.D.A., 147/1).

98. C.P. Curran in 'Memoirs of University College Dublin: the Jesuit tenure, 1883-1908' in Tierney (ed.), *Struggle with fortune*, p. 222.
99. Darlington MS, p. 9 (I.J.A.).
100. W.H. Gardiner and N.H. MacKenzie (ed.), *The poems of Gerard Manley Hopkins* (Oxford, 1970), no. 66, p. 101.
101. Evidence before *Royal Commission on university education in Ireland*, first report, 1901: under questioning he made it clear that he was referring to the physical structure and not to the quality of the students or staff.
102. *The poems of G.M. Hopkins*, no. 67, p. 101.
103. McKenna MS, ch. ix.

Chapter X

104. This period is dealt with in ch. xi of McKenna's MS vol. (I.J.A.).
105. McKenna, *ibid*.
106. *Ibid*.
107. The year only is given, 1896 (I.J.A.).
108. Del. to Meyer, 10 May 1896 (I.J.A.).
109. 1896, year only (I.J.A.).
110. Foley to Del., Nov. 1897 (I.J.A.).
111. McKenna, *loc. cit.*
112. Arthur Balfour to Del., 3 May 1890 (I.J.A.).
113. 1 July 1893(?) (I.J.A.): the year is not certain.
114. Morley to Del., 23 Apr. 1895 (I.J.A.).
115. Walsh to O'Dwyer, 31 Dec. 1896 (D.D.A., f 347/7).
116. 15 June 1896 (*ibid.*).
117. *F.Jn.*, 6 Oct. 1896.
118. T.M. Healy to O'Dwyer, 18 Mar. 1897 (L.D.A.).
119. Foley to Del., 18 Dec. 1896 (I.J.A.).
120. *A page of Irish history*, p. 142.
121. Minute bk. of Royal University, ii, 1887-91, p. 247.
122. Del. to Walsh, 27 Mar. 1896 (I.J.A.).

123. Province consultor's min. bk., 13 June 1896.
124. Owen Dudley Edwards, 'Belvedere in history' in J. Bowman & R. O'Donoghue (eds.), *Portraits, Belvedere College 1832-1982* (Dublin, 1982), p. 15: 'Finlay was one of the most extraordinary men of a truly extraordinary time — the Irish Renaissance — yet today he is in danger of oblivion. As educator, writer, administrator, economist, politician, agriculturist and Heaven knows how much more, he was pre-eminently the Renaissance Man of the Irish Renaissance.'
125. James Meenan (ed.), *Centenary history of the Literary and Historical Society of University College Dublin* (Tralee, 1955), p. 47; on Finlay's influence see, too, C.P. Curran, 'Memoirs of University College: the Jesuit tenure' in *Struggle with fortune*, pp 225-6; and Arthur Clery, *Dublin Essays* (Dublin, 1919), p. 55.
126. William Magennis, 'A disciple's sketch of Fr T. Finlay' in *The Belvederian*, ix, (Summer 1931), pp 19-20, 22; for the comment to George Moore see George O'Brien, 'Fr Thomas A. Finlay, S.J.' in *Studies*, xxix (Mar. 1940), p. 37.
127. These included 'Education and examination' in *Lyceum*, ii, pp 77 ff; 'Anomalies of our intermediate system', *ibid*, Oct. 1893, pp 2-5; 'Women's higher education in Ireland', Apr. 1893; 'University extension' and 'Some educational reformers' in Aug. 1891; and in vol. i, June 1888, 'Recent developments of the art of teaching'.
128. *Lyceum*, Sept. 1891-Sept. 1892.
129. Prov. consultors min. bk. 20 Feb. 1890. A letter was read from the General expressing criticism. 'There followed a series of consultations about the *Lyceum*, especially a review of Cardinal Gibbons' *Christian heritage*. The end was a suspension from writing of Frs Thomas and Peter Finlay. A letter

of apology was written to Cardinal Gibbons by order of Fr General'. Cardinal Gibbons replied on 7 May 1890 to the vice-provincial: 'The work *Our Christian heritage* received undue praise. I have no unkind feeling for the article in the *Lyceum*. ... Surprised that your Fr General should have taken the trouble to apologise.'
130. Fr L. Martin to provincial, 21 Mar. 1897 (I.J.A., in section entitled 'Generals' letters to the Irish province, 1895-1903', no. 96).
131. R.C.K. Ensor, *England 1870-1914* (Oxford, 1968 ed.), pp 308, 531, 339.
132. 'Resolutions of the Irish bishops in June 1889' in Dr Walsh, *Statement of the chief grievances of Irish Catholics in the matter of education, primary, intermediate and university* (Dublin, 1890), pp 345 ff.
133. Following Balfour's declaration in the debate on the address to the throne, 22 Jan. 1897, Dr Walsh and Bishop O'Dwyer exchanged a number of letters on its implications: 15, 23, 25 Jan.; 2, 11, 21, 23 Feb. (D.D.A., f 347/7).
134. *Report of royal commission on university education in Ireland* (Robertson commission); first report, app. 388.
135. Walsh to Del., 30 Oct. 1897 (I.J.A.).
136. Walsh to O'Dwyer, 13 Nov. (D.D.A., f 347/7).

PART THREE

Chapters XI to XVII

Chapter XI

1. Russell papers (I.J.A.).
2. *Ibid.*
3. Meenan (ed.), *Cent. hist. of L. and H. Society*, p. 43.
4. Henry Browne, professor of classics, joined the staff in 1890. Fr Darlington in his MS history of

the Catholic University and the policy of Fr Delany remarks that when Browne was converted to the Catholic church he asked Cardinal Manning whether he should continue his studies at Oxford. 'If you do, you will be damned' was the answer. Hopkins, on the other hand, went to Newman, not Manning. The answer was: 'Leave Oxford? Of course not! We need Oxford men'. Hence, Hopkins got his M.A., said Darlington, 'whilst Henry Browne (a first class Mods.) had to go back to Oxford in later years and get a pass degree' (I.J.A.).
5. John McErlean, Irish scholar and historian, later became archivist of the Irish Jesuit province. P.H. Pearse, teacher, lawyer, writer and poet, later led the insurrection of 1916 and was executed. James or Seamus Clandillon, an active member of the United Irish League, later achieved distinction for his renderings of Irish traditional airs.
6. 'Proceedings of Univ. College L. and H. Society' (I.J.A.).
7. *Cent. hist. L. and H.*, p. 44: reminiscences of Wm. Dawson from *National Student*, 1930.
8. 'Proceedings of Univ. College L. and H.' (I.J.A.).
9. *A page of Irish history*, pp 299 ff; *F.Jn.*, 1 Mar. 1894.
10. *Stephen Hero* (London, 1944), pp. 76, 77, 80, 81.
11. C.P. Curran, in *Struggle with fortune*, p. 227.
12. *Cent. hist. L. and H.*, p. 85: recollections of Eugene Sheehy.
13. Richard Ellmann (ed.), *Selected letters of James Joyce* (London, 1975), p. 99.
14. In *A page of Irish history*, p. 275.
15. Last editor of the magazine, brother-in-law to Tom Kettle and Sheehy-Skeffington, became secretary to Sir Horace Plunkett's Irish co-operative movement. Something of a political radical and religious agnostic, he died in 1927. See Conor Cruise O'Brien, *The states of Ireland* (London, 1972), pp 82, 84, 107, 109.

16. Apart from Skeffington and Pearse who died in 1916, almost all the others played a prominent part in the struggle for independence, or in the later life of the country, or in both. Clancy, mayor of Limerick, was killed by crown forces; P.J. Little became a government minister; O'Rahilly, president of University College Cork and a scholarly author on a number of subjects; Maurice Healy, a noted barrister and author; de Valera became both taoiseach, or prime minister, and president in turn; Dr McCartan, a candidate for presidency of Ireland; O'Connell, a general in the Free State army; O'Connor, prominent on the Republican side, was executed during the civil war; P. McGilligan, minister for finance and for foreign affairs; Costello, taoiseach; and MacNeill became leader of the Irish Volunteers, an eminent historian, and a minister in the Free State government.
17. *A page of history*, p. 244: a comment made on the occasion of his being congratulated by Prof. MacSweeney on his appointment to the position of secretary of the Dept. of Agricultural and Technical Instruction. Coyne had been professor of political economy.
18. W.P. Coyne to Del., 5 Oct. 1900 (I.J.A.).

Chapter XII

19. O'Dwyer to Bp. Donnelly, 1 Feb. 1898 (D.D.A., f 373/4).
20. Knox to O'Dwyer, 16 April, no year (L.D.A.).
21. N.U.I. pamphlets.
22. Flanagan to Dunraven, 28 Jan. 1899 (L.D.A.).
23. P.J. Walsh, *William J. Walsh, archbishop of Dublin* (Dublin, 1928), p. 553.
24. I.J.A.
25. O'Dwyer to Donnelly, 9 May 1899 (D.D.A., f 373/4).
26. *Royal commission on university*

education in Ireland; reports 1-2, p. 77.
27. Letters *passim* (I.J.A.); background information from obituary account at High Park.
28. Elizabeth Longford, *Victoria R.I.* (London, 1971), p. 555.
29. Lord Mayor to Delany, 16 Mar. 1900 (I.J.A.).
30. Generals' letters to Irish province, 1895-1900 (I.J.A.).
31. Fr Martin to Del., 10 June 1900 (I.J.A.).
32. Prov. consultor's min. bk., 11 Dec. 1900.
33. Letters of 13, 16, 18 Feb. (I.J.A.).
34. O'Dwyer to Del., 26 Feb. (I.J.A.).
35. Fr Pettit, it would appear, was ascribing attitudes to Dr Walsh which did not necessarily reflect His Grace's position. A later archbishop, Dr J.C. McQuaid, once commented wryly to a member of the medical profession how 'the archbishop would not approve' was readily ascribed to situations without he being in any way consulted on them.
36. Letter of provincial, 20 Aug. 1901 (I.J.A. and D.D.A., f 132/2).
37. Appended note by provincial, Fr J.F. Murphy (I.J.A.).
38. O'Dwyer to Bp. Donnelly, 18 Nov. 1901 (D.D.A., f 373/4).
39. *Royal comm. on univ. educ. in Ireland*; third report; p. xi.
40. M. Ward, *Insurrect. versus resurrect.*, pp 65-7.
41. Wyndham to Balfour, 29 Sept. 1901, in J.W. Mackail and G. Wyndham, *Life and letters of George Wyndham* (London, 1924), p. 427.
42. *Royal commiss.*, reports 1-2, 1901; 19 Sept. 1901, pp 16f, 20.
43. *Ibid.*, pp 19-20.
44. *Ibid.*, pp 20-21.
45. Incomplete, undated letter (L.D.A.).
46. McKenna MS, ch. xv.
47. P.J. Joyce, *John Healy, archbishop of Tuam* (Dublin, 1931), p. 179.

48. *Royal commiss.*, reports 1-2; 23 Sept. 1901, pp 76ff.
49. *Ibid.*, p. 77: The 3rd report contained supplementary evidence in which Delany stated that though all authority legally lay with the president, in practice he was aided in the interior management by a council of six members which was 'not merely consultative, but deliberative and elected by the collegiate body' (p. 359). The council met once a fortnight and, apart from Fr Finlay, all its members were laymen: Professors MacWeeney, Magennis, McClelland, Cadic, and Mr Bacon.
50. *Ibid.*, p. 75.
51. *Ibid.*, p. 338.
52. *Ibid.*, p. 78.
53. *Ibid.*, report 3, p. 360.
54. *Ibid.*, report 3, p. 361; The answer was: 'Certainly not. Such an arrangement would be entirely inadmissible. . . . I would regard any monopoly — whether lay or clerical — as disastrous. For the Jesuits I would ask only the same fair play which should be given to everyone else; that they should be judged singly on their individual merits, and treated accordingly, without any special favour or disfavour'. He thought that the positions of dean and president might be confined to clergymen in order to carry 'weight and influence with the Catholic people of the country and with the students in the institution'.
55. *Ibid.*
56. *Ibid.*, p. 359.
57. *Ibid.*, reports 1-2, p. 79.
58. *Ibid.*, p. 81.
59. *Ibid.*, report I, pp 81-2.
60. Quoted in Ward, *Insurrect. versus resurrection*, p. 68.
61. *Ibid.*, p. 61.
62. O'Dwyer to Donnelly, 9 Mar. 1902 (D.D.A., f 373/4).
63. *Ibid.*
64. Ward, *Insurrection versus resurrect.*, pp 73-4.
65. *Ibid.*, p. 67.
66. Prof. Dickie, who thought the recommended scheme denominational and, hence, out of harmony with all legislation since 1869.
67. *A page of Irish hist.*, pp 520-21.
68. McKenna MS, ch. xv.
69. Ward, *Insurrection*, p. 59.
70. *Ibid.*, p. 77.
71. *Hansard 4*, CLXXXVII, 30 Mar. to 4 May 1908.
72. Ward, *op. cit.* pp 74-6, and Prof. Dickey's comment on p. 78; see, too, *Royal commiss.*, third report, p. 588 — the written submission of E. Thompson, Esq., M.P., and elsewhere.
73. Del. to Walsh, 2 May and 30 Nov. 1903 (I.J.A.).
74. *Ibid.*, 29 Apr. 1904.
75. *Ibid.*, 31 May.
76. Quoted in John Biggs-Davison, *George Wyndham: a study in toryism* (London, 1951), p. 135.
77. In John Bithrey's memoirs, unpublished MS (I.J.A.); this part relates to interviews in 1961 with Fr M. Egan, S.J., a former lecturer at University College.
78. Biggs-Davison, *G. Wyndham*, p. 145.
79. *Ibid.*, p. 140.
80. L.D.A.
81. *Royal commission on Trinity College Dublin and the University of Dublin* (Fry commission); first report; app. 11, p. 421; and also McKenna, *op. cit.* ch. xv.
82. L.D.A. (bundle 33A).
83. His argument is presented in his pamphlet *A plea for fair play: Irish university education, facts and figures* (London, 1904), pp 2-14.
84. P.J. Walsh, *William J. Walsh, Archb. of Dublin*, pp 556-7.
85. Betty Balfour to Del., 15 June 1904 (I.J.A.).
86. Full title, *The present condition of university education in Ireland: a wrong to the country and an insult to Catholics* (Dublin, 1904), p. 19.
87. Quoted in Biggs-Davison, *op. cit.* p. 116.
88. *Ibid.*, p. 120.
89. *Ibid.*, p. 115.
90. *Ibid.*, p. 147.

91. Denis Gwynn, 'Sir Bertram Windle, 1858-1929, a centenary tribute' in *University Review*, ii, nos. 3 and 4 (1958-9), pp 48-58.
92. McKenna MS, ch. xvi.
93. See Desmond Bowen, *The Protestant crusade in Ireland, 1800-1870* (Dublin, 1978), pp xii, 264 ff, 304.
94. Resolution of the Irish bishops (I.J.A.).
95. 14 Sept. 1905 (I.J.A.).
96. Del. to Walsh, 18 July (I.J.A.).
97. *Ibid.*, 6 Aug.
98. *F.Jn.*, 2 May 1905.
99. Delany's summary notes on his efforts to secure a governing body for the college (I.J.A.).
100. *Ibid.* (I.J.A.): the meeting was held on 16 Nov. 1905.
101. *F.Jn.*, 22 Nov.
102. 25 July; notice of motion in Delany's papers (I.J.A.).

Chapter XIII

103. *Royal commiss. Trinity College* (Fry commiss.); first report; app. 23-4, 110-15, 408-13.
104. McKenna MS, ch. xviii.
105. *F.Jn.*, 31 July.
106. O'Dwyer to Del., 19 Aug. (I.J.A.).
107. *Royal commission* (Fry), first report, presented to both houses of parliament, 1906; *Parliamentary papers*, vol. 56 (N.L.I.), pp 121-22.
108. Del. to Healy, 21 Jan. 1907 (I.J.A.).
109. *A page of Irish hist.*, pp 535-6.
110. L.D.A. (folder L).
111. Healy to Del., 24 Jan. (I.J.A.).
112. *Hansard 4*, CLXIX, 72-3.
113. An incomplete, undated letter (L.D.A. bundle 33A).
114. Ross to O'Dwyer, 27 Jan. (L.D.A.).
115. Del. to Sweetman, 28 Jan. (I.J.A.).
116. Birrell came into office on 27 Jan.
117. *A page of Irish hist.*, p. 533.
118. Letter to Chief Baron Palles,

5 Mar. 1907 (I.J.A.).
119. *Ibid.*
120. Fr Peter Finlay had argued strongly in favour of a Palles type scheme before the Fry commission; and Delany pointed out that the majority of the staff at University College, including his own nephew, advocated the same solution.
121. Dublin University petitions to House of Commons (D.D.A., f 132/2).
122. To O'Dwyer, 18 April, no year (L.D.A.).
123. Quoted in *Cent. hist. L. and H.*, p. 101.
124. A.C. Hepburn, 'The Irish council bill and the fall of Sir Anthony MacDonnell, 1906-7' in *Irish Historical Studies*, xvii (Sept. 1971), p. 471.
125. Hepburn, *loc. cit.*, quoting MacDonnell in his cabinet paper of 28 Feb. 1907 (Public Record Office, cal. 37/38/26), p. 497.
126. Hepburn, *loc. cit.*, pp 496-7.
127. Quoted by F.S.L. Lyons in *Ireland since the famine* (London, 1973), p. 261.
128. Moriarty to Redmond, 17 May 1907 (N.L.I. Redmond papers, MS 15247), quoted in Hepburn, *loc. cit.*, p. 492.
129. Quoted from H.A.L. Fisher, *James Bryce* (London, 1927), p. 355, in John Wilson, *Life of Henry Campbell-Bannerman* (London, 1973), p. 115.
130. Quoted Hepburn, *loc. cit.*, p. 495 footnote.
131. *Ibid.*, pp. 496-7.
132. *Ibid.*, p. 496; Bryce papers, MS 19 (Bodlyn).
133. Quoted Hepburn, p. 486, from diary of John Burns.
134. Quoted in Wilson, *Henry Campbell-Bannerman*, pp 45 f.

Chapter XIV

135. *Cent. hist. L. and H.*, p. 51.
136. A. Clery, *Dublin Essays* (Dublin, 1919), pp 54, 55 ff.

137. *Cent. hist.*, p. 61.
138. *Ibid.*, p. 71.
139. C.P. Curran in broadcast talk of 2 May 1954, reproduced in *Struggle with fortune*, p. 221.
140. 9 Nov. 1905 (I.J.A.).
141. *Cent. hist.*, p. 91.
142. Frank Skeffington in *Irish Protestant*, 22 Nov. (I.J.A.).
143. Delany's memo of the occasion (I.J.A.).
144. *Cent. hist.*, pp 74 ff.
145. *Irish Times*, 23 Nov.
146. *Cent. hist.*, p. 75.
147. C.P. Curran, see *Struggle with fortune*, p. 222.
148. The *Irish Times* account ended at this point; the *Freeman's Journal* continued with the full report of the speech.
149. In introduction to *A book of Irish verse* (London, 1899), pp xxix, xxx.
150. *Dublin Essays*, p. 44.
151. *Cent. hist. L. and H.*, pp 72 ff.
152. 28 Jan. 1907 (I.J.A.).
153. Conor Cruise O'Brien, *States of Ireland* (Dublin, 1972), p. 80.
154. Almost all of the account which follows is based on Delany's typed version entitled 'A case for the opinion of counsel'; but it is supplemented by newspaper reports such as that of the *Daily Express* (Dublin) for 27 October (I.J.A.).
155. *Cent. hist.*, p. 91.
156. Letter of 28 Jan. 1907 (I.J.A.).
157. Memo for opinion of counsel (I.J.A.).
158. *Cent. hist.*: Ml. McGilligan's recollections, p. 115.
159. *A page of Irish hist.*, p. 548.
160. *Ibid.*, p. 546.
161. Delany's reply of 15 Nov. 1905 (I.J.A.).
162. *Cent. hist.*, pp 92-3.
163. 15 Mar. 1906 (I.J.A.).
164. Letter of registrar to the secretary of the committee of *St Stephen's*, 3 Apr. (I.J.A.).
165. *Cent. hist.*, p. 143.
166. *Ibid.*: McGilligan's recollections, p. 117; and see Jn. Sweetman's letter of Jan. 1907 in I.J.A.

167. *Cent. hist.*, W.G. Fallon's recollections, pp 100 ff.
168. *Ibid.*, p. 91.
169. *Ibid.*, p. 78.
170. Delany's memo on 'The title of the college and the magazine' (I.J.A.).
171. L. Ó Broin, *The Chief Secretary, Augustine Birrell in Ireland* (London, 1969), p. 3.
172. C.P. Curran, *art. cit.* in *Struggle with fortune*, pp 228-9.
173. McKenna MS, ch. xviii.
174. Resolution of 17 Dec. forwarded to the president (I.J.A.).

Chapter XV

175. C.P. Curran, *loc. cit.*, in *Struggle with fortune*, pp 226-7.
176. *A page of Irish hist.*, p. 465.
177. *Ibid.*
178. *Ibid.*, p. 466.
179. *Ibid.*, p. 468.
180. 8 Apr. 1908 (I.J.A.).
181. *Cent. hist. L. and H.*, p. 112.
182. *Ibid.*, p. 110.
183. Quoted in *A page of Irish hist.*, p. 548.
184. C.P. Curran, *James Joyce remembered* (Oxford, 1968), p. 62.
185. *Ibid.*, p. 60.
186. *Ibid.*, p. 61 (italics mine).
187. Quoted *ibid.*, p. 60.
188. Quoted *ibid.*, pp 59-60.
189. *Cent. hist.*, p. 317.

Chapter XVI.

190. L. Ó Broin, *The Chief Secretary: Augustine Birrell in Ireland* (London, 1969), pp 1, 3, 6 f.
191. *Ibid.*, p. 7.
192. Redmond to Birrell, 25 May 1907 (N.L.I. MS 15169), quoted in Gráinne O'Flynn 'Augustine Birrell and Archbishop William Walsh's influence on the founding of the National University of Ireland' in *Capuchin Annual*, 1976, p. 148.
193. O'Flynn, *ibid.*, p. 149: Birrell

met Redmond on 29 May. See, also,
Birrell, *Things past redress* (London,
1936), p. 201.
194. Ó Broin, *Chief Secretary*,
pp 17-18.
195. McKenna MS, ch. xix.
196. O Broin, p. 24.
197. Birrell, *Things past redress*,
p. 201.
198. Quoted by G. O'Flynn, *loc. cit.*
in *Capuchin Annual*, 1976, p. 150.
199. 31 Dec. 1907 (D.D.A., f 14 –
N.U.I.).
200. 6 Jan. (*ibid.*).
201. Birrell to Del., 11 Jan. (I.J.A.).
202. *Ibid.*, 19 Jan. (I.J.A.).
203. D.D.A., f 14.
204. Birrell to Redm., 20 Jan.,
quoted in O'Flynn, *loc. cit.* p. 152.
205. O'Flynn, *ibid.*, pp 152-3:
Walsh to Birrell, 23 Jan. 1908
(D.D.A., f 14).
206. 28 Jan. (I.J.A.).
207. Birrell, *Things past redress*,
p. 202.
208. O'Flynn, *loc. cit.*, p. 154.
209. *Ibid.*
210. *Hansard 4*, CLXXVII (30 Mar.-
4 May).
211. *Ibid.*, pp 388-9.
212. *Ibid.*, pp 331 ff (italics mine);
Delany was seventy-three not
seventy-six.
213. Dr Cox, a member of the
senate, and Dr Coffey, were both
professors in the Cecilia Street
Medical School. McGrath, afterwards Sir Joseph McGrath, was
secretary of the Royal University.
214. 15 Apr. (I.J.A.).
215. Meenan (ed.), *Cent. hist. L.
and H.*, pp 91-2.
216. W.B. Wells, *John Redmond*
(London, 1919), p. 132.
217. To Del., 4 Aug. 1908 (I.J.A.).
218. O'Flynn, *loc. cit.*, p. 155.
219. 'Let an experiment be tried
on a worthless body'.
220. Birrell, *Things past redress*,
p. 202.
221. O'Flynn, *loc. cit.*, p. 157.
222. *Ibid.*, p. 153.
223. *Hansard 4*, CXCIII, pp 527-33.
224. *Ibid.*, CLXXXVII, p. 778.

225. *Ibid.*, pp 806-11.
226. *Ibid.*, p. 817.
227. *Ibid.*, pp. 811 ff.
228. *Ibid.*, pp. 817-18.
229. *Ibid.*, pp. 792-802.
230. *Ibid.*, p. 791.
231. *Ibid.*, 31 Mar. p. 366; 11 May,
pp 836 ff.
232. *Ibid.*, 11 May, p. 770.
233. *Ibid.*, p. 400.
234. *Ibid.*, 30 July, pp 1659-60.
235. F.S.L. Lyons, *John Dillon*
(London, 1968), p. 305.
236. Quoted *F.Jn.*, 1 Aug. 1908.
237. *8 Edward VII*, c. 38; for brief
summary of the act see Fergal
McGrath, 'The university question'
in P.J. Corish (ed.), *A history of
Irish Catholicism* (Dublin, 1971),
pp 135-6, and N. Atkinson, *Irish
education* (Dublin, 1969), pp 140-1.

Chapter XVII

238. 'Get behind me Satan' (*Gospel St Matthew*, 16.23).
239. P.J. Joyce, *John Healy, archbishop of Tuam*, pp 185-7.
240. McKenna MS, ch. xx, provides
details of the occasion.
241. In his *Ireland in the new century* (London, 1904), Sir Horace
roused bitter criticism by his strictures on various aspects of Irish life,
particularly on the moral timidity
of the Irish people as compared to
their physical courage; this moral
cowardice he saw exemplified in
their intense dread of public opinion.
242. Plunkett to O'Dwyer, 9 Mar.
1904 (O'Dwyer MSS, L.D.A.; yellow
folder K).

Chapter XVIII

243. Diarmid Coffey, *Douglas Hyde*
(Dublin, 1938), pp 67 f, 74, 93.
244. Del. to O'Daly, 25 Nov.
(I.J.A.); he mentioned that he had
discussed his position with MacNeill.
245. Coffey, *op. cit.*, p. 93: 'It
would be difficult to imagine a

sentence more calculated to arouse
the indignation of patriotic Gaels'.
Coffey termed it a 'bombshell'.
246. These exist in rough copies.
247. Coffey, *op. cit.*, p. 95.
248. I.J.A. (italics mine).
249. G.K. Chesterton, *Irish impressions* (London, 1919), pp 56 ff.
250. Quoted by D.W. Miller, *Church, state and nation in Ireland, 1898-1921* (Dublin, 1973), p. 233.
251. D.D.A., f 13.
252. McKenna MS, ch. xx.
253. Coffey, *op. cit.*, p. 96.
254. Delany's memo on 'the essential Irish controversy' (I.J.A.).
255. Coffey, p. 98.
256. *Ibid.*, p. 99.
257. Meenan (ed.), *Cent. hist. L. and H.*, p. 91.
258. F.S.L. Lyons, *John Dillon*, pp 305-6.
259. 14 June (I.J.A.).
260. Denis Gwynn, 'Sir Bertram Windle, 1858-1929; a centenary tribute' in *University Review*, ii, nos 3 and 4 (1958-59), pp 49 ff.
261. D.D.A., f 7.
262. Coffey, *op. cit.*, p. 101.
263. Quoted in McKenna MS, ch. xx.
264. D.D.A., f 4.
265. Coffey, p. 105; italics mine.
266. Quoted in Frank O'Connor (ed.), *A book of Ireland* (London, 1959), pp 327-9.
267. The identification of Irish and Catholic was clearly, if amusingly, illustrated by G.K. Chesterton in *Irish impressions* (p. 156). He related an incident told him by the poet and writer, James Stephens. The latter described 'with great good humour' how a Catholic priest, at the close of a convivial conversation flavoured by plenty of good wine, said to him confidentially: 'You ought to be a Catholic. You can be saved without being a Catholic; but you can't be Irish without being a Catholic'.
268. John MacNeill, *Celtic Ireland* (Dublin, 1920), pp. xii-xiii, quoted in F.J. Byrne and F.X. Martin (eds.),

The scholar revolutionary, Eoin Mac Neill, 1867-1945 (Dublin, 1973), p. 282.

Chapter XIX

269. See Palles's letter to archbishop, 15 Dec. (D.D.A., f 13).
270. *Ibid.*
271. McKenna MS, ch. xx.
272. D.D.A., f 7.
273. *Ibid.*
274. Minute book Dublin commissioners (April 1909-April 1910), for Nov. 1909 (D.D.A., 124/2); the board of commissioners was established by the 1908 Act to help in the launching of the new university by having responsibility for such areas as the appointment of staff and schedule of salaries.
275. The story was related to the author by Professor Aubrey Gwynn, S.J., who was a member of the Leeson Street community with Delany for a number of years.
276. 18 Oct. 1909 (I.J.A.).
277. 29 Apr. 1909 (I.J.A.).
278. Min. bk. Dublin commiss. pp 2-7 (D.D.A., f 124/4).
279. The School of Irish Learning began its work at University College, Delany having placed its lecture halls at the disposal of Professor Strachan and Kuno Meyer. From the start, Delany had been one of the governors of the school and one of its staunchest supporters.
280. Consultors' min. bk., 14 June 1909 (I.J.A.): the announcement from the General that Delany was to continue as vice-provincial until 31 July and then become provincial.

PART FOUR

Chapters XX-XXII

Chapter XX

1. Quoted McKenna MS, ch. xxi.
2. Bithrey memoirs, specimen pages,

bk 9, pp 1-11 (A section of the MS is with Gráinne O'Flynn, Dublin; entire MS in I.J.A.).
3. Consultors' min. bk., 9 Feb. 1909.
4. McKenna MS, ch. xxi.
5. A favourite text was *Letter to Philippians*, ch. 4, vv 4-5: 'Rejoice always . . . for the Lord is near'.
6. Del. to Walsh, 14 May 1910 (I.J.A.).
7. Detail passed on to Fr Fergal McGrath, S.J., by his father, Sir Joseph McGrath, secretary of the Royal University.
8. D.D.A., f 2.
9. Consultors' min. bk., 9 Aug. 1909.
10. 28 Oct. (I.J.A.).
11. D.D.A., f 2 (N.U.I.).
12. Consult. min. bk., 9 Aug. 1909 (I.J.A.).
13. McKenna MS, ch. xxi.
14. Prof. Michael Tierney, under whom the movement of University College to an extensive site at Belfield was carried out.
15. Del. to Walsh, Aug. 1909 (no day); also letter of 28 Sept. (I.J.A.).
16. McKenna MS.
17. Del. to Walsh, 3 Feb. 1909 (I.J.A.).
18. McKenna MS, notes that the argument had previously been found deficient in English courts.
19. 8 May 1910.
20. Del. to Walsh, 14 May 1910 (I.J.A.).
21. Consult. min. bk., Oct. 1911; and Del. to Walsh, 11 Nov. 1911 (I.J.A.).
22. Del. to T.P. O'Neill, 13 July 1910 (I.J.A.).
23. McKenna, *ibid*.
24. Consult. min. bk., Dec. 1910 (I.J.A.).
25. Application to senate of National University (I.J.A.).
26. *Ibid*.
27. Addressed to governing body of Univ. College, 16 Apr. 1910 (I.J.A.).
28. McKenna MS.

29. Windle to Walsh, 8 July 1911 (D.D.A., f 21).
30. Consult. min. bk., 22 May 1912, which shows Finlay as first choice.
31. *Ibid*.
32. 30 Oct. 1912 (I.J.A.).

Chapter XXI

33. Belloc to Russell, 1 Jan. 1910 (I.J.A. Russell papers).
34. *Royal commiss. on univ. education in Ireland*, reports 1-2; 20 Sept. 1901, pp 24-5.
35. D.P. Moran in *The philosophy of Irish Ireland* (Dublin, 1905), quoted in F.S.L. Lyons, *Culture and anarchy in Ireland, 1890-1939* (Oxford, 1979), p. 61.
36. Lyons, *Culture and anarchy.*, p. 82.
37. *Ibid.*, p. 58.
38. C. Day Lewis, 'The conflict' in H. Peschmann (ed.), *The voice of poetry* (London, 1969), p. 68.
39. This brief account is summarised from McKenna MS.
40. Letters of 6, 8 Dec. 1911 (I.J.A.).
41. Even though he had actively canvassed for His Grace's appointment as chancellor, he yet felt somewhat aggrieved — to judge by his notes on 'An episode in the history of the Irish university question' (I.J.A.)— that one who had opposed a separate university should readily accept the chancellorship of it.
42. 18 June 1911 (I.J.A.).
43. 9 April 1919 (I.J.A.).
44. Shane Leslie, 'Democracy' in *Freeman's Journal*, 31 Mar. 1910, quoted in Joseph A. MacMahon, 'Catholic clergy and the social question 1891-1916' in *Studies*, Winter 1981, pp 274-5.
45. Mentioned in J.A. MacMahon, *loc. cit.*, p. 275. The interpretation of the clergy's position is drawn from MacMahon's article, pp 263-288, esp. pp 264, 268, 270, 274-5,

281. Other members of the clergy who were noted, in their writings and pronouncements, for a more progressive and understanding view of the social question and of socialism were Frs John Kelleher, James MacCaffrey, Peter Coffey, Michael O'Donnell, and Patrick Joy, S.J.; while among the bishops, Dr Walsh of Dublin was a strong advocate of a relationship of equality and mutual respect between employer and worker.
46. From W.H. Auden's poem 'A letter to Lord Byron' in *Collected longer poems* (London, 1968).
47. Chesterton, *Irish impressions*, p. 43.
48. *Clongownian*, 1924, p. 18.
49. *Ibid.*, pp 15 ff.
50. Alan Denson (ed.), *Letters from A.E.* (London, 1961), p. 63.
51. Interviewed by the author, 1974.

Chapter XXII

52. T. Corcoran, S.J., *The Clon-*

gowes record, 1814-1932 (Dublin, n.d.), pp 147-8
53. *Clongownian*, 1924, p. 15.
54. T. Brameld, 'Ethics of leadership' in C.A. Gibb (ed.), *Leadership* (London, 1969), p. 416.
55. *Clongownian*, 1924, p. 15.
56. *Ibid.*, p. 100.
57. *National Student*, pp 99-100.
58. *Ibid.*, p. 100.
59. The occasion was marked by the appearance of *A struggle with fortune: a centenary miscellany*; and by broadcast talks from Radio Eireann which featured C.P. Curran on 'The Jesuit tenure'.
60. 'Text of introductory address' in *Irish Jesuit year book*, 1956, pp 31 ff.
61. John Howley, 'Fr Joseph Darlington, S.J., 1850-1939' in *Studies*, xxviii, 1939, p. 503.
62. John MacNeill, *Celtic Ireland*, pp xii-xiii, quoted in F.J. Byrne and F.X. Martin (ed.), *The scholar revolutionary, Eoin MacNeill*, p. 282.
63. *Clongownian*, 1924, p. 18.

BIBLIOGRAPHY

SYNOPSIS

Primary Sources

I   Institutional archives, private papers, manuscripts
II   Representative published statements on the university question by Delany, Dr Walsh and Dr O'Dwyer
III   Parliamentary and other official publications
IV   Published memoirs and other works by contemporaries
V   Further publications containing relevant contemporary documents
VI   Newspapers, periodicals and scholarly journals (contemporary or dealing with contemporary issues)
VII   Works of reference

Secondary Sources

VIII Published writings containing references to Delany or special information
IX   Biographies of some contemporaries, and special studies
X   Works of a more general nature

PRIMARY SOURCES

I   Institutional archives, private papers, manuscripts

IRISH JESUIT ARCHIVES, DUBLIN
Fr William Delany papers
Fr Joseph Darlington papers
Fr Mathew Russell papers
Fr Gerard Manley Hopkins correspondence
Fr Lambert McKenna MS volume, 'Fr William Delany and his work for Irish education'
John Bithrey memoirs
Precis of Jesuit Generals' letters to Irish province 1895-1900
Province consultors minute-books (at Provincial's residence)
Memorials of the Irish Jesuit province: centenary year, 1814-1919 (printed volume, with some letters, for private circulation)

DUBLIN DIOCESAN ARCHIVES
Dr Edward McCabe papers (especially those relating to university education) and diary
Dr William J. Walsh papers, especially relating to education and the university question
Dr Bartholomew Woodlock papers relating to the university question
Minute-book of Dublin commissioners of National University of Ireland

ST STANISLAUS COLLEGE, TULLABEG, ARCHIVES (mainly at
CLONGOWES WOOD COLLEGE, Co Kildare)
Prefects of studies notebooks, and diary from Christmas 1881 to June 1886
Ministers' journals
William Delany's marking-book, some letters, part of a diary
Rules and instructions for masters and pupils
Various college prospectuses, 1840s-1880s
Programmes of dramatic and sporting activities
Printed catalogue of boys at Tullabeg 1818-1886, at Clongowes 1814-1900
Souvenir programme 1910
Typed and hand-written reminiscences of the college and church: one such,
    entitled 'Old Tullabeg', recalling the years before the advent of the
    railways

LIMERICK DIOCESAN ARCHIVES
Dr George Butler papers, especially relating to education
Dr E.T. O'Dwyer papers

NATIONAL LIBRARY OF IRELAND
William Monsell papers (MS 8318)

NATIONAL UNIVERSITY OF IRELAND OFFICE, DUBLIN
Minute-books of the Royal University of Ireland

II   Representative published statements on the university question by
      Delany, Dr Walsh and Dr O'Dwyer

William Delany, *Irish university education, facts and figures: a plea for fair
    play* (London, 1904; pamphlet N.L.I. 808, education, Ireland)

William J. Walsh, *Addresses by Most Rev Dr Walsh, Archbishop of Dublin*
    (Dublin, 1886)
    Memorandum on the Irish education question (Dublin, 1887)
    *Statement of the chief grievances of Irish Catholics in the matter of
    education, primary, intermediate and university* (Dublin, 1890)
    *The Irish university question, the Catholic case: selections from the
    speeches and writings (1885-1897) of the Archbishop of Dublin, with a
    historical sketch of the Irish university question* (Dublin, 1897)
Edward T. O'Dwyer, 'University education for Irish Catholics' in *Nineteenth
    Century* (London, Jan. 1899)
    *A letter . . . in answer to a sonnet and explanatory letter by R.Y. Tyrell,
    Esq* (Dublin, 1903)
    *The present condition of university education in Ireland: a wrong to
    the country and an insult to Catholics* (Dublin, 1904)

III   Parliamentary and other official publications

Hansard's parliamentary debates: third series, vol 300 (28 July 1885);
    fourth series, vol 187 (session March-May 1908).

*Report of royal commission of inquiry, primary education Ireland, 1868-
    70* (Powis commission), i [C-6], H.C. 1870.

Report of the educational endowments (Ireland) commission for 1887-8;
    and down to 1891-2; [C-5546], H.C. 1888, xxxix; etc.

Reports of the intermediate education board for Ireland for 1895; and down to 1907; [C-8034] , 1896 xxvii; etc.

Report of the royal commission on university education in Ireland (Robertson commission), [Cd-825-6] , [Cd-899-900] , [Cd 1228-9] , [Cd-1483-4] ; H.C. 1902, xxxi, xxxii; H.C. 1903, xxxii.

Report of royal commission on Trinity College Dublin and the University of Dublin (Fry commission), [Cd-3174] , [Cd-3176] , [Cd-3311-12] ; H.C. 1906 lvi, H.C. 1907, xli.

IV   Published memoirs and other works by contemporaries

Augustine Birrell, *Things past redress* (London, 1936)

M. McDonnell Bodkin, *Recollections of an Irish judge: press, bar and parliament* (London, 1914)

Randolph Churchill, *Intermediate education in Ireland* (Dublin, 1878)

A. Clery, *Dublin essays* (Dublin, 1919)

Clongownian 1910, 1914, 1919, 1924 (Dublin)

Conference of Catholic headmasters, printed report (Dublin 1883)

C.P. Curran, *James Joyce remembered* (Oxford, 1968)
    'Memoirs of University College Dublin: the Jesuit tenure' in M. Tierney (ed.), *Struggle with fortune* (Dublin, 1954)

'Educationist' (ed.) *The Irish intermediate education act of 1878, with an introduction* (Dublin, 1878, N.L.I.)

T. Finlay, 'William Delany, S.J.' in *Clongownian*, 1924

Bishop M. Fogarty, *The great Bishop of Limerick* (Dublin, 1917)

G. Fottrell, *Inaugural address . . . Literary and Historical Society of the Catholic University of Ireland*, 2 Dec. 1870 (Dublin, 1871)

H. Hennessy, *On freedom of education: an essay* (Dublin, 1859)

E. Howley, *The universities and secondary schools of Ireland, with proposals for their improvement* (Dublin, 1871)

J. Howley, 'Fr Joseph Darlington, S.J., 1850-1939' in *Studies*, xxviii, 1939

Intermediate and university education in Ireland, part I, by 'A committee of Irish Catholics' (Dublin, 1872)

James Joyce, *Stephen hero* (London, 1940)

T.M. Kettle, *Irish orators and oratory* (Dublin, 1917)

M.J.F. McCarthy, *Priests and people in Ireland* (Dublin, 1902)
    Education in Ireland (Dublin, 1901)

W. McDonald, *Reminiscences of a Maynooth professor* (London, 1925)

J. MacIvor, *Intermediate education in Ireland* (n.p., n.d.)

Lambert McKenna, 'The Catholic University of Ireland' in *Irish Ecclesiastical Record*, xxxi (1928)

John MacNeill, *Irish in the National University of Ireland: a plea for Irish education* (Dublin, 1909)
    Celtic Ireland, with introduction (Dublin, 1920)

'Our Whig inheritance' in *Ireland To-day*, , i, no 6 (Dublin, 1936)

Memorial to board of intermediate education from Catholic headmasters of Ireland, 1879

J.H.D. Miller, *Clericalised education in Ireland* (1907)

John Morley, *Life of William Ewart Gladstone* (3 vols, London, 1903)

John H. Newman, *The idea of a university defined and illustrated* (London, 1873)

H. Nowland, *Remarks addressed to W.H. Bellamy Esq., on state of education in Ireland* (Dublin, 1849)

F.H. O'Donnell, *Public education: its necessity, and the ideas involved in it. An essay on the principles of national instruction, with some of their applications to Irish university systems* (Dublin, 1867)

G. O'Neill, 'The centenary of Tullabeg' in *Clongownian*, 1919

Myles O'Reilly, *Two articles on education* (London, 1863)

M. O'Riordan, *Catholicity and progress in Ireland* (London, 1905)

Horace Plunkett, *Ireland in the new century* (London, 1904)

Secondary education in Ireland: a plea for reform, 1904, by association of secondary teachers of Ireland and university teachers of Ireland (Dublin)

W. Starkie, *Recent reforms in Irish education, primary and secondary, with a view to better coordination* (Dublin, 1902)

W. Steele, *Examination held at the Royal School of Portora, Easter 1861*

W. Whittle, *The university education question in Ireland: its difficulties and their solution* (Belfast, 1899)

B. Woodlock, *Educational dangers or the bearing of education on the future of Ireland* (Dublin, 1868)

V   Further publications containing relevant contemporary documents

Blackrock College Annual (Dublin), 1955-6, 1958-60, 1965-7

J. Bowman and R. O'Donoghue (eds.), *Portraits, Belvedere College 1832-1982* (Dublin, 1982)

T. Corcoran, *The Clongowes record, 1814-1932* (Dublin, n.d.)
Selected texts on education systems in Ireland from the close of the middle ages (Dublin, 1928)

P.J. Corish (ed.), 'Kirby papers' in *Archivium Hibernicum*, xxxii (1974)

Edward David, *Inside Asquith's cabinet; from the diaries of Charles Hobhouse* (London, 1977)

Alan Denson (ed.), *Letters from A.E.* (London, 1961)

R. Ellmann (ed.), *Selected letters of James Joyce* (London, 1975)

John Gerard (ed.), *Stonyhurst College, centenary record 1794-1894* (Belfast, 1894)

J. Stuart Maclure (ed.), *Educational documents, England and Wales, 1816-1968* (London, 1969)

J.W. Mackail and G. Wyndham, *Life and letters of George Wyndham*, (2 vols, London, 1924)

Peadar MacSuibhne, *Paul Cullen and his contemporaries, with their letters from 1820 to 1902*, (5 vols, Naas, 1961-77)

P.E. Moran, *The writings of Cardinal Cullen* (3 vols. Dublin, 1882)

G. Porter, *Archbishop Porter's letters* (London, 1891)

'Resolutions of the Irish bishops at Maynooth 1887' in *Irish Ecclesiastical Record*, 1887

M. Tierney (ed.), 'Correspondence concerning the disestablishment of the Church of Ireland, 1862-9' in *Collectanea Hibernica*, no 12 (1969)

VI   Newspapers, periodicals and scholarly journals: contemporary or dealing with contemporary issues

The Belvederian (Dublin), 1930-2

Blackrock College Annual (Dublin), 1955-6, 1958-9, 1960, 1965-7

Capuchin Annual (Dublin), 1976

The Catholic Mirror (Baltimore, U.S.A.), 1884

The Catholic University School centenary record, 1867-1967 (Dublin, 1967)

Clongownian (Naas), 1910, 1914, 1919, 1924

Collectanea Hibernica, 1969

Daily Express (Dublin), 1907

Freeman's Journal (Dublin), 1884, 1896, 1905, 1908, 1910

Hibernia (Dublin), 1882

History (London), xlii, 1958

Ireland To-day (Dublin), i, no. 6, 1936

Irish Catholic (Dublin), 1905

Irish Ecclesiastical Record (Dublin), 1887, 1928, 1951

Irish Historical Studies (Dublin), vol 17, 1971

Irish Jesuit Directory (Dublin), 1943-4

Irish Jesuit Year Book (Dublin), 1956

Irish Monthly (Dublin), 1942

Irish Protestant (Dublin), 1905

Irish Province News (Dublin), 1925-30, 1935, 1940

Limerick Reporter and Tipperary Vindicator (Limerick), 1859

Lyceum (Dublin), 1887-8, 1891-2

The Munster News (Limerick), 1889

The Munster Reporter, 1886

The Nation (Dublin), 1885

The National Student (Dublin), 1930

Nineteenth Century (London), 1899

An Phoblacht (Dublin), 1930

Recusant History: (London), 1980

Reportorium Novum: (Dublin), 1961-2

Studies (Dublin), 1939, 1941, 1943, 1948, 1961-2, 1970, 1981

Tablet (London), 1884

The Times (London), 1905

University Hall Record: jubilee number (Dublin), 1973

University Review: (Dublin), 1955, 1958

Victorian Studies (Indiana University) vol xv, no 3

VII   Works of reference

Catologi provinciae Hiberniae Societatis Jesu, 1875, 1877-96

Census of Ireland, 1861, 1881

Dictionary of National Biography (22 vols, London 1908-9)

A.P. Farrell, *The Jesuit code of liberal education: development and scope of the ratio studiorum* (Milwaukee, U.S.A., 1938)

F. Finnegan, *Limerick Jesuit centenary record, 1859-1959* (Limerick, 1959)

W.H. Gardiner (ed.), *Poems and prose of Gerard Manley Hopkins* (London, 1954)

C.A. Gibb (ed.), *Leadership* (London, 1969)

Samuel Lewis, *Topographical dictionary of Ireland* (2 vols, London, 1837)

H.M. Lynd, *England in the eighteen-eighties* (London, 1968)

Frank O'Connor (ed.), *A book of Ireland* (London, 1974 ed.)

Pigot, *Directory of Ireland* (Dublin, 1824)

Ratio atque institutio studiorum Societatis Jesu . . . quae scholas inferiores spectat (Rome, 1599, ed. 1926)

R. Williams, *Culture and society, 1780-1950* (London, 1963)

SECONDARY SOURCES

VIII   Published writings containing references to Delany or special information

A page of Irish history: the story of University College Dublin, 1883-1909 (Dublin, 1930), by Fathers of the Society of Jesus

F.J. Byrne and F.X. Martin (ed.), *The scholar revolutionary, Eoin MacNeill, 1867-1945* (Dublin, 1973)

J. Biggs-Davison, *George Wyndham: a study in toryism* (London, 1951)

D. Coffey, *Douglas Hyde* (Dublin, 1938)

R. Ellmann, *James Joyce* (Oxford, 1959)

S. Farragher, 'Blackrock and the intermediate act' in *Blackrock College*

Annual, 1958 (Dublin)

'Centenary education — intermediate education', ibid., 1960

'Fr Joseph Edouard Reffé, dean of studies, 1864-88', ibid., 1960

R.F. Foster, *Lord Randolph Churchill: a political life* (Oxford, 1981)

P.J. Joyce, *John Healy, Archbishop of Tuam* (Dublin, 1931)

F. McGrath, 'The university question' in P.J. Corish (ed.), *A history of Irish Catholicism*, vol 5 (Dublin 1971)

J. Meenan (ed.), *A centenary history of the Literary and Historical Society of University College Dublin* (Tralee, 1955)

G. O'Flynn, 'Augustine Birrell and Archbishop William Walsh's influence on the founding of the National University of Ireland' in *Capuchin Annual*, 1976 (Dublin)

W.F. Stockley, *Newman, education and Ireland* (Edinburgh, n.d.)

Michael Tierney (ed.), *Struggle with fortune: a centenary miscellany for Catholic University of Ireland 1854, University College Dublin 1954* (Dublin, 1954)

P.J. Walsh, *William J. Walsh, Archbishop of Dublin* (Dublin, 1928)

M. Ward, *Insurrection versus resurrection* (London, 1937)

IX   Biographies of some contemporaries, and special studies

D.A. Akenson, *The Irish education experiment: the national system of education in the nineteenth century* (Dublin, 1969)

J.J. Auchmuty, *Sir Thomas Wyse, 1791-1862: the life and career of an educator and diplomat* (London, 1939)

E. Boyd Barrett, *The Jesuit enigma* (New York, 1927)

A.C.F. Beales, 'The tradition in English Catholic education' in *Catholic Education: a handbook, 1962-3* (London, 1963)

D. Bowen, *The Protestant crusade in Ireland, 1800-70* (Dublin, 1978)

T. Brameld, 'Ethics of leadership' in C.A. Gibb (ed.), *Leadership* (London, 1969)

M. Brennan, 'Comment on Cardinal Newman and his attitude to the Catholic University' in *Irish Ecclesiastical Record*, Nov. 1951

Joseph Chamberlain, *A political memoir, 1880-92* (London, 1953)

G.K. Chesterton, *Irish impressions* (London, 1919)

T. Corcoran, 'Liberal studies and moral aims: a critical survey of Newman's position' in *Thought*, 1 (June, 1926)

P.J. Corish, 'Political problems, 1850-78' in P.J. Corish (ed.), *A history of Irish Catholicism*, vol 5 (Dublin, 1967)

V.T.H. Delany, *Christopher Palles, Lord Chief Baron of H.M. Courts of Exchequer in Ireland, 1874-1916, his life and times* (Dublin, 1960)

T. Dillon, 'The origin and early history of the national university', part I, in *University Review*, i, no 5 (Dublin, 1955)

R. Dudley Edwards, 'The beginnings of Irish intermediate education system, 1878-1883' in *Catholic University School centenary record, 1867-1967* (Dublin, 1967)

Owen Dudley Edwards, 'Belvedere in history' in J. Bowman & R. O'Donoghue (eds.), *Portraits, Belvedere College 1832-1982* (Dublin 1982)

H.O. Evenett, 'Catholics and the universities, 1850-1950' in G.A. Beck (ed.), *The English Catholics, 1850-1950* (London, 1950)

A. Gwynn, 'The Jesuits and University College' in M. Tierney (ed.), *Struggle with fortune* (Dublin, 1954)

D. Gwynn, 'Sir Bertram Windle, 1858-1929, a centenary tribute' in *University Review*, ii, nos 3 & 4 (Dublin, 1958-9)

McDonald Hastings, *The Jesuit child* (London, 1971)

C. Hayes, 'Cullen, Newman, and the Irish university' in *Recusant History*, vol, 15, no 3, May 1980

A.C. Hepburn, 'The Irish council bill and the fall of Sir Anthony Mac-Donnell, 1906-7' in *Irish Historical Studies*, xvii, Sept. 1971

C. Hollis, *Newman and the modern world* (London, 1967)

J.J. Horgan, 'Clongownians in Irish politics' in *Clongownian*, 1924

A.N. Jeffares (ed.), *Yeats, selected prose* (London, 1968)

D. Kerr, 'Catholic University School and Newman's university, 1850-1867' in *C.U.S. centenary record* (Dublin, 1967)

Earl of Longford and T.P. O'Neill, *Eamon de Valera* (Dublin, 1970)

Eliz. Longford, *Victoria R.I.* (London, 1971)

F.S.L. Lyons, *The Irish parliamentary party, 1890-1910* (London, 1951)
John Dillon (London, 1968)
Charles Stuart Parnell (London, 1977)
Culture and anarchy in Ireland, 1890-1939 (Oxford, 1979)

V.A. McClelland, *Cardinal Manning: his public life and influence, 1865-92* (Oxford, 1962)
'The liberal training of England's Catholic youth: William Joseph Petre (1847-93) and educational reform' in *Victorian Studies*, xv, no 3
'From Douai to Dublin: four hundred years of educational endeavour' in *Studies*, spring 1970
English Roman Catholics and higher education (Oxford, 1973)

Fergal McGrath, *Newman's university: idea and reality* (Dublin, 1931)
The Consecration of Learning (Dublin, 1961)

J.A. MacMahon, 'Catholic clergy and the social question, 1891-1916' in *Studies*, winter 1981

F.X. Martin (ed.), *1916 and University College Dublin* (Dublin, 1966)

David Mathew, *Lord Acton and his times* (London, 1968)
'Old Catholics and converts' in G.A. Beck (ed.), *The English Catholics, 1850-1950* (London, 1950)

C. Maxwell, *A history of Trinity College Dublin, 1591-1892* (Dublin, 1946)

D.W. Miller, *Church, state and nation in Ireland, 1898-1921* (Dublin, 1973)

T.W. Moody, 'The Irish university question in the nineteenth century' in *History*, xlii (1958)

T.W. Moody and T.C. Beckett, *Queen's, Belfast, 1845-1949: the history of a university* (2 vols, London, 1959)

T.J. Morrissey, 'Some Jesuit contributions to Irish education' (Ph.D. thesis, 2 vols, N.U.I., 1975)

C. Murray, 'The founding of a university' in *University Review*, ii, nos 3 & 4 (1958)

E.R. Norman, *The Catholic church and Ireland in the age of rebellion, 1859-73* (London, 1965)

C. Cruise O'Brien, *Parnell and his party, 1880-90* (Oxford, 1957)
The shaping of modern Ireland (London, 1960)
The states of Ireland (London, 1972)

L. Ó Broin, *The Chief Secretary, Augustine Birrell in Ireland* (London, 1969)

S. Ó Cathain, 'The Society of Jesus and education' in *Irish Jesuit Directory* (1943)

Dr A. O Rahilly, 'The Irish university question' in *Studies*, 1961

S. O Súilleabhain, 'Secondary education' in P.J. Corish (ed.), *A history of Irish Catholicism*, vol 5 (Dublin, 1971)

C. Scantlebury, 'The Jesuit houses in Ireland' in *Irish Jesuit Directory* (Dublin, 1944)

P. Sexton, 'Irish secondary teachers and their struggle for status, 1878-1937' (M.Ed., thesis, University of Birmingham, 1974)

W.B. Stanford and R.B. McDowell, *Mahaffy* (London, 1971)

W.B. Wells, *John Redmond* (London, 1919)

J.A. Whyte, 'Political problems 1850-1860' in P.J. Corish (ed.), *A history of Irish Catholicism*, iii (Dublin, 1967)

J. Wilson, *A life of Henry Campbell-Bannerman* (London, 1973)

X   Works of a more general nature

N. Atkinson, *Irish education, a history of educational institutions* (Dublin, 1969)

G. Balfour, *The education system of Great Britain and Ireland* (Oxford, 1903)

W.V. Bangert, *A history of the Society of Jesus* (St. Louis, U.S.A., 1972)

B. Bassett, *The English Jesuits, from Campion to Martindale* (London, 1967)

G.A. Beck (ed.), *The English Catholics, 1850-1950* (London, 1950)

J.C. Beckett, *The making of modern Ireland, 1603-1923* (London, 1965)

M.E.A. Boultwood and S.J. Curtis, *An introductory history of English education since 1800* (London, 1966)

T.J. Campbell, *The Jesuits* (New York, 1921)

A. de Blacam, 'Seventy years of history' in *Irish Monthly*, Jan. 1942

P.J. Dowling, *A history of Irish education* (Cork, 1971)

R.C.K. Ensor, *England, 1870-1914* (Oxford, 1936)

D. Gwynn, *A hundred years of Catholic emancipation, 1829-1929* (London, 1929)

M.P. Harney, *The Jesuits in history* (New York, 1941)

J.J. Lee, *The modernisation of Irish society, 1848-1918* (Dublin, 1973)

F.S.L. Lyons, *Ireland since the famine* (London, 1971)

J.A. Murphy, *Ireland in the twentieth century* (Dublin, 1975)

C. Petrie, *The Victorians* (London, 1960)
   Great beginnings in the age of Queen Victoria (London, 1967)

E. Strauss, *Irish nationalism and British democracy* (London, 1951)

W. Walsh, *The Jesuits in Great Britain* (London, 1903)

Abbreviations used in the notes:

C.W.C.A.	Clongowes Wood College archives, Co Kildare: section relating to St Stanislaus College, Tullabeg.
D.D.A.	Dublin archdiocesan archives, Clonliffe College.
F. Jn.	*Freeman's Journal.*
I.J.A.	Irish Jesuit archives, Leeson Street, Dublin; more particularly the Delany papers unless otherwise stated.
L.D.A.	Limerick diocesan archives, bishop's residence, Limerick. (The archives are only partly catalogued.)
McKenna MS	Uncompleted MS 'Fr William Delany and his work for Irish education', by Fr Lambert McKenna, S.J., in Irish Jesuit archives. McKenna, who knew Delany, had collected material from a variety of persons and sources during the 1920s.
N.L.I.	National Library of Ireland.

9, 350, 363, 386,
...er 270
...illiam 151
...und 41, 50, 51
...Tom 64 (See
...liam)
...m, SJ.
...01, 137

...masters
..., 35, 36, 61,
...st 31
...29—30,
..., 20, 31,
...passim
...17
...ms,

...195,
...230
...32,
...College

...iocesan 11
...1, 55
...Diocesan 11
...hop of 58 (See
...k, Dr.)
...atthew 139
...Thomas 136, 138,
...1 Tasmania 140
...th, Mr. 147
...nson, Dr. 321
...antis 162
...aden, W.H., *Collected
Shorter Poems* 321

Bacon John 150, 349,
351
Bacon Thomas F. 245,
251, 263, 272
Balfour, Arthur 129, 146
155, 168, 169, 170, 171,
181, 192, 195, 232, 236,
318
*Letter to a Manchester
Constituent* 169, 170
Balfour, Gerald 148, 173
206
Balfour, Lady (Betty), 8,
148, 205
Ball, Dr. J.T, Lord
Chancellor, 37, 58, 59, 82
Lord Chief Justice, 31
Baltimore 153
Plenary Council of 120
Barry Dr 145
Beaumont Lodge 18
Beckx Fr. Peter, SJ, 21,
23, 24, 25, 63

...cal Students'
...n 170
...wsletter 170
...m, Roger 374
...Hilaire 370, 371
...ere College 65
...ford, Lord Charles 51
...ningham University 236
...rell, Augustine 9, 39
167, 195, 232, 235, 241,
242 255, 273, 287, 288,
289, 290 292, 293, 294,
295, 296, 297, 299, 300,
301 303, 304, 305 306,
307, 308 310, 311, 312,
313, 315, 316 318, 363,
374 375
Bishops, American 120
'Bishops' National Catholic
College' 139
Bithrey, John 357, 358
Blackrock College 21 29,
36 65, 67 79 82, 84,
85 87, 93, 96, 102, 111,
139, 150 (See French
College, Blackrock)
Board of Education 289
Bodkin Judge Matthias
McDonnell — (See
McDonnell Bodkin)
Bodkin, Thomas 165 263,
270, 271, 272
Boland, John 335
Bonn scheme 226, 235
Bonn University 225, 228
Bournemouth 59 64
Brennan, Joseph 270
Bridges Robert 10
Bristol University 236
Browne, Fr (Prof.) Henry,
S.J. 150, 153, 158, 386
Browne, Fr. Thomas, SJ,
72, 74, 83, 133, 348, 349
Bryant, Mrs Sophie 217
Bryce James, 206, 222,
230, 232, 233, 235 236,
238, 241
plan 290, 307
proposals 320
scheme 309
Byrne, J.F. 261
Burke, Fr. 79
Burns, John 241
Butcher, Prof. Henry 177,
193, 194, 231, 300
Butler, Dr. (Bishop) 73
76 80, 82, 86 90 91,

92, 106, 107, 112, 125,
138 (See Limerick,
Bishop of)
Butler, W.F. 341
Butt Issac 32, 188

Cadogan, Lord 173, 192
Cahill, Fr. Edmund, SJ,
334
Cairns, Lord 35
Callan, Philip 51, 53
Cambridge University 92,
236, 280, 307
debating union 284
royal report on 50
students 137
Campbell, Sir George 52
Campbell, James 307
Campbell Bannerman
Henry 104, 241, 242,
288
Cannes 147
Canning, George 331
Carbery, Fr. Robert, SJ,
135, 148, 151 153, 157,
158
Carlow College — (see St.
Patrick's College, Carlow)
Carnarvon, Lord 105, 108,
110, 117
Carroll, D. 266
Carson, Sir Edward 189,
242, 311
Casey, Dr. 57, 69, 70-73,
79, 92, 139, 140
Cashel, Archbishop of 130
(See Croke, Dr. T.W.)
Castle Bellingham 202
Castletown, Lord 257 273,
319
Catholic Bishops' College
299
Catholic Club 178
Catholic Defence Society
227
Catholic Emancipation Act
(1829), 54, 364
Catholic Graduates and
Undergraduates'
Association 217, 218
Catholic Headmasters'
Association 9, 35 36, 61,
215
Catholic Medical School
170, 232, 253 (See
University School of
Medicine Cecilia Street)

Catholic Scholarship scheme 220
Catholic Truth Society 172
Catholic University of Cracow 175
Catholic University of Ireland 18, 25, 37, 38, 39, 40, 47, 49, 51, 57, 58, 60, 67, 68, 69, 72, 75, 76, 78, 88, 92, 93, 100, 102, 106, 107, 110, 117, 124, 155, 386
  library 125, 138
  magazine of 269
Catholic Young Man 345
Cavendish laboratory, 137
Chadwick, Mr and Mrs. 19
Chalons 18
Chandlery, Fr. J.P., SJ, 196, 197
Chicago newspaper 153
Christian World 295
Churchill, Randolph 9, 31, 32, 33, 34, 35, 36, 37, 49, 52, 105, 112, 117
Churchill, Winston 208, 230
Citizen's Reception Committee 175
Clancy George 166
Clancy, J J. 199
Clandillon, James 159, 160, 164
Clare Advocate, The 337
Clarke, Austin 386
Clarke, Prof. Kitson 11
Clery, Arthur E. 159, 160, 162, 165, 167, 218, 244, 255, 273, 386
Clonfert, Bishop of, 100, 177, 181 (*see* Healy, Dr. John)
Clongownian, The 379, 384
Clongowes Wood College 18, 62, 64, 73, 153, 159, 220, 381
  Archives 11
Clonliffe College — (*see* Holy Cross College, Clonliffe)
Coffey, Dr. Denis J. 231, 232, 299, 301, 302, 336, 346, 349
Coffey, Diarmid 342
College of Mount Carmel, Terenure 72
College of Surgeons 257
Collins, Michael 378
Collins, Sir William 311
Committee of Lay Catholics (*otherwise* of Catholic

Laymen) 192, 224, 227, 233 (*see* Fottrell, Synnott)
Conmee, Fr. J. SJ, 190, 191, 333, 360
Connolly, James 378
Conservative Party 39, 49, 123, 126, 168, 169, 289
  government 42
Contemporary Review 171, 175
Corcoran, Prof. T., SJ, *Clongowes Record 1814-1932* 381
Cork County Council 331
Corr Dr 73 (*See* Galway, Bishop of,)
Costello, John A. 166
County Councils, General Council of 293
Cox, A.E. 263 266, 272
Cox, Dr. M.J. 250, 299, 301, 336
Cox, Dr. M.F. 141
Coyne, W.P. 159, 162, 166
Cracow, Catholic University of 175
Crawford Lindsay 268
Creed Meredith, Sir James 269
Crescent College, Limerick 36
Croagh, parish priest of 170
Croke, Dr. T.W. 37, 52, 56, 73, 76, 84, 86, 106, 108, 110, 118, 122, 123, 125, 128, 129, 130 138 (*See* Cashel, Archbishop of)
Cross R.A. 53
Cruise, Dr. (*Later* Sir Francis), 82, 91, 92, 94, 95, 96, 97, 196, 210, 360
Cruise O'Brien, Francis 10, 165, 257, 259, 260, 261, 263 264, 265, 266, 267, 271, 272 282, 285, 287
Cullen, Archbishop Paul (later Cardinal), 11, 15, 40
Curran, C.P. 9 139, 166, 274, 286, 287
Curtis, Robert, SJ, 78, 79, 81, 83

Dale, F.H. 27
Daily Chronicle 210, 287
Daily Express, 259, 261 372
Daily Mail 154, 192
Dalton, Joseph S.J. 18
Darlington, Fr. Joseph S.J. 17, 137, 140 141, 153, 159 178, 179, 180, 191,

348, 3[...] 387
Davitt, Ca[...]
Dawson, W[...]
Dease, Edm[...]
Delany, Fr.[...]
  Delany, W[...]
Delany, Willi[...]
  Address by [...]
  Birthplace 1[...]
  Catholic Hea[...]
  Association, 9[...] 215
  Conversational[...]
  Diary Extract[...] 150–151
  English friends 9[...] 146, 147, 148 *e[...]*
  "Essential Irish"[...]
  Controversy 9 and [...] ch.XVIII
  Family 14, 61, 150[...] 196
  Fry Commission 229[...]
  Headmaster 20, 31,[...] 48, 61-64
  Honorary degree 102 [...]
  Illness 59, 61, 64, [...] 195, 370
  Intermediate Educatio[...] Act (1878) – ch. 11
  Issue of Womens' Rights [...] 9, and ch.XV
  Preacher 143–5
  Priest 143, 356
  Provincial 360-363, 365
  Range of Reading 29-30
  Robertson Commission 183-186
  Rome, 9, 18, 19, 20
  Royal University Act (1879) – see Ch.II.
  Student Protests see Ch.XIV
  Travel Abroad 9, 18-20, 59, 60, 64, 104
Dennehy, W.F. 373
de Valera, Eamon 166
Dickie, Prof. 177
Dilke, Charles 104
Dillon, John 129, 152, 160, 218, 271, 272, 289, 291, 294, 302, 303, 312, 335, 336, 343, 371
  Rev. Dr. 163 (*in Stephen Hero*)
  Fr. Nicholas (Henry) 305
Disraeli, Benjamin 42, 54, 55
Dominican Convent, Eccles St. 162, 215, 279
Donnelly, Dr. 172, 180,

218 (*See* Dublin, Auxiliary Bishop of)
Donovan, Robert 349
Douglas, Hon. Mrs. 19
Doyle, Charles 256
Drummond, Michael 177, 178, 179, 180, 191
Dublin Academic Council 341
Dublin, Archbishop of 101, 125, 126, 128, 129, 188, 222, 294, 316, 326 (*See* Walsh, Dr. William)
Auxiliary Bishop of 172, 180 (*See* Donnelly, Dr.)
Dublin Castle 103, 174, 195, 208
Dublin Corporation 174, 293
Dublin County Council 215, 227, 332, 365
Dublin Metropolitan Police 261
Dublin Review 219
Dublin University Scheme, 190, 192 (See also under University of Dublin and Walsh, Dr. William)
Dufferin, Lord 202
Dundalk College 79
Dunraven, Lord 169, 170, 198
Dunraven — Wyndham Scheme 199, 201
Education
Board of 289
Endowments Bill 110
equal opportunity in 7, 8, 33, 38, 102
improvement in secondary 29
intermediate 8, see Ch.II
Egan, Dr. John 70, 71, 73
Egan, Michael, S.J., 197, 198
Eglinton, John 286
Emly, Lord (Baron) 38, 53, 58, 81, 82, 85, 91, 99, 102, 111, 127, 132, 138, 198 (*see* Monsell, William)
Emo Park 31
Endowed Schools' Commission 28
Endowments
debate on 111
Errington, George 51, 55
Ewing, Prof. 177
Examinations
Public 34
Royal University 98, 99

Undergraduate 103
London University 26
Intermediate 32

Fawcett's Act (1873) 204
Feis Ceoil 329
Feis Thomond 337
Fermoy College 79
Fiesole 68
Finlay, Fr. Tom S.J., 8, 69, 77, 81, 98, 99, 110, 111, 140, 145, 151, 153, 162, 166, 216, 217, 273, 302, 303, 304, 305, 306, 314, 315, 316, 367, 369, 378, 379, 385
Fitzgibbon, Gerald 31, 32, 34
Lord Justice 110
Flanagan, Fr. I.J. 169, 170
Florence 68
Foley, Dr. 144, 145, 150, 347, 362, 363 (*see* Kildare and Leighlin, Bishop of)
Forster, W.E. 59
Fortnightly Review 385
Foster, R.F. 30
Fottrell, Mr. 224, 226, 227
Franciscan Friary, Limerick 305
Frost, Robert
The Poetry of Robert Frost 370
Franco - Prussian War 131
Freeman's Journal, 13, 51, 65, 66, 84, 86, 87, 89, 91, 92, 110, 127, 187, 193, 218, 225, 227, 237, 246, 250, 312, 322, 327, 331
French College, Blackrock 72, 73, 80, 81, 84, 85 (*see* Blackrock College)
French Fathers 67 (*see* Holy Ghost Congregation)
French Revolution,
Reflections on the by Edmund Burke 13
Fry Commission (1906) 155, 167, 222, 223, 282, 300, 372
First Report of 230, 282
Fry, Sir Edward 222, 231, 372
Fulton, Fr., S.J, 135

Gaelic Athletic Association 154, 161, 371
Gaelic League 9, 154, 160, 209, 213, 215, 219, 232, 247, 250, 321, 325, 326, 327, 328, 329, 330, 331,

333, 335, 336, 337, 338, 339, 342, 346, 351, 371
Gaelic Society(U.C.D.) 322
Galway, Bishop of 73 (*See* Corr, Dr.)
Gardiner Street Church, Dublin 20, 135, 142, 143, 145, 146, 147, 150, 153, 190, 191, 360
Gardiner, W.H.
Poems and Prose of G.M. Hopkins 355
Garibaldi 19, 37
General Council of County Councils 216
Gibbons, Cardinal 153
Gibson, Edward 31, 34, 51
Gillooly, Dr. (Bishop) 73, 82, 83
Gladstone 33, 41, 56, 105, 117, 118, 147, 169, 182, 188, 236
Government 59
Land Act (1870), 54.
University Bill (1873) 33, 42
Gogarty, Dr. O. St. John 165, 244
Grants 103—9
Grey, Edward Dwyer, 53, 56
Griffin, Sir Charles 158
Griffith Arthur, 148, 202, 213, 254, 255, 268
Gwynn, Edward 321
Gwynn, Capt. S.L. 307
Gwynn, Stephen 251
Gwynne, Fr. John, S.J. 367

Hackett, Felix 165, 244
Haldane, R.B. 168, 170, 289, 290, 308, 310
Hamilton, Sir Robert 87, 103, 104, 105, 108, 109, 110
Hamilton, Dr. Thomas 170, 175, 232, 237
Hannan, Miss 282
Hansard 307, 310
Harrington, T.C. 129
Hazel, Dr. 307, 309
Healy, Fr. James (of Little Bray) 31
Healy, Dr. John 7, 9, 85, 94, 100, 126, 127, 130, 131, 134, 138, 155, 176, 177, 180, 183, 227, 238, 291, 292, 315, 314 (*See* Clonfert, Bishop of, later Tuam, Archbishop of)

Healy, Maurice 166, 263, 265, 270, 271, 272, 284, 285, 287

Healy, T.M. 110, 149, 151, 251

Henry, Mitchell 51, 55

Hermes magazine 270

Hickey, Dr. 160, 321

Hicks-Beach, Sir Michael 32, 105, 106, 111, 126, 129

Higgins, Dr. 88

High Park Convent, Dublin 174

Hogan, Fr. (Dr.) Edmund, S.J. 140, 150, 153, 162, 328, 348

Holycross College, Clonliffe 72, 75, 76, 98, 108

Holy Ghost Congregation 67

Home Rule 126, 129, 130, 154, 161, 163, 169, 203, 209, 213, 236, 240, 242, 271, 288, 371, 378, 383, 384
Bill 129, 374

Home Rulers 148

Hopkins, Fr.GerardManley, S.J, 9, 10, 69, 78, 79, 80, 81, 82, 83, 84, 134, 139, 140, 141, 355, 386

Horne, Mr. 297

Hospital of Mercy 197

Howley, Prof. John *Studies* 387

Hughes, Fr. J. 16

'Hungarian policy' 202

Hutchinson, Joseph 227

Hutton, Mr. 310

Hyde, Douglas 213, 231, 321, 331, 333, 336, 339, 340, 342, 346
Religious Songs of Connacht 163

Intermediate Board 293

Intermediate Education Act, (1878) 9, 31, 34, 37, 48, 50, 51, 61, 183
introduction of 35

Intermediate Education Commission 321

Intermediate examination results 215

Ireland 196

Irish Agricultural Organisation Society 152

Irish Association of Women Graduates and Candidate Graduates 280, 282, 368

Irish Brigade 19, 37

Irish Catholic, The 250, 373

Irish College, Rome 100, 127

Irish, compulsory for University 321—341

Irish Conservatives 15, 49, 56

Irish Council Bill (1907) 240, 241, 242, 272, 273, 288, 301

Irish Ecclesiastical Record, 99

Irish Educational Review 305

Irish Homestead 152

Irish Independent, The 267, 372

Irish Learning, School of 329, 351

Irish Land Act (Balfour, 1891) 148

Irish Parliamentary Party 9, 35, 51, 108, 110, 129, 151, 221, 237, 242, 271, 315, 335, 374
Plan of Campaign 129, 130, 132

Irish Protestant 218, 251

Irish Sisters of Charity 16

Irish Times, The 227, 252, 372

Irish Universities Act (1908) 313 (*otherwise* referred to as National University Bill)

Irish University Bill (leading up to University Education (Ireland) Act (1879)) 31, 48—60

Irish Volunteers 344

Jackson, Prof. Henry 231

Jebb, Prof. (Sir Richard) 177, 181

Joint Board of Commissioners 349, 351

Joyce, James A. 9, 141, 157, 159, 160, 163, 164, 165
brother Stanislaus, 165
'Drama and Life' 164
Stephen Hero 163, 165, 286
Portrait of an Artist 244, 286

Kane, Sir Robert, 58

Kavanagh, Arthur 15, 49, 50, 51, 53

Kavanagh, Fr. (*otherwise* Dr.) James, 16, 74, 81, 82, 85, 87, 91, 94, 99, 100, 103, 118, 122, 125, 128, 179, 323

Keating, W.H. 127, 128

Keenan, Sir Patrick 29, 34, 35

Keller, Fr. S.J. 87

Kelleher, S.B. 231

Kelly, Fr. T. S.J. 65

Kennedy, Charles 364

Kennedy, Frank 364

Kennedy, H.B. 159

Kennedy, John E. 249, 250, 257, 263, 269

Kerr, Captain 19

Kerr, Lady A. 19

Kerrigan, Sarsfield 249, 250

Kettle, Thomas 159, 162, 164, 165, 166, 212, 213, 217, 218, 219, 240, 245, 246, 247, 250, 271, 285, 343, 386

Kieffer, Fr. S.J. 140

Kildare and Leighlin, Bishop of 144, 145 (*See* Foley, Dr.)

Kilkenny College -- (*See* St. Kieran's College, Kilkenny)

Killanin, Lord 31 (*See* Morris, Michael)

King Edward VII, 196
royal tour 197—8

Kingstown 197

Kipling, R. *Recessional* 154

Kirkpatrick Magee, William 286
Irish Literary Portraits 286

Kirby, Mgr. 100, 127

Klein, Dr. Martial L. 131, 132, 133, 166

Knox, E.H. 169, 239

Land League 130, 141, 209

Lane, Sir Hugh 380

Langdale, Charles 54, 68

Larkin, James 376

Leader 213, 249, 250, 281, 282

Lecky, Mr. 189

Leeds University 306

Leeson Street, Lower, No. 35: 363, 364, 369

Légion Francaise 159

Leinster College 326

Leman, Fr. 34
Leo XIII, Pope 130
Leslie, Shane 377
Liberal Party 39, 41, 50, 117, 168, 203, 231, 234, 240, 289
prime minister 38
government 40, 41, 126, 221
newspapers 291
Liberalism 140
Limerick 128
Limerick, Bishop of 68, 125, 126, 127, 129, 130, 148, 177, 181, 192, 193, 199, 229, 234 (*See* Butler, Dr. O'Dwyer, Edward Thomas)
County Council 337, 338
Manifesto 130
Mayor of 199
Literary and Historical Society 137, 158, 159, 164, 242, 244, 251, 257, 261, 262, 263, 264, 265, 267, 268, 270, 271, 272, 273, 274, 283, 284, 285, 287
History of, by Caher Davitt 270
Little Bray 31 (*See* Healy, Fr. James)
Little, Edward 268
Little, Frank 162
Little, Judge 35, 51, 52, 53
Little, P.J. 166, 257, 269, 270, 271, 302
Liverpool University 236 306
Logue, Cardinal 168, 178, 192, 218, 234, 291, 292, 317, 377
London University 25, 37, 48, 55, 161, 185
examinations 26, 42
Londonderry, Lady 25, 30
Lord 126, 127, 202
Loreto College, St. Stephen's Green 215, 279, 282, 367, 368
Loreto convents 162
Louvain University 138
Lowe, Robert 52
Lowther, Chief Secretary 54
Lucan Spa 195
L'Universe 312
Lyceum, The 133, 152, 162
Lyons, Prof. F.S.L. 371

MacAlister, Dr. 58
McCabe, Dr. (*otherwise* Archbishop or Cardinal) 37, 58, 60, 66, 70, 71, 72, 73, 82, 83, 85, 96, 100, 104, 134
McCartan, Patrick 166
McCarthy, A. 259
McCarthy, Justin 104, 105, 107
McClelland, Prof. (Dr.) 137, 300
McCormack, F. 266, 267
MacDonagh, Thomas 386
McDonald, Dr. Walter 99, 219, 220
McDonnell Bodkin, Judge Matthias 22, 34, 35, 160, 251, 379, 384
Mac Donnell, Sir Anthony 195, 198, 206, 207, 208, 231, 232, 240, 241
Mac Donnell, Lady 195
MacEnri, Dr. S.P. 323
McErlean, Fr. John S.J. 159
McGilligan, Patrick 166
McGrath, Joseph 28, 300, 301, 302
McGrath, Dr. Thomas 99
McGrath, William 268
McKean, John 307
McKenna, Fr. Lambert, S.J. 10, 29, 143, 144, 165, 378
MacNeice, Louis 'Autumn Journal' 355
MacNeill, Hugh 346
MacNeill, John 9, 166, 321, 322, 323, 325, 326, 329, 330, 331, 332, 339, 342, 344, 346, 350, 379, 380, 387
Celtic Ireland 163, 344, 380
Irish in the National University of Ireland 332
Phases of Irish History 163
McWeeney, H.C. 159
Madden, Justice 177, 181
Madden, Thomas 249, 250, 257
Magazine of the Catholic University of Ireland 269
Magazine of University College 269
Magee (Presbyterian) College, Derry 41, 103, 177, 194, 296, 297
Magennis, William 8, 162,

164, 166, 218, 350, 385
Mahaffy, Dr. J.P. 28, 31, 48, 199, 251, 321, 325
Mallac, Père 140
Manchester University 306
Mangan, James Clarence 165
Mangan, Timothy A. 261, 263, 266
Manning, Cardinal 120, 132, 152
Mannix, Dr. 291, 292
Mansion House 156, 250, 335
Marlborough, Duchess of 9, 30, 32, 52
Duke of 15, 30, 32, 34, 37, 49, 183
Martin, Fr. L. S.J. 175
Massie, Mr. 297
Mater Misericordiae Hospital 147
Maxwell, General 375
Maynooth College — (*See* St. Patrick's College, Maynooth)
Mayo, Lord 40
Meath, Earl of 245, 249, 250, 256, 269
Mentana (battle of) 19
Meredith, James 162
Meyer, Fr. S.J. 144
Miltown Park 74
Moffett, Dr. 58
Moffett, Rev. J.E. 372
Molloy, Dr. Gerald 37, 51, 57, 58, 72, 90, 108, 110, 111, 256
Moloney, Thomas P., K.C. 251
Monaghan Rural District Council 335
Monasterevan 18
Monsell Manuscripts 11
William 38, 41, 47 (*See* Emly, Lord)
Montague-Griffin, Mr. 130
Monteagle, Lord 170
Moore, George 151
Moore, William 307, 308
Moran, D.P. 213, 255, 282, 371
Moran, Dr. P.F. (*later* Cardinal) 15, 67, 73
Moriarty, D.M. 241
Morley, Florence 173 (*see* Agatha, Sr.)
Morley, John 9, 105, 147, 173, 174, 203, 312, 373
Mrs. 147, 174

Morning News, Belfast 89, 90
Morris, Michael 31 (*see* Killanin, Lord.)
Mulrany, Brother 153
Mungret College 81, 369
Munster News, The 337
Murphy, Fr. Andrew 215, 316
Murphy, Con 218
Murphy, Fr. Denis, S.J. 77, 140
Murphy, Fr. James F., S.J. 178
Murphy, William Martin 377

Nation, The 100
National Student, The 167
National College 93
National Education, Commissioner of 175
National Library 137, 286
National Student, The 385
National University 9, 11, 28, 128, 137, 223, 224, 233, 255, 306, 313, 320, 324, 328, 333, 335, 336, 340, 342, 345, 361, 384, 386
National University Legislation 316
National University Bill 1908 7, 195, 283, 287, 310-313 (*See* Irish Universities Act, 1908)
Nationalist Party 271
Nationist, The 166, 212, 217
Nettleship, Prof. 79
Neville, Dean Henry (*otherwise* Dr. or Monsignor) 53, 58, 60, 66, 67, 68, 72, 79, 85, 91, 94
New Ireland Review 162-3, 217, 227, 305, 316
Newman, Cardinal John Henry 18, 40, 41, 47, 57, 77, 100, 102, 140, 141, 161, 185, 226
Newman's University 136, 348, 363
Nixon, Dr (*later* Sir Christopher) 181, 231, 237, 250, 251, 252, 254, 367
Nolan, Fr. T.V., S.J. 365
Norfolk, Duke of 130, 132
Nutting scholarships (scheme) 215, 220

O'Brien, Lord Chief Justice 373
O'Byrne, G. 263
O'Byrne, J. 266
O'Carroll, Fr. John J. S.J. 77, 140
O'Connell, 'Ginger' J.J. 166, 272
O'Connor, Rory 166, 266, 267, 271
O'Conor Don 35, 36, 50, 51, 52, 56, 61, 170, 186
O'Daly, Patrick 321, 322, 323
O'Donnell, Bishop 347, 362, 363, 368 (*See* Raphoe, Bishop of)
O'Donnell, Dr. (*see* O'Donnell, Bishop)
O'Dwyer, Bishop Edward Thomas 47, 125, 126, 127, 128, 130, 134, 141, 149, 150, 168, 169, 171, 172, 176, 177, 180, 181, 182, 186, 187, 188, 189, 193, 199, 213, 215, 216, 226, 233, 234, 289, 320, 371, 377 (see Limerick, Bishop of)
A university for Catholics in relation to the material interests of Ireland 172
The present condition of university education in Ireland 207
O'Dwyer, Dr. — (*see* O'Dwyer, Bishop E.T. and Limerick, Bishop of)
O'Dwyer, Michael J. 72
O'Farrelly, Agnes 166, 282, 322
O'Hagan, Lord 35, 36, 53, 132, 363
Oireachtas 329
O'Neill, Fr. (Prof.) George, S.J. 158, 356-7
O'Neill, Patrick J. 227, 365 (*See* Dublin County Council)
O'Neill, Rev. 198 (*See* O'Neill, Fr. George)
O'Nowlan, T.P. 322, 323, 332
O'Rahilly, Alfred T. 166
Orange Society, Grand Master 372
O'Reilly, Fr. Edmund, S.J. 17
O'Reilly, Major Myles W. 37, 38
Ossory, Bishop of, 67

(*See* Moran, Dr. P.F., later Cardinal)
O'Sullivan, John Marcus 165, 228, 350
Oxford University 92, 140, 236, 307
All Souls College 177
Balliol College 79
debating union 284
royal report on 50
University College 177

Palles, Chief Baron 36, 37, 186, 187, 222, 223, 229, 231, 238, 256, 282, 317, 346, 347, 348, 349, 365, 373
Palmerston, Lord 38, 40
Park, Professor 98
Parnell, Charles Stewart 51, 104, 105, 110, 126, 129, 151, 169
Pascal, *Lettres Provinciales* 372
Pearse, Patrick H. 9, 159, 166, 217, 218, 323, 325, 330
Persico, Mgr. Ignatius 130
Pettit, Fr. 178, 191, 195
Phelan, Dr. 76 (*see* St. John's College, Waterford)
Phelan, Michael, S.J. 378
Phoblacht, An 344, 385
Phoenix Park 148
Pigott, J. 175, 176
Pius IX, Pope 140
Plunkett, David 31 (*see* Rathmore, Lord)
Plunkett, Sir Horace 152, 213, 320
Polin, Abbé 85
Pope Leo XIII 130
Pius IX 140
Portarlington, Lady 30
Lord 31, 52
Porter, Dr. 58, 131
Porter, Fr. G., S.J. 66, 67, 69, 72
Power, Fr. Cyril, S.J. 361, 379, 380
Primary education 219
Primary teachers diploma 219
Presbyterian General Assembly 304
Purbrick, Fr. S.J. 69, 131, 132, 133
Pye, Dr. 341

Queen Alexandra 196
royal tour 197-8
Queen Elizabeth I 41,

239
Queen's Colleges 39, 42, 50, 53, 55, 58, 59, 84, 86, 87, 97, 101, 103, 104, 126, 136, 170, 185, 203, 205, 207, 214, 228, 229, 280, 291, 297, 298, 305, 313
 Belfast 41, 98, 121, 131, 136, 170, 171, 177, 194, 198, 199, 200, 201, 204, 232, 255, 298, 313, 330, 346
 Cork 38, 39, 41, 57, 90, 111, 122, 136, 182, 200, 203, 207, 232, 233, 298, 313
 Dublin 235
 Estimates 155, 200
 Galway 39, 57, 90, 111, 122, 136, 158, 175, 182, 200, 203, 233, 298, 313, 346
Queen's University 42, 55, 171, 310, 345

Rahilly, T.F. 166
Raleigh, Sir Thomas 231
Raphoe, Bishop of 363 (*See* O'Donnell, Bishop)
Rathfarnham Castle 365
Rathmore, Lord 31
Redington, Mr. 58, 83
Redmond, John 218, 237, 239, 242, 288, 289, 294, 295, 303, 306, 307, 309, 311, 312, 371, 375
Reffé, Fr. 21, 36, 79, 80, 81, 82, 83, 84, 85, 97, 134
Review of Reviews 152
'Reviewer' 188, 189, 190
Rhys, Prof. 177
Ridgeway family 146, 147
Ridley, Lord 177
Robertson Commission, 1902 167, 173, 179-181, 199, 201, 211, 222, 223, 226, 230, 236, 237, 245, 280, 318, 345, 371
 Lord 177, 179, 181, 186, 187
 Report 199, 245
 Scheme 231
Roman College 19
Rome 18, 21, 24, 37, 61, 63, 67, 100, 101, 108, 149, 151, 165, 305, 313, 351, 358, 359
Ronan, Fr., S.J. 153

Ronayne, J.A. 263, 266, 271, 285
Ross, Earl of 58
Ross, Captain (*later* Sir John of Bladensburg, Earl of Ross) 102, 110, 111, 181, 233, 234, 373
Ross, Sir John, of Bladensburg 233, 234, 373 (*see* Ross, Captain, later Earl of)
Rothschild residence 168
Rotunda Hall 321, 327, 333
Royal Commission of Enquiry 1884-5 86
Royal Irish Constabulary 261
Royal Society 236
Royal University Act (1879) 42, 55 [*see* University Education (Ireland) Act (1879)]
Royal University of Ireland 7, 9, 11, 27, 37, 42, 47, 51, 59, 60, 61, 65, 68, 70, 71, 72, 79, 81, 85, 88, 89, 91, 92, 97, 98, 99, 102, 103, 111, 120, 126, 127, 132, 133, 135, 139, 140, 150, 153, 161, 166, 170, 171, 175, 176, 177, 178, 179, 183, 185, 186, 187, 192, 194, 196, 202, 205, 212, 217, 220, 223, 225, 228, 229, 231, 233-235, 245, 246, 247, 248, 249, 250, 251, 254, 256, 258, 259, 260, 268, 269, 279, 280, 293, 297, 298, 300, 318, 324, 328, 344, 345, 349, 351, 362, 364, 367, 368, 384, 385
Royal visit 196-198
Rucker, Sir Arthur 231
Russell, Dr. Charles 17
Russell, Lord Charles 17
Russell, George (A.E.) 342, 380
Russell, Lord John 40
Russell, Fr. Matthew S.J. 17, 130, 153, 157, 370
Ryan, Canon 331

St. Acheul 18
St. Ignatius College, Temple Street 68, 70, 71, 72, 80 (*see* Temple Street)
St. John Lateran Basilica 19

St. John's College, Waterford 76
St. Kieran's College, Kilkenny 70
St. Malachy's College, Belfast 79
St. Mary's College, Eccles St. 279, 367
St. Patrick's College, Carlow 16, 25, 72, 74, 85, 99, 145
St. Patrick's College, Maynooth 16, 17, 33, 72, 79, 85, 91, 93, 94, 96, 99, 100, 144, 145, 194, 196, 219, 233, 296, 297, 306, 311, 313, 314
St. Patrick's University 51
St. Stanislaus College, Tullabeg 8, 11, 18, 20, 22, 23, 24, 25, 26, 27, 28, 29, 30, 31, 34, 35, 36, 48, 61, 62, 64, 65, 69, 71, 72, 73, 88, 137, 302, 329, 357, 362, 365, 379, 381, 382, 384
St. Stephen's magazine 151, 257, 268, 269, 270
Salisbury, Lord 105, 175
Salmon, Dr. 171
Saxe Weimar, princes of 132
Scholarships 215, 216, 219, 299, 333, 366
 Catholic Scheme 220
 Nutting scholarships 220
 Catholic scholarship committee 351
 Travelling 366
 Funds 376
School of Medicine, Cecilia Street — (*see* University School of Medicine, Cecilia Street, *also* Catholic Medical School)
Scott, Rev. Robinson 58
Scottish Universities 236
Sexton, Thomas 110
Shaftesbury, Lord 202
Shaw, Judge 257, 310
Shaw, William 51
Sheehan, F. 260
Sheehy brothers 166
Sheehy, Eugene 257, 271
Sheehy, R.J. 266, 271
Sheehy-Skeffington, Francis J. 159, 160, 165, 166, 246, 260, 271, 279, 280
Sheffield University 236, 307

Shelbourne Hotel 192
Sherlock, David 51, 52
Sigerson, George 332
Simmonscourt Castle 216
Sinn Féin 140, 172, 242
Skeffington, Frank J. —
  see Sheehy Skeffington
Smith, Goldwin 241
Smith, Prof. Lorrain 177
Smith O'Brien W. 129
Smyth, P.J. 51
Society of Friends 373
Society of Jesus 18, 19, 64,
  74, 103, 124, 138, 178,
  357, 364
Sodality of the Blessed
  Virgin 158
Spencer, Lord 83, 86
Spoleto (defence of) 37
Starkie, Dr. W.J.M. 158,
  175, 177, 181, 184
Stead, W.H. 152
Stephens, T.A. 27
Stephenson, Fr. William,
  S.J. 379
Stonyhurst College, 25, 82
Stopford-Green, Alice 133,
  206, 350
Sturzo, Fr. S.J. 63, 64
Sullivan, O'Connell 263
Sullivan, T.D. 51, 54
Sullivan W.K. 38, 47, 58
Sweetman, John 235, 257,
  258, 261, 271
Synnott, N.J. 186, 192,
  193, 224, 225, 227, 304

Tablet, The 89, 90, 91,
  99, 111
Talbot, Edmund 304
TCD magazine 214
Teachers' Guild of Great
  Britain 368
Teacher Training College
  70
Temple Street 65, 69, 70,
  71, 72, 73, 76, 80,
  135, 139 (See St. Igna-
  tius College)
Thurles 118, 123
Tierney, Prof. Michael 7,
  386
Times, The 166, 198, 219,
  235, 250, 251, 306, 311
Tory Party 34, 41, 53,
  117, 132
  administration 40, 126
  cabinet ministers 386
  government 175
Traill, Dr. Anthony 171,
  230, 254, 289

Transport Union of Ireland
  376
Trinity College, Dublin —
  (see under University of
  Dublin)
Tristram, Dr. J.W. 372
Tuam, Archbishop of 177,
  227, 316 (See Healy,
  Dr. John)
Tuite, Fr. James, S.J. 26,
  61, 62, 63, 64, 65, 66,
  67, 68, 69, 70, 91
Tullabeg — see St. Stanis-
  laus College
Tyndall, Professor 15
Tyrell, Prof. R.Y. 214

Ulster Unionist Council 236
Unionists, Irish 169
Ulster, Northern 202, 374
United Irish League 242,
  257, 271, 302
United Irishman 254
University Club 336
University College, Cork
  339, 340, 341
University College, Dublin
  Passim (more particularly
  from ch. IV on)
University College, Galway
  340, 341
University Education,
  Council of 175
University Gazette 162
University Hall, Hatch
  Street 364, 369, 378
University of Dublin (otherwise Dublin University
  which had Trinity College
  as its sole constituent
  college) 10, 15, 18, 28,
  31, 36, 38, 41, 42, 47,
  50, 69, 71, 79, 80, 92,
  101, 111, 117, 118, 119,
  120, 122, 123, 128, 150,
  155, 160, 161, 171, 174,
  175, 176, 178, 179, 181,
  182, 185, 186, 187, 190,
  193, 194, 195, 198, 199,
  201, 204, 205, 206, 213,
  214, 215, 216, 219, 220,
  221, 222, 223, 224, 225,
  227, 228, 229, 230, 231,
  232, 233, 236, 239, 242,
  253, 254, 255, 256, 280,
  286, 288, 289, 290, 291,
  292, 304, 305, 306, 307,
  310, 311, 324, 330, 345,
  364
University of Ireland 228,
  299

University of London 236,
  306
University of Nancy 366
University of Wales 236
University School of Medicine, Cecilia Street 72,
  90, 111, 212, 217, 259,
  260, 267, 272, 279, 281,
  298, 302, 346, 348, 368
  (see Catholic Medical
  School)

Viceregal Lodge 110, 146,
  148, 283, 290
Victoria, Queen 120, 174
Victorian England, The
  Making of, by Prof. Kitson
  Clarke, 11

Walmesly, Fr., S.J. 369
Walsh, Archbishop of Dub-
  lin — see Walsh, Dr.
  William
Walsh, Dr. William 9, 35,
  36, 42, 47, 52, 58,
  59, 60, 73, 76, 79, 80,
  82, 83, 84, 85, 86, 87,
  88, 89, 90, 91, 92, 93,
  94, 95, 96, 97, 99, 100,
  101, 104, 105, 107, 108,
  109, 110, 111, 112, 117,
  118, 122, 126, 127, 128,
  133, 135, 138, 139, 140,
  148, 150, 156, 170, 171,
  173, 178, 179, 181, 187,
  191, 192, 194, 195, 196,
  199, 202, 209, 210, 213,
  214, 215, 219, 221, 224,
  226, 227, 237, 239, 283,
  284, 289, 290, 291, 292,
  294, 295, 296, 299, 300,
  303, 304, 305, 317, 318,
  332, 333, 339, 340, 341,
  346, 347, 348, 349, 350,
  362, 364, 365, 373
  Biography of 85
  Memorandum on the Irish
  Education Question 134
Walsh, Fr. J. S.J. 66
Walsh, Mgr. Parrick J. 85
Ward, Wilfrid, 177, 181,
  186, 193, 195, 219
Weld, Fr. S.J. 28, 37,
  57, 62, 63
Wexford County Council
  216
Westminster, Archbishop
  of 120 (see Manning,
  Cardinal)
Wheeler, Fr., S.J. 153
Whigs 53, 85, 86, 126,

141, 168
White, Miss 282 (*see* Alexandra College)
Whitty, Fr., S.J. 109, 130, 133
Windle, Prof. (Dr.) Bertram 209, 228, 230, 231, 237, 239, 339, 340, 368
Windsor 18

Winton House 363
Woodlock, Dr. 51, 53, 58, 73, 76, 82, 83, 84, 85, 94, 96, 98, (*See* Ardagh, Bishop of)
Workers' Republic 378
Wyndham, George 173, 181, 192, 193, 198, 199, 207, 208, 209, 210

Wyndham's Land Act (1903), 198, 370

XIX Century, The, magazine 168

Yeats, W.B. 17, 255, 284, 287
Young Ireland 242, 257, 271, 302

TOPICS IN MODERN IRISH HISTORY

General Editor: R. V. COMERFORD

Priest, Politics and Society in Post-Famine Ireland
A study of County Tipperary, 1850-91
JAMES O'SHEA

An analysis of the social origins of the
parochial clergy, their education and formation,
their financial resources, their social values and
affiliations and the complex and occasionally
decisive ways in which they participated
in political life.

Towards a National University: William Delany SJ (1835-1924)
An era of initiative in Irish education
THOMAS J. MORRISSEY SJ

FORTHCOMING TITLES

The Context of Fenianism: Irish Politics and Society, 1848-82
R. V. COMERFORD

The Moulds of Nationalism: a comparative study of
Irish political movements
H. H. VAN DER WUSTEN

WOLFHOUND PRESS

SERIES ISSN 0790-0783